The Changing Experience
of Women

Open University courses are prepared by a Course Team which for *The Changing Experience of Women* consisted of:

Richard Allen, Madeleine Arnot, Francis Aprahamian, Else Bartels, Veronica Beechey, Francis Berrigan, Sylvia Bently, Lynda Birke, Maria Burke, Ruth Carter, Judy Ekins, Barbara Hodgson, Susan Himmelweit, Gill Kirkup, Diana Leonard, Joan Mason, Jim Moore, Perry Morley, Rosemary O'Day, Stella Pilsworth, Ann Pointon, Sonja Ruehl, Mary Anne Speakman, Elizabeth Whitelegg, with assistance from, Lesley Doyal, Mary Ann Elston, Catherine Hall, Jalna Hanmer, and Janice Winship.

The Changing Experience of Women

Edited by Elizabeth Whitelegg, Madeleine
Arnot, Else Bartels, Veronica Beechey, Lynda
Birke, Susan Himmelweit, Diana Leonard,
Sonja Ruehl *and* Mary Anne Speakman.

Martin Robertson · Oxford
in association with
The Open University

First published in 1982 by Martin Robertson & Company Ltd.,
108 Cowley Road, Oxford OX4 1JF.

British Library Cataloguing in Publication Data

The changing experience of women.
  1. Women — Great Britain — Social
  conditions — Addresses, essays, lectures
  1. Whitelegg, E.   II. Arnot, M.
  305.4'2   HQ 1593

  ISBN 0-85520-517-2
  ISBN 0-85520-518-0 Pbk

Typeset by Pioneer in 10/11 pt English and Musica
Printed and bound in Great Britain

Contents

Introduction

This collection of readings reflects some of the main areas of current research and action around the position of women in Britain and forms part of a women's studies course at the Open University. Women's studies is a relatively new field that has emerged over the last ten years as part of the revival of feminism in Britain and elsewhere. There are now women's studies courses in a whole variety of educational institutions — in universities and schools, in colleges of further education and polytechnics, and in many kinds of formal and informal adult and continuing education programmes.

What is women's studies?

It is difficult to give a precise definition of women's studies. As a field of study it has grown out of the contemporary women's movement, yet the relationship between it and the women's movement is a complex one. Perhaps the only defining characteristic of women's studies is that it is concerned with and about women — with women's history, with the determinants of women's position in different societies, with how women have been culturally represented and written about in literature, with how femininity is constructed and women's experience is formed. There is certainly no single perspective within women's studies and people working in the field have used a variety of different approaches, and a number of different methods for doing research.

Where did women's studies come from?

Women have been studied in various ways and in a variety of contexts for many years, but women's studies as a field of study is more recent. Its beginning lies in the distinctive practice of the Women's Liberation Movement of using women-only consciousness-raising groups to explore women's common experience. (The stress on these groups being for women only came from the example of the Black Power movement in the United States which recognized that certain forms of oppression needed to be discussed in the absence of the dominant group.) These groups generated a good deal of shared knowledge about what it is like to be a woman — to be a mother, wife or daughter, to bear and raise children, to do paid work in a man's world, or a woman's world, to be a lesbian or a heterosexual woman. The knowledge coming from these groups has been the starting point for much feminist analysis, even if being grounded in woman's unrefined experience means that it rarely finds a place in the more academic women's studies literature.

A second source of feminist knowledge has been groups which feminists have set up to study and take action around particular problems affecting women. Groups have arisen around a whole range of issues, for example, women's health, sexism in children's books, women and the law, women's sexuality, women in science, feminist history. Campaigning organizations like the National Abortion Campaign, Women's Aid (which provides refuges for battered women), the National Council for Civil Liberties, and the Equal Opportunities Commission, as well as women's caucuses within particular industries (like women in the media), and in trade unions, have also stimulated a lot of research work on women. Sometimes this has been produced in the form of mimeographed papers and reports, sometimes it has led to conferences. Some published work appears in academic journals, some in newspapers, and quite a lot within the Women's Movement's own publications. The knowledge which is produced by such groups forms an important part of the material on which women's studies draws.

A third impetus for women's studies came from students and intellectuals of the New Left who were engaged in developing radical alternatives to established forms of knowledge within academic disciplines. There emerged within the social sciences and within history, for instance, a renewed interest in Marxist analysis, and a concern to develop perspectives which were adequate for understanding how people experienced social life 'from below'. At the same time there developed a strong interest in generating new frameworks for analysing culture and subjectivity, which led to a renewed interest in phenomenology, existentialism and psychoanalytic theory. Many of the endeavours to develop new and radical forms of analysis led people to transgress the established boundaries between academic disciplines, and to develop inter-disciplinary frameworks of analysis. One of the most notable absences within these new and radical perspectives, which feminists were quick to seize upon and to try to rectify within such critiques' own terms, was the absence of any concern for women's experience and for the sexual division of labour.

A final, related source of women's studies came from women students who after the student revolts of 1968, started to insist on courses on women being included in their institutions so that they could learn about their own position as part of their formal course-work. Although the response of the authorities to this was sometimes reluctant, if not hostile, a whole series of such courses eventually developed. Frequently these became options in degree programmes in a particular discipline — for example, courses on sexual divisions within sociology, on women in literature, and on the family in history. This was particularly true in universities in Britain, where the boundaries between disciplines are seen as the mark of elite status. It has been more possible to produce interdisciplinary courses in adult education, because it is less hidebound by disciplinary boundaries.

Teaching and learning women's studies

Women's studies as a field of academic study is subject to a number of contradictions. On the one hand, it developed out of specifically feminist concerns with women. It was part of a political project seeking to establish the rigorous and scholarly study of women in order to change their position. On the other hand, the very act of introducing women's studies into a higher education curriculum means that they are governed by academic criteria. While women's studies courses within curricula in higher education can undoubtedly retain a strong feminist orientation, the connection with grassroots feminism is inevitably broken as they become institutionalized.

A number of things follow from this. First, the subjective dimension, so important to the production of knowledge within feminist groups, is not easily incorporated into academic study, especially where time is limited and assessment is required. This is less of a problem within adult education, which generally allows its courses a flexibility denied to courses within an undergraduate curriculum. Secondly, not all students of women's studies courses have the same past history. There are differences as well as communalities of experience even between members of the same sex. And there are generally some men studying women's studies courses, to whose experiences the courses must try and speak. Finally, it is difficult to produce an interdisciplinary course within an academic curriculum which does not reproduce conventional divisions between disciplines.

The Changing Experience of Women and the Open University

The Open University is a unique institution in Britain providing opportunities for mature students who have no formal educational qualifications to do degree and non-degree work. It is itself, therefore, actively involved in changing the experience of many women. It is also now enabling students to *study* changes in the position of women by providing an interdisciplinary women's studies course, of which this book forms a part. This course is open to undergraduate students of the University as well as associate students who may enrol for a single course. Much Open University teaching takes place 'at a distance'. Students read teaching texts, watch television programmes and listen to audiovisual cassettes at home. They also receive some tutorial teaching and attend a Summer School. This collection is designed as set reading for the course, to be read in conjunction with teaching texts but it stands as a valuable collection in its own right.

The readings included in any collection are inevitably but a selection from a great deal of excellent material. Our main criterion has been to concentrate on Britain, with as a secondary criterion a focus on the post-war period — though we have included an initial historical section. Our other concern has been to use academic articles only where these were the best means to cover topics — hence there are no writings here on the cultural representation of women, since we are covering this area in the course through other media. Within this remit, the specially commissioned articles and reprints we have included cover most of the areas where feminist work is currently best developed, and thus provide an interesting and stimulating guide to the major areas of contemporary concern and scholarship.

PART ONE

The Historical Separation of Home and Workplace

Part One contains five articles which, by offering an historical perspective, enables the position of women in contemporary society to be set in context. Apart from their historical focus, the articles in this section are linked by a second theme, that of examining the relationship between women's position in the family and in employment, which has been structured by changes in society over a long timespan and at a broad level. Thus, the first two articles, which have been specially written for the book by Catherine Hall, detail the evolution of the separation between home and workplace during the Industrial Revolution. Two case studies have been chosen to illustrate this process and its results for working-class and middle-class women: the technological changes in factory production in the textile trades and the retail trades of nineteenth-century Birmingham. Sally Alexander's account of the trades in which women were employed in nineteenth century London provides a further case study, this time of the relationship between women's family roles and the paid employment into which they entered. The complex ways in which that relationship between family and work is structured are highlighted by Joan Scott and Louise Tilly who present a view that the changes in women's employment in the nineteenth century have to be understood in the context of the persistence of traditional, family oriented values from earlier periods, and that no direct or automatic connection can be assumed between economic changes and changes in values or ideologies. The section concludes with a discussion presented by Michèle Barrett and Mary McIntosh of the notion of the 'family wage', its history within wage bargaining strategies and the negative consequences for women of the adoption by trade union movements of the family wage as a central demand.

1.1   The butcher, the baker, the candlestickmaker: the shop and the family in the Industrial Revolution

CATHERINE HALL

In Mrs Gaskell's famous novel *Cranford,* Miss Matty, the kindhearted and genteel friend of the narrator, loses all her money in the collapse of a country bank. Faced with surviving on a tiny income, it is proposed to her that she could add to it by selling tea. She is assured that she could maintain her gentility and that only small alterations would need to be made to her home:

> The small dining-parlour was to be converted into a shop, without any of its degrading characteristics; a table was to be the counter; one window was to be retained unaltered, and the other changed into a glass door. [1]

Mrs Gaskell published *Cranford* in 1853, but she was describing the culture of a small country town in her childhood — looking back to those days before the face of England had been significantly altered by the growth of industrial towns and cities, of factory production and of new transport systems. A less obvious feature of that transformation, and one which Mrs Gaskell may have had in mind when she described the simple alterations needed to turn Miss Matty's dining parlour into a shop, were the changes which had taken place in the organization of shopping. Between 1780—1850, developments in the pattern of production, of distribution and of consumption combined to alter some of the physical characteristics of shops and the ways in which people acquired their food and clothing. These changes provided the necessary preconditions for the 'retailing revolution' of the second half of the nineteenth century — when consumer goods started to

Specially commissioned for this volume
© The Open University, 1982

be mass-produced and shops both increased in size and amalgamated into chains.[2] It is the shopkeepers themselves that we are primarily concerned with in this chapter — the butchers, bakers and candlestickmakers of the late eighteenth and early nineteenth century — and the changes which took place in the organization of the shop and the family. Furthermore, it is a substantial middle-class sector — those with their specialized shops on the high streets of the rapidly growing towns — whose custom came mainly from the local middle class. Their counterparts were the small shopkeepers running general stores who serviced the working-class population. Such small shops for the working classes were rapidly on the increase in the early nineteenth century. Rural immigrants, who had been able to grow a good deal of their own produce in the country, mainly had to rely on buying food in the towns and came to rely on local general shops. Markets and itinerant traders also continued to play an important part in retailing; they were the hawkers and sellers so powerfully portrayed by the journalist and commentator Mayhew in his series on London life in the 1850s.[3] Small shopkeepers and traders were certainly not a part of the middle class. Their links were far more with both the 'respectable' and the 'rough' working class who provided their clientèle and their neighbours.

High street traders, however, were a different matter. Their customers might range from the local gentry coming into town for business and services, to the best paid of the skilled artisans. They would primarily have relied, however, on the urban middle class — those merchants, manufacturers and professionals whose numbers were growing in an economy which was rapidly being industrialized — and on farmers. Such traders were running good-sized businesses, with none of the 'degrading characteristics' referred to by Miss Matty, and were themselves living the life of the middle class. The men were becoming the backbone of their churches and philanthropic and voluntary societies, they were mixing with professionals and small manufacturers and they were regarded as respected members of the community. Such small traders with their established tradition of retailing respectability, are nicely evoked in a memoir of a distinguished Birmingham Unitarian minister whose father was a draper. Though such men stood behind counters they had a 'quiet, gentlemanly dignity of bearing' which challenged the old adage that a tradesman could not be a gentleman.[4] Arnold Bennett placed a draper's establishment at the heart of his most popular novel *The Old Wives' Tale*. The shop was in St Luke's Square, the centre of Bursley's retail trade. The Square,

. . . contained five public-houses, a bank, a barber's, a confectioner's, three grocers', two chemists', an ironmonger's, a clothier's, and five drapers'. These were all the catalogue, St. Luke's Square had no room for minor establishments. The aristocracy of the Square undoubtedly consisted of the drapers (for the bank was impersonal); and among the five the shop of Baines stood supreme. No business establishment could possibly be more respected than that of Mr Baines was respected. And though John Baines had been bedridden for a dozen years, he still lived on the lips of admiring, ceremonious burgesses as 'our honoured fellow-townsman'.[5]

Businesses such as Baines the drapers were family affairs. Mrs Baines helped in the shop at busy times, but reserved Friday for pastry making and early Saturday morning for her own shopping. After her husband's illness, the shop was basically managed by one of the young men who had been apprenticed there and she continued to help when necessary.

But this sexual division of labour within the shopkeeping family, associated with a physical environment which combined work and home, was gradually changing in our period. From the late seventeenth century the wives of wealthy London tradesmen had been castigated by commentators such as Defoe for their attempts to be genteel.[6] The most prosperous were furnishing their living apartments elegantly, putting their servants into livery, and refusing to be seen in the shop themselves, as it was not considered ladylike. As the businesses of provincial tradesmen expanded in the late eighteenth and early nineteenth century, so their aspirations also grew. They increasingly wanted their homes to be separated from their workplace and their wives and daughters to be dependent on them; these had become powerful symbols of belonging to the middle class. By 1851 the numbers of lock-up shops in town centres, with their proprietors living elsewhere, were on the increase.[7] This separation between work and home had important effects on the organization of work within the family and the marking out of male and female spheres.[8] Men were increasingly associated with business and public activities which were physically and socially separated from the home; women with the home and with children.

For working-class families the separation between work and home was rooted in the changes in the organization of production. A family producing woollen cloth at home in the late eighteenth century, for example, with the wife spinning and the husband weaving, would by the mid-nineteenth century have been forced into factory production because they would not have been able to compete with the cheaper cloth produced by mechanised processes in the factory.[9] This separation between work and home, between the production of things and the reproduction of people, which has had such far-reaching effects on industrial capitalist societies, did of course take place at significantly different times in different trades. Some trades were mechanical much later tham others, and at mid-century many working-class men and women were still working inside the home. Industrial capitalism did not only mean factory production — it also brought with it a vast expansion of the sweated trades and of outwork.[10]

Within the middle class also the separation between production and reproduction was also a long, drawn out, and uneven process depending in part on the particular kinds of work which people were doing. Clergymen, for example, have never quite lived in their workplaces though they have often lived next door to them. Doctors and dentists, on the other hand, until the recent advent of health centres were still likely in the twentieth century to combine home and workplace. Large-scale manufacturers often lived next door to their factories so that they could easily oversee them — as did Mr Thornton in Mrs Gaskell's novel *North and South,* or indeed the first generation of the Greg family in Styal on whom it is thought Mrs Gaskell may have based her picture of the hard-nosed industrial capitalist.[11] For those small manufacturers who relied on workshop production, it was most convenient to combine home and workplace and many merchants had their warehouse at the back of their living quarters. Technological advances which revolutionized the labour process rarely forced those in middle class occupations to establish a home away from work, yet by the mid-nineteenth century this separation was becoming increasingly popular.

Take a town like Birmingham. Birmingham had grown from a population of around 35,000 in 1780 to a quarter of a million in 1850, its expansion being based on the metal trades for which it was famous. It had always been the pattern for the most prosperous members of the middle class to move to the small versions of the gentleman's country house which ringed the town when they could afford it. Joseph Priestly for example, the well-known scientist, theologian and minister of one of the Unitarian congregations in Birmingham, was living at Fair Hill about two miles from the town centre in the 1780s, and Dr William Withering, another member of the famous Birmingham Lunar Society and an eminent physician in the town, was living at Edgbaston Hall — a charming rural retreat away from the hustle and bustle of the town centre. By the 1820s and 30s they were being followed by families who were considerably less wealthy, but were looking for a modest version of country living in houses which were close enough to the town for the men to walk daily to their places of work. By the mid-1840s Edgbaston, the leafy suburb of Birmingham, carefully planned with restrictive leases that prevented the building of workshops in gardens or the opening of shops on the premises, was growing apace and the most popular domestic retreat of the growing Birmingham middle class.[12]

The domestic ideal which underpinned such a development was premissed on the notion of a male head of household who supported his dependent wife and children. The women and children were able to be sheltered from the anxieties of the competitive public world by living in their 'haven' or home — away from the political dangers associated with such movements as Chartism, and the business worries of the town. This ideal was popularized from the late eighteenth century particularly by evangelical Christians who believed that a proper religious household must form the basis of a reformed society.[13] The pulpit, the tract and the manual of behaviour provided some of the main vehicles for the promulgation of such ideas. The ideas were institutionalized in the new organizations formed by the middle classes — the self-improvement societies and the philanthropic societies, for example — in their business practices and in the new schools which they established for their sons, and eventually for their daughters.[14] Well-to-do shopkeepers were not slow to attach themselves to such ideas — ideas which called for significant changes in their established way of life 'above the shop'.

What was this established way of life? The records of the Cadbury family in Birmingham provide a valuable insight into the changing patterns of moderately successful shopkeepers over three generations.[15] Richard Tapper Cadbury, the originator of the Birmingham dynasty, arrived in the town in 1794, and having done his apprenticeship in Gloucester and served as a journeyman in London, he set up in business in Bull Street — a major Birmingham shopping street — as a silk mercer and draper. In 1800 he moved in with his wife and rapidly growing family above the shop. Elizabeth Cadbury was clearly actively engaged in the business, though she had not of course had access to the kind of training her husband had acquired. She helped in the shop when it was necessary, she looked after affairs when her husband was away and she organized the large household which included apprentices and female shop assistants as well as her own immediate family. That immediate family consisted of ten children — eight of whom survived, and her own mother who lived with them in her old age. In addition there were at least two women servants who helped with the organization of the household.

The provision of meals and linen for such a household, at a time when there were no mechanical aids and not even piped water, must have been an enormously time-consuming activity. It also has to be remembered that Elizabeth Cadbury had a baby every one to two years for the first fifteen years of her married life. Yet at the same time she was taking an active part in the business and living above the shop at a time when virtually no limitations existed on shop hours. This meant that household affairs had to be organized to fit in with those hours. In 1815, for example, when Richard was away in London buying fabrics for the shop, one of his letters to his wife included not only family news and inquiries about the children but also information about his commercial activities. He had already sent 'some coloured and scarlet whittles and scarves', some with the car men and others to go in the coach the next day. 'Bombazines I have been after', he told her, 'but I find it difficult to get all my colours. Such as I have met with are very nice and tomorrow I am to look out my black ones.' He was anxious to know whether she had had any news from Ireland about the linens; meanwhile he had ordered a bonnet for his daughter Sarah and assured his wife that the fresh eggs from Birmingham which she had sent had arrived safely.

In 1812 business was going sufficiently well for Richard Tapper Cadbury to take a modest second house in Islington Row, on the outskirts of the town and virtually in the country. The younger children went there to live with their nurse whilst their parents got away from the business as often as they could to visit them. The family kept pigeons, rabbits, a dog and a cat at the country house and since the garden was small, a second plot of land was rented nearby where strawberries and other fruit and vegetables were grown. Mrs Cadbury was now supervising two households and with her own older daughters she moved constantly between them. In 1827 she was unwell and soon after, Richard was glad to be able to report to his youngest daughter Emma that he had been gratified to find her well enough, 'to see her walk to town, and to bustle about all day without apparent fatigue.' The sons followed in their father's footsteps and were apprenticed — the eldest, Benjamin, to a draper in London in training to take over the family business. The second son, John, was apprenticed to a tea and coffee dealer in Leeds and in 1824, after a spell in London to gain more experience, he came back to Birmingham and set up in business next door to his father and brother.

The daughters, again like their mother, had no formal apprenticeship. Indeed there were very few trades where it was possible for girls to be apprenticed, since craft rules had always been concerned with the guarding of skills for men. But the Cadbury girls had informal domestic apprenticeships. They learnt to help their mother from a very early age and Maria and Ann would often assist their father in the shop. They were clearly brought up to see this as in no way reflecting on their femininity or gentility. Like their mother, they were no doubt just as much at home cooking, preserving, or preparing the house for winter by putting old extra carpets down. The business was a part of the life of every member of the family; as Elizabeth Cadbury wrote when, in 1828, the Bull Street premises were being altered and they were worried as to the effect this would have on the light in the parlour, '. . . I suppose we must not complain as it is for the business'.

Richard Tapper Cadbury's business was clearly doing quite well in the 1820s and he was publicly regarded as one of the substantial Birmingham tradesmen. But he could not afford to let matters drift, for around him the patterns of retailing were changing and this offered considerable opportunities. Despite the absence of a technological revolution in the retail trade, its organization was soon marked by the changes associated with the early development of industrial capitalism. Population growth and urbanization meant that there were large concentrations of people needing to buy. Factory production meant that some consumer items became much more easily and cheaply available — the Staffordshire pots for which the region was famous are examples of such items. In time the transport revolution meant that distribution networks could be established and transport speeded up. The traditional fairs and markets which had been central to eighteenth century consumer patterns were not specialized enough to supply the new demands. Sometimes consumers themselves tried to organize adequate supplies of what they saw as important items. A public subscription was established in Birmingham in 1791 to try to get a good fish shop set up in the town. This effort, together with other consumer-oriented activities, was lauded by James Bisset in his *Poetic Survey around Birmingham* of 1800.

> And Epicureans, then, may have their wish,
> And tho' an inland place, find good fresh fish,
> For many schemes suggested have been tried,
> To have our markets constantly supplied
> With ev'ry thing that's good, and cheap in reason,
> Fruit, fish or fowl, and rarities in season . . .[16]

Weekly markets remained very important for the sale of food-stuffs; in fact there was no national marketing system for food until after 1850, but gradually the markets became more organized. In the late eighteenth century a cattle market would often occupy the main street of a town one day a week, and this interfered considerably with other kinds of business and trading. Mrs Lucy Benton recalled New Street, which became one of Birmingham's main shopping streets, in the year 1817; there was an inn, the 'Old Crown' where the pig market was held:

> . . . all respectable females who traversed the street on market days had to turn into the middle of it to preserve their cleanliness, the footpaths being reserved for the special accommodation of the superior animal to whom the spot was devoted . . .[17]

Such an arrangement would hardly do for a town which depended economically on attracting buyers and selling its products to the rest of the country. The Birmingham markets were first centralized into the Bull Ring, and then construction of a market hall began in 1833, authorized by one of the town improvement acts and with a market committee responsible for its good order.[18]

Meanwhile shopkeepers were beginning to think about changing their practices. Larger towns meant the decline of custom based on kinship and on friendship — customers now had to be attracted from the streets and into the shops. This meant that the display of wares assumed a new importance and changes had to be made in the appearance of shops. John Cadbury was the first retailer in Birmingham to introduce plate glass windows which allowed for a much more attractive display. His friend Thomas Southall, who had a chemist's shop opposite, also had the new windows installed and the two of them would chat whilst they carefully polished them up in the mornings. A guide book to Birmingham in 1825 referred to the town as in 'the high tide of retail trade'. 'The shops' it continued, 'of the higher degrees are very handsomely fitted up; the form and sweep of the windows, and the style of the decorations, emulating those of the Metropolis.'[19] Superior shopkeepers began to advertise in the local press as another way of attracting trade, though some of the old-established families were shocked at this 'puffing', as it was called. Richard Tapper Cadbury made a regular practice of advertising in *Aris' Birmingham Gazette* and, like many other drapers, he would make a particular point of advertising when he had just brought in his new stock from London.

Contemporaries who commented on improvements in the organization of shopping tended to refer to the drapery business for it was the first branch of the trade to exhibit the characteristics of modern retailing systematically. Many traders in the eighteenth and early nineteenth century combined production and distribution; the butcher killed and cut his meat, the baker baked and sold his bread, the candlestickmaker produced his metal goods as well as retailing them. This combination of production and distribution, based on a large household which utilized the labour of all family members, was in decline at least in the large town by the mid-nineteenth century. Town butchers were increasingly specializing between killing and cutting on the one hand and retailing on the other. Candlestickmakers no longer existed as such; the production of hardware in workshops and small factories had become the staple trade of the Black Country and ironmongers would then sell these products. Baking, however, was still dominated by the independent master who baked and sold — the big change there had been from home baking. The draper had the advantage of being relatively free from production functions; the only item which required preparing for sale was thread. Developments in textile production, particularly cotton, meant that there was an expanding mass market for cloth and by the 1820s the drapery shops in towns and cities were bigger than any other shops. Drapers were able to concentrate their capital on shop improvements. They were frequently the first to introduce plate glass windows, window displays and gas lighting, and they also led the field in price ticketing and cash trading which were two of the next developments.[20]

Despite the advantages of his trade, however, Benjamin Head Cadbury, who took over the drapery business from his father, does not seem to have been such a good businessman as his brother, John. John not only introduced the latest retailing improvements in his tea and coffee shop but he also decided to branch out into the manufacture of cocoa as soon as he had the capital available. This production was not based on the household, however, rather he established a completely separate factory and ran the two sides of the business simultaneously for as long as he could. In 1826 he married his first wife Priscilla, but she died in 1828. Around 1830 the introduction of cocoa powder made possible an instant chocolate drink, and this led John in 1831 to set up a small factory around the corner from the shop. In 1832 he married for the second time. His wife Candia Barrow was the daughter of a Quaker shipping merchant. Initially the couple lived over the shop, but after the birth of their first son John they moved to Edgbaston and soon found the house which became the family home for nearly forty years. It was not a large house but they gradually altered and extended it. Their daughter Maria, in her recollections of her childhood, commented on the fact that her mother lived on the business premises initially; by the time that Maria was writing it was obviously something that had to be explained, and her account was that Candia liked to be beside her husband all the day in the early part of their marriage. There was no mention of the importance of her contribution to the work which had to be done. The profits from the shop and the factory were sufficient to warrant setting up a suburban home, but there was no money to spare. Candia could cook and she supervised the home wash once a fortnight in the back kitchen. But she was used to country living and it was these standards which they sought in their Edgbaston home, as Maria described it:

> . . . it was almost cottage like in appearance and too small without many alterations, but its countrylike surroundings decided our parents to take it, make more rooms, and lay out the gardens to their own taste . . . our Mother was exceedingly fond of gardening, but our Father was greatly occupied with business and town affairs and other interests and he had very little time during the week for his garden.

The house soon had a playroom, which was later turned into a schoolroom, and a nursery upstairs for the little ones. Such a differentiation between rooms had not been possible in the combined home/workplace in Bull Street. Suburban housing allowed for a different notion of childhood as well as a different role for women, and this differentiation of role was mirrored in the new definitions of physical space. Candia and her children's lives were focused on home and school, whilst her husband used the Edgbaston home as a happy family base for his business and public activities. 'Our dear Father was a very steady industrious man, noted for punctuality, and took great pride in his business, everything being arranged in beautiful order', wrote Maria. In 1847 John Cadbury opened larger premises for his cocoa production, some way from the shop but nearer to home. His time was increasingly spent at the factory whilst his brother Benjamin, who had recently come into partnership with him, managed the commercial side. Cocoa production provided a popular drink for temperance advocates in this period, and John and Candia were amongst the earliest supporters of the temperance movement. Indeed family habits clearly involved some small-scale advertising in themselves; when Maria was sent away to school her father sent some cocoa to the Misses Dymond who ran the school. Maria reported in one of her regular letters home that:

> Miriam Dymond told me that they liked Father's cocoas so much that they have persuaded their grocer to supply them regularly with it, and we have it regularly every 5th day morning for breakfast.

Meanwhile Richard Tapper Cadbury had decided to retire. At

64 he left the business in the hands of his eldest son Benjamin and bought a house in Edgbaston, where he lived with his wife and two remaining unmarried daughters on a 'modest competency'. He still went into town a great deal, however, in connection either with his public activities or his business interests. For his wife and daughters it was a very different matter. Once they had physically moved from the workplace it became marginal to their lives — the business was simply where the money came from, rather than something which occupied many of their working hours. It was Elizabeth's daughter-in-law, another Candia — Candia Wadkin, who now took over the responsibilities in the shop. The Bull Street house had been smartened up before Benjamin and Candia moved in and an effort was made to make it more comfortable as a home. Candia was impressed to find it so

. . . completely metamorphosed that it was almost difficult to recognize it as the old family mansion, the difference of furniture and the addition of window curtains have given the parlour quite another character, it now appears a much squarer room and more comfortable and had been dressed out with flowers . . . some hyacinths on the chimney piece are in full bloom in addition to this there are several plants in full blossom so that we have quite a country appearance . . .

Obviously every effort was being made to downplay the urban features of Bull Street life. The yard had been whitewashed and the upstairs sitting room and bedrooms comfortably fitted up. Candia was kept extremely busy with a growing family: she soon had six daughters and a son, and the same kind of business responsibilities that her mother-in-law had assumed. In the 1830s, for example, she gave Benjamin news of the shop when he was away: 'Customers have been flowing in very satisfactorily today and all has, I believe, gone on comfortably, all appear attentive, equally so or more anxious to be so than if thou wast at home . . .'

Candia was closely involved in the education of her children as were her sisters-in-law. The girls' education was started at home and then they went to a Birmingham day school before going to the same Quaker boarding school as their cousin Maria. They were given an early training in domesticity; dolls, prams, pincushions and workboxes figure prominently as presents, and they were taught to knit and to sew, to make their own clothes and to repair them. The family stayed in the Bull Street house until 1844 and then they too moved into the outskirts of Edgbaston; the last clear links were cut between the women and the family businesses. In 1846 Benjamin gave up the drapery business and went into partnership with John, presumably having decided that with the new, larger factory about to open there would be plenty of work and enough profits for the two of them.

The separation between home and work made substantial differences to the daily lives of both men and women in middle-class families. The Cadbury men still went to work every day and then came home to their families. This meant that there was a much clearer distinction between work-time and leisure-time and there was also a much clearer distinction between public and private life. As long as home and workplace were combined it must often have been difficult to categorize whether activities which went on there were 'public' or 'private' and indeed it would probably have been a pretty irrelevant question. Was feeding an apprentice, for example, who would usually have been the son of a friend and who would have generally been treated as one of the family, a business or domestic matter? The point is, of course, that they were one and the same thing, and one clear demonstration of this is that shopkeepers such as the Cadburys started to keep separate household accounts only when the separation had taken place between work and home. The physical separation of the two was the culmination of a long process during which time middle-class men's activities had become increasingly differentiated from those of middle-class women. Women's participation in family businesses had always tended to be an informal affair; the fact that married women had no property rights meant that the business was always legally owned by the husband as long as he lived. Only widows and spinsters could run their own businesses in their own names. Furthermore the training and skills had always been tied to masculinity — women were not apprenticed to drapers or to tea and coffee dealers. But the increasing complexity of the commercial world and its increasing formalization in this period meant that it was becoming more difficult for women to participate even informally. Furthermore, as new retailing skills became important, the training which encouraged these skills was not available for women. The informal 'picking up' of the business which was what women relied on was no longer necessarily enough.

But in addition to the increasing difficulty of women learning how to do business, there were the aspirations for a separate domestic sphere and the positive desire to move away from the shop if this were financially possible. Initially efforts were often made to make the shop more like a 'home' — as, for example when the Bull Street parlour was made more comfortable with curtains for Benjamin and Candia, and an attempt was made to make it look more countrylike by putting in flowers and plants. But in the end the only way to have a fully private home, where family time would not be interrupted by the apprentices, late customers or visiting business contacts, was by geographically dividing the home from the workplace. The most crucial effect of this in terms of sexual divisions was that it meant wives and daughters were no longer there to be called upon for help. Daughters were educated to be wives and mothers and to expect to be financially dependent on their husbands. This did not mean that women no longer had any financial relation to the business. Their money, acquired through marriage settlements, remained a vital source of capital. In fact John Cadbury's sons saved the family cocoa business, which went through a bad patch in the 1850s, by investing some money left to them by their mother. But the *direct* working relation of women to the business had gone and 'work' was now what their husbands did when they left the house in the morning.

Women were furthermore increasingly cut off from the variety of other *public* activities which their menfolk engaged in. 1780—1850 was the age of societies, when societies were formed in aid of every possible cause. These societies ranged from ones with a primarily political orientation to those concerned with commercial activities, self-education in its broadest sense and philanthropic works. It was exceedingly difficult for women to be involved in any of these except the philanthropic, and even there they were encouraged to participate privately and informally rather than being engaged in the public activities — the meetings and the dinners.[21] A typical day for John Cadbury might have involved an early rise, a walk with some of the children and the dogs, back home for breakfast, a walk into town to work, a morning in the shop or factory, a 12 o'clock meeting at the Public Office of the Street Commissioners (the oligarchic élite which was responsible for some aspects of town government up to 1851 and of which he was a member for many years), followed by something to eat in the respectable hostelry next door where street commissioners often gathered, an afternoon back at the business with a 5 o'clock philanthropic meeting of one of the many committees of which he was an active member, after which he would have returned home for what was left of the day. Candia, by contrast, would have spent her day in Edgbaston caring for the children both physically and educationally and supervising the household. In 1851, when they had six children, she had two female servants in the house and this was certainly not a generous number for a middle-class household, given the amount of domestic labour required in a pre-mechanical age.

If she had a little spare time she might have visited one or two poor families in whom she took a special interest, but as her daughter Maria recalled, she rarely left home:

Our precious Mother had a very busy home life with her five boys and one girl, living amongst them as much as possible; she was a lovingly watchful and affectionate wife and mother seldom visiting from home . . .

Candia's social life centred on her extended family and the Quaker network of Friends. Candia was indeed an essentially 'private person' whilst her husband was well known as a 'public man'. Such a social demarcation of male as 'public' and female as 'private' was both reinforced and encouraged by the physical separation between work and home.

Acknowledgements

This chapter is part of a larger research project, financed by the Social Science Research Council, and done jointly with Leonnore Davidoff, with whom all aspects of this article have been discussed. Thanks also to Veronica Beechey, Stuart Hall and Susan Meikle for their comments.

Notes

1. Gaskell, Mrs E. (1853) *Cranford.*
2. For an account of this process see Adburgham, A. (1964) *Shops and Shopping* 1800—1914, London; Davis, D. (1966) *A History of Shopping,* London; Alexander, D. (1970) *Retailing in England during the Industrial Revolution.* London.
3. Thompson, E.P. and Yeo, E. (1973) *The Unknown Mayhew. Selections from the Morning Chronicle 1849—50,* Harmondsworth.
4. Kenrick, J. (1854) *Memoir of the Rev. John Kentish.* Birmingham, p. 9.
5. Bennett, A. (1908) *The Old Wives Tale,* Pan edn (1964) London, p. 30.
6. See Davis, D. *op. cit.*
7. Alexander, D. *op. cit.*
8. This separation between the shop and the home was confined to the most prosperous tradesmen, while many shops still remain combined workplace and home in the late nineteenth century. See Vigne, T. and Howkins, A. 'The small shopkeeper in industrial and market towns', in G. Crossick (ed.) (1977) *The Lower Middle Class in Britain 1870—1914,* London.
9. See the companion article in this volume, Hall, C. 'The home turned upside down? The working-class family in cotton textiles in the early nineteenth century.'
10. See Samuel, R. (1977) 'The workshop of the world: steam power and hand technology in mid-Victorian Britain', *History Workshop* No. 3, Spring.

11. Gaskell, Mrs. E. (1854) *North and South*, Harmondsworth (1970). Rose, M.B. (1978) *The Gregs of Styal*, London.
12. Davidoff, L. and Hall, C. 'The architecture of public and private life: English middle class society in a provincial town 1780—1850', in A. Sutcliffe (ed.) *The pursuit of Urban History* (forthcoming).
13. Hall, C. (1979) 'The early formation of Victorian domestic ideology' in S. Buram (ed.) *Fit Work for Women*, London.
14. Hall, C. 'The active age of charity: men, women and philanthropy 1780—1850' (forthcoming).
15. The material on the Cadburys which forms most of the rest of the paper is drawn from the Cadbury Collection. The Collection, which is housed in Birmingham Reference Library, comprises a rich series of manuscripts plus drawings and illustrations.
16. Bisset, J. (1800) *A Poetic Survey around Birmingham*, Birmingham.
17. Benton, Mrs Lucy (1877) *Recollections of New Street in the year 1817*, Birmingham.
18. On the municipal history of Birmingham see Gill, C. (1952) *History of Birmingham* vol. 1, Oxford.
19. Drake, J. (1825) *The Picture of Birmingham*, Birmingham, p. 69.
20. Alexander, D. *op. cit.*
21. Hall, C. 'The active age of charity: men, women and philanthropy 1780—1850' (forthcoming). Prochaska, F.K. (1980) *Women and Philanthropy in Nineteenth Century England*, Oxford.

1.2 The home turned upside down? The working-class family in cotton textiles 1780—1850

CATHERINE HALL

In 1844 Friedrich Engels wrote an account of working-class life in Manchester — the heartland of the Manchester cotton industry — based on a combination of personal observation and documentary sources. One of the things he remarked upon, which troubled him greatly, was the way in which the introduction of machinery in the cotton mills was driving men out of work and encouraging the employment of women and children, who provided cheaper labour. Engels saw the employment of married women as something which would break up the family and have the most disastrous consequences for the social order:

> The employment of the wife dissolves the family utterly and of necessity, and this dissolution, in our present society, which is based upon the family, brings the most demoralising consequences for parents as well as children. A mother who has no time to trouble herself about her child, to perform the most ordinary loving services for it during its first year, who scarcely indeed sees it, can be no real mother to the child, must inevitably grow indifferent of it, treat it unlovingly like a stranger. The children who grow up under such conditions are utterly ruined for later family life, can never feel at home in the family which they themselves found . . .

In many cases, he continued, the family would not be entirely dissolved by the wife's employment but 'turned upside down. The wife supports the family, the husband sits at home, tends the children, sweeps the room and cooks.' These conditions, he argued, unsexed both sexes, leaving the men without their masculinity and the women without their true femininity.[1] Such an association between masculinity and paid employment on the one hand,

Specially commissioned for this volume
© The Open University, 1982

femininity and domestic labour and child care on the other was a middle-class one, commonplace in the mid-nineteenth century, but it is one which needs some explanation.

Engels himself, like many of his fellow social and political critics, looked back to the pre-industrial family economy with somewhat rose coloured spectacles. Yet in that pre-industrial economy all members of the family had worked. As long as that work had been done at home there was no question of castigating married women for being employed. It was the separation which took place between work and home, and the fact that women started going out into public places such as mills to work, so that it was no longer possible simply to combine employment with domesticity, that troubled many commentators. Furthermore the fact that women might get an independent wage in a factory was another source of worry. This financial independence gave the mill girls their notorious 'cheekiness' which was much remarked upon. It is very noticeable that there was never any public outcry about women's work as domestic servants for, despite what were in many cases appalling exploitative conditions of work, that work was private, carried out in other people's homes and thus not offending against Victorian notions of the woman as the 'angel in the house'. Similarly sweated work caused little concern until later in the nineteenth century. It was the factories and the mines, with their public presence and their mixed labour force, which forced questions about the propriety of married women's paid employment into the forefront of Victorian public life.

Women had always been centrally concerned with the production of textiles. The changes associated with the industrial revolution in textiles did not take women into a new kind of work, but rather fundamentally altered the ways in which their work was organized.

As Ivy Pinchbeck wrote in her classic study of women's work in the Industrial Revolution, from the earliest times 'the productive work of women has been of greater importance in the textile industry than in any other trade.'[2] Women had always been responsible for clothing the family, but as the textile industries were gradually reorganized on a commercial scale, so women had become wage earners rather than small independent producers. By the eighteenth century the production of cotton textiles had long been under the control of merchant capitalists, with the spinning and weaving being done as outwork. The transformation of the mid-eighteenth century was from cottage to factory production, and gave increasing control to the manufacturers at the expense of the workers. The pre-industrial family economy, although often in fact organized by mercantile capitalists rather than as small units of independent production, had been able to maintain considerable autonomy — as for example in the decision about hours of work and how to take time off.

The traditional division of labour in cotton textiles was for the father to superintend the weaving which would be done by himself and his sons, whilst his wife organized the initial processes of picking and cleaning the cotton, which would be done by the younger children, and the spinning which she herself would do perhaps with some help from her daughters. Wordsworth in his condemnation of the factory system and the ways in which it had destroyed the 'natural' economy of the family, later evoked a somewhat idyllic account of the mother at work, surrounded by her children who learnt as they laboured:

> The habitations empty! or perchance
> The Mother left alone — no helping hand
> To rock the cradle of her peevish babe;
> No daughters round her, busy at the wheel,
> Or in despatch of each day's little growth
> Of household occupation; no nice arts
> Of needle-work; no bustle at the fire,
> Where once the dinner was prepared with pride;
> Nothing to speed the day, or cheer the mind;
> Nothing to praise, to teach, or to command![3]

The father occupied the supervisory role in the household. He was seen as the head of the household and the master of the little community. As the weaver he was also the overall *organizer* and *discipliner* of labour. It was he who secured the raw cotton from the merchant and sold the finished cloth back.

Until the end of the seventeenth century the cotton industry, which was always centred in Lancashire, was of very minor importance in comparison to wool which had long been established as England's greatest export trade. From the end of the seventeenth century, however, cotton had become increasingly fashionable and by the mid-eighteenth century cotton imports were rapidly on the increase. The spinners in a family often could not produce enough to keep the weavers busy. It was generally assumed that one weaver could occupy three spinners, so sometimes a family would employ neighbouring spinsters to do some extra work.[4] The shortage of yarn led to attempts to invent quicker methods of spinning, and the first of these to be successful on any scale was Hargreaves' spinning jenny which was patented in 1770. The late eighteenth century was a period of major technological innovation — though of course many of the new inventions were not taken up. The jenny multiplied the number of spindles that could be worked by one spinner and increased the production of weft enormously. Initially it was possible to use the jenny at home and, therefore, it led to little change in the organization of work. Gradually, however, larger jennies were designed which had to be assembled in small workshops or factories. At the same time Arkwright's frame came into use which was powered by water and spun a thread which was strong enough for the warp. In 1779 Crompton introduced his mule — the third major invention — which produced an even better thread. The increasing importance of, first water power, and then in the last decades of the eighteenth century steam power, meant that factory production became more important and spinning moved from the home into the factories.[5] Weaving for the moment stayed at home.

The move from the home to the factory involved a crucial change in the sexual division of labour. Spinning at home, as has been seen, was the prerogative of women. But, as Pinchbeck describes, the technological changes which were introduced had vital social consequences. As she puts it:

> . . . when the number of spindles was considerably increased the jennies were gathered into small workshops and worked by men, and after the appearance of the mule in 1779, women spinners were soon superseded. . . . Heavier machines required the strength of men, and spinning on the mule quickly became highly skilled work monopolized by a new class of men spinners. Thus, within the space of one generation, what had been women's hereditary occupation was radically changed . . .[6]

Pinchbeck's account assumes that women could not manage the machines physically and that mule spinning soon became defined as a *skilled male* occupation, therefore excluding women. This raises important questions about the definition of strength and skill and the way in which both attributes belong to men. Why was it that men became the spinners in the factories when women had been the spinners in the home? Initially it was women and children who worked the jennies in the early factories, but with the introduction of the mule their labour was displaced in favour of relatively highly paid male operatives.

Pinchbeck explains this with reference to physical strength — the need for such strength necessitated the employment of men and this has become the standard explanation. This is not, however, an entirely straightforward issue. Men develop the kinds of strength they do partly because of the kinds of work which they do, just as women are encouraged to develop their manual dexterity because it is seen as a feminine attribute. There is evidence to show that bodily differences between men and women have to be understood socially as well as biologically. As Cynthia Cockburn suggests:

> A small physical *difference* in size, strength and reproductive function is developed into an increasing relative physical *advantage* to men and vastly multiplied by differential access to technology . . . The appropriation of muscle, capability, tools and machinery by men is an important source of women's subordination, indeed it is a part of the process by which females are constituted as women . . .[7]

The explanation of the displacement of women spinners in terms of male skill is also open to question. Women's work is almost invariably characterised by low pay, lack of craft traditions, weak unions and unskilled status. As Anne Phillips and Barbara Taylor argue, this might have more to do with definitions of what is male and what is female than with an 'objective' judgment about skill:

> . . . the classification of women's jobs as unskilled and men's jobs as skilled or semi-skilled frequently bears little relation to the actual amount of training or ability required for them. Skill definitions are saturated with sexual bias. The work of women is often deemed inferior simply because it is women who do it. Women workers carry into the workplace their status as subordinate individuals, and this status comes to define the value of the work they do. Far from being an objective economic fact, skill is often an ideological category imposed on certain types of work by virtue of the sex and power of the workers who perform it.[8]

Clearly men had to develop the skills associated with spinning since traditionally it had been women's work. Nevertheless they were soon able to monopolize mule spinning in the factories.[9] Lazonick explains this in terms of their established social position and the way in which they were able to carry their supervisory role from the home into the factory. The early factory spinners, who were women and children, needed no auxiliaries. As the machines became more complex, however, each spinner employed two or three assistants over whom he had direct authority. He usually paid them himself out of his own gross wages. Lazonick argues that the moment at which the spinners took on a supervisory role was the moment at which male spinners established their dominance. The men often employed their own wives, children or other close relatives as their underlings so that 'it was the authority of the father carried over from his social position in the family which suited the adult male to the job of mule spinning'.[10]

It was this which allowed the persistence of a kind of family economy in the factory which Smelser was the first to comment on and which, it has recently been argued, survived in varied forms for very much longer than is usually thought.[11] It seems that in the 1820s and 30s there was an increasing tendency for the manufacturer to take over employing the piecer, or assistant, rather than the spinner, and this threatened to limit the authority of the spinners. But in the 1840s this threat was lifted and the superior status of the mule spinner was confirmed, which included his authority over his family's labour.[12]

The mule spinners did not leave their dominance to chance. Until the 1820s the exclusion of women from spinning tended to be informal and piecemeal, but the heartfelt protest of one male trade union official in 1824 who appealed for the preservation of the position of the head of the household would find many echoes. 'We do not,' he said, 'stand opposed to women working, but we do enter our protest against the principles on which they are employed. The women, in nine cases out of ten, have only themselves to support — while the men, generally have families.'[13]

Girls' employment, meanwhile, meant that they were 'rendered independent of their natural guardians', who often had to become dependent on them. In time the spinners decided to form a national organization and the exclusive practices of their trade were one of their earliest concerns. Craft unions, like the gilds before them, took the limitations on entry to the trade as essential to the protection of their position. At their meeting in the Isle of Man in 1829 the spinners stipulated 'that no person or persons be learned or allowed to spin except the son, brother, or orphan nephew of spinners.'[14] Those women spinners who had managed to maintain their position were advised to form their own union. From then on the entry to the trade was very tightly controlled and the days of the female spinners were indeed numbered.

So far we have seen little evidence of the home being turned upside down. Indeed the patriarchal authority of the father had been maintained in the family by a reorganization of the sexual division of labour. Men had gone into mule spinning in the factory because it was the important job. Those men who became spinners had not for the most part been weavers previously; rather they tended to be immigrants from the countryside or from Ireland who were coming into the towns seeking work.[15] Meanwhile what was happening to the weavers? Weaving, as has been seen, had traditionally been men's work in the pre-industrial economy and often involved supervising the family as a productive unit. The mechanisation of spinning in the late eighteenth century meant that there was an increased demand for handloom weavers and for a short period they were able to earn good wages — this was the so-called 'golden age' of the handloom weaver. This period of prosperity was later somewhat mythologized as in this description by Radcliffe written in 1828:

> Their dwellings and small gardens clean and neat — all the family well clad — the men with each a watch in his pocket, and the women dressed to their own fancy, — the church crowded to excess every Sunday, — every house well-furnished with a clock in elegant mahogany or fancy case, — handsome tea services in Staffordshire ware . . . . Birmingham, Potteries, and Sheffield wares for necessary use and ornament . . . . many cottage families had their cow . . .[16]

But these standards were not to last. As E. P. Thompson has described in his classic account of the decline of the handloom weavers, wages started to be cut from the 1790s and this was possible because of the enormous number of unskilled immigrants who came into the trade and the gradual collapse of customary rights and craft protection. Women, particularly those displaced by factory spinning, and children were brought into weaving, especially during the Napoleonic wars, and weaving became

> . . . an employment to the whole family, even when spinning was withdrawn from the home. The young children winding bobbins, older children watching for faults, picking over the cloth, or helping to throw the shuttle in the broad-loom; adolescents working a second or third loom; the wife taking a turn at weaving in and among her domestic employments. The family was together . . .

Such togetherness may have had its tensions but was surely preferable to the employment of both adults and children in factories, which became the unpopular alternative when weaving no longer provided a way of making a living.[17] The position of the handloom weavers was already in decline when power looms began to be introduced. Experiments had been made with power-looms since the 1780s but it was not until the 1830s and 40s that they were introduced on a large scale. It was women and children who were employed on these looms, and very few adult males. Indeed the weavers with their tradition of independence strongly resisted factory employment until 'poverty broke down all defences'. As the Select Committee on the weavers of 1834, which had been set up to consider their collective protests, remarked:

> . . . no man would like to work in a power-loom, they do not like it, there is such a clattering and noise it would almost make some men mad; and next, he would have to be subject to a discipline that a hand-loom weaver can never submit to.[18]

Even if they had been prepared to submit, it would have been very difficult for the weavers to find factory employment. Indeed in the early 1830s between one third and a half of the labour force in the cotton mills was under 21. The employment of women and children as weavers, to the exclusion of men, represented a decisive break with the traditional sexual division of labour in the family. A child could earn more in the factory than his/her father could earn at home on the loom. Furthermore it was the masters who employed these hands. Consequently, as Smelser argued, 'the weaving innovations altered the traditional form of the family economy more radically than did the spinning improvements.[19] The men who had been at the heads of productive households were unemployed or deriving a pittance from their work whilst their wives and children were driven out to the factories. It was this that Engels was referring to when he described the home as 'turned upside down'.

His was far from the only voice raised in concern about the 'inversion' of male and female roles. The idea of a dependent wife, whose main task was to care for the home and children, had become increasingly popular amongst the middle classes in early nineteenth century England. Such an ideal became more realistically possible as informal working partnerships between husband and wife ceased to be the major form of business organization and were replaced by partnerships between men, whilst the separation between workplace and home became an aspiration for significant sections of the wealthier bourgeoisie. Middle-class philanthropists, who took it upon themselves to improve the manners and morals of the working classes, were amongst the first to carry bourgeois notions of the perfect family to the working class. As the Registrar General defined it in his introduction to the 1851 Census, the perfect English family in its 'essential type' was composed of, 'husband, wife, children and servants, or, less perfectly but more commonly, of husband, wife, and children'.[20]

The less perfect family might at least aspire to a non-working wife, for the middle-class critique of working wives and the belief that their employment endangered the very structure of English society, had long been current.

The 1840s saw what has been described as a 'coincidence of interests' between philanthropists, the state — representing the collective interests of capital — and the male working class who were represented by the trade union movement and Chartism — which co-operated to reduce female and child labour and to limit the length of the working day.[21]

The ten hours movement could be seen as having compromised with the philanthropists, seeing the restriction of women's and children's factory hours as the only way to achieve a reduction of hours for men as well.

At the same time of course the men were responding to prevalent ideas amongst the respectable about the proper place of women. As Joseph Corbett a button burnisher in Birmingham for over 40 years said when commenting on the unfortunate effects of his mother's necessary employment and the absence of proper domestic instruction for working class women:

> To the best of her ability she performed the important duties of a wife and mother. She was lamentably deficient in domestic knowledge; in that most important of all human instruction, how to make the home and the fire-side to possess a charm for her husband and children she had never received one single lesson . . . Poor thing, the power to make home cheerful and comfortable was never given to her. She knew not the value of cherishing in my father's mind a love of domestic objects . . . Not one moment's happiness did I ever see under my father's roof . . .[22]

In fact the extent of married women's employment was exaggerated in the context of fears about the imminent collapse of the family. In 1833 the majority of female textile workers were girls between 16 and 21 and only 25 per cent of female cotton workers were married in the Lancashire district in 1841. Scott and Tilly argue that, 'it looks as though as industrialization advanced . . . fewer married women worked'; they may well be underestimating the degree of married women's paid labour because of the difficulty of taking casual employment such as charring or laundry work into account, or indeed that traditional method for women of making a living — being a landlady.[23] In the cotton towns the presence of some married women working provided employment for others — as tea-makers, washerwomen, nurses or needlewomen. Hewitt estimates that in 1851 approximately 27 per cent of the cotton operatives in the Lancashire district were either married or widowed, and of course widows were an important group of working women. Her investigation into middle class fears about female operatives reveals the extent of the prejudice, for example about the open enjoyment of sexual relations, which underpinned the assumptions made about the likely depravity associated with women's paid work.[24]

The effects of mechanization on the sexual division of labour in the two major processes in cotton textile production — spinning and weaving — were, therefore, on the face of it significantly different. In spinning, male authority was maintained by men's appropriation of what had previously been women's work; in weaving, women and children were brought in to operate the new power looms and men were for a time displaced. Men's position as the head of the household and the breadwinner was challenged. This state of affairs, which so disturbed middle-class observers, did not, however, last very long. The combination of successive factory acts, which initially restricted and finally more or less prevented the employment of child labour, together with the pressure on married women not to work, meant a gradual reorganization of the labour force and the increasing employment of men. Women remained very important in weaving, and the unusual situation was found in Lancashire of men and women working together, apparently for equal pay. A careful examination of male and female weaving, however, reveals differences in status which meant that men nearly always earned more.[25] Weavers earned considerably less than spinners, yet even amongst the male weavers demands were being made by the middle of the nineteenth century for a 'family wage' and some of the women seem to have supported this. In 1853, for example, Mrs Fletcher of Preston urged that 'every man should earn enough money to keep himself and his family without the necessity of sending his wife into the mill.[26] The idea of the family wage was an adaptation from the bourgeois ideal of a family in which the wife and children could be financially dependent on the husband and father. Respectable women should not work for money. Such an ideal represented a financial impossibility for most working-class families and its existence had important effects on the evaluation of men's and women's work. It became a recognized part of trade union bargaining that men were negotiating for a wage which would support a dependent wife and family — whereas women were working for 'pin money'. In fact, of course, married women entered employment because it was economically essential for the survival of the family, and Anderson's data on working-class families in Preston makes this abundantly clear.[27] Single women and widows had to earn to survive. But the existence of such an ideal, which legitimated low pay for women, regardless of whether they were unmarried or married, whether they were able to be dependents or were supporting others, on the grounds that they did not really *need* to work, clearly had effects in terms of increasingly marginalizing their work and reducing their status relative to men.

Nevertheless more women remained in relatively skilled work in the textile industry than in any other branch of manufacturing, and this gave them a certain strength, which was reflected in women's political activities up to the 1840s. After mid-century, however, the stabilization of the patterns of male and female work, the decline of militant working class politics, the weight of the most skilled and respectable sections of the male working class in trade union politics and the pervasiveness of domestic ideology with its inflexible notions of male and female spheres all contributed to a 'near-total absence of women from the public and organized life of the working class between the 1840s and the 1890s.'[28] The emphasis here has to be on *public* and *organized* since in the informal networks of working class communities women were absolutely central. Furthermore the traditions of women's relative independence proved very important in the later development of suffrage politics.

The transformation from family production to factory production, from small independent producers or commercial capitalists to largescale industrial capitalism provoked, as can be seen, a period of transition and re-accommodation in the sexual division of labour. The break up of the family economy, with the threat this could present to the male head of household, who was already faced with a loss of control over his own labour, demanded a re-assertion of male authority. The shift from home production to factory production, the separation of work from home, the concept of the individual wage and the new organization of labour within the factory all posed questions for working men and women about their relations to manufacturers and to each other. The new equilibrium, which was established around mid-century and coincided with the defeat of Chartism, had its work and its home dimensions, now no longer combined in one set of social relations. The social relations of the 'golden age' of Victorian prosperity were constructed around negotiated settlements between the skilled male working class and capital on the one hand, and the continued subordination of women within the working class family on the other.

Acknowledgement

Thanks to Sally Alexander, Veronica Beechey and Sue Himmelweit for comments.

Notes

1. Engels, F. (1962) 'The condition of the working class in England' in *Karl Marx and Friedrich Engels on Britain,* Moscow, pp. 175—80. Engels was most unusual for his time in the political interest which he took in the 'woman question'. His critique of marriage and the family *The Origin of the Family, Private Property and the State* first published in 1844 has provided a starting point for most socialist analysis of the family.
2. Pinchbeck, I. (1981) *Women Workers and the Industrial Revolution 1750—1850* London, p. 111.
3. Wordsworth, W. *The Excursion, Book 8* quoted in E. P. Thompson (1963) *The Making of the English Working Class,* London, p. 343.
4. Clark, A. (1968) *Working Life of Women in the Seventeenth Century,* London.
5. Pinchbeck, I. *op. cit.*
6. Ibid, p. 148.
7. Cockburn, C. (1981) 'The material of male power', *Feminist Review,* No. 9, p. 44.
8. Phillips, A. and Taylor, B. (1980) 'Sex and skill: notes towards a feminist economics', *Feminist Review,* no. 6, p. 79.
9. It is important to note that it was *mule spinning* which men monopolized. Mules were highly technical and delicate machines. Women continued in throstle and ring spinning which had a different labour process and did not require the same kind of trained labour force.
10. Lazonick, W.H. (1976) 'Historical origins of the sex based division of labour under capitalism: a study of the British textile industry during the Industrial Revolution'. Harvard Institute of Economic Research Discussion Paper, No. 497, p. 13.
11. Smelser, N.J. (1959) *Social Change in the Industrial Revolution,* London.
12. Joyce, P. (1980) *Work, Society and Politics: The Culture of the Factory in later Victorian England,* Brighton.
13. Quoted in Smelser, *op. cit,* p. 232.
14. Quoted in Liddington, J. and Norris, J. (1978) *One Hand Tied Behind Us. The Rise of the Women's Suffrage Movement,* London, p. 51.
15. Anderson, M. (1971) *Family Structure in Nineteenth Century Lancashire,* Cambridge.
16. Quoted in Thompson, *op. cit,* p. 276.
17. *Ibid,* p. 306.
18. *Ibid,* p. 307.
19. Smelser *op. cit,* p. 201.
20. *Census of Great Britain 1851* (1854) Population Tables, Part 2, Vol. 1, London.
21. See Barrett, M. and McIntosh, M. 'The "family wage"' (article in this volume).
22. Quoted in Pike, Royston, E. (1966) *Human Documents of the Industrial Revolution in Britain,* London, (1980) p. 234.

23. See Scott, J.W. and Tilly, L.A. 'Women's work and the family in nineteenth-century Europe' (article in this volume).

24. Hewitt, M. (1958) *Wives and Mothers in Victorian England,* London.

25. Joyce, P. *op. cit.*

26. Quoted in Liddington, J. and Norris, J. *op. cit,* p. 53.

27. Anderson, M. *Family Structure in Nineteenth Century Lancashire, op. cit.*

28. Joyce, P. *op. cit,* see Thompson, D.'s article 'Women and nineteenth century radical politics: a lost dimension' in J. Mitchell and A. Oakley (1976) *The Rights and Wrongs of Women,* Harmondsworth.

1.3 Women's work in nineteenth-century London: a study of the years 1820—50

SALLY ALEXANDER

Introduction

Most historians define the working class *de facto* as working men. Occupations, skills, wages, relations of production, the labour process itself, are discussed as if social production were an exclusive male prerogative. Consciously or unconsciously, the world has been conceived in the image of the bourgeois family — the husband is the breadwinner and the wife remains at home attending to housework and child-care. Both the household itself, and women's domestic labour within it are presented as the unchanging backcloth to the world of real historical activity. The labour historian has ignored women as workers — on the labour market and within the household. Consequently women's contribution to production and to the reproduction and maintenance of the labour force as well, has been dismissed. This is partly because the labour and economic historians who first wrote about the working class, wrote about the organized and articulate labour movement, accessible through its trade union records, its newspapers and the occasional autobiography. Only recently have the inaccessible areas of working-class life been approached, but even here the focus has remained on the working man. In every respect women's participation in history has been marginalized.[1]

Feminist history releases women from their obscurity as the wives, mothers and daughters of working men. This does not just mean that family life, housework, the reproduction of the labour force, the transmission of ideology etc. can be added to an already constituted history, but the history of production itself will be rewritten. For the history of production under capitalism, from a feminist perspective, is not simply the class struggle between the

Source: Alexander, S. (1976) Women's work in nineteenth-century London: a study of the years 1820—50, in *The Rights and Wrongs of Women*, Mitchell, J. and Oakley, A. (eds), Penguin, Harmondsworth, extracts from Chapter 2

producer and the owner of the means of production. It is also the development of a particular form of the sexual division of labour in relation to that struggle.

The focus of this article is women's waged work in London in the early Victorian period. London in the period of the industrial revolution has been chosen for two reasons. Firstly, because it offers a wide survey of women's employments within a reasonably manageable geographic unit; and because it illustrates the multiple effects of industrial change on women's work, reminding us that the industrial revolution brought with it more than just machinery and the factory system. [. . .]

The working woman emerged as a 'social problem' in the thirties and forties. Indeed, it is as though the Victorians discovered her, so swiftly and urgently did she become the object of public concern. The dislocations of modern industry, the rapid increase in population, the herding of the population into the towns, drama-tized class antagonisms and forced the condition of the working classes onto the attention of the propertied class as a mass of documentary evidence reveals. The effect of these dislocations upon working-class wives and children became one major focal point of this anxiety. The short-time movement (the struggle of the factory operatives in the Lancashire and Yorkshire textile mills to limit the working day), in particular Sadler's Commission of 1832, first highlighted the problem of the female factory operative. Ten years later, the Children's Employment Commission (1842—3) exposed a string of female occupations in the mines and the traditional outwork trades, where wages and conditions were no less degrading than those in the textile mill. These revelations shattered middle-class complacency and aroused the reformatory zeal of Evangelical and Utilitarian philanthropists. And it is from the philanthropists, as well as factory inspectors, that we receive most of our information on women's work.

This sense of shock at 'the condition of England', as contempo-raries termed it, in particular the apparent destruction of the working-class family, cannot be understood simply from the terrible conditions in the factories alone.[2] The British Industrial Revolution did not take place in a neutral political context. Its formative years, 1790 to 1815, were years in which England was engaged in counter-revolutionary war against France. Jacobinism (the ideology of the French Revolutionaries) and industrial discontent were fused by England's rulers into an indiscriminate image of 'sedition'. Any political or industrial activity among the working class was severely repressed. Out of this repression emerged the distinctive features of Victorian middle-class ideology — a blend of political economy and evangelicalism. The one an ideology appropriate to the 'take off' of the forces of production — the industrial revolution; the other a doctrine demonstrating the fixity of the relations of production. While political economy asserted that the laws of capitalist production were the laws of nature herself, evangelicalism sanctified the family, along with industriousness, obedience and piety, as the main bulwark against revolution. The Victorian ideal of womanhood originated in this counter-revolutionary ideology. The woman, as wife and mother, was the pivot of the family, and consequently the guardian of all Christian (and domestic) virtues. Women's waged work, therefore, was discussed insofar as it harmonized with the home, the family and domestic virtue.

Because of women's very special responsibility for society's well-being, it was the woman working outside the home who received most attention from the parliamentary commissioners, and to push through legislative reform, emphasis was placed, not on the hours of work, rates of pay, and dangers from unsafe machinery — although all these were mentioned — but on the moral and spiritual degradation said to accompany female employment; especially the mingling of the sexes and the neglect of domestic comforts. 'In the male the moral effects of the system are very sad, but in the female they are infinitely worse', Lord Shaftesbury solemnly declared to a silent House of Lords, at the end of his two-hour speech advocating the abolition of women and children's work in the mines . . . 'not alone upon themselves, but upon their families, upon society, and, I may add, upon the country itself. It is bad enough if you corrupt the man, but if you corrupt the woman, you poison the waters of life at the very fountain.'[3]

Respectable opinion echoed Lord Shaftesbury's sentiments. Both evangelicalism and political economy attributed the sufferings of the poor to their own moral pollution. Their viciousness was variously ascribed to drink, licentiousness, idleness and all manner of vice and depravity, for which religion, temperance, thrift, cleanliness, industriousness and self help were advocated as the most potent remedies. But, if there was any reason for these evils — beyond the innate moral depravity of the individuals concerned — the one that commended itself most readily was the negligence and ignorance of the working-class wife and mother. It is true that enlightened public opinion — enlightened, that is, by an acquaint-ance with the poor acquired through visiting them for religious or reformatory purposes — recognized that the crowded courts, tenements and rookeries of the cities, so deplored by Octavia Hill and her associates, hardly stimulated the domestic virtues nurtured in the suburban villa.[4] Nevertheless, the very squalor of working-class housing could be blamed upon the slender acquaintance with domestic economy possessed by working women whose 'want of management' drove their husbands to the alehouses and their children onto the streets. The remedy was succinctly expressed by Mrs Austin, an ardent advocate of 'industrial' education for the working girl — 'our object', she wrote in the 1850s, 'is to improve the servants of the rich, and the wives of the poor'.[5]

Every Victorian inquiry into the working class is steeped in the ideology we have been discussing. The poor were seldom allowed to speak for themselves. 'What the poor are to the poor is little known,' Dickens wrote in the 1840s, 'excepting to themselves and God.'[6] And if this was true of the poor as a whole, it was doubly true of working-class women who almost disappear under the relentless scrutiny of the middle class. It was not that the Victorians did not expect women of the lower classes to work. On the contrary, work was the sole corrective and just retribution for poverty; it was rather that only those sorts of work that coincided with a woman's natural sphere were to be encouraged. Such discrimination had little to do with the danger or unpleasantness of the work concerned. There was not much to choose for example — if our criteria is risk to life or health — between work in the mines, and work in the London dressmaking trades. But no one suggested that sweated needlework should be prohibited to women. To uncover the real situation of the working woman herself in the Victorian period, then, we have to pick our way through a labyrinth of middle-class moralism and mystification and resolve questions, not only that contemporaries did not answer, but in many cases did not even ask.

This applies in particular to women's employment in London. Some trades it is true, received a great deal of local attention. The declining Spitalfields silk industry was investigated as part of the national inquiries into the handloom weavers; dressmakers and needlewomen received the notice of a House of Lords Select Committee; while starving needlewomen and prostitutes were the subject of a host of pamphlets. But the factory girls of Manchester and the West Riding who so traumatized observers in the 1840s could have no place in London where few trades were transformed by the factory system until the twentieth century. (The high cost of rent in central London combined with the high cost of fuel and its transportation, inhibited the earlier development of the factory system.) What changes did occur in the sexual division of labour as a result of a change in the production or labour process, took place beneath the surface, in the workshop, or the home. Most women workers in London were domestic servants, washerwomen, needlewomen or occupied in some other sort of home work. Many married women worked with their husbands in his trade. These traditional forms of women's work were quite compatible with the

Victorian's deification of the home, and so passed almost unnoticed.

Material proof that women's work was not just less noticeable in London but often completely overlooked, is found in the Census of 1851. The number of women over twenty who are listed as being without occupation is 432,000, i.e. 57 per cent of all women over twenty living in London. In round numbers, this figure of 432,000 is broken down as follows: 317,000 wives 'not otherwise described', 27,000 widows 'not otherwise described', 43,000 children and relatives at home 'not otherwise described', 26,000 persons of rank or property, 7,000 paupers, prisoners and vagrants, 13,000 'of no specified occupations or conditions'.[7] If we exclude the 26,000 propertied at one end, the 7,000 paupers etc. at the other, and a proportion of propertied widows and dependent relatives in between, that still leaves over 50 per cent of women 'with no occupation'. And yet among the vast majority of the working class, all members of the family were expected to contribute to the family income, for even when the wages of the male workers were relatively high they were rarely regular.[8] We know therefore that 50 per cent of adult women would not have been able to live without any independent source of income. Obviously the statistics require explanation.

There were several reasons why the occupations of working-class women might not have been declared in the Census, some more speculative than others. The work of married women for instance, was often hidden behind that of their husbands. Alice Clark, Dorothy George and Ivy Pinchbeck have shown that although the separation of workplace and home (introduced by merchant capitalism) was one of the factors reducing the opportunities for women to learn a skill or to manage a small workshop business, nevertheless, the process was gradual, especially in the numerous and diverse London trades which, well into the nineteenth century, were characteristically conducted in small workshops, often on a family basis. Some women were listed in the Census as innkeepers', shopkeepers', butchers', bakers' and shoemakers' etc. wives; but often a wife's connection with her husband's trade would not have been mentioned. Many trade societies forbade the entry of women. Also, because the head of the household filled in the Census, he — especially if he was a skilled artisan or aspiring tradesman — probably thought of his wife as a housewife and mother and not as a worker.[9]

Wives of skilled workmen may be glimpsed, however, through conversations recorded by Mayhew. Sawyers' wives and children, for instance, did not 'as a general rule . . . go *out* to work', (my italics),[10] and coachmen's wives were not in regular employ for the slop-tailors, because, as one confided in Mayhew, 'we keep our wives too respectable for that'.[11] Nevertheless, according to Mayhew, 'some few of the wives of the better class of workmen take in washing or keep small "general shops"'.[12] Taking in washing, needlework, or other sorts of outwork was the least disruptive way of supplementing the family income when extra expenses were incurred, or during the seasonal or enforced unemployment which existed in most London trades. Home work did not unnecessarily interrupt a man's domestic routine, since the wife could fit it in among her household chores; it simply meant she worked a very long day.

But only a minority of women would have been married to skilled artisans or small tradesmen. Mayhew estimated that about 10 per cent of every trade were society men, and Edward Thompson has outlined the 30s. line of privilege in London, while suggesting that Mayhew's 10 per cent was probably an exaggeration, 5 or 6 per cent being a more realistic figure.[13] Society men were becoming more and more confined to the 'honourable' sectors of every trade in the 1840s (i.e. those who produced expensive well-made goods for the luxury and West End market), whereas workers in the unorganized, dishonourable sectors were rapidly expanding in the period 1815—40, and they made a much more precarious living. Women (and children) of this class always had to contribute to the family income. Indeed, in the 1830s and 1840s, a time of severe economic hardship, the London poor drew more closely together, and it was often the household and not the individual worker, or even separate families, that was the economic unit. A mixture of washing, cleaning, charring as well as various sorts of home- or slop-work, in addition to domestic labour, occupied most women throughout their working lives. The diversity and indeterminancy of this spasmodic, casual and irregular employment was not easily condensed and classified into a Census occupation.

Other women who were scarcely recorded in the Census, though we know of their existence through Mayhew, were the street traders, market workers, entertainers, scavengers, mudlarks;[14] also those who earned a few pence here and there, looking after a neighbour's children, running errands, minding a crossing, sweeping the streets, in fact, most of the women discussed in the final section of this chapter. Lastly, perhaps the most desperate source of income for women, and one which provoked a great deal of prurient debate and pious attention was prostitution. This too was often intermittent and supplementary and found no place in the Census.

Despite the fact that working women emerge only fitfully through the filter of Victorian moralism; in spite of the tendency to view women as the wives and dependents of working men rather than workers in their own right; in spite of the particular problems of uncovering women's employment in London; nevertheless, some distinguishing characteristics are beginning to appear.

Firstly, London offered no single staple employment for women comparable to that in the northern textile towns; secondly, in a city of skilled trades and small workshops, women, although long since excluded from formal apprenticeship, often worked with their husband in his trade; thirdly, much women's work outside small workshop production was intermittent and casual, which meant that most women's working lives were spent in a variety of partial occupations most of which escaped the rigid classifications of the Census.

These features of women's work must be looked at against the wider background of the London labour market, and the sexual division of labour within it, but first, to help fix the locality, a brief descriptive sketch of London follows. [. . .]

London trades and the sexual division of labour

Women's waged work was not immediately conspicuous in London in the early Victorian period. Women were not found in the skilled and heavy work in shipbuilding and engineering, two of London's staple industries in the first half of the nineteenth century. Neither were they employed in the docks and warehouses, nor their subsidiary trades. There were no women in the public utilities, (gas, building etc.) or transport, nor in most semi-processing and extractive industries — sugar refining, soap manufacture, blacking, copper and lead working and the 'noxious' trades — which were London's principal factory trades in this period. Finally, women were excluded from the professions, the civil service, clerical work, the scientific trades, and had been excluded from the old guild crafts (e.g. jewellers, precious instrument makers, carriage builders etc.) since the fourteenth and fifteenth centuries. If women were not in the heavy or skilled industries, in public service or factory, in the professions or clerical work, then where were they to be found?

The 1851 Census tells us (in round numbers) that 140,000 women over twenty, (or 18 per cent of women of that age group) were employed in domestic service; 125,000 (16.3 per cent) were in clothing and shoemaking; 11,000 (1.9 per cent) were teachers and 9,000 (1.2 per cent) worked in the silk industry. The bulk of the remainder were employed either in other branches of manufacture, (artificial-flower making, straw-hat and bonnet making, tailoresses, etc.) or as licensed victuallers, shopkeepers, innkeepers and lodging-house keepers, or else they were listed as the wives of tradesmen and manufacturing workers. Bearing in mind the insufficiency of the 1851 Census as a source, we can see that women's work fell into four principal categories: firstly, all aspects of domestic and household labour — washing, cooking, charring, sewing, mending, laundry work, mangling, ironing etc; secondly, child-care, and training; thirdly, the distribution and retail of food and other articles of regular consumption; and finally, specific skills in manufacture based upon the sexual division of labour established when production (both for sale and domestic use) had been organized within the household. That is to say: the sexual division of labour on the labour market originated with, and paralleled that within the family.

This sketch of women's waged work in London is not an oversimplification. A closer examination of the Census and other sources apparently reveals a wider variety of women's work. Arthur J. Munby, for instance, a careful observer of working-class women, wrote in June 1861:

> London Bridge, more than any place I know here, seems to be the great thoroughfare for young working women and girls. One meets them at every step: young women carrying large bundles of umbrella frames home to be covered; young women carrying cages full of hats, which yet want the silk and the binding, coster-girls often dirty and sordid, going to fill their empty baskets, and above all female sackmakers.[15]

And in the same year Munby met or noticed female mudlarks, brick-makers, milk-girls, shirt-collar makers, a porter, a consumptive embroiderer, a draper's shop assistant as well as servants and some agricultural labourers from the country. Mayhew also talked with women in heavy manual work: dustwomen, milkgirls, porters, market girls. Nevertheless, most women's work fitted into the categories described above. Poverty had always forced some women to seek employment in heavy, unpleasant, irregular work, especially those women outside the family, or with no male wage coming in regularly. Dorothy George wrote of women among the eighteenth-century London poor, for instance, that there is no work 'too heavy or disagreeable to be done by women provided it is also low paid'.[16] And an investigation by the Statistical Society into the poorer classes in St George's in the East, uncovered the same characteristics of women's employment in 1848. Whereas men's wages

> varied as usual, with the degree of skill required in the several trades, the lowest being those of the sailors, 11s 10d per week

beside rations, and of the mere labourers, 15s. 7d. per week, on
the average; the highest those of the gunsmiths, 41s. 9d. per
week; the general average being 20s. 2d. per week . . .

The average wage of single women and widows was only 6s. 10d.
The average earnings of 'widows with encumbrance' was 9s. 11d.
The report blamed those 'limited means' on the 'narrow range of
employments available for female hands, especially if unaccompanied by a vigorous frame and habits of bodily exertion'.[17]
Although the sexual division of labour was seldom static on the
London labour market, the designation 'women's work' always
meant work that was unskilled, overcrowded and low paid.
Consequently men in the relatively highly paid skilled trades,
especially in the honourable sectors, jealously resisted the entry of
women into their trades and excluded them from their trade
societies. Indeed, such was the force of custom and tradition in the
structure of the London labour market that the appearance of
women into a previously male-dominated trade or skill indicated a
down-grading of the work involved, and this was generally achieved
through a change in the production process itself.

The capitalist mode of production and the sexual division of labour

The sexual division of labour — both within and between the
London trades — in the 1830s and 1840s had been established in
the period of manufacture (roughly from the sixteenth to the
eighteenth century). It was predetermined by the division of labour
that had existed within the family when the household had been
the unit of production. The epoch of modern industry, far from
challenging this division, further demarcated and rigidified it.
Historically many steps in this process must be left to the
imagination. Its progress anyway varied from trade to trade and
was modified by local custom. But a schematic outline can be
given of the way in which capitalist production, as it emerged and
matured, structured the sexual division of labour.

Capitalist production developed within the interstices of the
feudal mode of production; it emerged alongside of, but also in
opposition to, small peasant agriculture and independent handicrafts. Capitalist production first manifests itself in the simultaneous
employment and co-operative labour of a large number of labourers
by one capitalist. Co-operation based on division of labour assumes
its characteristic form in manufacture, which, as a mode of
production arose from the breakdown of the handicrafts system.[18]

Each step in the development of capitalist production is marked by a further refinement in the division of labour, so that what distinguishes the labour process in manufacture from that in handicrafts is that whereas the worker in the latter produces a commodity, the detail labourer in manufacture produces only part of a commodity.[19] [. . .]

The accumulation of capital was held back by the handicraft base of manufacture, which enabled skilled workmen to exert some control over the labour process through combination in a trade society. Entry into the trade was restricted and knowledge of the skills involved in the work process was confined to those who entered formal apprenticeship. But these limited privileges were gained at the expense of the 'unskilled'. Excluded from trade societies, most workers were denied a specialized training, and hence lacked bargaining power against capital. The transition from handicrafts to manufacture relegated most women to this position.

By the fifteenth century many craft guilds were excluding women, except for the wives and widows of master craftsmen. Even when women were admitted there is little to indicate that they had ever been formally trained in the technical skills of the labour process itself.[20] But the guilds had been organizations of master craftsmen. With the accumulation of capital, and demarcation of economic classes within a handicraft, the practice of a craft or trade required more capital. The proportion of masters to journeymen altered on the one hand, while on the other, the impoverished craftsmen (masters or journeymen) practised their trade outside the jurisdiction of the guilds. As more journeymen became wage-earners at their masters' workshops, they organized themselves into societies to protect their interests, which, insofar as they preserved work customs etc., coincided with the master craftsmen against the domination of merchant capital and the encroachment of the unskilled. These journeyman societies also excluded women. Women, who were now denied access to socially recognized skills, formed a source of cheap labour power for the unskilled unorganized branches of production developing outside the corporate guilds. This pool of female labour formed one basis of the industrial reserve army, which was at once both a precondition and necessary product of the accumulation of capital.[21]

Women's vulnerability as wage-workers stemmed from their child-bearing capacity upon which 'natural' foundation the sexual division of labour within the family was based. Because, in its early organization (the putting-out, or domestic system), capitalism seized the household or the family as the economic and often the productive unit, the sexual division of labour was utilized and sustained as production was transferred from the family to the market-place.

The pre-industrial family had a patriarchal structure. This was true of the working-class family in the period of manufacture (sixteenth to eighteenth centuries), whether the family was employed directly on the land or in an urban craft or trade, or in a rural domestic trade. The father was head of the household, his craft or trade most often determined the family's principal source of income, and his authority was sanctioned by both the law of God and the law of Nature. Nevertheless (except among the very wealthy minority), every member of the family participated in production and contributed to the family income. A woman's work in the home was different from her husband's, but no less vital. (All women were married or widowed in the pre-industrial period except for those in service.) Her time was allocated between domestic labour and work in production for sale, according to the family's economic needs. And sometimes a woman's economic contribution to family income was considerable (especially in rural industries). But a wife's responsibility for the well-being of her husband and children always came before her work in social production, and in a patriarchal culture, this was seen to follow naturally from her role in biological reproduction.[22]

The intervention of capitalism into the sexual division of labour within the patriarchal family confirmed the economic subordination of the wife. By distinguishing between production for use and production for exchange and by progressively subordinating the former to the latter, by confining production for use to the private world of the home and female labour, and production for exchange increasingly to the workshop outside the home and male labour, capitalism ensured the economic dependence of women upon their husbands or fathers for a substantial part of their lives. In these conditions, each further step in the development of capitalist production — breakdown of the handicraft's system, division of labour, exclusion from the skilled craft guilds, separation of workshop and home, formation of trade societies — further undermined women's position on the labour market. Manufacture provided the economic conditions for the hierarchy of labour powers, but it was the transference of the sexual division of labour from the family into social production which ensured that it was women who moved into the subordinate and auxiliary positions within it. (The other main area of women's employment, domestic and personal service, cannot be analysed in these terms, since it remained outside capitalist production proper arguably into the twentieth century. This did not prevent it however, from sharing the general characteristics of women's work, low pay and low status).

This reservoir of female labour was an immediate source of cheap labour power ready for utilization by capitalist production when a revolution in the mode of production altered the technical base of the labour process. For as long as production depended upon the workman's skilled manipulation of the instruments of labour, the capitalist could not dislodge his skilled workmen. Only the decomposition of that skill into its constituent parts, which was brought about by a revolution in the instruments of labour, could break up workmen's control over the labour process. It was this revolutionary progress in the division of labour which marked the advent of the epoch of modern industry. Machinery and the factory system abolished the material base for the traditional hierarchy of labour powers and so for the first time the possibility of the introduction of cheap unskilled labour on a large scale. [. . .]

In this sense, modern industry was a direct challenge to the traditional sexual division of labour in social production. In the Lancashire textile industry, for instance, women and children were the earliest recruits into the factories. But in London the ways in which the labour power of women was utilized in the transition from manufacture to modern industry was more complicated, because that transition itself, when it was made at all, was made differently in each trade.

Some traditional areas of the London economy, the small, specialized and luxury trades for instance, which depended on proximity to their markets and skilled handicraftsmen, were not at all affected by modern industry. Indeed in a few cases, they had been only minimally affected by the transition from handicrafts to manufacture. There were still handfuls of women working in these skilled crafts — engraving, precious metals, instrument makers, watchmakers, etc. — who served as a reminder of the position that women had once occupied in production during the handicraft era. Yet even in the trades most directly affected by the industrial revolution there was no single process of adaption. Of those which had transferred to the factory, there were one or two in which the introduction of machinery at certain stages in the labour process was forcing a realignment in the sexual division of labour. In the Spitalfields silk industry, for example, William Wallis, a weaver, states that 'the winding is almost wholly done by machinery now consequently it is performed by girls only', and that '. . . winding under these circumstances obtains the best wage of any other branch of trade in Spitalfields'.[23] But, on the whole, those trades with a potential or actual mass market found that the high costs of rent and fuel and its transportation in central London, made the introduction of machinery and factories quite impracticable. Other techniques with which to counter provincial factory and foreign competition were found. The large supply of cheap labour favoured the development of sweated outwork and other slop-work, not modern industry proper. [. . .]

Notes

1. For a lucid statement of the purpose and need for a feminist history, see Anna Davin, 'Women and history', in Michelene Wandor (ed.), (1971) *The Body Politic,* Stage 1.
2. For accessible contemporary accounts of the breakdown of the family, see Leon Faucher, (1969) *Manchester in 1844,* Frank Cass, pp. 47—8; Friedrich Engels (1962) 'The condition of the working class in England', *Marx and Engels on Britain,* Moscow, pp. 162—3, 174—82; for Marx's view of the material effects of modern industry on the family, see *Capital,* Dona Torr (ed.) (1971) Vol. 1, Allen & Unwin, pp. 495—6.
3. Lord Shaftesbury was an Evangelical Tory and social reformer. His speech to the House of Commons, 7 June 1842, is cited in Ivy Pinchbeck (1969) *Women Workers and the Industrial Revolution, 1750—1850,* Frank Cass, p. 267.
4. For contemporary views of the effects of density of population, see for example, John Simon, *Report on the Sanitary Condition of the City of London 1849—50,* p. 86. 'It is no uncommon thing, in a room of twelve foot square or less, to find three or four families *styed* together (perhaps with infectious diseases among them) filling the same space day and night — men, women and children, in the promiscuous intimacy of cattle. Of these inmates, it is mainly superfluous to observe, that in all offices of nature they are gregarious and public, that every instinct of personal or sexual decency is stifled, that every nakedness of life is uncovered.'
5. Mrs Austin, (1857) *Two Lectures on Girls' Schools, and on the Training of Working Women* p. 12. Hannah More (education), Elizabeth Fry (prisons), Mary Carpenter (Ragged Schools), Louisa Twining (workhouses), Octavia Hill (housing and charity reform) all advocated 'industrial training' in the form of housework and needlework for their 'fallen' sisters. These women opened up social work as an appropriate activity for middle-class women. Mrs Jameson's lecture, 'The Communion of Labour' (1855) was the most influential expression of the sentiments embodied in such activities. The links between evangelicalism, respectable philanthropy and early feminism have yet to be elucidated.
6. Charles Dickens, *Bleak House,* Household edn. p. 56.
7. 1851 Census, Vol. 3, Parliamentary Papers (PP), 1852—3, LXXXVIII, Table 2, p. 8.
8. For seasonality and irregularity in the London trades in the nineteenth century, see Gareth Stedman Jones (1971) *Outcast London.* Oxford

University Press Chs. 1—5; H. Mayhew (1861) *London Labour and the London Poor*, 4 volumes, Vol. 2, pp. 297—323. On p. 322, Mayhew wrote, 'I am led to believe there is considerable truth in the statement lately put forward by the working classes, that only one third of the operatives of this country are fully employed, while another third are partially employed, and the remaining third wholly unemployed'.

9. The preface to the 1841 Census stated that, 'the number of women about 20 years of age, without any occupation returned, consists generally of unmarried women living with their parents, and of the wives of professional men or shopkeepers, living upon the earnings, but not considered as carrying on the occupation of their husbands'. (PP, 1844, XXVII, p. 9).

10. Thompson, E. and Yeo, E. (1971) *The Unknown Mayhew*, The Merlin Press, p. 394. (Pelican, 1973). Henry Mayhew was a nineteenth-century journalist and friend of the poor.

11. H. Mayhew, *op. cit*, Vol. 3, p. 344.

12. E. Thompson and E. Yeo, *op. cit*, p. 407.

13. H. Mayhew, *op. cit*, Vol. 3, p. 221: 'As a general rule I may remark that I find the society men of every trade comprise about one tenth of the whole . . . if the non-society men are neither so skilful nor well-conducted as the others, at least they are quite as important a body from the fact that they constitute the main portion of the trade.' See E. Thompson and E. Yeo, *op. cit*, pp. 218—19, 409—10; Iorwerth Prothero, 'Chartism in London', *Past and Present*, no. 44, 1969; and E. Thompson (1968) *The Making of the English Working Class*, Pelican, p. 277.

14. H. Mayhew, *op. cit*, Vol. 2, p. 155. Mudlarks are 'compelled, in order to obtain the articles they seek, to wade sometimes up to their middle through the mud left on the shore by the retiring tide . . . They may be seen of all ages from mere childhood to positive decrepitude, crawling among the barges at the various wharfs along the river . . . mudlarks collect whatever they happen to find, such as coal, bits of old iron, rope, bones, and copper nails . . . They sell to the poor'.

15. Hudson, D. (ed.) (1972) *Munby, Man of Two Worlds*, J. Murray, p. 99.

16. George, D. (1930) *London Life in the Eighteenth Century*, Kegan Paul, p. 170.

17. 'Report of an Investigation into the State of the Poorer Classes of St George's in the East', *Journal of the Statistical Society of London*, August 1848, p. 203. Of the women's occupations only one gun-polisher, one yeast maker, and one coal wharf keeper fall outside the conventional category of 'women's work'.

18. Handicraft guilds excluded division of labour within the workshop by their refusal to sell labour power as a commodity to the merchant capitalist. See Marx, K. *op. cit*, pp. 352—3.

19. Ibid, p. 341. 'The collective labourer, formed by the combination of a number of detail labourers, is the machinery specially characteristic of the manufacturing period.'

20. Clark, A. (1968) *Working Life of Women in the Seventeenth Century*, Frank Cass, especially pp. 154—61.
21. Marx, K. *op. cit.* p. 646.
22. See Laslett, P. (1971) *The World We Have Lost*, Methuen, Ch. 1; Clark, A. *op. cit.* p. 156, for women and marriage. Spinning for example, women's most important industrial work in the manufacturing period was ideal 'employment for odd minutes and the mechanical character of its movements which made no great tax on eye or brain, rendered it the most adaptable of all domestic arts to the necessities of the mother'. (Ibid, p. 9.)
23. Select Committee on Handloom Weavers, PP. 1834, X, p. 4359.

1.4 Women's work and the family in nineteenth-century Europe

JOAN SCOTT AND LOUISE TILLY

There is a great deal of confusion about the history of women's work outside the home and about the origin and meaning of woman's traditional place within the home. Most interpretations of either question depend on assumptions about the other. Usually, women at home in any time period are assumed to be non-productive, the antithesis of women at work. In addition, most general works on women and the family assume that the history of women's employment, like the history of women's legal and political rights, can be understood as a gradual evolution from a traditional place at home to a modern position in the world of work. Some historians cite changes in employment opportunities created by industrialization as the precursors of legal emancipation. Others stress political rights as the source of improved economic status. In both cases, legal-political and economic 'emancipation' usually are linked to changes in cultural values. Thus William Goode, whose *World Revolution and Family Patterns* makes temporal and geographic comparisons of family patterns, remarks on what he calls 'the statistically unusual status of western women today, that is, their high participation in work outside of the home.' He maintains that previous civilizations did not use female labour because of restrictive cultural definitions. 'I believe,' Goode writes, 'that the crucial crystallizing variable — i.e. the necessary but not sufficient cause of the betterment of the western woman's position — was ideological: the gradual logical philosophical extension to women of originally Protestant notions about the rights and responsibilities of the individual undermined the traditional idea of "woman's proper place".'[1]

Yet Goode makes no systematic effort to validate his statements with historical data. If, however, notions about individual rights did transform cultural values and lead to the extension of rights to women, and if work opportunities for women stemmed from the

Source: Scott, J. and Tilly, L. (1975), Women's work and the family in nineteenth-century Europe, in *Comparative Studies in Society and History* No. 17, C.U.P. as reprinted in *Family History*. Charles E. Rosenberg (ed.) (1975) University of Pennsylvania Press

same source, we should be able to trace an increase in the number of women working as they gained political rights. The only long period for which there are any reliable labour force statistics for any populations (whether of cities or countries) is the nineteenth and twentieth centuries. These should serve our purpose, however, since women gained political rights in most European countries only in the twentieth century. If we examine the figures for three European countries during the nineteenth and twentieth centuries, we find no confirmation of Goode's belief. In Great Britain, a Protestant country, the civil status of women was reformed through the married women's property acts of the late nineteenth century and political emancipation in the form of suffrage came in 1918. In 1851 and 1861, about 25 per cent of British women worked; in 1921, the figure was still about 25 per cent. In both Catholic France and Italy, women's legal rights within the family were severely limited until after World War II. Immediately after the war, constitutional changes granted women the right to vote. In France, in 1866, 25 per cent of women worked; in 1896, 33 per cent worked and in 1954, 30 per cent worked, down from a high of 42 per cent in 1921. In Italy, the highest percentage for women's employment outside the home (before 1964) was in 1901.[2]

There are several conclusions to be drawn from these figures. First, there was little relationship between women's political rights and women's work. The right to vote did not increase the size of the female labour force, neither did the numbers of women in the labour force dramatically increase just prior to their gaining the vote. Moreover, great numbers of women worked outside the home during most of the nineteenth century, long before they enjoyed civil and political rights. Finally, rather than a steady increase in the size of the female labour force, the pattern was one of increase followed by decline. [. . .]

The women who worked in great numbers in the nineteenth century were overwhelmingly members of the working and peasant classes. Most held jobs in domestic service, garmentmaking or the textile industry. In 1841 and still in 1911, most English working women were engaged in domestic or other personal service occupations. In 1911, 35 per cent were servants (including laundresses), 19.5 per cent were textile workers and 15.6 per cent were engaged in the dressmaking trades.[3] In Milan, according to the Censuses of 1881, 1901, and 1911, a similar concentration of women in domestic service existed, with garmentmaking ranking second and textiles much less important than in England.[4] Similarly in France, (excluding agriculture) textiles, garmentmaking, and domestic service were the chief areas of female employment. In France, 69 per cent of working women outside agriculture were employed in these three fields in 1866: domestic service, 28 per cent; garmentmaking, 21 per cent; textiles, 20 per cent. In 1896, the proportions were altered, but the total was 59 per cent; domestic service, 19 per cent; garmentmaking, 26 per cent; textiles, 14 per cent.[5]

Despite very different rates of industrialization in England, France, and Italy, the evidence strongly suggests that women in all three cases did not participate in factory work (except in textiles) in large numbers. Rather, economic and social changes associated with urban and industrial development seem to have generated employment opportunities in a few traditional sectors in which women worked at jobs similar to household tasks. The economic changes leading to high employment of women included the early industrialization of textiles and the nineteenth-century pattern of urbanization, with cities acting as producers of and markets for consumer goods and as places of employment for domestic servants.[6] The expansion of consumer goods production involved the growth of a large piecework garment industry. Production moved from the workshops of craftsmen to the homes of people who sewed together precut garments. This change in the process of production generated employment opportunities for large numbers of women. The subsequent decline of this method of producing ready-made goods and its replacement by factory production, as well as the decline of textiles and the growth of heavy industry, led to lower female participation in the work forces of all three countries we have examined.

The kinds of jobs available to women were not only limited in number and kind, they also were segregated, that is, they were held almost exclusively by women.[7] The women who held these jobs were usually young and single. In Milan, about 75 per cent of women aged fifteen to twenty worked in 1881 and 1901. In female age groups over twenty, employment in textile manufacture and garmentmaking declined sharply, presumably as women stopped work after marriage. The only female occupation with appreciable proportions (50 per cent or more) of workers over thirty years of age was domestic service, in which celibacy prevailed.[8] In Great Britain, similar age patterns are evident in the scattered available data. Most women operatives in the Lancashire cotton mills in 1833 were between sixteen and twenty-one years old. Only 25 per cent of female cotton workers were married in the Lancashire districts in 1841. Hewitt argues for an increase in proportions, either married or widowed, among cotton operatives peaking sometime in the 1890s and declining thereafter. The highest fraction of married women in this occupation was about one third.[9] The much less specialized labour force of London in the

1880s was aged primarily between fifteen and twenty-five years.[10]

When Census figures finally provide marital status, some big national differences can be noted. In 1911, while 69 per cent of all single women in Britain worked, only 9.6 per cent of married women did.[11] In 1896, 52 per cent of all French single women were in the labour force, and 38 per cent of married women.[12] Although our evidence is impressionistic and scattered, it looks as though fewer married women worked as industrialization advanced (at least in the pre-1914 period). Thus Britain, the more advanced industrial country in 1911, had the lower proportion of married women workers; on the other hand, in France, where both agriculture and manufacturing were organized on a smaller scale than in Britain, more married women were in the labour force.

Why did women work in the nineteenth century and why was the female labour force predominantly young and single? To answer these questions we must first examine the relationship of these women to their families of origin (the families into which they were born), not to their families of procreation (the family launched at marriage). We must ask not only how husbands regarded their wives' roles, but what prompted families to send their *daughters* out into the job market as garment workers or domestic servants.

The parents of these young women workers during industrialization were mostly peasants and, to a lesser extent, urban workers. When we examine the geographic and social origins of domestic servants, one of the largest groups of women workers, their rural origins are clear. Two-thirds of all the domestic servants in England in 1851 were daughters of rural labourers. For France, we have no aggregate numbers, but local studies suggest similar patterns. In his study of Melun, for example, Chatelain found that in 1872, 54 per cent of female domestic servants were either migrants from rural areas or foreigners.[13] Theresa McBride calculated that in Versailles from 1825 to 1853, 57.7 per cent of female domestic servants were daughters of peasants. In Bordeaux, a similar proportion was obtained: 52.8 per cent. In Milan, at the end of the nineteenth century, servants were less likely to be city born than any other category of workers.[14]

If cultural values were involved in the decisions of rural and lower class families to send their daughters to work, we must ask what values they were. Goode's loose references to 'values' obscure an important distinction between modern middle-class values and pre-industrial lower class values. Goode assumes that the idea of 'woman's proper place,' with its connotations of complete economic dependency and idealized femininity is a traditional value. In fact, it is a rather recently accepted middle-class value not at all inconsistent with notions of 'the rights and responsibilities of the individual.' The hierarchical division of labour within the family which assigned the husband the role of breadwinner and the wife the role of domestic manager and moral guardian emerged clearly only in the nineteenth century and was associated with the growth of the middle class and the diffusion of its values.[15] On the other hand, as we will demonstrate at length below, traditional ideas about women, held by peasant and labouring families, did not find feminine and economic functions incompatible. In the pre-industrial Europe described by Peter Laslett and in contemporary pre-modern societies studied by anthropologists, the household or the family is the crucial economic unit.[16] Whether or not all work is done at home, all family members are expected to work. It is simply assumed that women will work, for their contribution is valued as necessary for the survival of the family unit. The poor, the illiterate, the economically and politically powerless of the past operated according to values which fully justified the employment of women outside the home. [. . .]

Our examination of the evidence on women's work in the nineteenth century has led us to a different understanding of the process which led to the relatively high employment of women outside the home in nineteenth-century Europe. *The model we use posits a continuity of traditional values and behaviour in changing circumstances. Old values coexist with and are used by people to adapt to extensive structural changes.* This assumes that people perceive and act on the changes they experience in terms of ideas and attitudes they already hold. These ideas eventually change, but not as directly or immediately as Goode and Engels would have us believe. Behaviour is less the product of new ideas than of the effects of old ideas operating in new or changing contexts.[17]

Traditional families then, operating on long-held values, sent their daughters to take advantage of increased opportunities generated by industrialization and urbanization. Industrial development did not affect all areas of a given country at the same time. Rather, the process can best be illustrated by an image of 'islands of development' within an underdeveloped sea, islands which drew population to them from the [. . .] less developed areas.[18] The values of the less developed sector were imported into the developing sector and there were extended, adapted, and only gradually transformed.

As peasant values were imported, so was the behaviour they directed. And work for the wives and daughters of the poor was a familiar experience in pre-industrial societies. No change in values, then, was necessary to permit lower class women to work outside the home during the nineteenth century. Neither did industrialization 'emancipate' these women by permitting more of them to work outside the home. And, given the fluctuations in the size of the female labour force especially, it is difficult to see any direct connection between the work of peasant and working-class women and the political enfranchisement of all women.

Since most women workers were of rural origin, an attempt at reconstructing the historical experience of women workers during the early stages of industrialization should begin by examining the peasant or family economy whose values and economic needs sent them into the job market.

Commentators on many different areas of Europe offer strikingly similar descriptions of peasant social organization. Anthropologist and social historians seem to agree that regardless of country, 'the peasantry is a pre-industrial social entity which carries over into contemporary society specific elements of a different, older, social structure, economy and culture'. The crucial unit of organization is the family, whose 'solidarity provides the basic framework for mutual aid, control and socialization'. The family's work is usually directed to the family farm, property considered to belong to the group rather than to a single individual. 'The individual, the family and the farm appear as an indivisible whole . . . . Peasant property is, at least *de facto,* family property. The head of the family appears as the manager rather than the proprietor of family land.'[19]

These descriptions of Eastern European peasants are echoed by Michael Anderson in his comparison of rural Lancashire and rural Ireland early in the nineteenth century. He suggests that in both cases the basis of 'functional family solidarity . . . was the absolute *interdependence* of family members such that neither fathers nor sons had any scope for alternatives to the family as a source of provision for a number of crucially important needs'.[20] Italian evidence confirms the pattern. Although in late nineteenth century Lombardy a kind of *frereche* (brothers and their families living together and working the land together) was a frequent alternative to the nuclear family, the household was the basic unit of production. All members of the family contributed what they could either by work on the farm, or, in the case of women and the young, by work in nearby urban areas or in rural textile mills. Their earnings were turned over to the head of the household; in the case of brothers joined in one household, the elder usually acted as head. He took care of financial matters and contractual relationships in the interests of all.[21] For Normandy in the eighteenth century, Gouesse's recent study has described the gradual evolution of reasons given for marriage when an ecclesiastical dispensation had to be applied for. At the end of that century, grounds such as 'seeking well-being,' or 'desire to live happily' became more common. Goesse considers these differences of expression rather superficial; what all these declarations meant, although few stated this explicitly, was that one had to be married in order to live. 'The married couple was the simple community of work, the elementary unit.' In nineteenth century Brittany, 'all the inhabitants of the farm formed a working community . . . linked one to the other like the crew of a ship.'[22]

Despite differences in systems of inheritance and differences in the amount of land available, the theory of the peasant economy developed by Chayanov for nineteenth century Russia applies elsewhere. The basis of this system is the family, or more precisely the household — in Russia, all those 'having eaten from one pot'. It has a dual role as a unit of production and consumption. The motivations of its members, unlike capitalist aims, involve 'securing the needs of the family rather than . . . making a profit'. The family's basic problem is organizing the work of its members to meet its annual budget and 'a single wish to save or invest capital if economic conditions allow'.[23]

Members of the family or household have clearly defined duties, based in part on their age and position in the family and in part on their sex. Sex role differentiation clearly existed in such peasant societies. Men and women not only performed different tasks, but they occupied different space.[24] Most often, although by no means always, men worked the fields while women managed the house, raised and cared for animals, tended a garden, and marketed surplus dairy products, poultry, and vegetables. There was also seasonal work in the fields at planting and harvest times.[25] [. . .]

Women laboured not only on the farm, but at all sorts of other work, depending in part on what was available to them. In most areas their activity was an extension of their household functions of food provision, animal husbandry, and clothesmaking. Documentation of this can be found in almost every family monograph in the six volumes of Le Play's *Les Ouvriers Européens*. There was the wife of a French vineyard worker, for example, whose principal activity involved the care of a cow. 'She gathers hay for it, cares for it and carries its milk to town to sell.' Another wife worked with her husband during harvest seasons and 'washed laundry and did other work . . . for farmers and landowners in the neighbourhood'. She also wove linen 'for her family and for sale'. Other women sewed gloves or clothing; some took in infants to nurse as well.[26] In the regions surrounding the silk-weaving city of Lyon, the wives and daughters of farmers tended worms and reeled silk.[27] Similarly, in Lombardy, seasonal preoccupation with the care of the hungry worms filled the time of women and children in the household.[28]

Work of this type was a traditional way of supplementing the family income. Indeed, Le Play insisted on including all activities of family members in his budgets because, he argued, 'the small activities undertaken by the family are a significant supplement to the earning of the principal worker'.

[. . .]

In non-farming and some urban families a similar situation seems to have prevailed. In fact, Chayanov's description of the peasant economy seems a fitting characterization of pre-industrial working class social arrangements. In *The World We Have Lost,* Peter Laslett describes the household as the centre of production. The workshop was not separated from the home and everyone's place was at home. In the weaver's household, for example, children did carding and combing, older daughters and wives spun, while the father wove. In the urban worker's home, a similar division of labour often existed. Among Parisian laundry workers, for example, the entire family was expected to work, although women were uniquely responsible for soaping and ironing. This kind of business, in fact, was as well run by women as by men. And parents willed their shops and their clientele to their daughters as frequently as to their sons.[29] Wives of craftsmen sometimes assisted their husbands at their work of tailoring, shoemaking, and baking. Sometimes they kept shop selling the goods and keeping accounts. The wives of skilled cutlery workers served as intermediaries between their husbands and their masters. They not only picked up materials for their husbands to work on at home and transported finished products back to the employer, but they also negotiated work loads and wages.[30]

When the husband worked away from home, women engaged in enterprises of their own. Like their rural counterparts, urban working-class women contributed to the family economy by tending vegetable gardens, raising animals (usually some pigs and hens), and marketing the surplus. Some women set up cafés in their homes, others sold the food and beverages they had prepared outside. A Sheffield knife maker's wife prepared a 'fermented drink called 'pop', which she bottled and sold in summer to the inhabitants of the city'.[31] These are early nineteenth century examples, but Alice Clark refers to gardening and the garment trades in seventeenth century England; she cites another expedient of poor women, 'selling perishable articles of food from door to door'[32] This practice continued in the nineteenth century. Le Play details the work of a German miner's wife who 'transported foodstuffs on her back. Two times a week she goes to [the city] where she buys wheat, potatoes, etc. which she carries (10 kilometers) . . . Some of this food is for her household, some is delivered to wealthy persons in town, the rest is sold [for a small profit] at the market'.[33] Among the popular classes in eighteenth century Paris and Bordeaux, 'it was generally accepted that womenfolk had an important part to play in the domestic economy. Most took a job to bring in an additional income'.[34] [. . .]

The indispensable role of women was demonstrated, too, by the fact that in many communities, widows could manage to farm alone (with the assistance of a few hired hands) whereas widowers found the task almost impossible.[35] It is also demonstrated vividly in times of financial hardship. Hufton insists that women were the first to feel the physical effects of deprivation, in part because they denied themselves food in order to feed the rest of the family. Other observers describe a similar situation. The report Anderson cites from Lancashire is representative of conditions in Italy, England, and France: 'an observation made by medical men, that the parents have lost their health much more generally than the children and particularly, that the mothers who most of all starve themselves, have got pale and emaciated'.[36]

The role women played in the family economy usually gave them a great deal of power within the family. Scattered historical sources complement the more systematic work of contemporary anthropologists on this point. All indicate that while men assume primacy in public roles, it is women who prevail in the domestic sphere. Hufton even suggests they enjoyed 'social supremacy' within the family.[37] Her suggestion echoes Le Play's first-hand observation. In the course of his extensive study of European working-class urban and rural families (carried out from the 1840—70s), he was struck by the woman's role. 'Women are treated with deference, they often . . . exercise a preponderant influence on the affairs of the family (La communauté)'.

[. . .]

The key to the women's power, limited almost exclusively, of course, to the family arena, lay in her management of the household. In some areas, wives of craftsmen kept business accounts, as did the wives or daughters of farmers.[38] Their familiarity with figures was a function of their role as keeper of the household's accounts, for the woman was usually the chief buyer for the household in the market place, and often the chief trader as well. Primitive as this accounting was, it was a tool for dealing with the outside world. Working-class women also often held the purse strings, making financial decisions, and even determining the weekly allowance their husbands received for wine and tobacco.

[. . .]

It is important here to stress that we speak here of married women. Whatever power these women enjoyed was a function of their participation in a mutual endeavour, and of the particular role they played as a function of their sex and marital status. Their influence was confined to the domestic sphere, but that sphere bulked large in the economic and social life of the family. In this situation, women were working partners in the family enterprise.

Daughters in lower class families were early socialized to assume family and work responsibilities. 'Daughters . . . begin as soon as their strength permits to help their mother in all her work'.[39] Frequently they were sent out of the household to work as agricultural labourers or domestic servants. Others were apprenticed to women who taught them to weave or sew. In areas of rural Switzerland where cottage industry was also practised, daughters were a most desirable asset. It was they who could be spared to spin and weave while their mothers worked at home; and they gave their earnings, 'as a matter of course to the economic unit, the maintenance of whose property had priority over individual happiness'. Whatever her specific job, a young girl early on learned the meaning of the saying,'woman's work is never done'. And she was prepared to work hard for most of her life. [. . .]

Women's work was in the interest of the family economy. Their roles, like those of their husbands, brothers and fathers, could be modified and adjusted to meet difficult times or changing circumstances. [. . .]

This means that traditional families employed a variety of strategies to promote the well-being of the family unit. Sometimes the whole family hired itself out as farm hands, sometimes this was done only by men, at other times by one or more children. Supplemental work in domestic industry was frequently resorted to by mothers of families in time of greater need or economic crises. That is why such work was so often seasonal or undertaken sporadically. The custom of sending children of both sexes out to serve on other farms, or to work in nearby cities, was yet another expedient — a way of temporarily extending the family beyond its own limited resources in order to increase those resources and thereby guarantee economic survival.

As major structural changes affected the countries of Europe (in the late eighteenth century in England, much later in France and Italy) these strategies were adapted and new ones were developed, in the face of new pressures and opportunities, to attain the traditional goals of the family economy. In the nineteenth century, Western European population growth was causing land shortages in some areas. In addition, rationalized large-scale agriculture was putting marginally productive lands under great competitive pressure. New forms and methods of industrial production also transformed the location and nature of the work done by rural and urban craftsmen. In this situation, it became increasingly necessary for family members, but particularly for children, to work away from home. The development of domestic industry and rurally-located textile mills, and the expansion of urban populations (with their increased demand for consumer goods and domestic services), provided opportunities for these people to work.

In Lombardy, for example, peasants had long practised labour-intensive farming on small-holdings. During the nineteenth century, peasants were increasingly unable to support their growing families on these holdings. They seized options similar to the temporary expedients they had customarily employed. Women and girls, whose work on the farm was less productive than that of men, went to work in nearby rural silk mills. Others went to Milan as domestic servants or garment workers, into what were essentially self-exploitative, low-paying, marginally-productive jobs. The point was to make enough money to send home.[41] [. . .]

Similar examples can be drawn from non-farming families as well. The first industrial revolution in England broke the locational unity of home and workshop by transferring, first spinning and then weaving, into factories. Neil Smelser's study of *Social Change in the Industrial Revolution* shows, however, that in the first British textile factories the family as a work unit was imported into the mills. 'Masters allowed the operative spinners to hire their own assistants . . . the spinners chose their wives, children, near relatives or relatives of the proprietors. Many children, especially the youngest, entered the mill at the express request of their parents.[42] Of course, this extension of the family economy into factories in early industrialization declined after the 1820s, with increased differentiation and specialization of work. But the initial adjustment to a changed economic structure involved old values operating in new settings.[. . .] Long before the nineteenth century, lower-class families had sent their daughters out to work. The continuation of this practice, and of the values and assumptions underlying it is evident not only in the fact of large numbers of single women working but also in the age structure of the female labour force, in the kinds of work these women did, and in their personal behaviour.

The fact that European female labour forces consisted primarily of young, single women—girls, in the language of their contemporaries—is itself an indication of the persistence of familial values. Daughters were expendable in rural and urban households, certainly more expendable than their mothers and, depending on the work of the family, their brothers. When work had to be done away from home and when its duration was uncertain, the family interest was best served by sending forth its daughters. Domestic service, the chief resort of most rural girls, was a traditional area of employment. It was often a secure form of migration since a young girl was assured a place to live, food, and a family. There were risks involved also; servant unemployment and servant exploitation were real. Nevertheless, during the nineteenth century, though many more girls were sent into service and moved farther from home than had traditionally been the case, the move itself was not unprecedented. Domestic service was an acceptable employment partly because it afforded the protection of a family and membership in a household.[43]

This was true not only of domestic service, but of other forms of female employment. In Italy and France, textile factory owners attempted to provide 'family' conditions for their girls. Rules of conduct limited their activity and nuns supervised the establishments, acting as substitute parents. *In loco parentis* for some factory owners sometimes even meant arranging suitable marriages for their female operatives.[44] [. . .]

We do not wish to argue that the factory dormitory was a beneficient institution. The fact that it used the family as model for work and social relationships, and the fact that the practice did serve the *family* interest to some degree, is, however, important.

In the needle trades, which flourished in urban centres, similar practices developed. The rise of ready-made clothing production involved a two-fold transformation of garmentmaking. First, piecework at home replaced workshop organization. Only later (in England by 1850, in France by the 1870s depending on the city and the industry, and in Italy, still later) did new machinery permit the reorganization of the garment industry in factories. In the period when piecework expanded, women found ample opportunity for work. Those who already lived in cities customarily took their work home. Migrants, however, needed homes. So enterprising women with a little capital turned their homes into lodging houses for pieceworkers in their employ. While these often provided exploitative and miserable living conditions, they nonetheless offered a household for a young girl, a household in which she could do similar work to what she or her mother had done at home.[45]

Domestic service, garmentmaking, and even textile manufacturing, the three areas in which female labour was overwhelmingly concentrated, were all traditional areas of women's work. The kind of work parents sent their daughters to do, in other words, did not involve a radical departure from the past. [. . .]

As parents sent daughters off with traditional expectations, so the daughters attempted to fulfil them. Evidence for the persistence of familial values is found in the continuing contributions made by working daughters to their families. In some cases, as we have seen, factories sent the girls' wages directly home to their parents. In others, girls simply sent most of their money home themselves. In England, it was not until the 1890s that single working girls living at home kept some of their own money.[46] [. . .]

In Lancashire 'considerable contact was maintained' between migrants and their families. Money was sent home, members of the family were brought to the city to live by family members who had 'travelled', and sometimes even 'reverse migration' occurred.[47] [. . .]

The cultural values which sent young girls out to work for their families also informed their personal behaviour. The increase, noted by historians and demographers, in illegitimate birth rates in many European cities from about 1750 to 1850 can be seen, paradoxically, as yet another demonstration of the persistence of old attitudes in new settings.[48] Alliances with young men may have begun in the city as at home, the girls seeking potential husbands in the hope of establishing a family of their own. The difference, of course, was that social customs enforceable at home could not be controlled in the city.[. . .]

The loneliness and isolation of the city was clearly one pressure for marriage. So was the desire to escape domestic service and become her own mistress in her own home as her mother had been. The conditions of domestic service, which usually demanded that servants be unmarried, also contributed to illicit liaisons and led many a domestic to abandon her child. This had long been true; what was different in nineteenth century Europe was that the great increase in the proportions of women employed in domestic service outstripped increased employment in manufacturing. This meant that, proportionately, more women than ever before were employed in this sector, which was particularly conducive to the production of illegitimate children.

Yet another motive for marriage was economic. Girls in factories were said to be fairly well paid, but most girls did not work in factories. Women in the needle trades and other piecework industries barely made enough to support themselves. (Wages constantly fluctuated in these consumer product trades and declined after the 1830s in both England and France. Women in these trades were also paid half of what men received for comparable work, often because it was assumed that women's wages were part of a family wage, an assumption which did not always correspond with reality.)[49] In the rural households they came from, subsistence depended on multiple contributions. The logical move for a single girl whose circumstances took her far from her family, and whose wages were insufficient either to support herself or to enable her to send money home, would be to find a husband; together they might be able to subsist. [. . .]

Even among prostitutes, many of whom were destitute or unemployed servants and pieceworkers, a peculiar blend of old and new attitudes was evident. In pre-industrial society, lower class women developed endless resources for obtaining food for their families. Begging was not unheard of and flirtations and sexual favours were an acknowledged way of obtaining bread or flour in time of scarcity. Similarly, in nineteenth century London, prostitutes interviewed by Mayhew explained their 'shame' as a way of providing food for their families. One, the mother of an illegitimate boy, explained that to keep herself and her son from starving she was 'forced to resort to prostitution'. Another described the 'glorious dinner' her solicitations had brought. And a daughter explained her prostitution to the author of *My Secret Life* as her way of enabling the rest of the family to eat: 'Well, what do you let men fuck you for? Sausage rolls?' 'Yes, meat-pies and pastry too.'[50]

Not all single working girls were abandoned with illegitimate children, nor, despite the alarm of middle class-observers, did most become prostitutes. Many got married and most left the labour force when they did. Both the predominance of young single girls in the female labour force and the absence of older married women reflect the persistence of traditional familial values. When they married, daughters were no longer expected to contribute their wages to their parents' household. Marriage meant to transfer from one family to another and the assumption of some new roles. Single girls, however, carried the values and practices of their mothers into their own marriages. The traditional role of a married woman, her vital economic function within the family economy, sent her into the labour force when her earnings were needed by the household budget. When the income of her husband and children was sufficient for the family's needs, she left the labour force. Mothers of young children would sometimes leave the labour force only after their oldest child went out to work. Over the developmental cycle of the family, this pattern is valid, but in cases of temporary need, such as sickness, or in the case of the death of a money earner, the married woman would go back to work.[51] [. . .]

Although increasingly the location of work in factories or shops outside the home made such work more feasible for single women, some married women continued to find jobs. Industrialization only gradually transformed occupational opportunities. Old jobs persisted for many years alongside the new. Women who married industrial workers and who lived in cities imported old styles of behaviour into new contexts. Much of the work performed by married women was temporary. Anderson describes varieties of domestic employment for married women in Preston in 1851. Many helped their husbands, others ran 'a little provision shop or beer house'. Well over a third of those who worked, he continues, 'were employed in non-factory occupations. Many others also worked irregularly or part time' and often were not even listed in official records as having an occupation. Indeed, Anderson's formulation for Lancashire, that 'patterns of family structure in towns can only be explained as hangovers from rural patterns', has much wider application.[52] Whether in the cities and towns of Europe or in America, the work patterns of married women resembled older, pre-industrial practices. [. . .]

Whether they worked outside the home or not, married women defined their role within the framework of the family economy. Married working-class women, in fact, seem almost an internal backwater of pre-industrial values within the working-class family. Long after their husbands and children had begun to adopt some of the individualistic values associated with industrialization, these women continued the self-sacrificing, self-exploitative work that so impressed Le Play and was characteristic of the peasant or household economy. Surely this (and not the fact that 'husbands gave purpose to married women among the poor') is the meaning of the testimony of a women from York cited by Peter Stearns: 'If there's anything extra to buy such as a pair of boots for one of the children, me and the children goes without dinner — or mebbe only 'as a cop o' tea and a bit o' bread, but Him allers takes 'is dinner to work, and I never tell 'im.'[53] As long as her role is economically functional for her family, familial values make sense for the lower-class woman. And the role of provider and financial manager, of seamstress and occasional wage earner was economically functional for a long time in working-class families.

Perhaps most illustrative is this case history which embodies the collective portrait we have just presented. Fransesca F. was born in about 1817 in a rural area of Moravia and remained at home until she was eleven.[54] She had a typical childhood for a girl of her class. She learned from her mother how to keep house and help on the farm, and she learned at school how to read, write, figure and, most important of all, sew. At eleven, she was sent into domestic service in a neighbouring town. She worked successively in several different houses, increasing her earnings as she changed jobs. At one house she acquired a speciality as a seamstress. She saved some money, but sent most of it home, and she returned home (to visit and renew her passport) at least once a year.

Until her eighteenth year, Francesca's experience was not unlike young girls' of earlier generations. Her decision to 'seek her fortune in Vienna', though, began a new phase of her life. With the good wishes of her parents, she paid her coach passage out of her savings and three days after she arrived she found a job as a maid. She lived for six months with the bourgeois family which employed her. Then she left for a better position, which she held until her master died (six months), and on-to yet another job as a domestic for a year.

At twenty, attracted by the opportunities for work available in a big city and tired of domestic service, she apprenticed herself to a wool weaver. He went bankrupt after a year and she found another job. That one she quit because the work was unsteady and she began sewing gloves for a small manufacturer. Glovemaking was a prospering piecework industry and Francesca had to work 'at home'. Home was a boarding house where she shared her bed with another working girl of 'dubious character.' Unhappy with these arrangements, Fransesca happily met a young cabinetmaker, himself of rural origin with whom she began living. (The practice of sleeping with one's fiancé was not uncommon in rural Moravia according to Le Play.) She soon had a child whom she cared for while she sewed gloves, all the while saving money for her marriage. (Viennese authorities at this time required that workers show they could support a family before they were permitted to marry. The task of accumulating savings usually fell to the future bride.)

Three years after she met the cabinetmaker, they were married. Francesca paid all the expenses of the wedding and provided what was essentially her own dowry — all the linens and household furnishings they needed. The daughter of rural peasants, Francesca was now the mother of an urban working-class family. Although the care of her children and the management of her household consumed much of her time, she still managed to earn wages in 1853, by doing the equivalent of 125 full days of work, making gloves. (Although it amounted in Le Play's calculation to 125 days, Francesca sewed gloves part of the day during most of the year.)

As long as piecework was available to her, Francesca F. could supplement her husband's wage with her own work. With the decline of such domestic work, however, and the rise of factories, it would become increasingly difficult for the mother of five young children to leave her household responsibilities in order to earn a wage. Economic conditions in Vienna in the 1850s still made it possible for Francesca to fulfil the role expected of a woman of the popular classes.

Traditional values did not persist indefinitely in modern or modernizing contexts. As families adapted customary strategies to deal with new situations they became involved in new experiences which altered relationships within the family and the perceptions of those relationships. As the process of change involved retention of old values and practices, it also transformed them, but in a more gradual and complex manner than either Goode or Engels implied.

The major transformation involved the replacement of familial values with individualistic ones. These stressed the notion that the individual was owner of him or herself rather than a part of a social or moral whole.[55] They involved what Anderson calls 'an instrumental orientation' of family members to their families 'requiring reciprocation for their contribution in the very short run.'[56] These attitudes developed differently in different places depending in part on specific circumstances. Nonetheless, the evidence indicates an underlying similarity in the process and the final outcome. Sons first, and only later daughters, were permitted to keep some of their earnings. They were granted allowances by their parents in some cases; in others a specified family contribution was set; in still others the child decided what portion of the pay would be sent home (and it diminished and became increasingly irregular over time). Anderson points out that in Preston, high factory wages of children reversed normal dependencies and made parents dependent on their children. The tensions created by the different priorities of parents and children led to feuds. And in these situations children often left home voluntarily and gladly and 'became unrestrained masters of their destiny.'[57]

Long distance and permanent migration also ultimately undermined family ties. This, coupled with the pressures of low wages and permanent urban living, and the forced independence of large numbers of young girls, clearly fostered calculating, self-seeking attitudes among them. They began to look upon certain jobs as avenues of social and occupational mobility, rather than as a temporary means to earn some money for the family. Domestic service remained a major occupation for women until the twentieth century in most of Europe. (In fact, in the mid-nineteenth century the number of women employed as domestics increased tremendously.) Nonetheless, as it embodied traditional female employment, a position as a servant also began to mean an opportunity for geographic and occupational mobility. Once the trip to the city and the period of adjustment to urban life had been accomplished under the auspices of service, a young girl could seek better and more remunerative work.[58] Her prospects for marrying someone who made better money in the city also increased immeasurably.

Their new experiences and the difficulties, and disillusionment they experienced, clearly developed in young women a more individualistic and instrumental orientation. They lived and worked with peers increasingly. They wanted to save their money for clothes and amusements. They learned to look out for their own advantage, to value every penny they earned, to place their own desires and interests above those of their families.

Decreased infant mortality and increased educational opportunity also modified family work strategies. And instead of sending all their children out to work for the family welfare, parents began to invest in their children's futures by keeping them out of the work force and sending them to school. (Clearly this strategy was adopted earlier for sons than daughters — the exact history of the process remains to be described.) The family ethic at once sponsored intergenerational mobility and a new individualistic attitude as well.[59]

A number of factors, then, were involved in the waning of the family economy. They included the location of job opportunities, increased standards of living and higher wages, proximity to economic change, increased exposure and adherence to bourgeois standards as chances for mobility into the bourgeoisie increased, ethnic variations in work patterns and family organization, and different rates of development for different regions and countries. The decline of the family as a productive unit can be dated variously for various places, classes, and ethnic groups. It reached the European peasant and working classes only during the nineteenth century, and, in some areas like Southern Italy, rural Ireland, and rural France, not until the twentieth century. The usefulness of the family model as a unit of analysis for social relationships and economic decision making, however, has not disappeared.[60]

A great deal more work is needed on the redefinition of family relationships and on the changes in the definition of women's work and women's place that accompanied it. Clearly many things changed. The rising standard of living and increased wages for men, which enabled them to support their families, made it less necessary for married women to work outside the home. (In early industrialization, such work also exacted great costs in terms of infant and child mortality.)[61] Even for single women, economic change reduced traditional work opportunities, while new jobs opened up for those with more education. After World War I, for example, domestic service was much less important an area of employment for young women. A smaller number of permanent servants who followed that occupation as a profession replaced the steady stream of young women who had constituted the domestic servant population.[62] The rise of factory garment production seems to have limited available work for women in

Milan and elsewhere.[63] On the other hand, the growth of new jobs in expanding government services, in support services for business, in commerce, in health services, and in teaching provided work opportunities primarily for single women, and especially for those with at least a basic education.[64]

There is evidence also that women's role in the household, whether as wives or as daughters, was modified with time. In Britain, women in working-class families began to lose control over finances early in the twentieth century, but the process was not complete until World War II. Working girls began to receive spending money of their own only at the end of the nineteenth century. After about 1914, more and more single girls kept more and more of their wages, and wives began to receive a household allowance from their husbands, who kept the rest and determined how it was spent.[65] The rhetoric of some working-class organizations also suggests a change in ideas about family roles. Labour unions demanded higher wages for men so that they could support families and keep their wives at home. Some socialist newspapers described the ideal society as one in which 'good socialist wives' would stay at home and care for the health and education of 'good socialist children.'[66]

The changes that affected women's work and women's place in the family late in the nineteenth and in the twentieth centuries are subjects which are virtually unexplored by historians. They cannot be understood, however, apart from the historical context we have presented. It was European peasant and working-class families which experienced at first hand the structural changes of the nineteenth century. These experiences were anything but uniform. They were differentiated geographically, ethnically, and temporally, and they involved complex patterns of family dynamics and family decision making. The first contacts with structural change in all cases, however, involved adjustments of traditional strategies and were informed by values rooted in the family economy. It is only in these terms that we can begin to understand the work of the vast majority of women during the nineteenth century. We must examine *their* experience in the light of *their* familial values and not our individualistic ones. The families whose wives and daughters constituted the bulk of the female labour force in Western Europe during most of the nineteenth century simply did not value the 'rights and responsibilities of the individual' which Goode invokes. Their values cannot be logically or historically tied to the political enfranchisement of women. The confusion about women's work and women's place begins to be resolved when assumptions are tested against historical data. The evolutionary model which assumes a single and similar experience for all women, an experience in which political and economic factors move together, must be discarded in the light of historical evidence.

Notes

1. William Goode, *World Revolution and Family Patterns* (New York, 1963), p. 56. Ivy Pinchbeck makes the opposite point (that occupational changes played a large part in women's emancipation) in the preface to the reprinted edition of her book, *Women Workers and the Industrial Revolution, 1750—1850* (New York, 1969), p. v.
2. T. Deldycke, H. Gelders, J. M. Limbor, *La Population active et sa structure*, under the supervision of P. Bairoch (Brussells, 1969), pp. 29—31. The figures given for Italy indicate that 1881 had an even higher proportion of women working. The 1901 Census, however, has been shown to be more reliable, especially in designating occupation. In 1881, Census categories tended to overestimate the numbers of women working. In 1901 about 32.5 per cent of Italian women worked.
3. I. Pinchbeck, *Women Workers*, p. 315; E. L. Hutchins, *Women in Modern Industry* (London, 1915), p. 84.
4. Louise A. Tilly, 'Women at Work in Milan, Italy — 1880-World War I' (Paper presented to the American Historical Association Annual Meeting, New Orleans, December 28, 1972). The national distribution of women workers, in Italy as a whole, showed textiles more important than domestic service as an employer of women. Domestic servants were disproportionately concentrated in cities, textile production outside cities.
5. Calculated from data in Deldycke *et al.*, *La Population active*, p. 174. Agricultural activity was unimportant in England and in the city of Milan, so French figures are made comparable by excluding agriculture.
6. By industrialization we mean the process by which secondary and tertiary economic activity, over time, gain in importance in an economy. This is accompanied by an increased scale of these activities and consequent increasing productivity *per capita.*
7. See Edward Gross, 'Plus ça change . . .? The Sexual Structure of Occupations over Time', *Social Problems* 16 (Fall, 1968), pp. 198—206.
8. Census data from 1871 to 1901 analysed in Louise A. Tilly, 'The Working Class of Milan, 1881—1911' (Ph.D. diss., University of Toronto, 1974).
9. Miriam Cohen, 'The Liberation of Working Class Women in England?' (Paper, History Department, University of Michigan), p. 15; Hutchins, *Women in Modern Industry*, pp. 81—2; Edward Cadbury, M. Cecile Matheson and George Shann, *Woman's Work and Wages. A Phase of Life in An Industrial City* (Chicago, 1907), p. 219; Margaret Hewitt, *Wives and Mothers in Victorian Industry* (London, 1958), p. 17.
10. Pinchbeck, *Women Workers*, pp. 197—8.

11. Deldycke *et al,* p. 169.
12. *Ibid,* p. 185.
13. Abel Chatelain, 'Migrations et domesticité feminine urbaine en France, XVIII siècle-XX siècle' *Revue d'Histoire économique et sociale* 47 (1969), p. 521; E. Royston Pyke, *Golden Times* (New York, 1970), p. 156.
14. Teresa McBride, 'Rural Tradition and the Process of Modernization: Domestic servants in Nineteenth Century France' (Ph.D. diss., Rutgers University, 1973), p. 85; Tilly, 'Working Class of Milan', pp. 129—30. McBride found that in Versailles in the same period only 19.5 per cent of female domestic servants were from working-class families.
15. Philippe Ariès, *Centuries of Childhood: A Social History of Family Life,* trans. Robert Baldick (London, 1962); J. A. Banks, *Prosperity and Parenthood. A Study of Family Planning Among the Victorian Middle Classes* (London, 1954); J. A. and Olive Banks, *Feminism and Family Planning in Victorian England* (New York, 1964), all associate the idea of these separate feminine characteristics with the middle class. John Stuart Mill made a compelling argument for granting political equality to women while recognizing feminine preferences and qualities which distinguish women from men. See J. S. and H. T. Mill, *Essays on Sex Equality,* ed. Alice Rossi (Chicago, 1971). For analysis of hierarchical patterns, see Susan Rogers, 'Woman's Place: Sexual Differentiation as Related to the Distribution of Power', (Paper, Anthropology Dept. Northwestern University, April, 1974).
16. Peter Laslett, *The World We Have Lost* (New York, 1965). Among the many anthropological and historical studies of pre-industrial societies are George Foster, 'Peasant Society and the Image of the Limited Good', *American Anthropologist* 67 (April, 1965), pp. 293—315; Conrad Arensberg and Solon Kimball, *Family and Community in Ireland* (Cambridge, Mass., 1968); Ronald Blythe, *Akenfield, Portrait of an English Village* (New York, 1968); Edgar Morin, *The Red and the White: Report from a French Village* (New York, 1970); Mack Walker, *German Home Towns: Community, State and General Estates, 1648—1871* (New York, 1971).
17. Our notion is a variation of the one presented by Bert Hoselitz: 'On the whole, the persistance of traditions in social behaviour . . . may be an important factor mitigating the many dislocations and disorganizations which tend to accompany rapid industrialization and technical change', Bert Hoselitz and Wilbert Moore, *Industrialization and Society* (Paris, 1966), p. 15.
18. W. Arthur Lewis, 'Economic Development with Unlimited Supplies of Labour', in *The Economics of Underdevelopment,* (eds) A. N. Agarwala and S. P. Singh (New York, 1963), p. 408.
19. Teodor Shanin, 'The Peasantry as a Political Factor', in *Peasants and Peasant Societies; Selected Readings,* ed. T. Shanin (Penguin Books, 1971), pp. 241—44. A similar analysis of the peasant family in mid-twentieth century can be found in Henri Mendras, *The Vanishing Peasant. Innovation and Change in French Agriculture,* trans. Jean

Lerner (Cambridge, Mass., 1970), p. 76: 'The family and the enterprise coincide: the head of the family is at the same time the head of the enterprise. Indeed, he is the one because he is the other . . . he lives his professional and his family life as an indivisible entity. The members of his family are also his fellow workers.'

20. Michael Anderson, *Family Structure in Nineteenth Century Lancashire* (Cambridge, 1971), p. 96.

21. Giunta per la Inchiesta Agraria e sulle condizioni della Classe agricola. *Atti* (Rome, 1882), Vol. vi, Fasc. ii, 552, 559; Fasc. iii, pp. 87, 175—76, 373, 504, 575.

22. Y. Brekilien, *La vie quotidienne des paysans en Bretagne au XIX siècle* (Paris, 1966), p.37. Jean-Marie Gouesse, 'Parenté, famille et marriage en Normandie aux XVIIe et XVIIIe siècles, *Annales, Economies, Sociétés, Civilisations* 27e Année, (July—October, 1972), pp.146—7.

23. Basile Kerblay, 'Chayanov and the Theory of Peasantry as a Specific Type of Economy,' Shanin *Peasants and Peasant Societies,* p. 151, and *A. V. Chayanov on the Theory of Peasant Economy,* eds. Daniel Thorner, Basile Kerblay and R. E. F. Smith (Homewood, Ill., 1966), pp. 21, 60. See also Henriette Dussourd, *Au même pot et Au même feu: etude sur les communautés familiales agricoles du centre de la France* (Moulins, 1962).

24. For the most part, men worked outside the home. They performed public functions for the family and the farm. Women, on the other hand, presided over the interior of the household and over the private affairs of family life. Separate spheres and separate roles did not, however, imply discrimination or hierarchy. It appears, on the contrary, that neither sphere was subordinated to the other. This interpretation is, however, still a matter of dispute among anthropologists. See Lucienne A. Roubin, 'Espace masculin, espace feminin en communauté provencale'. *Annales, E. S. C.* 26 (March—April, 1970), 540; Rogers, 'Woman's Place', and Rayna Reiter, 'Men and Women in the South of France: Public and Private Domains' (Paper, New School for Social Research, 1973).

25. Pinchbeck, *Women Workers,* part 1 *passim.,* Alain Girard and Henri Bastide, 'Le budget-temps de la femme mariée à la campagne.' *Population* 14 (1959), pp. 253—84.

26. *Ibid.,* 6:pp. 145, 127, and 5: p. 261, respectively.

27. Arthur Dunham, *The Industrial Revolution in France* (New York, 1935), p. 170.

28. Marie Hall Ets, *Rosa, The Life of an Italian Immigrant* (Minneapolis, 1970).

29. Le Play, *Les ouvriers européens,* 5: p. 386.

30. *Ibid.,* 3: p. 281. Le Play adds that 'For each day of work . . . the women transport twice, a weight of about 210 kilograms a distance of one kilometer' (3: p. 161).

31. *Ibid.,* 3: p. 325.

32. Alice Clark, *The Working Life of Women in the Seventeenth Century* (London, 1919), pp. 150, 209.

33. Le Play, *Les ouvriers européens,* 3: pp. 106—7.
34. Alan Forrest, 'The Condition of the Poor in Revolutionary Bordeaux', *Past and Present* 59 (1973), pp. 151—52.
35. Susan Rogers, 'The Acceptance of Female Roles in Rural France', (Paper, Anthropology Dept., Northwestern University, 1972), pp. 95—96; Anderson, *Family Structure,* p. 95; Leonard Covello, *The Social Background of the Italo-American School Child* (Leiden, 1967), quotes a Sicilian proverb: 'If the father is dead, the family suffers; if the mother dies, the family cannot exist', (pp. 208—9). A French version of this is, 'Tant vaut la femme, tant vaut la ferme,' quoted in Plan de Travail, 1946—7, *La Role de la femme dans la vie rurale* (Paris, 1946).
36. Hufton, 'Women in Revolution,' pp. 91—3, Tilly, 'Working Class of Milan,' p. 259, Anderson, *Family Structure,* p. 77, Laura Ohren, 'The Welfare of Women in Labouring Families: England, 1860—1950,' *Feminist Studies* 1 (Winter—Spring, 1973): pp. 107—25.
37. Hufton, 'Women in Revolution', p. 93, Susan Rogers, 'Female Forms of Power and the Myth of Male Dominance: A Model of Female/ Male Interaction' (Paper, Anthropology Dept., Northwestern University, 1973); Rémi Clignet, *Many Wives, Many Powers: Authority and Power in Polygynous Families* (Evanston, 1970); Ernestine Friedl, 'The Position of Women: Appearance and Reality', *Anthropological Quarterly* 40 (1967); pp. 97—108; Evelyn Michaelson and Walter Goldschmidt, 'Female Roles and Male Dominance Among Peasants', *Southwestern Journal of Anthropology* 27 (1971); pp. 330—52; Rayna Reiter, 'Modernization in the South of France: The Village and Beyond,' *Anthropological Quarterly* 45 (1972); pp. 35—53, Joyce Riegelhaupt, 'Salaoio Women: An Analysis of Informal and Formal Political and Economic Roles of Portuguese Peasant Women', *Anthropological Quarterly* 40 (1967); pp. 127—38. See also Olwen Hufton, 'Women and the Family Economy in Nineteenth Century France' (Paper, University of Reading, 1973).
38. That sometimes management roles implied literacy as well is indicated in a manuscript communicated to us by Judith Silver Frandzel, University of New Hampshire. It is the account book of a farm in Besse-sur-Barge, Sarthe, undated but from the 1840s, kept exclusively by the daughter of the family. She lists everything, from sale of animals and land to purchase of handkerchiefs, kitchen utensils or jewelry, for which money was spent or received.
39. Le Play, *Les ouvriers européens,* 3: p. 111.
40. Rudolf Braun, 'The Impact of Cottage Industry on an Agricultural Population', in *The Rise of Capitalism,* ed. David Landes (New York, 1966), p. 63.
41. Tilly, 'Women at Work'; this pattern of behaviour also confirmed for pre-World War I Piedmont, another province of northern Italy, by interviews with several women who went, as young as age ten, to the city of Turin as domestic servants.
42. Neil Smelser, *Social Change in the Industrial Revolution: An application of Theory to the British Cotton Industry* (Chicago,

1959), pp. 188−89.

43. Chatelain, 'Migrations,' p. 508.

44. Ets, *Rosa*, pp. 87−115; Italy, Ufficio del Lavoro, *Rapporti sulla ispezione del lavoro, 1 dicembre 1906−30 giugno* (1908) (pubblicazione del Ufficio del Lavoro, Serie C, 1909), pp. 64, 93−94, describes the dormitories and work arrangements in north Italian textile mills; Evelyne Sullerot, *Histoire et sociologie du travail féminin* (Paris, 1968), pp. 91−94; Michelle Perrot, *Les Ouvriers en Grève, France 1871−1890* (Paris, 1974), pp. 213, 328. Recent interpretations of similar American cases are to be found in John Kasson, 'The Factory as Republican Community: The Early History of Lowell, Mass.' (Paper read at American Studies Convention, October, 1973), and Alice Kessler Harris, 'Stratifying by Sex: Notes on the History of Working Women,' (Working Paper, Hofstra University, 1974).

45. Eileen Yeo and E. P. Thompson, *The Unknown Mayhew* (New York, 1972), pp. 116−80. See also, Henry Mayhew, *London Labour and the London Poor*, 4 vols. (London, 1861; reprinted London, 1967). Sullerot, *Travail féminin*, p. 100, describes the household-like organization of seamstresses in small shops, in which the *patronne* and workers ate *en famille*, with the less skilled workers dismissed, like children, before dessert.

46. Stearns, *Women in Britain*, p. 110.

47. Anderson, *Family Structure*, p. 153.

48. Cf. Edward Shorter, 'Illegitimacy, Sexual Revolution and Social Change in Europe, 1750−1900,' *Journal of Interdisciplinary History* 2 (1971); pp. 237−72; 'Capitalism, Culture and Sexuality: Some Competing Models', *Social Science Quarterly* (1972): pp. 338−56, and, most recently, 'Female Emancipation, Birth Control and Fertility in European History', *American Historical Review* 78 (1973): pp. 605−40. Shorter has argued that the increase in illegitimate fertility which began in the mid-eighteenth to late nineteenth centuries in Europe was preceded by a dramatic change in values. This change, he says, was stimulated by rebellion against parental authority and by exposure to 'market values' when young women broke with 'old traditions' and went out to work. The change was expressed in a new sexual 'liberation' of young working girls. They sought self-fulfilment and self-expression in sexual encounters. In the absence of contraception, they became pregnant and bore illegitimate children. We find Shorter's speculations imaginative but incorrect. He makes unfounded assumptions about preindustrial family relationships and about patterns of work in these families. The actual historical experience of young women working in the nineteenth century was not what Shorter assumes it was. When one examines their history and finds that peasant values and family interests sent them to work, and when one examines the kinds of work they did and the pay they received, it is impossible to agree with Shorter that their experience was either radically different from that of women in the past, or was in any sense 'emancipating'.

Shorter cannot demonstrate that the attitudes changed; he deduces that they did. We show that the behaviour from which Shorter deduced changed values was consonant with older values operating in changed circumstances. Illegitimacy rose at least partly as a consequence of a compositional change in population, i.e., the increasing presence of many more young women in sexually vulnerable situations as workers in cities, removed from family protection and assistance. Under these circumstances, illicit liaisons can be seen as alternate families and illegitimate children the consequence of an attempt to constitute the family work unit in a situation in which legal marriage sometimes could not be afforded, or at other times was not felt necessary. Far from their own parents and the community which could have enforced compliance with an agreement to marriage which preceded sexual relations, women were more likely to bear illegitimate children. This is discussed more fully in the text. See J. DePauw, 'Amour illegitime et société à Nantes au XVIIIe siècle,' *Annales, Economies, Sociétés, Civilisations* 27e Année (July—October, 1972); pp. 1155—82, esp. 1163. De Pauw shows (1166) that promises of marriage in cases of illegitimacy increased as both illegitimacy and the unions between social equals in the eighteenth century which produced the bastards increased. (In each subsequent version of his argument, Shorter has become less qualified and more insistent about the logic of his argument. Logic, however, ought not to be confused with actual historical experience and Shorter has little solid evidence from the past to support his speculation.) See Louise Tilly, Joan Scott and Miriam Cohen, 'Women's Work and European Fertility Patterns' (Paper, 1973).

49. Charles Booth, *Life and Labour of the People of London* (London, 1902); Yeo and Thompson, *The Unknown Mayhew*, pp. 116—80; France, Direction du Travail, *Les associations professionelles ouvrières* (1903), 4: pp. 797—805; P. Leroy-Beaulieu, *Le travail des femmes au XIXe siècle* (Paris, 1873), pp. 50—145.

50. Yeo and Thompson, *The Unknown Mayhew*, pp. 141, 148, 169; E. M. Sigsworth and J. J. Wylie, 'A Study of Victorian Prostitution and Venereal Disease,' in Vicinus, *Suffer and Be Still*, p. 81.

51. Chayanov and other economic studies of peasantry remark on the concept of 'target income.' On the demographic reflections of the developmental cycle see Lutz Berkner, 'The Stem Family and the Developmental Cycle of the Peasant Household: An Eighteenth-Century Austrian Example', *American Historical Review* 77 (April, 1972); pp. 398—418. Lynn Lees is working on urban applications of the developmental cycle concept with English and Irish workers' families.

52. Anderson, *Family Structure*, pp. 71, 79 respectively.

53. Stearns, 'Women in Britain', in Vicinus, p. 106.

54. Le Play, *Les ouvriers européens*, 5: pp. 9, 16—17, 45, 50—54.

55. C. B. MacPherson, *The Political Theory of Possessive Individualism. Hobbes to Locke* (Oxford paperback, 1964), p. 3.

56. Anderson, *Family Structure*, pp. 131—132.

57. *Ibid.*

58. McBride 'Rural Tradition': Chatelain 'Migrations', makes a similar point.

59. For an important discussion of changes in family strategies, see Charles Tilly, 'Population and Pedagogy in France', *History of Education Quarterly* 13 (Summer, 1973); pp. 113—28.

60. See, for example, Marc Nerlove, 'Economic Growth and Population: Perspectives of the New Home Economics', (Unpublished Draft, Northwestern University, 1973).

61. Hewitt, *Wives and Mothers,* pp. 99—122 and Appendix I. For France, see the debate surrounding the passage of the Loi Roussel in 1874, regulating wet nursing.

62. Chatelain, 'Migrations', McBride, 'Rural Tradition', p. 20. Domestic service continued, at the same time, to be the channel of geographic mobility of small rural population groups, sometimes in international migration streams.

63. Tilly, 'Women at Work'.

64. Holcombe, *Victorian Ladies.*

65. Stearns, 'Women in Britain', p. 116.

66. These particular attitudes were expressed in *Le Reveil des Verriers* in an 1893 article, entitled 'La Femme socialiste', but they are representative of many such attitudes expressed in the working class press. See M. Guilbert, 'La Presence des femmes dans les professions: incidences sur l'action syndicale avant 1914', *Le Mouvement Social* no. 63 (1968); 129. For Italy, see *La Difesa delle Lavoratrici* (a socialist newspaper for women), 11 May 1912, for a socialist view of women's role as mothers. See also Theodore Zeldin, *France 1850—1950. Ambition, Love and Politics* (Oxford, 1973), 1: p. 346.

1.5 The 'family wage'

MICHELE BARRETT AND MARY MCINTOSH

Introduction

The notion of a 'family wage' has been in the past a divisive issue (Land 1980), though lately it has been less discussed. It is the idea that an adult man ought to earn enough to enable him to support a wife and children. It has often, though not always, had support in the labour movement and has often, though again not always, been opposed by feminists. In so far as the balance of the labour movement has historically been in favour of it and the tendency of the present women's movement is to oppose it, it is clearly a divisive and important political issue for both socialists and feminists today. In this paper we address some of the arguments about the history and desirability of a 'family wage' system, and also question the usefulness of this notion as a description of the means by which the reproduction of the working class has in fact been accomplished.

The idea of the 'family wage' has tended to be identified with that of the 'living wage': a living wage is one on which a man can keep himself, his wife and children at a decent level. Although at times some socialists have toyed with the idea of a wage that varied with the scale of a man's family responsibilities [. . .], on the whole the trade union movement in Britain has seen this as a way of keeping the general level of wages down and has sought to achieve for all its members a wage adequate to support a family (see, for instance, Royal Commission on Equal Pay, 1946, para. 363).

Today the idea of a family wage is so much taken for granted that it is standard trade union practice to draw up pay claims for low-paid workers which refer to the need to maintain the level of living of a standard married man with two children. The newspapers routinely supply us with calculations of the effects of tax changes or price changes for the same man married with two children. [. . .]

The principle is articulated most clearly in a social security system that differentiates radically between breadwinners and their dependents,[1] providing insurance benefits for a man's dependents but not for a wife's and no supplementary benefit to a

Source: Barrett, M. and McIntosh, M. (1980) 'The "family wage": some problems for socialists and feminists', *Capital and Class*, II, Summer, pp. 51–72

wife or a 'cohabiting' woman at all. [. . .]

Since equal pay legislation was introduced in 1970, the conventional wisdom on all sides has been to take for granted that discussions should be couched in terms of the wage form: 'equal pay for work of equal value' or at least for (in the words of the Act) 'like work', 'the rate for the job' and so forth. Yet it was not always so. Although the Trades Union Congress adopted the principle of equal pay in 1888 and much of the public discussion revolved round the question of whether women's work *was* in fact worth as much as men's, nevertheless such discussions always dealt also with the question of needs and family responsibilities. Thus it was in a minority report of the 1919 War Cabinet Committee on Women in Industry (the Atkin Report) that Beatrice Webb first put forward proposals for child allowances as a way of enabling equal pay for men and women without endangering the maintenance of children. The 1946 Royal Commission on Equal Pay devoted much time to considering the dependents of employed women, and also to the argument that 'most women . . . unlike most men, do not expect either now or in the future, to support a married partner or a family of children out of the proceeds of their labour; on the contrary most of them look forward to being themselves supported in the relatively near future' (para. 362). So earlier discussions of equal pay always recognized that it would cause immense problems for the principle of the male worker as family breadwinner.

Recently, however, the trade union movement has tried to have its cake and eat it too. While day-to-day bargaining has routinely used the argument of family needs, the official pronouncements of the TUC in relation to equal pay have tended to play down this consideration and emphasize the wage as payment for work performed. Thus, as Bea Campbell and Val Charlton so lucidly put it (1979, p. 32): 'The Labour Movement has managed to combine a commitment to equal pay with a commitment to the family wage; you can't have both.'

History of the idea

Before we present our arguments against such a commitment to the family wage, it is worthwhile examining how the idea became so widely accepted and what were the various group interests involved. For the idea of the family wage is associated historically with the development of the modern relation between the family and social production and with the modern sex-structured labour market and the marginal position of women, especially in industrial production. The early period of factory production was marked by the employment of men, women and children from a very young age. During the course of the nineteenth century children became excluded almost totally from the factories and from all other full-time paid work. Women became marginalized in many fields of factory production, became located in specifically female occupations and sectors, and many women spent much or even the whole of their married lives outside of regular waged employment altogether (Gardiner 1974). Children became more dependent and in need of greater and longer care; women too became more dependent and more taken up with the tasks of caring for children and other family members.

[Marx and subsequent] Marxist historians have tended to see the introduction of female and child labour into factories, mines and so on, in the context of the process of deskilling set in motion by the mechanization of capitalist production. [Employers forced up profits] through the extension of the working day, and many contemporary sources document the almost incredibly long hours worked by labourers in the first decades of machine production.

By the 1830s, however, it was becoming apparent that these conditions were incompatible with the reproduction of a working class fit to carry out its task:[the extension of the working day and increased intensity of labour foundered] on the physical condition of the working class. Hence it became imperative, both from the point of view of the capitalist class as a whole and from the point of view of the working class, to protect the life and health of the industrial proletariat. There has been dispute as to whether the measures subsequently taken to assure the adequate reproduction of the working class are to be understood as the fruit of successful class struggle on the part of the working class, or as successful collective control by capital of the instruments of production — the labourers themselves. Certainly it seems the case that there was a coincidence of interests, though not of course a formal alliance, between bourgeois philanthropists and the bourgeois state on the one hand and the emergent Chartist and trade union movement on the other. The Factory Acts of the 1840s, limiting the length of the working day, the protective legislation aimed at the reduction of female and child labour and, later in the century, the introduction of elementary education all formed part of this process.

It is worth noting, in relation to the demand for a family wage, that the relegation of women to the home cannot be explained solely with reference to the 'needs of capitalism' but was the object of struggle, and therefore choice, of the working class. It was presumably open to the working class organizations of the 1830s and 1840s to struggle for better conditions of reproduction of the class through some other means. In textile districts, for instance, the high level of women's employment and aggregate family income meant that practices like eating shop-made pies and puddings, and having the day-care of infants, the washing and basic cleaning done by women who specialized in these jobs were common among the working class. Improved standards of home life do not necessarily involve more unpaid domestic labour. It appears, however, that the organizations of the working class colluded with pressure from the bourgeoisie to structure the working population along the lines of gender.

What was most forcibly articulated in bourgeois philanthropy was the degeneration of the family caused by the conditions in which mothers undertook wage labour, the way in which working wives neglected the home and so drove their husbands to the ale-house, the moral impropriety of men and women and young people all working together in the same place, the moral danger of the influx of independent single girls to the factory towns (Hutchins and Harrison 1911, Pinchbeck 1930, Hewitt 1958, Davidoff *et al.* 1976, p. 167). But a further and more important dimension to their arguments was the attempt to establish the idea of the hard-working man who was responsible for the support of his wife and children. [. . .]

Robert Gray has pointed to the ways in which ideas about the 'respectable artisan' involved a particular life-style which emphasized home-ownership, domesticity, the woman's place in the home. He says:

> Economic structure and ideology were mutually reinforcing in perpetuating the sexual division of labour in industry, the home and society. The exclusion of women and the demand for a breadwinner's wage for men was an industrial bargaining strategy, enabling men to make sectional gains while women provided employers with a pool of casual labour at below-subsistence wages. For women confronted by the limited opportunities of this labour market, marriage could afford better chances of survival; moreover, the time devoted to household tasks could have an appreciable effect on the living standards of even the poorest families (Gray 1980).

So Gray sees these as ideas which, although found among the bourgeois reformers and philanthropists, were also a response of the would-be 'respectable' male workers to their own economic and social environment.

In the trade union movement, at that stage a movement largely of the 'skilled' male upper strata, an association between reducing competition in paid work and women as dependent homemakers was explicitly articulated. For instance, a speaker at the 1877 Trades Union Congress said that men

> had the future of their country and their children to consider and it was their duty as men and as husbands to use their utmost efforts to bring about a condition of things, where their wives could be in their proper sphere at home, instead of being dragged into competition for livelihood against the great and strong men of the world (Henry Broadhurst, quoted in Ramelson 1967, p. 103).

Housework and childcare (with the large families and primitive domestic technology of the day) were indeed heavy and time-consuming tasks and it was, in many ways, a fortunate woman whose husband earned enough to enable her to do this work in the day-time rather than after a day's paid work. It was for this reason that Hutchins and Harrison (1911), historians of the Factory Acts, castigated the 'women's rights opposition' to protective legislation for 'transferring their own grievance (against being excluded from the professions) to a class whose troubles are little known and less understood by them. . . . Not exclusion but exploitation, is the trouble here' (1911, p. 184). [. . .]

Hutchins and Harrison were wrong to accept the 'protective' rhetoric of the short-time movement (especially as they were well aware that it was a tactic designed to bring about a reduction of overall factory hours), for the factory acts did not attempt to limit the exploitation of women in the whole range of employment, but only in specific kinds of jobs, which happened to be in the places where men also worked. As Sally Alexander has noted: 'There was not much to choose — if our criteria are risk to life or health — between work in the mines and work in the London dressmaking trades. But no one suggested that sweated needlework should be prohibited to women' (1976, p. 63).

There does not seem to be much evidence about what working-class women at the time themselves thought about the factory acts or about being excluded from the 'skilled' male trades. Their voices were little heard in the debates, for they were unorganized and unrepresented, it was left to others to speak of their rights or of their sufferings — even when it was recognized that their exploitation at work was so great precisely because they were unorganized and disunited. It seems likely that some women would have welcomed the shortening of their hours, others feared that it might bring about either a reduction in their wages or their displacement from the better jobs and that the married and young single women would think of an improvement in men's wages as some sort of compensation for the weakening of their own position and be glad that men offered to shoulder family responsibilities which they were less and less able to carry.

But whatever the response to their immediate situation may have been, the eventual outcome of this demand for a family wage and its persistence as an ideal, has placed the working class and the women of this class in a worse position than if it had continued to be assumed that husband and wife would both earn wages. Certainly it was a demand that found support mainly among bourgeois reformers and the upper strata of male workers. On the other hand, the bitter opposition of many employers to the factory legislation and even more to its implementation, suggests that individual capitalists did not favour the exclusion of women from the factories. Yet it seems clear that the collective interests of capital as a whole, as eventually articulated in state policies, lay in establishing the principle, if not the practice, of the male breadwinner and that the state has played an important part in fostering this idea.

The myth of the family wage

Attacking the family wage is a bit like an atheist attacking god the father: She wants to say that it does not exist, that the false belief that it does has evil consequences and that even if it did exist it would not be a good thing. We shall look first at the evidence that there has never in fact been a family wage system for the support of the wives, children and other non-waged relatives of working men.

Official statistics of women's labour-force participation are notoriously unrevealing of the real extent to which women engage in paid work. [. . .]

Oral history (for instance, Taylor 1977) is beginning to fill out the picture for the early decades of this century, when few married women were employed within the factories, but many seem to have made ends meet by out work, charring, laundry or taking in boarders (see also Scott and Tilly 1978, p. 25 and Davidoff 1979). It seems likely that it has never been possible for the majority of working-class families to manage on one income. [. . .]

The Liberal reforms of the first decade of the twentieth century reflected such a recognition, and the arguments raised then (about pensions, insurance and so on) paved the way for the inter-war years' debate on the question of family allowances. This period, during which Eleanor Rathbone campaigned tirelessly for the principle of family allowances, was crucially important for the formation of the modern 'welfare state' as outlined in the Beveridge Report of 1942. Rathbone was particularly insistent that the poverty documented by researchers such as Booth and Rowntree arose from the attempt to fit the support of families of varying sizes and stages of dependency to the 'Procrustean bed' of the adult male wage.

Recent historical work on social policy (notably that of Hilary Land and Pat Thane) demonstrates the force of Rathbone's arguments. In pointing to the essential contribution of working-class women to the family income, and to the dire poverty of the many women who were financially responsible for the support of their children or other people, such work has exploded, in Hilary Land's terms, 'the myth of the male breadwinner'. For whatever arguments and political conclusions we may draw from the history of the demand for a male 'family wage', there is one point that is certain: this notion does not serve as an accurate description of the means by which the working class had been supported and reproduced.

The fact is that today, as in the past, many male wage-earners do not have dependents and many of the unwaged members of the working class do not have breadwinners. Taking the population as a whole, the household consisting of a man, woman and children is far from being the typical household: in 1976 it represented only 30 per cent of all households, with one-woman-one-man households another 30 per cent and one-person households 20 per cent (Family Expenditure Survey for 1976). Only 79 per cent of men aged 20 to 65 are married and only 42 per cent of those have dependent children, so that the supposed justification for the family wage — the children — in reality exists only for a third of adult men of working age. An increasing proportion of married women work for wages: the official figure for their economic activity rate (including the over-60s) is now 50 per cent and for the age group 35-54 it rises to 68 per cent, almost as high as for unmarried women (Department of Employment Gazette, June 1977).

It is not surprising, then, to find that, taking households as a whole, the wages or salaries of 'heads of household' (some of whom are women anyway) contribute only 51 per cent of household income, the rest coming from other sources such as state benefits, self-employment and investments, and from the wages and salaries of wives (11.4 per cent) and other household members (10.8 per cent) (Family Expenditure Survey for 1976).

It is clear that many men supposedly earning a family wage do not have any dependents; it is less easy to say how many unwaged people there are who are unsupported. Among the great advances in welfare during this century has been the fact that increasingly, category by category, starting with the old age pension in 1908, unwaged individuals have become eligible for social security support, though often means-tested and set at a mean and minimal level. Only for children and married women — and a few married men — are there substantial exceptions to this eligibility. Apart from the universal child benefit, children and married women are denied individual access to supplementary benefit support and are expected to rely on their parent or husband. Nevertheless, despite child and supplementary benefits, invalid care allowances and retirement pensions, there is ample evidence of extreme poverty among those — predominantly women — who have sole care of children or of disabled people and also among old people — again often women — who are not subsidized by a wage-earner but rely entirely on their pension. For such people the family wage system provides no support or protection.

However, perhaps even more important than the inadequacy of the household structure to sharing the wage around the working class is the inadequacy of the size of the wage to supporting an entire household. This is evidenced most starkly in that modern revival of the Speenhamland system of poor relief, the Family Income Supplement — a long-term benefit available to families with children where the 'head' is in full-time low-paid work. There are almost a hundred thousand families that qualify because the 'head's' wages are simply not enough to support the family even at the exiguous levels laid down. The research that foreshadowed the introduction of FIS found that twice as many families would fall to this level, or close to it, but for the earnings of the wife (DHSS 1971, p. 12).

At higher levels, too, wives' earnings are an essential part of the household budget. Higher income couples more often have the wife in employment as well as the husband and a study in 1974 found that out of eleven million couples with the husband under 65 there were seven million wives in employment who contributed an average of a quarter of the household's income. The same study found that there were in Britain over half a million couples where the wife was the sole or primary earner. The report concluded that 'while economic role reversal is uncommon, role sharing is the norm' (DHSS Economic Advisor's Office 1976). The importance of wives' earnings, together with the uncertainty of marriage (given the high divorce rate) and of the husband's employment, means that they cannot be expected to be dependents who work only for 'extras'.

The case against the family wage

The question we have to confront, then, is whether this idea of the family wage represents an ideal that we should aim to realize or a myth that we should aim to destroy. [. . .]

Jane Humphries (1977a and b) has argued that the case against the working-class family is 'not proven'; defence of the family was, she insists, based on a correct perception of the material advantages it carried for the working class. According to Humphries the family wage system provides [among other benefits] a non-degrading form of support for non-labouring members of the working class. [. . .]

Leaving aside our disagreements with the argument that the working class as a whole would benefit from the family wage system,[2] we concentrate here on the specific situation of women. Such a system would enforce the dependency and oppression of all women and subject unsupported women, especially mothers, to severe poverty. [. . .]

A number of feminist arguments can be raised against a wage structure predicated upon the dependence of a married woman on her husband. There is no shortage of evidence to support the suggestion that financial dependence carries in its train a significant degree of ideological subordination. Studies by Laura Oren (1974) and others have shown that women's levels of consumption within the family tend to be lower than those of men, and the degrading aspects of a struggle over the distribution of the wage within the family have been explored by Pauline Hunt (1978) — and there are stark examples in *Coal Is Our Life* (Dennis *et al.* 1956). Hilary Land has pointed out that women who return to wage labour after a period of child-bearing have lost ground and go back to lower wage rates: '. . . marriage and motherhood', she comments, '. . . effectively "deskill" women' (1978, p. 282). Indeed the assumption of a male family wage affects all women's wages adversely, since even single women suffer from the lower rates of pay, poorer working conditions and constraints on promotion generally applied to women wage workers. Marriage and motherhood are not, in any case, a secure livelihood: for many women the consequences of divorce are a much lower standard of living and a structurally disadvantaged place in the labour market. The numbers of married women who stay with their husbands through financial necessity alone cannot be gauged accurately, but the numbers of women taking up the opportunity to resort to refuges for battered wives may indicate that many women previously had literally nowhere to go.

Even if married women were better off under a family wage

system, those who were not married would be worse off. At the end of the 19th century only 85 per cent of women married, and often later than now (today the figure is 95 per cent, but many of these divorce). The plight of the 'surplus women' in the bourgeois class has been widely canvassed, but that of those in the working class has to be gleaned from papers relating to the poor law. Unmarried mothers, widows and deserted wives were in the direst straits. Even the most respectable, the widow, was subjected to the 'workhouse test' before she could obtain relief, on the grounds that 'a man in receipt of regular weekly wages may be fairly called upon to secure his widow . . . against dependence upon Poor Law relief' (3rd Annual Report of the Local Government Board 1873—4, p. 185, quoted in Finer (1974) Vol. 2, p. 123). Deserting husbands and putative fathers were also expected to pay maintenance (for unmarried mothers from 1844 and for deserted wives from 1878), but it was unlikely that they often did so. Indeed, many thousands of these 'liable relatives' were imprisoned for failing to reimburse the poor law authorities for the maintenance of their dependents. The Finer Report on One-Parent Families has documented the fact that maintenance is still rarely and irregularly paid today and that many men, and their dependents, suffer real hardship from the fact that men are expected to maintain two consecutive families simultaneously. When poor relief in the 19th century and supplementary benefit today are granted to a single woman, she is subject to a cohabitation rule, on the assumption that if she shares a household with a man he should be supporting her. The expectation of dependence on a man can thus have disastrous consequences for the woman who has no man to depend upon, yet provisions for state support show a remorseless determination to enforce that expectation wherever possible.

Dispute rages about exactly what economic or sociological theory best explains women's position in the wage-labour market, their concentration in a limited range of sectors and occupations and their lower average pay (see, for instance, Beechey 1978; Bruegel 1979). This is not the place to enlarge on that discussion. It is sufficient for our purposes to note that there is broad agreement that domestic responsibilities and the supposed possibility of dependence upon a husband (and in the nineteenth century on a father) must figure largely in the explanation. Furthermore, the belief that women reduce men's wages by undercutting has served to justify trade union pressure to exclude them from work, or at least from the better-paid trades.

Nevertheless, as the Cadbury team found in their (1907) investigations, the argument for giving a woman only one-third or half the pay of a man 'because her wage is an auxiliary one, because she is subsidized by the other members of a family', was 'not borne out by the facts'. Most women lived off their earnings; many had dependent parents or siblings, and those who had not still required more than one-third or half what a man required to feed, house and clothe themselves. Many of the women the Cadbury team interviewed were obliged to maintain the minimum standard of living or even less (Auchmuty 1975, pp. 113—14).

Part of the ideal model of the family wage and women's peripheral place in wage-work is the idea of women's domestic responsibilities. [. . .] The need of a man for a clean cheerful home and a meal prepared on his return from work was one of the powerful arguments for restricting the hours and types of paid work that women should do. Low wages, dependence and housework for women are a trio of mutually reinforcing ideas, each justifying and producing the conditions for the others. [. . .]

Many feminists have argued that the enforcement of domestic responsibilities, especially childcare and doing the man's housework, lies at the root of women's oppression. Childcare has been thought, by non-feminists, to be an inalienable task of women and both to justify and explain most of the division of labour and the differences between men and women. Yet it is interesting that childhood as a period of prolonged dependence and childcare as a separate task are relatively recent and developed hand-in-hand with dependent motherhood. However, in this century, as women have lived longer and concentrated their childbearing into a few early years of life (the youngest child usually starts school before the mother is 35) the appeal to motherhood as a justification for dependence has become less plausible (even to those who think that privatized mothering is the only way to bring up children). Yet the risk of marriage and motherhood is often mobilized as a justification for not training women and not giving them better-paid and supervisory jobs.

Responsibility for caring for the old and the mentally and physically handicapped also falls most naturally to female relatives, (especially married women) who can expect support from their husbands if they have to give up paid work or reduce the number of hours they do. Even the responsibility for ordinary housework is seen as linked to dependence, at least in the world-view of the Department of Health and Social Security who expect a husband to support a disabled wife who can do 'her' housework but will give her a pension if she is so disabled that she cannot perform 'normal household duties'. In fact, however, housework seems to fall to women's lot whether or not they are dependent and whether or not they go out to work (Boulding 1976, p. 112, Hunt, 1968, p. 176). Wilmott and Young (1973, p. 113) found that while the men in their sample of couples aged 30 to 50 spent an average of 10 hours a week on household tasks, women in full-time jobs spent 23 hours, those in part-time jobs 35 hours and those not in paid work 45 hours. Other studies covering the more heavily burdened age groups have found the hours that women spend much longer than this, but all are agreed that even when in full-time jobs outside, women spend far more time than men on work at home.[3] This does not square with the argument put by Jane Humphries that it is women staying at home that makes available the [benefits of] domestic production. It seems that women are obliged to work a good deal at this form of production in any case.

We have argued that the demand for the family wage, and the belief that it exists, enforces the dependence and oppression of all women. If the demand were actually realized and married women no longer went into paid employment, married couples might possibly be as well off in purely financial terms; but the women would not necessarily get their share, and if they did, it would be under conditions of subordination to their husbands. And single women, especially mothers, would be at an acute economic disadvantage. Hence, if the men of the working class struggle for a family wage, they do so in opposition to one of the central demands of the women's liberation movement and against the interests of working-class women. [. . .]

Furthermore, acceptance of the family wage system involves the principle that the obligation to support non-labouring members of the working class should fall on the shoulders of the labouring individuals rather than being met [by the state]. In this respect the demand for support from the state is one that stimulates revolutionary class consciousness. For although Jane Humphries is right to point out that working-class organizations fiercely resisted the state provision of support as embodied in the 'new poor law' of 1834, there is no evidence that this represented a principled preference for a family system of support over a state system. Outrage against the 'workhouse test' was directed against its degrading and offensive form rather than against the principle of poor relief in general, which had been accepted as a right since the introduction of the Elizabethan poor law. (Humphries herself quotes a working-class man's denunciation of the 1834 poor law in which he speaks of the 'right' of poor people to parish relief as being of 'more than two centuries' standing' (1977b, p. 29).) The parish system was preferred to the bureaucratic inhumanity of the nineteenth-century poor law. So too in the twentieth century the working class has struggled for state support, in the form of old-age pensions, unemployment and sickness benefit, family allowances and so on; yet it has resisted and criticized means-testing, red tape and offensive treatment in the administration of this support. It is true that radical analysis has recognized that centralized state support for non-labourers makes for state control over the labour force and gives the state power to determine who shall be obliged to work for wages. Yet that recognition does not mean that state support stultifies the working class, since it leads to a demand for greater control over its conditions and administration.

The demand for state support renders more visible the irrationality and inadequacy of the wage in capitalist production. This indeed formed the basis of Rathbone's campaign for family allowances, since she demonstrated that the assumed family wage in fact catered (in the early decades of the twentieth century) for approximately three million 'phantom' wives and sixteen million 'phantom' children, the fictitious dependents of men who were in fact bachelors, and left six-and-a-quarter million children insufficiently fed and clothed (1949, pp. 15–16). The fact is that the family wage system has never been adequate to ensure the reproduction of the working class. The belief that it does, or that it could be perfected if only men's wages were raised, merely masks the fact that the capitalist wage system can never meet the needs of the working class. So the belief leads to attempts to reform it that cannot succeed and that do not improve the chances of more radical change.

Problems of the current crisis

In the post-war period there have been remarkable changes in women's wage-work participation, so that by now the principle of women's dependence is beginning to lose some of its pernicious power, though the apparently more benign principle of the family wage seems, curiously, to have survived unscathed. The urgent question is: how many of the gains that women have made in challenging dependence, and that non-employed members of the working class have made in claiming support through the state rather than through dependence on kin, will be lost during the course of the restructuring attendant upon the current crisis?

It is well known that women stand to be particularly hard hit by cuts in public spending. On the one hand, they are often employed in threatened public-service jobs, on the other, they rely more on publicly provided health, education and welfare services to keep them afloat and enable them to go out to work. It is less clear in what ways women's employment in private sectors of manufacturing and services are likely to be affected by the recession. Their still-marginal position in the labour force (and much of the increase in married women's employment during the 1970s was in part-time work) makes them more easily disposed of. They are often doing jobs that are either very routine or associated with an obsolescent technology, which will disappear as more advanced technologies are adopted. On the other hand, their potential for lower wages may mean that they will be substituted for higher-paid men as restructuring proceeds.

The survival of the idea of the family wage means that there is a real risk of a concerted effort to push women back into dependence and deny them the right to employment. A bourgeois state intent on saving public spending and on strengthening the ideological role of the family could well find allies among those male sections of the trade union movement that fear dilution and deskilling as a result of competition from married women and that have traditionally relied upon the idea of the family wage both as a bargaining counter and as a righteous rallying point for their rank and file membership.

We hope we have said enough by now to indicate how disastrous such an alliance would be. [. . .] The family wage ideal has never worked. Families relying on one wage have always been the hardest up. Changes in the age of marriage, the expectation of life and the timing of childbearing mean that women are bound to go on seeking employment. If the labour movement does not allow them to do so on the same basis as men and fight for them to get the same pay, conditions and job-security, then they will be found increasingly in the 'informal economy' and the poorly-organized, badly-paid sectors. The existence and expansion of such sectors threatens the gains made in the better organized sectors. In other words, women *do* threaten men's jobs, but the only way to prevent this is to challenge that distinction, to welcome them on the same conditions, not vainly to wish them away. It is time that men as well as women became disenchanted with the fantasy world of the family wage.

Notes

Michèle Barrett and Mary McIntosh teach sociology at The City University, London and at Essex University.

An earlier version of this paper was read at the Leeds CSE conference in July 1979 and at the CSE Sex and Class group in October 1979. We have learned a great deal from the discussions at both these meetings and also from the comments sent to us by *Capital and Class* and by the following people: Sally Alexander, Irene Bruegel, Bob Connell, Sue Himmelweit, Jane Humphries, Hilary Land, Kerry Schott, Judy Wajeman and Elizabeth Wilson.

1. Indeed at present the distinction is between men and married or cohabiting women, but it seems likely that 'man' will soon be translated euphemistically as 'breadwinner' to conform with EEC rules against sex discrimination (Rights of Women, 1979).
2. See the longer version from which this extract is taken: 'The "family wage": some problems for socialists and feminists', *Capital and Class*, II (Summer 1980) pp. 51—72.
3. Interestingly too, a study in the United States found that men's 'help' in the home did not reduce the amount of women's work commensurately: When men helped with physical childcare, women spent even more time on it; when men put in time preparing meals, women only gained half that time (Leibowitz, 1975, p. 223).

References

Alexander, Sally (1976) 'Women's work in nineteenth-century London, a study of the years 1820—50' in Mitchell and Oakley.

Atkin Report (1919) *Report of the War Cabinet Committee on Women in Industry*, Cmd. 135, HMSO, London.

Auchmuty, Rosemary (1975) 'Spinsters and trade unions in Victorian Britain' in Curthoys.

Beechey, Veronica (1978) 'Some notes on female wage labour in capitalist production', *Capital and Class*, III.

Blaxall, M. and Reagan, B. (1976) *Women and the Workplace*, University of Chicago Press.

Boulding, E. (1976) 'Familial constraints on women's work roles' in Blaxall and Reagan.

Bruegel, Irene (1979) 'Women as a reserve army of labour', *Feminist Review* No. 3.

Campbell, Beatrix and Charlton, Valerie (undated) 'Work to rule — wages and the family', *Red Rag* (1979).

Curthoys, Anne, Eade, Susan, and Spearitt, Peter (eds) (1975) *Women at Work* Australian Society for the Study of Labour History, Canberra.

Davidoff, Leonore (1979) 'The separation of home and work?' in Burman, S. (ed.) *Fit Work for Women*, Croom Helm, London.

Davidoff, Leonore, *et al.* (1976) 'Landscape with figures' in Mitchell and Oakley.

Dennis, N., Henriques, F. and Slaughter, C. (1956) *Coal is Our Life*, Eyre and Spottiswoode, London.

Department of Health and Social Security (1971) *Two-Parent Families: A Study of their Resources and Needs in 1968, 1969 and 1970*, DHSS Statistical Report Series, No. 14, HMSO, London.

Department of Health and Social Security, Economic Adviser's Office (1976) 'Wives as Sole and Joint Breadwinners' (Mimeo).

Finer Report (1974) Report of the Committee on One-Parent Families, *Cmnd. 5629,* HMSO, London.

Gardiner, J. (1974) 'Women's work in the Industrial Revolution' in Allen, S., Sanders, L. and Wallis, J. (eds) *Conditions of Illusion,* Feminist Books, Leeds.

Gray, R. Q. (1980) *The Aristocracy of Labour in Nineteenth Century Britain c. 1850—1900,* Macmillan, Studies in Economic and Social History, London.

Hartman, Mary and Banner, Lois W. (1974) (eds) *Clio's Consciousness Raised,* Harper and Row, New York.

Hewitt, Margaret (1958) *Wives and Mothers in Victorian Industry,* Rockliff, London.

Humphries, Jane (1977a) 'Class struggle and the persistence of the working class family', *Cambridge Journal of Economics,* Vol. 1. No. 3.

Humphries, Jane (1977b) 'The working class family, women's liberation and class struggle: the case of nineteenth century British history', *The Review of Radical Political Economics,* Vol. 9. No. 3.

Hunt, Audrey (1968) *A Survey of Women's Employment,* Office of Population Censuses and Surveys, London.

Hunt, Pauline (1978) 'Cash transactions and household tasks: domestic behaviour in relation to industrial employment', *Sociological Review,* Vol. 26, No. 3.

Hutchins, B. L. and Harrison, A. (1911) *A History of Factory Legislation,* (2nd edn) P. S. King and Son, London.

Land, Hilary (1978) 'Who cares for the family?' *Journal of Social Policy,* Vol. 7, Part 3.

Land, Hilary (1980) *The Family Wage* (The Eleanor Rathbone Memorial Lecture for 1979) Liverpool University Press, Liverpool.

Leibowitz, A. (1975) 'Women's work in the home', in Lloyd.

Lloyd, C. (ed.) (1975) *Sex Discrimination and the Division of Labour,* New York, Columbia University Press.

Mitchell, Juliet and Oakley, Ann (1976) *The Rights and Wrongs of Women,* Penguin, Harmondsworth.

Oren, Laura (1974) 'The welfare of women in labouring families: England, 1860—1950' in Hartman and Banner.

Pinchbeck, Ivy (1930) *Women Workers and the Industrial Revolution,* reprinted 1969, Frank Cass, London.

Ramelson, M. (1967) *The Petticoat Rebellion,* Lawrence and Wishart, London.

Rathbone, Eleanor (1949) *Family Allowances* (a new edition of *The Disinherited Family*) George Allen and Unwin, London.

Rights of Women and Women's Liberation Campaign for Financial and Legal Independence (1979) 'Disaggregation Now!' *Feminist Review* Number 2.

Royal Commission on Equal Pay (1946) *Report* HMSO, London, Cmd. 6937.

Scott, Joan W. and Tilly, Louise A. (1978) *Women, Work and Family,* Holt, Rinehart and Winston, New York.

Taylor, Sandra (1977) 'The effect of marriage on job possibilities for women and the ideology of the home: Nottingham 1890—1930', *Oral History*, Vol. 5, No. 1.

Thane, Pat (1978) 'Women and the poor law in Victorian and Edwardian England', *History Workshop Journal*, No. 6.

Wilmott, Peter and Young, Michael (1973) *The Symmetrical Family*, Routledge and Kegan Paul, London.

PART TWO

Employment and Training

Although the readings in the first section have stressed the inter-connections between workplace and home for determining women's position in society, in the second and third sections of the book we have chosen a selection of articles which will highlight each in turn. Thus, Part Two, Employment and Training, turns to a consideration of some aspects of women's paid work. The historical interest begun in Part One is continued in the article by Gail Braybon in her examination of the need for women's labour during the first world war. Irene Bruegel brings us up to date by discussing the competing theories which have attempted to explain changes in women's employment in more recent years, and a discussion of the current introduction of new technology into the office and its effects on secretarial work and office organization is given by Janine Morgall. Rita Arditti outlines the current position of women in scientific occupations in the United States and reflects upon her own personal biography as a geneticist. The last article in this section is a new piece by Ann Wickham and is concerned with recent issues in the training of girls and women, and the ways in which this is determined by state policy, made especially pertinent by the unemployment crisis Britain now faces.

2.1 The need for women's labour in the First World War

GAIL BRAYBON

An outline of the expansion of women's labour

The immediate effect of the outbreak of war was a drastic increase in unemployment, and many of the industries worst hit were those which, in peacetime, employed large numbers of women. As an economy measure wealthy households dismissed servants, and cut their orders to 'luxury' trades like jewellery, millinery or dress-making; women employed as fish-gutters found themselves out of work as the fishing fleets withdrew from areas patrolled by German ships; many industries, including the cotton trade, contracted as employers and clients hesitated, awaiting developments in the war and in the economy. One contemporary author, I. O. Andrews, estimated that 44.4 per cent of all women workers were un-employed for a brief time in September 1914,[1] and the Central Committee on Women's Employment (a labour body) issued figures on unemployment and short-time working which revealed the full extent of the problem that autumn. In dressmaking, only 34 per cent of women workers in large firms were working full-time, and 31 per cent of women in small firms; in boots and shoes a mere 13 per cent of women workers were in full-time work, and the equivalent percentages for other trades were: printing and books, 26 per cent; jam and sweets, 39 per cent; furnishing and upholstery, 18½ per cent; furs and skins, 33 per cent.[2]

The position of women was considered to be serious, and at this time industry, government and unions had no idea that within weeks there would be a labour shortage. Efforts were put into organizing some form of relief work for the female unemployed: 'Queen Mary's Work Fund' was set up, followed by 'Queen Mary's Workrooms', which were to be administered by the Central Committee for Women's Employment, itself set up on 20 August by such stalwarts of the labour movement as Mary Macarthur, Susan Lawrence, Margaret Bondfield and Marion Phillips, to

Source: Braybon, G. (1981) *Women Workers in the First World War.* Croom Helm, London, Chapter 2

mitigate the worst effects of unemployment by providing needle-work for women who had been laid off. Sylvia Pankhurst pointed out that the wages paid at the sewing workrooms were only 10s a week, which was virtually a sweated rate, but the aim was to provide as many women as possible with some form of subsistence without the taint of charity,[3] while the Committee continued to press for the early placing of government clothing and supplies contracts with industry.

Many of the traditional 'women's trades' — cotton, linen, silk, lace, tailoring, dressmaking, millinery, hat-making, pottery and fish-gutting — did not speedily recover,[4] but the irony was that even by November 1914 there was a labour shortage in some sections of industry. Men too had been unemployed in the chaotic months of August and September, including skilled engineers, and many of them enlisted. As the engineering and chemical industries began to expand munitions production, it soon emerged that there was a shortage of skilled labour. The problem became increasingly evident in 1915.[5]

During the winter and spring of 1914—15 government contracts did give employment to many women, as industries which traditionally employed them expanded to supply the troops with equipment: the leather, hosiery, boot, kitbag, medical dressing and tailoring industries all took on more women,[6] but such extra labour was for jobs which were usually regarded as women's in peacetime. Very few women were, at this time, employed on work normally done by men in any industry, and the engineering industry, although short of labour, was loath to employ women. By 1915, however, women were being employed in non-industrial jobs which were new to them: they replaced men in offices and in the transport system, where custom rather than skill had led to the notion that these were men's trades. [. . .]

As men enlisted, women were indeed employed as van drivers, window-cleaners, shop assistants, etc, but they were often informally taking the places of husbands, fathers or brothers: major industries remained wary about using them, unions remained worried about the effect of female labour on wages and security, and the women themselves were given little opportunity for training.

'Substitution', the extensive use of women in place of men, in industry really began in the summer of 1915 on a limited scale. Women were being employed in the munitions industry in quite large numbers by August 1915, but on jobs like shell-filling (which they had done before the war) or on processes formerly deemed just above their capabilities. They were confined to simple repetition work for the most part.[7] But once the terms of substitution became established, and unions and employers came to grudging agreement about the use of women in many industries, the expansion of women's labour began in earnest. In March 1915 there was still a surplus of unemployed women[8] and the government was sufficiently concerned to launch a national scheme for the registration of women who wanted paid work; the rush of women into engineering and explosives began in the autumn of 1915[9] and by 1916 there was actually a shortage of female labour in the textile and clothing trades, as women moved into more lucrative munitions work.[10] This rapid expansion in munitions continued in 1916 and 1917, and women also increasingly replaced men in private, non-munitions industries, like grain milling, sugar refining, brewing, building, surface mining and shipyards. London dressmakers found it so hard to get female apprentices by 1917, because of the competition offered by other industries, that they contacted the LCC and labour exchanges with a view to planning shorter, more regular hours for their workers — the first time such trades had ever been driven to consider improvements. In 1917, the *Labour Gazette* estimated that 1 in 3 working women was 'replacing' a male worker in industry.[11]

The background to this expansion was the introduction of conscription for men in January 1916. At first there were many exemptions — older and married men were not called up, nor were skilled workers in munitions industries. But as casualties increased abroad, and women's industrial capabilities became more evident to the government at home, the blanket exemption of skilled men from conscription by union was withdrawn and the Manpower Bill was passed in February 1918, cancelling all previous exemptions; from that time all munitions workers (male) under 25 were liable for conscription.[12] By 1917 women were spread throughout industry, on various processes, and the last year of the war saw a levelling-off in the demand for them, and the development of their use on some skilled processes not previously open to them.

The real increase in numbers of women employed came in the years 1915 to 1917, and the most striking instances were in munitions. Woolwich Arsenal, for example, employed 125 women in 1914, and 25,000 in 1917.[13] In July 1914, 3,276,000 women were classed as employed (not including small dressmaking establishments, domestic service, the self-employed, and those employed by husbands), and in April 1917 the figure had increased to 4,507,000. By April 1918, only another 300,000 women were employed, and the total stood at 4,808,000.[14] There was in fact a slackening in demand for certain munitions by 1917—18, and a small number of factories were already closing or changing back to pre-war production. In some industries and areas there was still a demand for more women workers, but in spite of suggestions in 1918 that there should be a 'Womanpower' Bill to conscript women for industry, such measures were never necessary.[15] By early 1918 women war workers were already being dismissed and the peak of their employment was over.

A much debated point throughout the war, and one of some interest now, is 'where the women came from'. Who were the new recruits to industry in general and the munitions industry in particular? Although statistics show that the numbers of women in industry, transport and the professions increased drastically, they do not show the extent of transference between trades. The figures quoted by Kirkaldy for 1914 (3,276,000 women at work) do not include domestic service or small dressmaking establishments, which accounted for many thousands more women. If these unnoted workers then moved into the official trades they were *not* new workers who had previously been unemployed. In fact, it does seem that a large number of women who went into the munitions industry were from other trades or were married women returning to work. I. O. Andrews, decided that the increase of women in munitions was accounted for by the transference of women from slack to busy trades, the return of married women, the movement of workers from low-paid industries, the entrance of some older women or girls straight from school, and a very few middle- or upper-class women, for, as she said drily, 'in spite of impressions to the contrary, the proportion of previously unoccupied upper- and middle-class women entering "war work" was by no means large.'[16] There was a romantic idea, commonly held, that the classes came together through women's work, or, as Hammond wrote: 'to the popular imagination there have been pictured the figures of duchesses and other ladies of fine breeding running the lathes in munition factories or pouring the deadly TNT into endless rows of shells.'[17] The idea was fuelled by the press, and by such patriotic writers as L. K. Yates, whose book, *A Woman's Part*, is full of breathless descriptions of the wonders of women's work, and who wrote, on the subject of women's background:

They have come from the office and the shop, from domestic service and the dressmaker's room, from the High Schools and the Colleges, and from the quietude of the stately homes of the leisured rich . . . Even in the early days of the advent of women in the munitions shops, I have seen working together, side by side, the daughter of an earl, a shopkeeper's widow, a graduate from Girton, a domestic servant, and a young woman from a lonely farm in Rhodesia, whose husband had joined the colours. Social status, so stiff a barrier in this country in pre-war days,

was forgotten in the factory, as in the trenches, and they were all
working together as the members of a united family.[18]

Such a picture was far from accurate, both in terms of the social
background of the workers in most factories, and the relations
between the women when there were middle- or upper-class women
present. Hammond estimated that over 200,000 women who went
into industry during the war came from domestic service, and that
many others had been outworkers, self-employed, or wives who
had left work.[19] The *Labour Gazette* concluded from a survey of
444,000 insured women workers that 70 per cent had changed their
trade during the war, and that 23 per cent moved from one kind of
factory work to another, 22 per cent were previously unemployed
(this would have included school-leavers and married women who
had retired from work), 16 per cent came from domestic service,
and 7 per cent from other non-industrial work.[20] Kirkaldy also
noted how many came from domestic service, or the clothing
trades, as did the Factory Inspector's report for 1914, and the
writers of the draft interim report of the British Association for the
Advancement of Science on *Outlets for Labour After the War,*[21]
although the latter also revealed that when middle-class women
did enter industry for patriotic reasons they invariably chose
munitions rather than any other trade. Barbara Drake drew
attention to another feature: as older women left the standard
women's trades like cotton or dressmaking for 'men's work', their
places were invariably taken by young girls,[22] which was an ominous
sign for women hoping to return to their old jobs after the war. She
too believed that about a quarter of the women in munitions came
from domestic service. Reports in newspapers often mentioned ex-
servants, and in this case they do not seem to have exaggerated the
truth, as such women flooded into all kinds of jobs as well as
munitions. *Common Cause*, the suffragist newspaper, described
the work of several 'street housemaids',[23] one of whom was a
former servant who had married, taken in washing, and then
moved to this job of road-sweeping — she liked the freedom, the
fresh air, and the fact that there was no one to nag her. The
Yorkshire Observer looked at the social background of those on a
course for munitions workers at Bradford Technical College, and
discovered women from domestic service, dressmaking, other
factories, the laundry trade, nursing, and those who were wives of
engineers.[24] The *Daily Chronicle*, even in 1915, reported that
Nottingham lace-makers were turning to munitions work,[25] and
there were appeals at various times in the press for women not to
leave the textile mills for the munitions shops.[26] Before the war
cotton had been one of the most popular trades for women, and

the wages had been comparatively good, but it could not compete with the engineering and explosives industries, which appeared to offer new opportunities and more money. Domestic service, already an unpopular trade, became the last job anyone wanted during the war.[27]

Most women who went into munitions, or other 'men's jobs', therefore, had been workers before. The middle-class women who took up war work were few, and were not necessarily popular with their companions. Monica Cosens, herself a volunteer for the war period only, commented: 'there is no denying immediately a new volunteer comes into a street [the gangway between the machines] there is defiance in the air. She is not gently treated.'[28] There could be a vast gulf between the classes.

One group did come into its own during the war: married women. Previously told that they should not work, and that their role was in the home, they were now invited back to industry, and made up a large proportion of workers in many areas, particularly since some firms had a definite preference for soldiers' wives as workers.[29] Married women made up 40 per cent of all working women throughout the country: in Leeds 44 per cent of women in the four main engineering firms were married, although in 1911 only 15 per cent of women workers in the area had been married.[30]

The main effect of the war was, therefore, to bring about the transference of women between the trades, and the return of those previously excluded; there were not really hundreds of thousands of completely new workers in industry as might be assumed at first from the statistics.

The role of the state

It is all too easy with an outline description of women's expanding employment prospects to give the impression that such expansion was inevitable, consistent within each industry, and smooth-running. In fact, the situation was more complex. [. . .]

The question of female labour lay at the heart of the government's efforts to organize war production, and the way the government attempted to control industry had a major effect on women's prospects and popularity.

This was the first time England had fought a war so greedy for men and resources, and to a large extent the machinery for coping with it was experimental. [. . .]

The structure of control during the First World War was, ironically, at the same time autocratic and inadequate: both the heavy-handedness of the government and the gaps in legislation had a serious effect on the position of women workers. A look at the government's role in the organization of the munitions industry reveals the dichotomy, and shows why the labour movement felt oppressed by an alliance of state and employers. The government did take control of the supplies of raw materials and food, but I am largely concerned with the way it attempted to organize the munitions industry. It is important to bear in mind the original strict definition of the term 'dilution of skilled labour', as set out by the Ministry of Munitions and as recognized by the engineering industry. Circular 129, issued by the Ministry in September 1915, stated that:

(1) The employment of skilled men should be confined to work which could not be efficiently performed by less skilled labour or by women.
(2) Women should be employed on all classes of work for which they are suitable.
(3) Semi-skilled and unskilled men should be employed on any work which does not necessitate the employment of skilled men and for which women are unsuitable.[31]

In November 1914 the ASE (the main craft union of the engineers) and the Employers' Federation signed the Crayford Agreement, after trouble about the introduction of women on to some processes at Vickers, Crayford. The fact that Vickers wished to recruit female labour was seen as an early intimation of the labour shortage to come, and immediate union complaints about the threat which female labour posed alerted the government to the idea that munitions production probably depended upon some kind of official policy on wartime substitution and post-war job security. It duly set up the Committee on Production in Engineering and Shipbuilding in February 1915, to act as Court of Arbitration on industrial disputes and to look into the use of less skilled labour. Employers were demanding the abandonment of the usual union regulations regarding the use of female and non-union labour, with guarantees that established conditions would return when peace came. The engineering union suggested the use of colonial labour (white), reallocation of men around the country, and the recall of skilled men who had enlisted in the army. The Committee on Production came firmly down on the side of the employers, suggesting the abolition of output restrictions (standard practice amongst engineers, designed to guard against any reduction in piece rates if they produced 'too much'), the use of female labour, and a ban on labour stoppages. It also suggested that appropriate piece rates be fixed, and that the changes should be for the war period only.[32]

On 4 March 1915, the Engineering Employers' Federation and the engineering unions duly signed the *Shells and Fuses Agreement*. Theoretically it was a compromise, designed to prevent the flooding of industry with female substitutes, and to stop the unions holding out against any change in traditional practice. In fact, the unions' retreat from their total opposition to female labour left the way open for further erosion of demarcation and skill in the years to come. The points accepted in the *Shells and Fuses Agreement* were as follows:

(1) men engaged in the making of tools and gauges should be skilled men, as should those who set up machines;
(2) such men could be drawn from other branches of the engineering trade, as long as they had the necessary qualifications, and should be paid the standard 'rate for the district' on that job (wages before the war were arranged on a local basis by union branches and firms, not nationally, and could vary from area to area);
(3) lists of such men should be given to the local unions;
(4) transferred workers should be the first to be discharged;
(5) there should be no displacement of skilled men by less skilled, unless alternative skilled work could be found;
(6) the operations done by skilled men which *could* be done by semi-skilled or female labour should be performed by them during the war: rates would be the usual district rate for the job;
(7) the removal of restrictions should not harm workpeople, or unions;
(8) after the war, pre-war conditions should return;
(9) the proposals offered should not lead to any permanent substitution by semi-skilled or female labour;
(10) employers should not take advantage of any wartime agreements afterwards;
(11) employers should agree to distribute government work throughout the country (thus avoiding the situation where some firms demanded overtime while other factories were on short time);
(12) overtime should be reduced wherever possible;
(13) semi-skilled or female labour should be the first discharged.[33]

Spring-summer 1915 was the key time for the negotiations between unions and employers and for the emergence of government policy on munitions production and the control of labour. On 9 March Parliament passed a Bill allowing the government to take control of munitions factories,[34] and on 19 March the *Shells and Fuses Agreement* was followed up by a government/union contract, the *Treasury Agreement.* This was designed to deal particularly with the substitution of semi-skilled for skilled workers in engineering, and confirmed that skilled men were to work on skilled processes alone, instead of doing a variety of jobs which *included* skilled work, as before. The unions also agreed that there would be no strikes (arbitration would take place instead) and that processes would be accelerated. In return they were promised that there would be no decrease in skilled men's wage rates, and that women replacing them would receive the fully skilled tradesman's rate.

Problems became evident almost immediately. The government was overseeing the formal relationship between employers and unions, yet the guarantees given to the workmen were inadequate. This had repercussions for women as well. There was never any full analysis of what was meant by the terms 'skilled', 'semi-skilled' and 'unskilled' work. As processes were altered for war production and jobs were subdivided employers could claim that women who were only doing *part* of a skilled man's job were not entitled to full rates. [. . .]

Thus there was no guarantee that women would not be employed at far cheaper rates on *parts* of skilled work. Nor, at this stage, did the government make any promises at all about the rates for semi-skilled or unskilled work done by women, and within a few days of the *Treasury Agreement* the Employers' Federation issued a note to its members stating that women should be paid the district rate for youths, not adult men, on semi- or unskilled work they were introduced to.[35]

This system of the state's partial control of the munitions industry, which gave power over unions, men and women, without offering full guarantees on wages and prospects, continued to develop throughout 1915. The Ministry of Munitions was set up in June, replacing the earlier ineffective local armament committees, and was designed to organize all aspects of national munitions production. In the same month the first Munitions Act was passed. This embodied the terms of the *Treasury Agreement,* and confirmed the existence of 'controlled establishments' (munitions factories temporarily under government control), set limits on the profits armaments firms could make, limited wage rises, and shelved the engineering unions' standard workshop practices — including union limitation of production and the ban on female labour. It also introduced the Leaving Certificate, one of the most unpopular measures ever tried by the government. Men or women working in munitions could not leave their jobs unless they obtained a Leaving Certificate from their employer; without one, they could not get work with any other employers (even in munitions) for the next six weeks. This ended the 'freedom of the individual' to seek alternative employment if he or she felt underpaid or exploited.[36] Factories in the same area might have widely differing wages and conditions, yet workers could not take up better positions without the permission of their employer in the form of a Leaving Certificate, which was, of course, usually denied.

There remained no guarantee on wages, except on jobs where women were completely replacing fully skilled tradesmen, when the same piece rates were payable (although not the same time rates). The Central Munitions Labour Supply Committee was set up in September 1915 to discuss wages and conditions, and plan a Dilution Scheme. It drew up 5 'L' Circulars on wages and other aspects of substitution in engineering. Women on skilled work 'customarily done by men' were entitled to equal time and piece rates; women replacing other men were supposed to have equal piece rates, and a guaranteed minimum on time rates of £1 a week, women on jobs not previously done by men were to be paid according to the piece rates or premium bonus rates of equivalent jobs in the area. Unfortunately, L2 and L3, the circulars dealing with women's work in men's trades, were not made mandatory at this time, and still there was no investigation into what constituted skilled work. Even when the Munitions Act was amended in November 1915, L2 and L3 were only put into practice in controlled establishments, not in private munitions factories. In addition, as there was no guaranteed *time rate* except for women who were proved to be doing the work of fully skilled tradesmen, the majority of women workers found that they were promptly put on time rate, at whatever their employers chose to pay, in order to avoid equal piece rates. Furthermore, the £1 minimum set for women on unskilled or semi-skilled men's work tended to become the standard, rather than the minimum, wage on time rate.[37]

In March 1916, the government set up Special Arbitration Tribunals to deal with wage disputes concerning women and unskilled men — but they could only *recommend* rates for women, not enforce them. But at last this same year, Order 49 secured equal time and piece rates for women doing *part* of work customarily done by fully skilled men, and Order 447 consolidated awards made by the Special Arbitration Tribunals for women on work *not* recognized as men's work before the war — but even so these did not apply in every munitions factory. A new Substitution Scheme was introduced in September 1916 to increase further the use of female labour, even on skilled work which was accepted by the unions, but when in 1917 it was proposed to extend Dilution to private factories (where there were no safeguards on wages and conditions) the labour movement rebelled. The May Strikes followed, the idea was abandoned, and the Leaving Certificate, which had for so long been encouraging discontent, was abolished.

The above, very brief, description of government schemes for organizing labour shows the way in which the government attempted to interfere in industry to an unprecedented extent. The same years which saw the introduction of the Leaving Certificate, and the almost compulsory abandonment of standard union practices in munitions, also saw the use of military conscription and press censorship, both of which were closely linked with what went on in industry. Conscription, introduced in 1916, was after all designed to set up a system which sorted the sheep from the goats: the less skilled, replaceable men were to be taken to fight, while skilled engineers were entitled, until 1918, to exemption, a fact which led to much resentment amongst men in other trades. Not only did this force men to go to war, it divided the unions, and it offered employers a stick to hold over skilled men who protested about wages — a man unemployed was immediately liable to be conscripted. Press censorship, in the meantime, meant that the nation knew neither what was happening in the trenches, nor what was going on in the shipyards or engineering shops: strikes could not be honestly reported, and the government even suppressed the newspapers of the Clyde shop stewards when they became too critical of government policy.[38]

The fact that, in the midst of this fairly autocratic regime, there were gaps in the government's control of wages and conditions of labour is obviously not merely accidental. The government was more concerned about keeping armament firms profitable, and munitions production steady, than with offering permanent guarantees to male workers or ensuring that women (who were vote-less) had equal pay. When factories were threatened with closure the government paid attention to workers' grievances, as during the May Strikes in 1917, but generally the labour movement remained fragmented, and failed to oppose substitution or dilution schemes on a consistent basis. It was divided in its attitude to women, to craft status, to military exemptions and, often, to the war itself, and its stand against government policy was rarely united. The state, meanwhile, had become an employer, and was working with other employers to keep up production: the links between the Ministry of Munitions and private businessmen were strong.

However, it would be untrue to suggest that the government's failure to secure good wages and job security was entirely deliberate. Some efforts *were* made to give skilled workmen in engineering (though not in other trades) safeguards, and promises were made about the return of pre-war conditions. Furthermore, the gaps which existed in state control did not simply adversely affect wages: they extended to other aspects of industry in which the government and employers could well have done with further, efficient organization. The recruitment of women for munitions or any other trade was never properly organized: labour exchanges were not fully utilized, women were sent to areas where there was no accommodation available, skilled women were sent to unskilled jobs, etc. Nor was there any attempt to standardize training schemes: some firms trained their own workers from the beginning, others took women who had been on government courses at technical colleges and training factories, or to classes set up by private bodies. Recruitment too remained a haphazard matter, as the government relied to a large extent on the press to arouse women's enthusiasm for war work and send them looking for jobs.[39] The disorganized nature of the labour market lasted from the first weeks of the war, when skilled men were allowed to enlist in the army (which would not release them again), right through to 1918—19, when, in spite of the existence of the Ministry of Reconstruction and schemes for the payment of dole, the demobilization of men and women was chaotic.

Such omissions in state control were partly due to the problems involved in setting up the machinery for war production, machinery which did not exist in 1914 and had to be developed from scratch. There was also the fact that many Ministers and politicians remained extremely reluctant to interfere in industry at all, and were loath to set up any more controls than were absolutely necessary. As E. M. H. Lloyd wrote, a few years after the war:

> The idea that industry would have to be deliberately organized for war production encountered subconscious resistance in a government committed to the doctrines of free trade and individualism. It is not surprising that the necessity for state intervention was only gradually admitted by Ministers who had spent the greater part of their political careers in exploding the fallacies of protectionism on one hand and socialism on the other.[40]

The early assumption was that private firms could cope with supplies for war, making their own agreements with workers about overtime and any extra labour required. When it became evident that the government *would* have to play a part, there were two conflicting ideals in the minds of Ministers: first, that 'every private interest must be subordinated to the successful prosecution of the war,' and, secondly, 'there must be as little interference as possible with the normal channels of trade.'[41] The question became, what degree of interference was allowable? There was, as Lloyd pointed out, an almost universal bias against the concept of state control in industry, and the systems introduced were piecemeal or a matter of compromise. Autocratic though certain aspects of government actions were, schemes were nevertheless ill-organized. To quote Lloyd again: 'the development of wartime control was thus due almost entirely to the overwhelming force of circumstance, and hardly at all to a deliberate policy of state intervention, consciously thought out and consistently applied.'[42]

So there was an unfortunate and ironic juxtaposition between new, authoritarian machinery for running a war (which involved extensive co-operation between government and armament firms), together with the curtailment of precious union freedoms and, on the other, the legacy of government non-interference in the recruitment of workers and the bargains struck by employers and unions. Only in the munitions industry was limited control classed as being acceptable. The same uneasy background characterized the work of the Health of Munition Workers Committee, which noted the over-long hours and made suggestions for improvements, yet did not even do enough to change the munitions industry, let alone the conditions of other factories.

Thus munitions employers did have a trapped, potentially vulnerable work-force, and the nature of government control in munitions, together with the complete lack of government interest in maintaining safeguards on wages and conditions in other industries, mapped out the way in which women were received into industry. It also explained to some extent the way in which they were welcomed or opposed by unions and employers: these feelings were superimposed upon the standard ideas about women's role in industry.

Notes

1. I. O. Andrews, *The Economic Effects of the World War upon Women and Children in Great Britain* (Oxford University Press, 1921), Ch. III.
2. Sylvia Pankhurst, *The Home Front* (Hutchinson, 1932), Ch. VI.
3. Pankhurst, *The Home Front*, Ch. III; Andrews, *The Effects of War*, Ch. III; G. D. H. Cole, *Labour in Wartime* (Bell & Sons, 1915), Ch. VIII.
4. M. B. Hammond, *British Labour Conditions and Legislation during the War* (Oxford University Press, 1919), Ch. III.
5. Cole, *Labour in Wartime*, Chs. III and VII; Hammond, *British Labour Conditions*, Ch. IV; Andrews, *Effects of the War*, Ch. IV;

Barbara Drake, *Women in the Engineering Trades* (Fabian Research Dept., 1917).

6. Andrews, *Effects of the War,* Ch. IV; Hammond, *British Labour Conditions,* Ch. VI.
7. Andrews, *Effects of the War,* Ch. IV; Hammond, *British Labour Conditions,* Ch. VI.
8. Cole, *Labour in Wartime,* Ch. VIII.
9. Andrews, *Effects of the War,* Ch. IV; Hammond, *British Labour Conditions,* Ch. VI.
10. Andrews, *Effects of the War,* Ch. IV.
11. Andrews, *Effects of the War,* Ch. IV.
12. Cole, *Trade Unionism and Munitions* (Clarendon, 1923), Ch. VIII; Hinton, *The First Shop Stewards* (Allen & Unwin, 1973), Ch. I.
13. Andrews, *Effects of the War,* Ch. IV.
14. A. W. Kirkaldy, *Industry and Finance* (Isaac Pitman, 1921), vol. II, section I.
15. Demands for female conscription are indicative of resentment towards women who were not working rather than proof of any labour shortage.
16. Andrews, *Effects of the War,* Ch. IV, p. 77.
17. Hammond, *British Labour Conditions,* p. 171.
18. L. K. Yates, *A Woman's Part* (Hodder & Stoughton, 1918), p. 9.
19. Hammond, *British Labour Conditions,* Ch. VI.
20. Andrews, *Effects of the War,* Ch. IV; *Labour Gazette,* December 1917.
21. Kirkaldy, *Industry and Finance,* vol. II, section I; BAAS, *Outlets for Labour,* p. 7.
22. Drake, *Women in the Engineering Trades.*
23. *Common Cause,* 1 Oct. 1915, 'Street Housemaids'.
24. *Yorkshire Observer,* 31 Aug. 1916, 'War Work in the West Riding'.
25. *Daily Chronicle,* 3 Dec. 1915, 'Lace Hands Make Grenades'.
26. E.g. *Yorkshire Observer,* 7 July 1916, 'Keighley's Need of More Women Workers', an appeal from the Mayor; *Manchester Guardian,* 22 Nov. 1915, 'Labour Shortage in the Cotton Trade': an appeal for the Women of Rochdale to go back to cotton.
27. *The Times,* 18 Oct. 1916, for example, 'Women in the Labour Market'. See also interviews with women at the Imperial War Museum, Dept. of Sound Records. Amongst several munitions workers, an army clothing worker, a crane driver and other substitutes, previous employment had been as weavers, clothing workers or other factory workers, and servants.
28. Monica Cosens, *Lloyd George's Munition Girls* (Hutchinson, 1917), p. 108.
29. In soldiers' wives they could guarantee a sense of patriotism, as well as loyalty to the firm, and it was obvious that such women would readily relinquish their jobs to returning men.
30. Kirkaldy, *Industry and Finance,* vol. II, section I.
31. Hammond, *British Labour Conditions,* p. 143.

32. Cole, *Labour in Wartime,* Ch. VII; Cole, *Trade Unionism and Munitions,* Ch. V.
33. Cole, *Trade Unionism and Munitions,* Ch. V.
34. In Controlled Establishments:
    (a) 4/5 net profits over and above average profits of the two years preceding war should be paid to the Exchequer (but certain allowances granted);
    (b) no change in wage rates allowed unless changes submitted to Ministry of Munitions;
    (c) abandonment of workshop practices which hinder production, but safeguards to be restored after the war;
    (d) everyone subject to the control of the Ministry of Munitions — hours, conditions, wages.
    (Hammond, *British Labour Conditions,* Ch. V.) In February 1917, 4,285 Controlled Establishments existed, with approximately 2 million workers (Hammond, Ch. V).
35. Drake, *Women in the Engineering Trades.*
36. This 'freedom' may seem illusory, yet it was of significance, particularly when so much work was available for anyone who wished to go into munitions. It should be seen in relative terms.
37. The minimum rate was raised to 24s for a 48-hour week in 1917.
38. Hinton, *The First Shop Stewards Movement*; B. Pribicevik, *The Shop Stewards' Movement and Workshop Control* (Blackwell, 1959); Jose Harris, *William Beveridge* (Benn, 1977).
39. The press relayed simple appeals for women to come forward, e.g. *Daily Express,* 2 Oct. 1916, 'Women and their Work': recruiting for the London General Omnibus Co., describing job, pay, conditions, etc.
40. E. M. H. Lloyd, *Experiments in State Control* (Clarendon, 1924), p. 22.
41. Lloyd, *Experiments in State Control,* Ch. XXI.
42. Lloyd, *Experiments in State Control,* p. 260. Lloyd added that further control would have been politically and psychologically impossible.

2.2 Women as a reserve army of labour: a note on recent British experience

IRENE BRUEGEL

The idea that women workers are particularly useful to capital as a reserve army of labour — to be brought in and thrown out of wage labour as the interests of capital dictate — has a wide currency amongst marxists and feminists (Bland *et al.* 1978, Beechey 1978, Counter Information Services 1976, Adamson *et al.* 1976). Such a theory clearly has important implications: it places the specificity of female labour within a general marxist model of capital accumulation and so provides some material basis for the differentiation of male and female wage labour, and it also shows up the similarities between the situation of women as wage labourers and that of other groups of workers such as immigrants.

The theory has, however, been challenged. While no one disputes that women have provided a reservoir of labour to be tapped in times of boom and labour shortage, some marxist-feminists have questioned the assumption that female labour is particularly 'disposable' in times of economic crisis. This note examines the argument in the light of the experiences of women workers in Britain in the years 1974—8. It concludes that, taken as a whole, women's employment opportunities have been protected from the worst effects of the crisis by the continued expansion of service work in the period. Nevertheless, individually, women have been more susceptible to redundancy when compared to men in similar circumstances. Thus the reserve army of labour model holds, but the simple version needs qualification.

Marx and the industrial reserve army

Marx (1867) saw the expansion of a reserve army of labour as an inevitable outcome of the process of capital accumulation (*Capital*, Vol. I). As capital accumulated, it threw certain workers out of

Source: Bruegel, I., (1979) Women as a reserve army of labour: a note on recent British experience, *Feminist Review*, No. 3, pp. 12—23

employment into a reserve army; conversely, in order to accumulate, capital needed a reserve army of labour. Without such a reserve, capital accumulation would cause wages to rise, and the process of accumulation would itself be threatened as surplus value was squeezed. While Marx did note that certain workers — the pauperized lumpen-proletariat — might bear the brunt of unemployment, he was concerned to show how the expansion of capitalism inevitably drew more and more people into a labour reserve of potential, marginal and transitory employment, rather than to identify any group of workers as particularly vulnerable. Marx did not consider women as a group in his reserve army of labour model. Nevertheless, the extension of women's involvement in wage labour in all Western economies clearly fits the picture of the continued expansion of the reserve army drawn by Marx.

Braverman (1974) and Kolko (1978) both argue this in relation to the United States. In Britain the net expansion of 2.5 million workers achieved between 1951 and 1971 was made up almost entirely (2.2 million) of women coming into wage labour. This expansion meant, as Marx argued it would, that wages, particularly in those industries where women predominate, have been kept down. The process becomes self-fuelling. Increasingly, the maintenance of family living standards has come to depend on two or more wage packets,[1] and all adult female labour has become potential wage labour — as many as a quarter of mothers of pre-school children are now employed (Office of Population Census and Surveys 1978).

In the sense of providing a labour *reserve*, women's labour power has clearly become an important part of what Marx saw as the industrial reserve army.

The hypothesis of greater 'disposability'

This is not really at issue. What is in dispute is whether or not women bear, to a disproportionate extent, the burden of unemployment in times of crisis, whether they are *more* 'disposable'. This is what the notion of women as a reserve army of labour has come to mean, notwithstanding Marx's use of the term.

There are a number of grounds on which one would indeed expect that women's labour power would be more readily dispensed with in times of redundancy (Barron and Norris 1976, MacKay *et al.* 1971) concluded in their study of the engineering industry that 'there was a greater propensity to dismiss females in preference to males in a redundancy situation'.[2] They point to the fact that redundancy procedures often stipulated that, after people over the age of retirement, part-time and married women workers should be picked out for the sack. The seniority principle of last in, first out would also tend to discriminate against women, even if there was no explicit discrimination (Jenness *et al.* 1975).[3] Daniel and Stilgoe (1978) found that half of the firms in their recent survey of 300 companies operated the seniority principle in making redundancies. A Department of Employment Survey of redundancies in 1975—6 (Department of Employment 1978) does confirm the vulnerability of shorter service workers, despite the bias in the Redundancy Payments Act which tends to increase the vulnerability of older (and hence more long-serving) workers. Significantly, the survey does not distinguish between male and female workers.

The fact that women tend to work in smaller, less unionized workplaces may also make them more vulnerable to redundancy. However, the poor record of many unions in fighting redundancies, particularly amongst part-time women workers (Counter Information Services 1976), suggests that lower levels of unionization may not be a particularly important handicap as such.

MacKay *et al.* (1971) also saw the higher rates of redundancy amongst women as a reflection of their lower levels of skill; employers are likely to keep on skilled men or put them on short time when work is slack because their skills are not easily replaced and, on dismissal, they may move elsewhere.[4] Women, on the other hand, can be more easily replaced or re-engaged when trade picks up, so there is much less of a deterrent to giving them the sack. The dependency of working wives, which forces them to live where their husbands work, contributes to this pattern. Twilight shifts in particular are closed down and started up again on the basis of a captive, relatively immobile workforce of married women. In the United States, where there is in any case more job mobility, the lesser mobility of married women is seen to contribute to higher levels of unemployment amongst women (Ferber and Lowry 1976, Niemi 1976).

The current pattern of limiting redundancies by freezing appointments (Daniel and Stilgoe 1978) may also increase the relative vulnerability of women workers. This is because family responsibilities often force women to leave work for a period; as a result, at any given point in time, women workers are more likely to be looking for work than men.[5]

Moreover, ideology in the form of the notion that a woman's place is in the home may well contribute to a greater vulnerability of women to unemployment. The onslaught on married women working — blaming them, in effect, for the level of unemployment amongst men — is perhaps not as strong as it was in the 1930s.[6] Nevertheless, it is still evident,[7] with youth unemployment in particular being 'explained' by the tendency of married women to work. Unemployment amongst women is never considered the personal and social problem which male unemployment is.[8] As a result, women's confidence in their right to work is weaker than men's, and may well contribute to a higher 'voluntary' redundancy rate as well as fuelling discriminatory practices by managements and unions.

These arguments, taken together, suggest that, other things being equal, one could expect women to be more vulnerable to unemployment than men. However, Gardiner (1976) and Milkman (1976) suggest different ways in which everything is not equal, in which female labour is quite distinct from male labour. Gardiner argues that the cheapness of female labour would lead capital to substitute women for men, rather than sack women in preference to men. This is indeed Marx's argument, and such a fear certainly underlay attempts by organized workers to exclude women from large areas of employment. Such a fear indeed led the Trades Union Congress into endorsing the provisions which forced unemployed women into domestic service before the war (Lewenhak 1977). In this way women could be prevented from competing for men's jobs. However, it is not at all clear that such substitution (of women for men) would be especially common in periods of slump; the returns on, and the possibilities of, substituting women for men are greater when the economy is expanding.[9]

Gardiner's argument also conflicts with the point Milkman makes; namely that the sexual division of wage labour is so rigid as to preclude both the substitution of male by female labour (as in Gardiner's account) and the effective substitution of female by male labour (as in the 'women as a dispensable labour force' account). What Milkman is arguing is that the segregation of women into women's work is of such ideological importance that it cannot be breached, even where it would yield capital cheaper labour.[10] Hence for Milkman the pattern of women's employment and unemployment over the cycle of booms and slumps simply reflects the fortunes of 'women's' industries and occupations. While the degree of segregation is great (Hakim 1978), Milkman's argument cannot be sustained. As is shown below, the effect of a slump in any given industry is different for women than for men. Secondly, the pattern of segregation of women's work and men's work is not naturally determined, nor easily explained by 'ideology'. It reflects, in part, economic factors, and follows, in some degree, the dual labour market division (Barron and Norris 1976). This means that women tend to be recruited to less stable areas of employment (Baudouin *et al.* 1978); a job is 'women's work' partly *because* it does not offer stable and continuous employment.[11]

Catering work in schools and colleges is a prime example of the use of female labour for 'unstable and seasonal work'.

Unemployment amongst women

If one looks at figures for women's unemployment over recent years, both in Britain and elsewhere, there seems to be little basis for either Gardiner's or Milkman's objections to the reserve army model. Between 1974 and 1978 in Britain, the official rate of unemployment amongst women increased more than three times as fast as that of men. In Holland, Italy, Spain and Belgium (OECD 1976, Werneke 1978) the rate of increase in unemployment was also greater amongst women than men. In other countries the level of unemployment amongst women is higher, although the rate of increase is on a par.[12] However, there are always severe problems in using the official statistics of unemployment as a measure of the effects of crisis on women's employment. In Britain, only women registered at the labour exchange are counted as unemployed.[13] Given this narrow definition, something like half the women who say they are looking for work are not counted as unemployed (General Household Survey 1976, Dex 1978). This complicates the assessments of changes over time (quite apart from hiding the real extent of unemployment amongst women), because it is likely that the proportion of unemployed women who do register does vary over time (General Household Survey 1974, 1976). Given a shift in unemployment towards younger people and hence towards single women, the proportion of women registering has probably risen (Moore, Rhodes *et al.* 1978). To some extent then, the fast rise in official unemployment amongst women overestimates the real rise.

Nevertheless, from what evidence there is, it would seem that 'real' unemployment amongst women has risen faster than amongst men, the rise being particularly fast amongst single women.[14] Moore, Rhodes *et al's* estimates of the real unemployment level suggest that women have been disproportionately affected; while women are only 41 per cent of the labour force, they accounted for 53 per cent of the net rise in real unemployment. Thus the unemployment figures, even allowing for changes in registration, do not substantiate Gardiner's argument. Neither, however, can they be said to prove the disposability model, because it is single women who appear to have been particularly badly affected, while the hypotheses outlined above tend to emphasize the particular vulnerability of married women workers (Beechey 1978), rather than women workers as a whole. However, even figures derived from surveys pose problems for measuring unemployment amongst 'housewives', and the survey figures could well underestimate the impact of a crisis on married women's employment. This is because unemployed housewives who would otherwise work may not consider themselves to be looking for work in a climate of restricted employment, childcare facilities, transport provisions and so on, and so would not therefore be counted as unemployed by a survey such as that undertaken by the General Household Survey. Because of the difficulties with any of the measures of unemployment, in this note employment figures rather than unemployment figures will be used to analyse the impact of the crisis on women's employment opportunities.

Trends of women's employment

In attempting to evaluate a 'disposability' model, it is important to clarify exactly what the model proposes. On the one hand, the idea that women might cushion men from the full impact of recession could be taken to imply that women's employment opportunities, taken as a whole, deteriorate relative to men's in times of recession. On the other hand, it can be taken to mean that any individual woman is more susceptible to redundancy and unemployment than a man in an equivalent situation would be. This distinction is important.

At first glance the first form of the model appears to have little validity. In the years 1974—8 female employment *rose* by 145,000

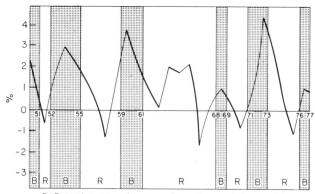

R – Recession years when unemployment as a whole was rising.

B – Boom years when unemployment as a whole was stagnant or falling.

Figure 1   Annual changes in female employment, 1950—78 (June-June), Great Britain

Source: Department of Employment

jobs, while the number of men at work fell by 361,000, a pattern repeated in a number of countries. However, this pattern is simply a reflection of the long-term trend towards an increasingly female labour force. In 1951 only 32 per cent of the labour force were women; by 1977 over 40 per cent were. Had there been no recession and past trends had continued, then the rise in women's employment between 1974 and 1978 would have been greater than the 145,000 jobs created. This point is illustrated in Figure 1, which shows how in each recession since the war the rate of growth of female employment slowed down relative to periods of expansion. If one takes into account the increasing need and desire for women to seek paid work, then it is far from clear that the rise in female employment over the last few years really signals a lesser deterioration in women's employment prospects relative to men's. The number of women seeking work between 1974 and 1977 increased faster, at 4 per cent, than the number of jobs created (1.5 per cent). Moore, Rhodes *et al.* (1978) calculated the shortfall in male jobs relative to male workers between 1973 and 1977 to be 615,000; for the smaller female labour force the shortfall is some 680,000.

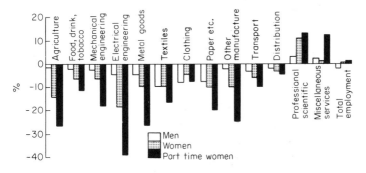

Figure 2   Changes in employment by industry, 1974—7
(percentage change for each group), Great Britain

Source: Department of Employment

Turning to the second form of the 'disposability' model, Figure 2 makes it clear that in every industry[15] employing a substantial number of women and where employment declined between 1974 and 1977, the rate of employment decline was greater for women than for men. Of the major industries, only construction, public and miscellaneous services and the public administration sector, where reclassification has distorted the picture,[16] do not conform to this trend. In manufacturing as a whole, women lost nearly 9 per cent of their jobs, in a period when male manufacturing jobs fell by less than 5 per cent. The losses were particularly great in the new growth sectors such as electronics. Similar trends are found throughout Western manufacturing (OECD 1976, Baudouin *et al.* 1978). What kept women's employment buoyant as a whole was the continued expansion of parts of the service sector (Figure 3), for example, professional and scientific and miscellaneous services.

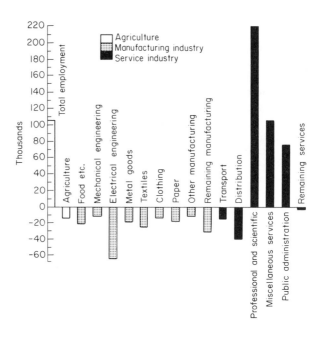

Figure 3   Components of change in women's employment, 1974–7
Great Britain, change by industry

Source: Department of Employment

The growth of these matched the falls in employment elsewhere, despite public sector cuts.[17] To a degree, then, Ruth Milkman is right; the particular pattern of women's employment, the concentration in a limited range of the expanding service sector, has limited the impact of the recession on women's opportunities as a whole. If women had not been concentrated in 'women's work' — catering, nursing, teaching, cleaning — but had been distributed amongst industries in the same way as men, then the impact of the 1974–7 crisis would have been far greater — a decline of jobs of almost half a million, compared to an actual increase in the period of 140,000.[18] Thus, as in the United States (OECD 1976), the 'favourable' industrial distribution of women has cushioned women's employment, *taken as a whole*, against the worst effects of the crisis.

In manufacturing the impact of the crisis has fallen dispro-portionately on women. As in all previous post-war recessions, women's employment has fallen faster than men's (Figure 4), in a way which conforms to the reserve army model. Comparing one

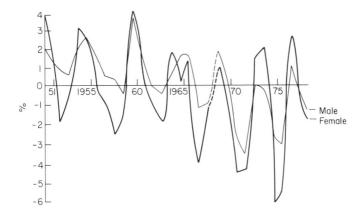

Figure 4   Annual change in manufacturing employment, male and female, 1950–78, Great Britain

period of recession with another, women appear to be becoming less vulnerable than they were in the 1950s. This may well be due to a shift away from the declining textile and clothing sectors and into more stable clerical and administrative employment. What it does show is that the vulnerability of women industrial workers to recession is not a recent phenomenon attributable to recent legislative changes such as the Equal Pay Act.

Part-time work

It is part-time women workers who have been made to bear the brunt of the decline in employment. The pattern in electrical engineering shows this up particularly well. Between 1974 and 1977, 38,000 unskilled and semi-skilled jobs were lost; 18,000 of these were part-time jobs done by women. This represents a 40 per cent decline for part-time women workers, compared to a 5 per cent job loss amongst men. The 'selection' of women for redundancy does not imply any breakdown in the sex stereotyping of jobs — men taking women's work — as Milkman's argument implies. Rather, it highlights the function of part-time employment in a capitalist economy. Wherever short-term fluctuations in demand for labour are expected, whether the fluctuations are from day to day, month to month, or year to year, the cost of dealing with such fluctuations for the capitalist is less when women, particularly part-time women, have been employed (Hurstfield 1978). This phenomenon is well illustrated by the mini-boom of 1973—4; part-time employment of women in manufacturing increased by 15 per cent in that year, to fall subsequently by 10 per cent in 1974—5 and 8 per cent in 1975—6. In every industry where employment declined between 1974 and 1977, the rate of decline for part-time women exceeded that of men and full-time women (Figure 2). It is part-time women workers, who form an increasing proportion of women workers (40 per cent are now part-time), who conform most closely to the model of women as a disposable reserve army. Nevertheless, in certain areas of work, their numbers are still increasing rapidly.

Conclusion

Over the last few years there have been two conflicting processes at work affecting women's employment. On the one hand, within any given industry or job, women, particularly part-time women workers, have suffered from greater rates of job loss than men. This has come about partly, no doubt, through explicit or barely veiled discriminatory policies, but more important, probably, has been the exploitation of the weaknesses of married women's labour market position, weaknesses which derive in one way or another from a primary definition of women as housewives and mothers. On the other hand, the continued expansion of parts of the service sector on the basis of the availability of cheap female labour has mitigated the effects of the crisis on women's employment opportunities. It is important to recognize that the 'protection' that women's jobs have had through the expansion of the service sector is a protection based on the cheapness of female labour. The low pay offered to women in the expanding service sectors virtually precludes any wholesale takeover by men, even when unemployment is high. Given certain technological constraints which have until now made the service sectors highly labour intensive (Braverman 1974, Harris and Taylor 1978), the service sector did require a 'reserve army' of cheap labour to draw on to expand its output. As a result, in virtually all capitalist countries the expansion of service industry went hand in hand with the expansion of women's paid employment in the post-war years. Since services were less vulnerable to recession than other sectors of employment, they have afforded women a certain protection from unemployment in times of recession. However, with the development of microprocessors this 'protection' is likely to wear thin, since the advantages women offer to capital — cheap and relatively docile labour — become less and less relevant (Counter Information Services 1979, Downing and Barker 1979). Moreover, the type of work women do — low level, repetitive and boring — is probably more susceptible to rationalization, whether it is manufacturing or service work, than ever before. In Germany, where rationalization of office work has gone further than in Britain (Cooley 1979), service work no longer protects women's employment as a whole from the impact of crisis (Däubler-Gmelin 1977); the degree of protection in the United States is also significantly less than in Britain (OECD 1976). Thus the analysis in this note must be seen in its historical perspective.

While it is probably true for all periods that the marginal position of married women in the labour force has made them, individual for individual, more vulnerable to redundancy than male workers, the particular form of capitalist expansion and restructuring over the last thirty years — the expansion of labour-intensive public and private services and administrative occupations — greatly extended the employment opportunities of women. The result was that women's employment continued to expand even when men's jobs were being cut back fast.

The long-term shift towards women in the workforce cushioned women's employment against the shorter-term (cyclical) recessions. The signs are that this particular phase of capital restructuring may be over; that one of the bases of the long-term expansion of female employment — the cheapness of female employment — may be declining in relative significance, given new technological developments. Hence many groups of women who have traditionally regarded their jobs as secure will find themselves threatened with rationalization on a scale comparable to the wholesale elimination of jobs in the traditional male strongholds — mining, railways, docks. The implications of this analysis are not that the solution lies in attempting to equalize the incidence of increasing unemployment between men and women. Rather, it is that the fight for jobs will increasingly be a fight for women's jobs. Thus if the labour movement is to be able effectively to resist unemployment, now more than ever before it urgently needs to devise more effective strategies of defending women's jobs and the right of women to work.

Notes

1. This point comes out very clearly in the Royal Commission on the Distribution of Income and Wealth (Research Report 6, 1978). When wives do not go out to work, the chances of a family in Britain today being in poverty are almost one in three; where wives work, the chances are nearer one in fourteen.
2. MacKay *et al.*, p. 375, give the following figures for redundancies in Birmingham and Glasgow over the 1959—66 period:

| | Average quarterly redundancy rate | |
	Birmingham	Glasgow
skilled men	0.1	0.6
all men	0.2	0.5
all women	0.9	0.6

3. The degree to which 'last in, first out' (LIFO) loads redundancy on to women depends on how the procedure is applied. If it was adopted company or plant wide, then women would indeed be particularly vulnerable. It seems in practice that unless the whole plant is closed, redundancies tend to be brought in shop by shop. Given the high level of job segregation within a workplace, this means that the LIFO procedure would tend to be applied separately to groups of men and women and would not necessarily lead to a higher rate of redundancy amongst women. As Jenness *et al.* (1975) point out, where women have broken through into male dominated jobs, as in the United States steelworks, the LIFO procedure will work against them.
4. British statistics on short-time working do not distinguish between men and women. Däubler-Gmelin's research in Germany shows that men are far more likely to be put on short time than women but far less likely to be made redundant.
5. This is reflected in turnover figures. These show that over industry as a whole, for every one hundred women in work, nearly forty are taken on in a year, compared to thirty men; at the same time, nearly forty leave, compared to thirty men (Department of Employment Gazette, November 1978).
6. Rowbotham 1973, Milkman 1976, Humphries 1976 all present evidence of hostility to married women workers in Britain and the United States in the 1930s. In both countries various bars were put on married women working; nevertheless, the long-term expansion in women's wage labour was not halted.
7. Occasional calls are made even today to sack married women. In 1977 the Daily Mail ran a campaign, 'Weed out the Working Wives', but no major party has explicitly questioned the right of married women to work.

8. None of the major studies of the impact of unemployment in Britain consider unemployed women. Government figures for unemployment amongst women are seriously inadequate and, even more disturbing, the various job creation schemes show a distinct bias towards male workers; in 1976, 84 per cent of the young people on the Job Creation Scheme were boys, despite the fact that unemployment levels for girls are equally bad. One of the ill-fated Manpower Services Commission's posters did feature a girl, but the problem of youth unemployment is seen as a problem of boys out on the streets, of potential disruption to the social order; hence the emphasis in the Youth Opportunities Programme on training and integrating boys into work roles.

9. The process of substitution is rarely one where a woman takes on a job that was previously held by a man. More often substitution takes place in the context of capital restructuring, of bringing in new machinery which transforms a skilled job into a semi-skilled or unskilled one, or of moving jobs around the country. In either case the substitution of female for male labour, while bringing in long-term savings in wage costs, requires capital investment. Such investments are unlikely to be made where output is stagnant and wage rises are restricted.

10. Milkman maintains that it is 'ideologically' important to retain the image of women as dependent and passive, despite the drive to exploit their labour power. Milkman sees this contradiction only being resolved by segregating women into 'women's work'.

11. This is not to say that all areas of unstable employment are filled by women. Immigrant men fulfil a similar role in the economy; the construction industry, with very large fluctuations in demand for labour, is almost wholly dependent on male immigrant labour (Baudouin 1978). Nor are all areas of women's work highly unstable, but in general women's work is characterized by a greater degree of instability in employment.

12. The OECD gives the following figures of relative unemployment rates (1975):

	Australia	France	Germany	Italy	Belgium	United States
male	3.2	3.5	4.5	2.9	4.4	8.0
female	5.0	7.9	5.2	4.9	9.9	9.2

13. This is justified on the grounds that: 'many married women who state they are seeking work may be expressing a future intention rather than a current activity. In practice they are more inclined to attach conditions to the work they are prepared to take — working hours, ease of travel, availability of nursery schools and so on — and they can only be described as unemployed in a restricted sense.' (Cmnd. 5157, Unemployment Statistics: Report of the Interdepartmental Working Party 1972)

14. Calculating from the General Household Survey data 1974 and 1976:

                                                         1974—6

change in total male unemployment (registered and unregistered)   +10%

change in total female unemployment (registered and unregistered)   +28%

change in single female unemployment (registered and unregistered)   +42%

15. The data used are the Department of Employment annual census (June) of employment by industry, analysed at the 27-industry Standard Industrial Classification level. Unfortunately, data on occupational groups are not available on an annual basis. Such information would have been helpful for the analysis because the jobs (occupations) women do within an industry tend to be very different from those of men. In theory, the higher rate of job loss for women within each industry could be due to the particular vulnerability of the *jobs* that women do, rather than the vulnerability of women in any particular area of work. This point has been checked as far as possible with the published statistics for the electrical engineering industry. When the broadly defined industry is disaggregated into its nine constituent industries, the pattern of higher job loss for women in each of the declining industries remains; similarly, when each occupation within electrical engineering is analysed from the annual returns, there is still a tendency for women to suffer a higher rate of job loss in each of the declining occupations.

16. Some sixty to seventy thousand workers in public administration were reclassified into other services in the period under review.

17. Despite the public sector cuts, net employment in the public services has continued to grow, albeit at a much slower rate than previously. In the year 1977—8 the growth in female employment has been so slow that it has barely matched the declines elsewhere. See Hughes (1978) for a further discussion.

18. This is calculated using a 'shift and share' analysis. Expected growth in total employment on the basis of the male distribution is

$$\underset{i}{\leq} \left(\frac{M_i}{M} \cdot F \right) R_{fi}$$

    where M   =   total male employment 1974

            M_i =   male employment in industry in 1974

            F   =   total female employment 1974

            R_{fi} =   rate of change of female employment in industry in 1974—7

References

Adamson, O., Brown, C., Harrison, J. and Price, J. (1976) 'Women's Oppression Under Capitalism' *Revolutionary Communist*, No.5.

Barron, R.D. and Norris, G.M. (1976) 'Sexual Divisions and the Dual Labour Market' in Barker, D. and Allen, S. (eds) *Dependence and Exploitation in Work and Marriage*, London: Longman.

Baudouin, T., Collin, M. and Guillerm, D. (1978) 'Women and Immigrants: Marginal Workers' in Crouch, C. and Pizzorno,A. *The Resurgence of Class Conflict*, Vol.2, London: Macmillan.

Beechey, V. (1978) 'Women and Production' in Kuhn,A. and Wolpe,A.M. (eds) *Feminism and Materialism*, London: Routledge & Kegan Paul.

Bland, L., Brunsdon, C., Hobson, D. and Winship, J. (1978) 'Women Inside and Outside the Relations of Production' in Women's Studies Group, *Women Take Issue*, London: Hutchinson.

Braverman, H. (1974) *Labor and Monopoly Capital*, New York: Monthly Review.

Cooley, M. (1979) 'Computers, Politics and Unemployment' *European Computing Review*, 1979.

Counter Information Services (1976) *Women Under Attack*, London.

Counter Information Services (1979) *The New Technology*, London.

Daniel, W. and Stilgoe, E. (1978) *The Effects of the Employment Protection Act*, London: Policy Studies Institute.

Däubler-Gmelin, H. (1977) *Frauenarbeitslosigkeit*, Hamburg: Rowolt.

Department of Employment (1978) 'Age and Redundancy',*Employment Gazette*, September 1978.

Dex,S. (1978) 'Measuring Women's Unemployment', *Social and Economic Administration*, Summer 1978.

Downing, H. and Barker, J. (1979) 'Office Automation, Word Processing and the Transformation of Patriarchal Relations' Paper to CSE Microprocessors Group January 1979 (mimeo) *Capital and Class* (forthcoming).

Ferber, M. and Lowry, H. (1976) 'Women, the New Reserve Army' in Blaxall, M. and Reagan, B. (eds) *Women and the Workplace*, Chicago: University of Chicago Press.

Gardiner, J. (1976) 'Women and Unemployment' *Red Rag*, No. 10.

Hakim, C. (1978) 'Sexual Divisions in the Labour Force' *Employment Gazette*, November 1978.

Harris, D. F. and Taylor, F. J. (1978) *The Service Sector*, London: Centre for Environmental Studies, Research Series, No. 25.

Hughes, J. (1978) 'A Rakes Progress' in Barrett Brown, M. and Hughes, J. (eds) *Full Employment — Priority*, Nottingham: Spokesman Books.

Humphries, J. (1976) 'Women as Scapegoats and Safety Valves' *Review of Radical Political Economy*, 1976.

Hurstfield, J. (1978) *The Part-Time Trap*, London: Low Pay Unit.

Jenness, L., Hill, H., Reid, N. M., Lovell, F. and Davenport, S. E. (1975) *Last Hired, First Fired*, New York: Pathfinder.

Kolko, G. (1978) 'Working Wives, Their Effect on the Structure of the Working Class', *Science and Society*, Fall 1978.

Lewenhak, S. (1977) *Women and Trade Unions*, London: Benn.

Mackay, D. I., Boddy, D., Brack, J., Diack, J.A. and Jones, N. (1971) *Labour Market Under Different Employment Conditions,* London: George Allen & Unwin.

Marx, K. (1867) *Capital,* Vol.I, ch. 25.

Milkman, R. (1976) 'Women's Work and Economic Crisis', *Review of Radical Political Economy,* 1976.

Moore, B., Rhodes, J., Tarling, F. and Wilkinson, F. (1978) *Economic Policy Review,* University of Cambridge, Department of Applied Economics.

Niemi, B. (1976) 'Geographical Immobility and Labour Force Mobility: A Study of Female Unemployment', in C. B. Lloyd (ed.) *Sex Discrimination and the Division of Labour,* New York: Columbia University Press.

Office of Population Census and Surveys, (1974,1976) *General Household Survey.*

Office of Population Census and Surveys (1978) 'The Changing Circumstances of Women', *Population Trends,* 1978.

Organisation for Economic Cooperation and Development (1976) *The 1974-5 Recession and the Employment of Women,* Paris.

Rowbotham, S. (1973) *Hidden From History,* London: Pluto Press.

Royal Commission on the Distribution of Income and Wealth (1978) Report No. 6. *Lower Incomes,* Cmnd. 7175, London: HMSO.

Unemployment Statistics (1972) Report of an Interdepartmental Working Party, Cmnd.5157,London: HMSO.

Werneke, D. (1978) 'The Economic Slowdown and Women's Employment' *International Labour Review,* January-February 1978.

2.3 Typing our way to freedom: is it true that new office technology can liberate women?

JANINE MORGALL

Foreword

The most frightening reactions to technology one can encounter in today's office are passivity, helplessness and resignation. At union meetings, courses, secretary groups, study groups and in offices one meets these reactions all too often. I've yet to talk with anyone who believes that the new office technology can be stopped in the long run. Most people feel that it is unavoidable, and in many offices defensive measures are being taken, such as demands for a certain number of rest periods, special glasses for working at Visual Display Units (VDUs) and specifications for office furniture. In other words except for individual attempts at passive resistance, there is a basic acceptance of the new technology as it is marketed by manufacturers, and clerical workers are trying to make the best of it.

What is lacking in my opinion is:
1. a pooling of the collective experience of office technology so far;
2. a review of the state of the art by those who have actually operated these new machines;
3. a creative offensive

New technology should be met with ideas and feasible plans for its utilization, not by unchallenged acceptance.

For women the realities of today's clerical labour market are harsh. Its characteristics are a division of labour by sex segregation, low-paying dead-end jobs, and a double work role because of their responsibility in the family. These are indeed realities but must not

Source: Morgall, J. (1981). Originally published in Swedish as 'med tangentvalsen mot friheten eller kan den nya kontorstekniken frigöra kvinnorna?' in *Kvinnovetenskaplig Tidskrift* nummer 1−2 1981, Centre for Women Researchers and Women's Research in Lund, Sweden

be *excuses* for lack of collective response to the restructuring of their profession.

My interest in office technology stems from my many years as a clerical worker, private secretary, shop steward and most recently as a student of sociology. I feel more and more burdened by what I see as an inevitable and almost irreversible course which the technology is taking.

The purpose of this chapter is to look at office technology from a woman's perspective and to discuss what I consider to be the most serious problems and some realistic suggestions for avoiding them.

Introduction

Technology is neither neutral nor value-free. Technological innovations reflect the political, social and economic conditions of the societies which create and put them to use. Technology can be used to eliminate inequalities in society or to exploit them further depending on the motives and goals of those in power.

In the clerical sector, where women have traditionally held subordinate positions, technology *could* be used as a tool to liberate women so that they can play a more active and responsible role in their work place.

Women stand only to gain from the liberating potential of office technology. There are, however, no signs of this occurring, and this is not surprising when one considers the past relations between technological innovations and women clerical workers.

The new microprocessor-based technology is coming into offices where there is already a division of labour characterized by sex segregation. Far from eliminating the differences between 'men's' and 'women's' work, it appears that technology can now reinforce these barriers and make them more rigid.

This chapter begins with a short description of the feminization, rationalization and mechanization of office work in the United States. It will attempt to show how the creation of new occupations and changes in the organizational structure resulting from technological innovation have been used to widen the gap in the sexual division of labour, rather than minimize it. The typewriter and computer will be used as examples. The word-processor will then be singled out as an example of the new technology showing how management can exploit it in order to further the division of labour and how these machines can be used by clerical workers to break down existing divisions.

The benefits of the new technology will be discussed, and in the conclusion I will suggest ways of realizing these benefits for women clerical workers. It is not only a case of avoiding disastrous consequences for women, but also of improving their position on the job market. I do not have any answers, only suggestions.

Criticism is welcome, especially from women clerical workers with whom I would like to share ideas for developing a strategy which will utilize technology as a tool for women's liberation.

This article is about women clerical workers . . . share it with them!

The feminization of office work

During the last decades of the nineteenth century many US corporations underwent a period of rapid growth, marked by the development of monopoly capital. This was a time when a large part of the country's capital increasingly became concentrated into the hands of a few entrepreneurs, who used it to enlarge enterprises (Braverman,1974). As a result, there was a demand for an expanded office structure, and a sharp increase in the amount of general office work (note this was not a proliferation of the small offices of the nineteenth century where capital was not so concentrated but an entirely new structure). To fill this need in commercial concerns for literate labour in large numbers, employers turned to the great untapped pool of educated female labour.

Three interesting developments helped American women to break into office work:

1. the shortage of male clerical workers due to the American Civil War;
2. the discovery that women worked for less pay than men;
3. the general acceptance in the late 1890s of the typewriter (Davies 1974).

There was a fear that women would take work away from men, In 1900, an article appeared in the *Ladies Home Journal* warning women that the physical strain of office work was too much for them. As the need for low-paid office workers increased, a shift in ideology occurred, condoning women office workers so long as they knew their place, and that place was 'at the typewriter' (Davies 1974). It is an interesting fact that the profession of typist was sex-neutral but very quickly became identified as women's work.

As clerical work became more and more a female occupation, its function and status declined (Hagerty and Tighe 1978). Women were relegated to the low-paying routine tasks, while a new exclusively male managerial layer developed and continued to grow. With groups of five or six female typists working under one male supervisor, the pattern of male supremacy was clearly reinforced in the office hierarchy. Women did not step into the jobs previously held by men. Instead office work was adjusted so that women performed only the routine and subservient functions (Benet 1973).

Modern office work became the process of acquiring, storing, transforming, presenting and sending information. It became women's work to transform, store and send information and men's work to acquire information, assimilate and manipulate existing information and generate new information.

Women did not improve their position in society by entering into office work. They were paid less than men, there was no career ladder for them and they were given the routine and less responsible tasks. Their position in the office became a reflection of the patriarchal society they lived in.

The rationalization of office work

With an increase in the volume of work and the number of employees came a need to systematize and control office work. In the early twentieth-century books on office management the message was clear . . . the purpose of the office was to control the enterprise; the purpose of office management was to control the office (Braverman, 1974).

Rationalization or 'scientific management' was originally used to analyse and eventually control the work process in the factory. This method used time and motion studies to break tasks down into their smallest components. These components were then measured for length of time and extent of movement. Once the smallest units were identified, ways were found to cut down the time and the movement needed. Rationalization helped speed up the work process and reduced the amount of decision-making left to the workers, thus increasing the amount in the hands of management.

These techniques were soon applied to office procedures. As long as offices were small in relation to production, clerical work was more or less self-supervising. As offices expanded, the need to make office work more efficient gained importance. Under scientific management, decision-making and judgment on how work should be carried out became centralized in the hands of the office manager.

Every office process was studied closely. Daily records were kept of the production of each clerk. Every office employee became the object of interference from management. Once all phases of office procedure had been studied, management set out to rationalize the work process. The figures arrived at by the metering of all procedures were in many cases used as the statistical base for piecework payments. Clerical operations became standardized.

It is important to note that mechanization in the late nineteenth and early twentieth century was taken as given (the typewriter and early versions of adding and dictating machines) and no great advances in technical development were expected.

In the early part of the twentieth century the office layout was given much attention. In order to 'save time away from the desk' offices were designed with all necessary facilities i.e. water coolers, toilets etc. in close proximity. Thus was born the sedentary tradition of clerical work. All motions or energies not directed to the increase of capital were considered 'wasted' or 'misspent' (Braverman 1974). Office work proved easier to rationalize than factory work.

Scientific management in the office meant that planning and decision-making became concentrated into fewer hands. Mental labour was further subdivided into conception and execution. The elimination of thought from the work of office labour took place as a result of:

1. the reduction of mental labour into a repetitious performance of the same small set of functions, and
2. an increase in the number of clerical categories where nothing but manual labour was performed.

Second and third generation office managers reduced work into abstract labour. They viewed all human labour, both factory and office, as simple motion components; a finite motion of hands, feet, and eyes. Efficiency and fragmentation of jobs led to white collar alienation (Popkin 1975).

The mechanization of office work

The mechanization of the office occurred in three stages:

1. early mechanization consisting of the typewriter and adding machines.
2. punched card data processing, and
3. computers.

Rationalization combined with mechanization resulted in the regimentation of office work. Jobs became more standardized to meet the requirements of the machine (Hagerty and Tighe 1978).

With the introduction of machines, machine-pacing became available to the office and was a method used by management to increase productivity in the office, as it once had been applied in the factory. The standardization of office work into small units provided management with an automatic accounting of the size of the work-load and the amount done by each operator (Braverman 1974).

Mechanization made possible new organizational models such as typing and steno pools. As early as the late 1880s there were typing pools in England (Delgado 1979). Organizing work in this way contributed to a more efficient use of machines, and to centralization of the work process which increased management's control over the workers (Hagerty and Tighe 1978).

Many offices instituted the use of conveyer belts to move the work from one station to the next. A segregation of functions and an impersonal atmosphere developed. Offices began to resemble factories. Office workers were no longer considered skilled workers, they became as interchangeable as factory workers. An example of this is evident in the growth in agencies which market temporary office workers.

During the Second World War the first operational computer (the ENIAC) was used to perform some of the complex calculations required by the Manhattan Project (the wartime efforts to design and build the first nuclear weapons). The programming task was considered 'clerical' and a group of one hundred young women were hired to do what was considered 'women's work'. The women designed the programme necessary for the bomb calculations in a few months by 'crawling around the ENIAC's massive frame, locating burnt-out vacuum tubes, shorted connections, and other non-clerical "bugs" ' (Kraft 1979).

Programming became 'men's work' from the time it was recognized as intellectually demanding and creative, and that a broad knowledge of abstract logic, mathematics, electrical circuits and machines was required.

It is one of the ironies of programming that women pioneered in the occupation, largely by accident, only to make it attractive to men once the work was redefined as creative and important. The further irony, however, as we shall see, is that the men who followed women pioneers — and effectively eased them out of the industry — eventually had their work reduced into something that was genuinely like clerical labour. It was at this point that women were allowed to re-enter the occupation they created (Kraft 1979, p. 4-5).

In the early 1970s, due to an increased division of labour accompanied by fragmentation, standardization and deskilling, women re-entered the field of programming. In the US in 1970 approximately 20% of computer programmers were women, but the polarization of the occupation is obvious when one considers that men dominate in the most skilled suboccupations.

There was never any doubt about the sex of keypunchers. Keypunching was immediately recognized as a job for the 'girls' because it was a keyboard machine. In most instances women lacking formal education did this work. Keypunching is a dead-end occupation which rarely leads to advancement. Keypunching has remained women's work.

Computers have increasingly created higher-level clerical jobs, both within and without the electronic processing unit. The higher-level jobs of computer operator, programmer and systems analyst became men's work, and the lower-level jobs of keypuncher, sorters and coders became women's work.

The new technology

The heart of what is known as 'the new technology' is the microprocessor — a miniature electronic circuit no bigger than a postage stamp. With the development of the microprocessor, computers which previously required several rooms can now be made to fit it into a briefcase. The microprocessor has cut the cost of computer 'memory' a thousandfold since 1970. Pocket calculators and electronic watches are rearranged — it can be done in many cases by pressing a button. No more cut and paste jobs, no more correction fluid, no more retyping entire pages.

Word processing machines have a printing speed of up to 425 lines per minute and a memory which can store basic drafts and letters for later use. There are a number of devices available for storing information typed on the keyboard. One of these is the 'floppy disc', a single one of which can hold up to 100 pages of text. By typing in the correct code, the text is brought up onto the screen so the operator can revise and edit it. IBM estimates that the use of word processors could increase typists' productivity by almost 150 per cent. In many cases word processing equipment is creating factory-like conditions in the office, but they *could* be used as a tool for saving secretaries and typists from boring routine tasks.

Word processors as a tool for management

Word processors can be used as a tool for management to increase control of the work force (in this case women) and further widen the gap between 'men's' and 'women's' work by deskilling qualified female clerical workers.

Secretarial work can be divided up into two parts: typing and administrative routine. In an attempt to rationalize and cut costs the trend is to divide these tasks, the typing work being taken over by typing pools equipped with word processors, and the administrative tasks being taken over by 'administrative support centres' which handle secretarial functions such as filing, answering the telephone, making plane reservations, typing chores of a personal and confidential nature, etc. The expected ratio is four to eight principals to one secretary — which involves tremendous cut-backs in the clerical labour force (Braverman 1974).

Estimates from Germany suggest an overall decrease in clerical jobs by 1990 of 40 per cent, and in France a cut-back of 30 per cent is expected in the financial sector within the next ten years (APEX 1979). In Denmark the office workers union (HK) expects 75,000 office jobs to disappear within the next few years as a result of word processing (*Aktuelt*, 1979).

Word processors will require typists, but the total number of jobs on the market may decrease. The need for highly skilled typists will decrease as programmes for the layout of tables and text are devised and stored in the machines' memory.

Some reports claim that word processors will create more jobs than they destroy — this is a fallacy. It depends on how these machines are used and what the purpose of installing them in the first place is. In other words if the goal is to eliminate boring and repetitive tasks and increase productivity, using the time saved for more qualified work, then it could be imagined that both new skills and therefore new jobs will be created. If, however, the goal is to centralize the work process, quantify and monitor work increasing productivity and using the time saved to increase the work load, and intensify the work process, the result will most likely be a drop in the total number of jobs.

Some manufacturers claim that word processors will require highly skilled operators, thus bringing about an increase in the skill-level of typists. The contrary is true. It takes a trained typist about a week to learn how to use the machine and about six months to reach top efficiency. These machines deskill those who are required to work full-time on them, performing monotonous tasks and who are denied physical mobility and involvement in their work. Once the machine's 'memory' is developed with standard paragraphs and letters, word processors can reduce typing to an almost completely mechanical task.

Word processors can be used to increase managerial control over the work process itself. These machines can be programmed so that when one typing job is finished the next will come up immediately on the screen. The device which makes this possible is called a 'prompter'. These machines can be equipped with counters that register the number of key depressions per day, they can also be used to collect information on the speed and/or accuracy of individual workers. When a word processor enters the office an automated time and motion man may come along with it.

In order to capitalize on their investment, management may decide to increase shiftwork and speed up the work process. A piece rate system may be introduced which, as we have seen in industry, leads to competition, alienation and a continuous struggle over what a 'fair' rate is. The introduction of involuntary part-time work (breaking down full-time jobs into part-time jobs) is a serious and very real threat for female clerical workers.

In Scandinavia today more than 50 per cent of all women are active in the labour market. *One half* of these women are working part-time and the trend is continuing especially in the clerical sector. In the Danish Shop and Office Workers Union 37 per cent of the women members as opposed to 1 per cent of the male workers work part-time. This trend is very significant at this critical time of increased office automation.

Because of the occupational health hazards caused by sitting full-time at word processors with visual display screens, the unions are asking that a maximum of four hours per day be the limit for any one operator. Instead of filling the rest of the day with diversified clerical tasks, an employer may be tempted to divide full-time jobs up into two part-time jobs. This will give the advantage of a fresh work force twice a day, the disadvantage being that these jobs are women's jobs and will in most cases weaken women's commitment to the labour market and to union activities.

Among feminists in Denmark there is a fear that this will lead to further splits in the already sex-segregated work force — full-time work equals men's work and part-time work equals women's work, thus putting women at an obvious disadvantage for promotion and the possibility for more responsible tasks. A movement for a six-hour day with full salary compensation of *both* men and women is mobilizing.

One result of the introduction of word processing equipment is that many secretaries and typists complain of an unnecessary increase in their workload. It appears that persons initiating work are becoming less orderly in their thinking as a result of the ease with which their secretaries can make corrections. These persons overestimate the productivity gains and there are cases where they 'create' additional work for the clerical staff.

The present level of lightweight portable terminals makes it possible for computer terminals to communicate with large central computers via telephone which makes work at home a reality. The potential for pushing women back into traditional roles would be disastrous not to mention the destruction of the labour unions and the opportunity for management to have absolute control over the work process.

How word processors could be used

Word processing machines can assist secretaries and typists in their daily work. They can increase productivity and bring about a shorter working week. Word processors will save secretaries' and typists' time in correcting and editing documents. That time should then be used for more responsible and challenging administrative tasks, for the training in new skills and for union activity. Word processors should be a tool in liberating women office workers from low-paid dead-end jobs. *Women must ensure that it is their brain-power and not their manual dexterity that is drawn on.*

The first step in introducing word processors should be an analysis of the needs of the office to determine whether a word processor would really expedite the work to be done. A common pitfall is an enchantment with the 'new technology', disregarding actual needs. Envisaged savings can in fact quickly be eaten up by concomitant usages to which the machine is put which are not strictly necessary. A good example of a machine creating the need is the photocopy machine. Whereas twenty years ago one or two carbon copies were often sufficient, today most documents are photocopied in many more copies than is absolutely necessary.

Word processors should not be allowed to create typing pools where none existed previously. They should be the tools of the clerical staff to be used when needed, integrated with other office duties.

No-one should be made to sit at a word processor all day because:

1. it can deskill clerical workers and undermine their education and training;
2. it can lead to shift work, speed-up and a piece-rate system;
3. it will cause health problems as it creates monotonous, sedentary, fast-paced work.

As many of the office staff as possible should learn to operate the machine. No-one should be made to work at a machine if not properly trained. Management often (in an attempt to save time and money) may send only one person on a training course and then expect that person to educate the others. This is a burden to the one sent on the course and unfair to those who have to receive 'second hand' instructions. Free instruction by the manufacturer for all potential operators should be a condition of the purchase.

The work force should be kept together. 'Natural wastage' should not even be a consideration since it gives management an incentive to force people out. As positions become vacant they must be filled again.

It must be clear that anyone who is not able to work on word processing equipment for medical reasons (there are cases of eye problems and allergic reactions to the screen) must not be fired or laid off. This goes especially for older workers with weakened eyesight. Some industries in England have specified that persons over forty-five should not use VDUs (Harman 1979). This approach sorts out people rather than eliminating occupational hazards. It is the machines that must adapt to the needs of people not *vice versa.*

The benefits of new technology

It must at all times be remembered that the *reasons,* the *goals* and *ideology* which support the introduction of technology are the basic underlying factors in determining whether the consequences will be harmful or beneficial for women clerical workers. For the new technology to have beneficial effects for women presupposes an active participation from them.

New jobs

It is projected that since microelectronic-based technology will increase productivity, it is expected to lead to economic growth and also new jobs.

In the past, rapid technological advancement has generally been accompanied by high rates of job creation. When new technology poured forth after the Second World War the number of jobs increased and unemployment hit low levels in the industrial economies (Norman, 1980). New technology will make it possible for us to handle and exploit more information than now. This can increase jobs in the field of information usage.

New options for relocating industry and employment become possible because it is now technically feasible and sometimes economically profitable to decentralize the processing. It could create new employment opportunities in sparsely populated areas and in areas with high unemployment.

New skills

Computers have increasingly created higher-level clerical jobs both within and without the electronic data-processing unit. Lack of software skills is already seen as a bottleneck in the application of microelectronics and demands for these skills will probably increase (Hult 1980).

Data bases and retrieval systems will require clerks to page through routine files and data banks to build up dockets of information relevant to particular problems for which their principals are engaged. This is a new form of creative and imaginative work requiring a higher calibre of staff than is needed in most clerical jobs today (Sleigh *et al,* 1979).

Many word processors can do much more than simple editing, for example sorting and mathematical programs can be performed. Exploring and utilizing the machines to capacity could lead to more qualified and interesting work, upgrading the operators and increasing their knowledge and control over the work process.

New organizational models

There is now the possibility of job sharing and reduced work hours for *both* men and women due to the productive gains expected from the new technology. Part-time and flexitime work for men will give them the opportunity to take a more active part in family life and will improve women's opportunities on the labour market.

Eliminating the drudgery of routine and monotonous jobs creates the possibility for a new division of labour whereby responsibility and decision-making can be dealt with collectively. New systems of work organization such as small work groups will be possible.

How to realize the benefits of the new technology

It is essential that women participate in the debate and decision-making process with regard to new technology. This can be done at work, through unions and in women's groups. Women clerical workers must break their dependence on leaders to do all the thinking, and push for co-determination in the office. These goals should include the right to make decisions about how work is set up, staffing and personnel politics.

When technology breaks down traditional demarcation lines at work it is a time to suggest ways of redistributing occupations on non-sexist lines. Word processors can hook up to large central computers and can communicate with computer terminals. As the barriers between word processing and computer programming lessen, women should seize their chance to get into programming and systems analysis, and take advantage of any available courses in advanced functions.

Encouraging male clerks to learn to operate word processors

could be a step in the redistribution of the existing work. If previously non-typing male clerks began typing some of their own correspondence (or first drafts of manuscripts) this could be a time saver for female clerks. Such a move is extremely individual and the implications are dependent on the factors present in each separate work place.

An important step is to insist on the establishment of and participation in *ad hoc* committees with the task of evaluating all new technology. These committees can make suggestions for eliminating the negative results of the introduction of new equipment and making suggestions for how best to exploit the benefits with special consideration for women. Training programmes should be provided in order to learn new skills which can help break down labour divisions and counteract the dead-end nature of most female clerical jobs.

Unions, although necessary in ensuring certain basic rights, support management's right to organize and distribute work. This limits what they can do. They can be counted on to help minimize the employment implications and to support health and safety measures, but must be pressured into challenging the authority of existing office hierarchies.

Permanent committees dealing with trends in technological innovations must be established in the unions. Again women must make their presence felt. The union is an excellent place to tap the collective experiences of its members, and thus discover the positive and negative applications of new technology.

Unions can be used to exert pressure on the computer industry. Manufacturers have the technology and the resources to develop safe equipment and to stop production of monitoring devices and 'prompters'.

Unions and women's groups should begin to criticize manufacturers and distributors for their sexist advertising. The majority of brochures for word processing equipment contain photographs of women *sitting down* at word processors and men, with documents in hand, *standing over them* instructing and pointing. On the other hand more advanced computer equipment inevitably features men as operators.

Technology agreements (made between unions and employers regarding guidelines for usage of new equipment) are important tools for ensuring co-determination at the work place, they can ensure the right to information about new technology in the planning stages; participation in determining new organizational systems; and the possibility for appointing data shop stewards for this extremely important area.

Because women as a group will be disproportionately affected by the new technology, it may be necessary for governments to develop policy measures for the labour market and compensatory education to help women overcome the difficulties (Hult 1980).

Conclusion

Due to the rising costs of labour, the falling prices of office equipment and the supposed low productivity in the office sector, the new microprocessor-based technology is expected to change the organizational structure of the office. Women as a group will be disproportionately affected, because (except for managerial posts) clerical work is predominantly women's work.

What is desperately needed now is for female clerical workers to become aware of their subordinate position on the labour market as a reflection of their position in society and the family, and to make every effort to change both.

In deciding how best the technology can help women's position in the clerical sector, female office workers cannot expect help or guidance from the firms designing the equipment, from their employers or from their unions. The technology being introduced in offices today incorporates the values and expectations of an already functioning and accepted division of labour based on sex segregation. The new technology will at best retain the *status quo* but threatens to limit women's career possibilities in the office of the future even further. The new technology can be used in centralizing, monitoring and machine-pacing work. It could also be used to improve women's place on the job market.

Even if one is committed to finding ways of developing the liberating potential of technology, there are no existing structures or models to look to. The struggle that lies ahead requires a re-evaluation of the uses of the new technology, together with a formulation of an occupational/political ideology which will free women from boring and repetitive work in the office, instead of creating factory-like conditions which further limit the possibilities of breaking down sex segregation at work. It is fundamental for the struggle ahead that women believe that they can make an impact. The direction technology is taking today is neither unshakable nor irreversible.

There is always a range of possibilities or alternatives that are delimited over time — as some are selected and others denied — by the social choices of those with the power to choose, choices which reflect their intentions, ideology, social position, and relations with other people in society. In short, technology bears the social 'imprint' of its authors (Noble, 1979; pp. 18—19).

Women must be made to see that they can be the 'authors'.

References

Maskine nedlægger 75,000 kontor job *Aktuelt*, Fredag 2 marts 1979.

APEX (1979) *Office Technology: the Trade Union Response* First report of the APEX word processing working party London: APEX.

Barron, Iann and Curnow, Ray (1979) *The Future with Microelectronics: Forecasting the Effects of Information Technology*, London: Frances Pinter Ltd.

Benet, Mary Kathleen (1973) *The Secretarial Ghetto*, New York: McGraw Hill.

Bliven, Bruce Jr. (1954) *The Wonderful Writing Machine*, New York: Random House.

Braverman, Harry (1974) *Labor and Monopoly Capital: the Degradation of Work in the Twentieth Century*, New York: Monthly Review Press.

CIS Report (1979) *The New Technology*, London: Counter Information Services.

Davies, Margery (1974) 'Woman's Place is at the Typewriter', *Radical America*, Vol. 8, No. 4, July—August.

Delgado, Alan (1979) *The Enormous File: a Social History of the Office*, London: John Murray Publishers.

Hagerty, Eileen M. and Tighe, Joan E. (1978) Office Automation and the Clerical Worker. Speech presented at MIT Lecture Series: 'Technology and Work: the worker's perspective.'

Harman, Chris (1979) *Is a Machine After Your Job?* London: SWP.

Hult, Marit (1980) *Technological Change and Women Workers: the development of microelectronics*, Submitted to the World Conference of the United Nations Decade for Women, Copenhagen Denmark 14—30 July 1980 (A/CONF.94/26).

Kraft, Philip (1979) 'The Industrialization of Computer Programming: from Programming to Software Production' in Zimbalist (1981).

Markoff, John and Stewart, Jon (1979) 'The Microprocessor Revolution, an Office on the Head of a Pin', *In These Times* March 7—13.

Noble, David F. (1979) 'Social Choice in Machine Design: the Case of Automatically Controlled Machine Tools', in Zimbalist (1981).

Norman, Colin (1980) *Microelectronics at Work: Productivity and Jobs in the World Economy*, Washington DC: Worldwatch Paper 39.

Popkin, Maggi (1975) 'Raises Not Roses', *The Second Wave*, Vol. 4, No. 1.

Sleigh, J., Boatwright, B., Irwin, P., Stanvon, R. (1979) *The Manpower Implications of Micro-electronic Technology*, London: Dept. of Employment.

Zimbalist, Andrew (ed.) (1981) *Case Studies on the Labor Process*, New York: Monthly Review Press.

2.4   Feminism and science

RITA ARDITTI

This article examines what it has been and continues to be like for women to be scientists in the masculinized world of science. It explores the powerful and positive potential of feminism in developing a truly humane science of the future.

'Women drink water while men drink wine'

In *A Room of One's Own*, published in 1929, Virginia Woolf describes a visit to Oxbridge, an imaginary centre of learning in England. She is walking through a grass plot when a man stops her: only the Fellows and Scholars are allowed to walk in the turf path; she should walk in the gravel. She steps into the library and instantly a kindly gentleman informs her that 'ladies are only admitted to the library if accompanied by a Fellow of the college'. Eating in Oxbridge she notices that the male scholars are served delicious foods and their wine glasses are quickly refilled. At the women's dining hall the food is plain and there is only water in the glasses. Why did men drink wine and women water? Why was one sex so prosperous and the other so poor? She reflects that if there had been more support for women, maybe 'we could have been sitting at our ease tonight and the subject of our talk might have been archaeology, botany, anthropology, physics, the nature of the atom, mathematics, astronomy, relativity, geography'.

All through history while male scholars conversed, debated and contributed to the disciplines of their choice, women provided the services that made that work possible. A non-sexist history of science (still to be written) would show the extent to which our culture has been built on the bodies and labour of women. [. . .]

During the Renaissance, the new science that followed from the work of Copernicus, Kepler and Galileo provided an alternative vision of the world and general impetus to question the established social order. Women's education became a lively topic of discussion. [. . .]

Source: Arditti, R. (1979) 'Feminism and science', in *Science and Liberation*. Arditti, R., Brennan, P. and Cavrak, S. (eds) South End Press, Boston, pp. 350—367

As new ideas in science were developed, strong women inspired and nurtured the male scientists who were creating the basis of science as we know it now. Sister Celeste, Galileo's oldest daughter, followed every detail of his work for eleven years. Her support allowed him to continue his work whenever despair came over him. Her death was a blow from which he never recovered. Kepler relied on his wife, Barbara, to help him keep up his strength and good spirits. Descartes acknowledged the inspiration and encouragement he received from Elizabeth of Bohemia by dedicating his work to her: 'in her alone were united those generally separated talents for metaphysics and for mathematics which are so characteristically operative in the Cartesian system'.[1] [. . .]

In the western scientific milieu [of the 17th century] a particular ideology and organization evolved following Francis Bacon's ideas. Nature (female) was the enemy, and science was the instrument for its control and domination — a way of recovering the lost dignity of 'man'.[2] Nature was to be conquered. A group of male scholars, devoted to scientific research and the pursuit of wisdom, would guide society. From this vision, his 'House of Solomon', derived the European scientific societies, mainly the British Royal Society and the French Royal Academy. Membership was open to 'men of all professions . . . students, soldiers, shopkeepers, farmers, courtiers and sailors, all mutually assisting each other'.[3] Membership in the societies was considered proof of scientific ability. [. . .]

In 1903 Marie Curie received the Nobel prize for her work on radioactivity together with Henri Becquerel and Pierre Curie. In 1904 she started receiving a salary for the first time in her career. Marie Curie is practically the only woman scientist given the worldwide recognition traditionally accorded to male scientists who are considered competent. Her devotion to scientific research, her inability for small talk and her seriousness made her quite unpopular among many of her colleagues. Her talent elicited mixed feelings. When in 1910, she published her *Treatise on Radioactivity*, Rutherford reviewed it favourably in *Nature* magazine, but in a private letter to a friend he expressed his true feelings: 'Altogether I feel that the poor woman has laboured tremendously, and her volumes will be very useful for a year or two to save the researcher from hunting up his own literature, a saving which I think is not altogether advantageous'.[4] At the height of her career she presented her candidacy for membership in the French Academy of Science. According to the customs of the time she went from house to house and from laboratory to laboratory visiting the members of the Academy and asking for their support. But the Academy was not moved, she was a woman and as such was not eligible. A few days before her name appeared before the

Academy as a candidate, its members reaffirmed in plenary session 'the immutable tradition against the election of women'.[5] [. . .]

Current times

Today, discrimination against women is still overt and socially acceptable within the academic community. Among 207,500 science and engineering PhDs in the US labour force 93.1 per cent are white and 92.1 per cent are male. Only 0.8 per cent are black, 0.6 per cent Latin, 0.04 per cent Native American while East Asians who make up 0.7 per cent of the US population comprise 5 per cent of science and engineering PhDs.[6] Women scientists (8 per cent of the total) have markedly lower salaries than men and are concentrated in certain fields: four-fifths are life scientists, psychologists, or social scientists. The unemployment rates for women in science are two to five times higher than for men in the same field with comparable training and experience. [. . .]

Discrimination against females starts early. Young females in the seventh through to twelfth grades 'tend' to lose interest in mathematics. Later in college they feel they lack the necessary fundamental skills and avoid science courses whenever possible.

In order to become a scientist, both women and men have to learn to behave in a way that will be acceptable and recognizable to other people in the field. Years of informal role learning are necessary before we complete the socialization process that transforms us into 'the scientist'. [. . .]

While it is accepted that women can efficiently perform technical and data-gathering functions, there is a general feeling that the truly original work, the work that 'makes a difference', is produced by male scientists. That truly creative work is beyond women's capabilities. This debilitating thought has in effect prevented many women from ever fully exploring their abilities or believing in themselves. However, such a view of creativity ignores the realities of the organization of work in the scientific world. The image of the distracted and genial scientist, oblivious to practical details, devoting heart and soul to finding a solution to a research problem, is an image that bears little resemblance to what actually takes place. What is essential is a knowledge of how to operate within a certain framework and follow the often implicit rules. [. . .]

The position of women in research laboratories is suspiciously similar to the position we have in the nuclear family. The laboratories resemble a patriarchal household, with the 'head' of the laboratory usually male, women in marginal positions without independent status, job security or benefits, and younger students playing child-like roles. A woman in a research laboratory is often expected to perform 'mothering' functions, the supportive and nurturing functions that nobody else will take on. [. . .]

One mechanism that ensures the perpetuation of this exploitative situation is the alienation that many women who do research feel. This alienation originates from the contradiction between the work experience and what one has been told or taught to believe. Having become a scientist, having 'made it' in a man's profession, one is supposed to have overcome the disadvantages of belonging to the female sex. On the other hand, the day-to-day experience of being in a subordinate position (even if one is doing scientific work) negates the previous optimistic viewpoint. As a result many women feel ambivalent about their own capabilities. Having been taught that when there is something wrong in a situation it is likely to be our fault, we keep reticent about our confusion. Consequently, we do not join forces to oppose the oppressive situation.

The personal is political

One of the central ideas of feminism, *the personal is political,* allows us to see how the exploitation of women is perpetuated. By reflecting on our personal experiences, we begin to gain an understanding of how oppressive patterns are allowed to run our lives. Nothing clamorous need happen. Things go as usual. Our lives are filled with what is familiar. And the thread of oppression binds us without our even noticing it. We know very little about the experiences of women in the sciences. Only recently have women begun to speak up.

In my own case it took many long years before I could see what the situation clearly was. I became attracted to biology in the fifties because it seemed a field that offered the promise of scientific rigour and at the same time relevant knowledge useful to my own life. As a student at Rome University in Italy, I decided to become a geneticist. Genetics related to people; its internal logic, its consistence and its elegance delighted me. In my early years I dismissed manifestations of hostility from some of my teachers and colleagues toward me as 'personality' problems, and I immersed myself completely in the genetics of micro-organisms. It never occurred to me that my sex had anything to do with some of the difficulties I encountered — this in spite of the fact that I was one of the few women doing that type of research and that I had picked up sexual innuendoes from some of my teachers. I cannot offer any reasonable explanation for my blindness.

As the years went by, however, I began to notice that women scientists had special problems, such as lack of advancement. They seemed to be stuck in the same position while men were moving ahead rapidly. The few women who were around did not show up at meetings or participate actively in them. Family obligations seemed to tear them apart.

Before long, I was one of them, struggling with my own marriage, childcare arrangements, and the need to keep focused on my work. At the same time, I was receiving all kinds of mixed messages from husband and colleagues. I also began to notice the particular situation of women scientists married to men in the same field of research. All had secondary positions to their husbands regardless of ability, and their loyalties as wives had led them to accept a precarious work situation in which their research had become dependent on their marriages. They did the day-to-day work necessary to produce a solid piece of research, and the credit would invariably go to their husbands. Naively, I thought I was safe from exploitation because my husband (soon my ex-husband) worked in a different field. I did not know then that all men are potential 'husbands'. By this I mean that the pattern of accommodations and expectations that I had observed between women scientists married to men in the same field, could and would also arise with male colleagues. This led to confusion and disappointment.

In the late sixties in the USA, I got involved in the movement against the war in Vietnam and began meeting with a group of scientists who were questioning the role of science in the war. Our analysis soon led us into discussions about the contradictions of trying to do humane science in an inhumane society. Scientific laboratories were supposedly dedicated to the discovery of new knowledge. Which kind of knowledge, we asked, and for what purposes? Who benefits from it? And what are the allegiances of the scientific community? These were exciting meetings, and I felt I was getting in touch with deep questions that would in some way or other alter the course of my life.

At about the same time I started to read and reflect about women. I had once attended a women's group meeting where questions had been raised regarding our position in society and statements had been made about our lives being 'political'. It took me almost a year before I was ready for another meeting like that, but in the interim I did a lot of thinking and, more importantly, I began to observe everyday situations in a new way. I realized how my professional training had often led me to disassociate myself from other women, especially if they were not professional women. I had grown to accept feelings of inadequacy and isolation as a normal part of life. Next, I sadly discovered that my questioning colleagues so ready to fight against the war did not have any understanding of how their own behaviour was a declaration of war against women. They branded me as 'difficult' and 'over-sensitive'. 'What do you mean women's issues when there is a war going on?' Comparisons were made about whose oppression was 'worse', and women were always at the losing end. It finally dawned on me that you do not discuss how to overthrow oppression with your oppressors. I started to reach out to other women, and after an initial period, we found that indeed we had many common experiences and could validate each other's perceptions. We were not crazy. We all had received destructive messages, and we all had deep insecurities regarding our role as scientists. On the surface we had all been led to believe that we were 'one of the boys' but we feared being found out: we 'knew' we were inadequate. Would they know?

Exploring my feelings in a safe context allowed me to remember experiences that I had buried deep down and I saw them with a fresh eye. I understood why blood had flushed to my cheeks when the head of my department, years ago, running into me one Saturday morning in the cold room of the laboratory had exclaimed affectionately: 'What are you doing here? You should be home with your child!' I remembered how tense I would get before making a public presentation about my work, and I realized why. Most of the time I would be judged as much for my appearance as for the quality of my work. I was told many times, jokingly, that with my new awareness I had to give up my female 'privileges'. What this meant was that I was not supposed to ask for help if I needed it and that if I did I would be most likely ridiculed for being 'weak'. Carrying a 25-gallon flask of distilled water was not easy for me (I am a short person) but once my colleagues decided I was 'liberated', I was on my own.

Talking with other women made the difference between sanity and insanity. I knew that my own life had to conform to my changing awareness and that the next task was to start looking for alternatives. The elitism of the research laboratories suffocated me. Concomitant with my personal growth was a new interest and delight in teaching. In my search for alternatives I read some of Rachel Carson's work. Her words, as she accepted the National Book Award for her book, *The Sea Around Us*, spoke directly to me:

Many people have commented with surprise on the fact that a work of science should have a large popular sale. But this notion, that 'science' is something that belongs in a separate compartment of its own, apart from every day life, is one that I should like to challenge. We live in a scientific age, yet we assume that knowledge of science is the prerogative of only a small number of human beings, isolated and priestlike in their laboratories. This is not true. That materials of science are the materials of life itself. Science is part of the reality of living; it is the what, the how and the why for everything in our experience.[7]

When I found out that Rachel Carson was looked upon with suspicion by the scientific community because she did not have a PhD and because she was so deeply concerned with educating the public, I laughed and I cried. Here was somebody who had done more than anybody else I was aware of to integrate science with public concerns, and she was mistrusted and put down! My ideas about my own future began to change. It became clear to me that my interest in doing research in genetics of micro-organisms was minimal and that I enjoyed working with people. Teaching became a source of deep satisfaction and continuous learning. I decided to put my energies into trying to change some of the oppressive conditions that I and many others had encountered. Learning about the social and political implications of science, with a focus on women, became a priority. Learning about power relations is also learning about how to change them.

Learning about the past and present position of women in science and understanding my own experiences made me realize that feminism and science (my two main interests) did not mix easily, and that some of the fundamental ideas and insights from the women's movement run contrary to the way science is now. The potential of feminism in the development of a truly humane science became an issue to explore.

Feminism and science

While lack of encouragement and blatant sexism have prevented women from fully participating in the sciences, the dehumanization of science has also played an important role in keeping women away. Women, generally more in touch with their feelings, often raise uncomfortable questions about 'detached scientific objectivity'. The prevalent mode in science today presents serious problems for people who have human concerns, as many women have. 'Objectivity' applied to people often leads to objectifying them, or perceiving only their object aspects. As mentioned before, the scientific community is composed mainly of white males who have been socialized into the professional value system. Professionalism, an elitist concept, provides the means to control others and to maintain privilege over them. It divides economic and occupational groups into the thinkers at the top and the unthinking masses at the bottom.[8] It protects scientists from external evaluation or even egalitarian discussions with the people affected by their work and dependent upon their performance.

As scientists we are taught to approach problems with a purely cerebral attitude and *not* to bother with the consequences or ramifications of our work. We are taught to 'keep things separate': scientific inquiry on the one hand and human concerns on the other. This way of working leaves little room for our development as human beings and opens the door to the creation of exploitative technologies. We stand powerless, producing knowledge that can be used against people. Nuclear weapons, chemical weapons, recent advances in the life sciences have all been developed by scientists who gave their energies to the narrow task before them without concern for the larger issues that would affect the community at large. It is clear that scientific inquiry without concern for the pressing social problems of our time will only create new ones. We do not live in a vacuum. Scientists will have to deal with new concepts (like being accountable) and seek closer contact with other parts of the community. More and more people are beginning to question the right of scientists to divest themselves of responsibility for the direction of their work and the use of scientific results.

Because of our experience as women in a patriarchal culture, we know, first hand, that a purely mechanistic approach does not add much to knowledge. Scientists have studied us as the reproductive system of the species, and we have been reduced to our reproductive organs, our secondary sexual characteristics and/or sexual behaviour. 'Scientific' rationalizations are offered for the secondary status of women, racial minorities, and poor people. Sociobiology, the study of sex differences, and anthropology contain our own cultural myths about women. Sexism is rampant in the hard and soft sciences.[9] For women to take the place of male scientists and not to advocate a humanistic and committed science would be a tragic mistake. A man-centred science serves a man-centred society — we have to question the process by which scientific work is accomplished as well as its product. We have to question the professionalism that keeps people separate.

Out of the experience of support groups in the women's movement some of us have learned that the conditions under which people are able to work creatively and joyfully are practically non-existent in the scientific milieu. We know now that in order to communicate clearly it is essential to feel that one is being listened to with attention and interest, that qualities that one may seem to lack can be developed, and that leadership skills can be learned, if there is an interest in sharing them. All this runs against the competitive patterns prevalent in the research environment.

A feminist perspective in science would involve the creation of an environment that maximizes the development of minds and bodies and encourages positive attitudes towards one's own biological identity. It would involve the conversion from an exploitative 'value free' technology to a commitment to a humane technology: to preventive medicine, fair distribution of material goods and educational opportunities. The concept of self-help would be fully accepted and fostered by the scientific community. The whole area of reproductive research, contraception and sex differences would be revamped to eliminate sexist stereotypes. Females would no longer be considered the sole reproductive units of the species.

A feminist perspective would not necessarily hail new technological developments as 'liberating' because it would realize that oppression is not the result of biological or natural conditions but of social constructs. Technology would be assessed for the impact it has in bringing meaningful change in social relations.

Feminism is also a special form of 'knowing'. By eliminating the division between intellect and emotion, scientists can perform intellectual tasks without becoming intellectual robots. We do not know how science would have evolved if women had been full participants in its development. There seems to be a connection between the specialization and reduction, the indifference to values and the masculinization of science.

Since science does not progress only by inductive analytical knowledge, the importance of imagination and emotion in the creative process should be obvious. The role of intuition in science is consistently undervalued in a science which is exploited for corporate, military and political reasons. A feminist perspective would re-introduce and re-legitimize the intuitive approach. The benefits of this in terms of new knowledge might well be incalculable.

Adrienne Rich notes that Virginia Woolf suggested that 'women entering the professions must bring with them the education — unofficial, unpaid for, unvalued by society — of their female experience, if they are not to become subject to the dehumanizing forces of competition, money lust, the lure of personal fame and individual aggrandizement, and "unreal loyalties".'[10] Rich adds: 'in other words, we must choose what we will accept and what we will reject of institutions already structured and defined by patriarchal values . . . We need to consciously and critically select what is genuinely viable and what we can use from the masculine, intellectual tradition, as we possess ourselves of the knowledge, skills and perspectives that can refine our goal of self-determination and discipline and wisdom . . . In fact, it is in the realm of the apparently unimpeachable sciences that the greatest modifications and revaluations will undoubtedly occur. It may well be in the domain that has proved least hospitable or attractive to women — theoretical science — that the impact of feminism and of women-centred culture will have the most revolutionary impact'.

Today, in science we know 'more and more' about 'less and less'. Science as an instrument of wealth and power has become obsessed with the discovery of facts and the development of technologies. The emphasis on the analytical method as the only way of knowing has led to a mechanistic view of Nature and human beings. We should remember that the concept of evolution, for instance, did not emerge from developments in the field of genetics or biochemistry but from 'inspired guesses based on a sort of awareness of complex relationships in natural situations. The modern scientific techniques have served merely to verify the theory and to elaborate its details'.[11]

The task that seems of primary importance — for women and men — is to convert science from what it is today, a social institution with a conservative function and a defensive stand, into a liberating and healthy activity. Science needs a soul which would show respect and love for its subjects of study and would stress harmony and communication with the rest of the universe. When science fulfils its potential and becomes a tool for human liberation, we will not have to worry about women 'fitting' into it because we will probably be at the forefront of that 'new' science.

Notes

1. H.J. Mozans, *Woman in Science*, Cambridge, Massachusetts, MIT Press, 1974, p.370.

2. Joseph Haberer, *Politics and the Community of Science*, New York, Van Nostrand-Reinhold, 1969.

3. Rene Dubos, *The Dreams of Reason: Science and Utopias*, New York, Columbia University Press, 1961, p.34.

4. Robert William Reid, *Marie Curie*, New York, Saturday Review Press, 1974.

5. Mozans, *op. cit.*, p.230.

6. Betty Vetter, 'Women and Minority Scientists,' editorial in *Science*, 189, September 5, 1975, p.75.

7. Paul Brooks, *The House of Life: Rachel Carson at Work*, New York, Fawcett-Crest, 1974, pp. 116-17.

8. Mary McKenney, 'Class Attitudes and Professionalism,' in *Quest*, 3, Spring 1977, pp. 48-58.

9. Evelyn Reed, *Sexism and Science*, New York, Pathfinder Press, 1978; R. Hubbard, M.S. Henifen, and B. Fried, *Women Look at Biology*

Looking at Women, Cambridge, Schenkman, 1979.
10. Adrienne Rich, 'Toward a Woman-centered University,' in Florence Howe, *Women and the Power to Change,* New York, McGraw-Hill, 1975, p.15.
11. Dubos, *op. cit.,* p.116.

2.5 The state and training programmes for women

ANN WICKHAM

Introduction

Increasingly in the post-war period state institutions in Britain have become involved in the development of training. This chapter examines the growth of state intervention in training in relation to women. It argues that training is important, not just because it is as an entry requirement for many jobs, but also because it is an important element in the production of gender differences at work. Training and the notion of skill that it carries helps structure work differentiation between the sexes and stimulates the subjective subordination experienced by women in the work place. It is therefore important to show the extent to which state involvement in the training area has opened up features favourable to women. The chapter argues that although state training policy has changed over time, and there have been reports dealing with the specific training problems of women, these have seldom been acted on.

Through the impetus of feminist research it is increasingly realized that the working class is neither a homogenous category nor one that is innocent of gender relations. One problem is the existence of an organized labour movement which is male-dominated and fails to represent specifically female demands in its negotiations. But struggles in and around the labour process also produce gender divisions between workers. A recent paper recognizes that:

> . . . men organize to exclude women from certain jobs, struggle with women over entry to certain occupations, and [. . .] the presence of women in some jobs has materially damaged men's chances. Such conflict may be put down to 'false consciousness' and not seeing that capital is the real enemy. But in fact material advantages accrue to men from women's disadvantaged position at work.[1]

Specially commissioned for this volume
©The Open University, 1982

The authors also comment on men's control over technology and the question of skill. In both cases these are elements which are the outcome of class struggle but also of gender struggle. Work skills, especially in relation to industry, have traditionally been seen in terms of craft skills and craft workers have almost overwhelmingly been male workers. The assets which women bring to their work have been persistently devalued. As Phillips and Taylor[2] note, skilled work has become almost by definition that work which women do not do. This definition of skill is seldom challenged although as Pollert emphasizes in a study of female tobacco workers:

> The irony comes when a system of so-called non-discriminatory 'objective' job 'measurement', aimed at getting rid of the awkward 'interference' of ideological judgements, succeeds in rooting them more deeply . . . . One might legitimately inquire why such a job as hand stemming (in practice, female) in Group A should be rated lower than security patrols (in practice, male) in Group D. One job might hold more responsibility and danger but the other involves more patience and physical discomfort.[3]

In other words, the definition of a skill is socially constructed and whilst the concept of 'skilled work' may be used by working-class men for their own benefit in maintaining privileges in relation to employers, it can also be used against women whose work, once defined as low skilled, is also low paid. These practices help reinforce subjective perceptions of women's marginal place in the labour market and their dependence in the home.

Training is traditionally seen as the means through which skills can be acquired and the apprenticeship system is at the basis of this approach. In the post-war period more and more training schemes have been introduced at different levels and for different periods of time, culminating in the present youth training programmes of the Manpower Services Commission (MSC). Such schemes are presumed to pass on those technical skills which the economy requires. However, in many cases it seems clear that training involves the acquisition of social attributes required in the labour process — work discipline, for instance — just as much as technical skills. When women have no access to training it effectively excludes them from many occupations, whether it is technical or social skills that are required, or even if training qualifications are being used solely as a form of entry requirement without reference to their content. Undoubtedly the absence of schemes for women is important when women want to enter what have been male-dominated occupations. However, it is essential not to overemphasize the impact of training. One must realize that even if women replicated the training available to men it is unlikely that they would gain an equal place on the labour market given the existence of competition from males, and when they are faced by male-dominated unions, male employers and a capitalist system that has profited from the use of women as a marginal, low-paid labour force.

Despite this, the extension of training opportunities to women could be of benefit to some and their entrance into less marginal areas of economic activity could help weaken the dominance of the belief that the place of women is in the home.

Early developments

For much of the post-war period little attention was paid to the training of women workers. In the pre-war period, state involvement in training in general was minimal. After the First World War instructional factories were set up for ex-servicemen. In the 1920s training centres were used to deal with unemployment and in the Second World War they were used to provide rapid training for hurriedly mobilized workers. In the fifties, however, there was even a decline in the number of such training places and the main concern expressed in government circles was for apprentices, that is mainly male workers.[4] However, labour shortages, technological changes and a 'baby boom' prompted more wide-ranging considerations which were embodied in the assumption that 'upskilling' (the need to increase the skills of the workforce) was essential for economic growth.

In 1956 a sub-committee was set up under the Ministry of Labour which produced the Carr Report *Training for Skill*[5] in 1958. In this report, which was concerned with the adequacy of the training of young workers for industry, only one short section dealt with opportunities for girls. It was assumed in the report that girls would marry and therefore would not need training. The main concern expressed was for the above average female grammar school pupil who might be expected to make a sustained contribution to the labour force. In this the Report both reflected much of the current thinking about women in other areas of social policy and anticipated the relative neglect of women's training over the next decade.

In terms of school education, for instance, the Crowther Report[6] published in 1959 (the year after the Carr Report) also assumed that the main interest of girls was in their future role of wives and mothers. Similarly the Newsom Report[7] in 1963 concentrated upon marriage as the more important vocational concern of girls, despite mounting evidence of the importance of women workers within the economy.

The emphasis upon marriage and the notion of the dependence of the woman upon the male wage earner which was implicit in so many areas of British welfare state policy[8] reduced the pressure for any further training provision for women even when, as in the Crowther Report, the paucity of women's day release opportunities was specifically commented upon. Curricula differentiation in the schools both taught girls that their main interests were in the home and closed them off from many of those training opportunities which existed. The clustering of girls in arts subjects is well known,[9] yet various apprenticeships and forms of training often require a maths or science qualification. Thus even when girls did enter further education and training, it was likely to be in areas defined as 'female', such as secretarial work or nursery nursing.

Whilst many government reports and the whole thrust of the welfare system emphasized the place of women in the home, the development of training opportunities for women would remain a rhetorical commitment. When changes were intitiated in the 1960s and the government started to introduce training legislation, the issue of provision for women was still not regarded as one of importance. In 1964 an Industrial Training Bill[10] was brought into Parliament which marked a revolution in state thinking in relation to training. Until then, training had mainly been left to the efforts of individual firms. However, this *ad hoc* process was now considered inadequate, especially in the face of overseas industrial competition. Industrial Training Boards were to be set up which would help establish an overall training policy and oversee its implementation. A levy system was to spread the cost across industry. Yet in the debate around this Bill, the problem was conceptualized in almost exclusively male terms and the absence of reference to the numbers of women entering employment was publicly noted.[11] The dominance of human capital theory in this period reinforced this emphasis on men. Education and training were regarded as an investment which would later produce calculable returns. However, only men were regarded as producing economic returns. The benefit of any investment in women was regarded as social and not economic.[12] This approach both legitimated and reinforced women's perceived marginality in the world of work and their role in the home.

State policy towards the training of women in the seventies

The Industrial Training Bill, which set up training boards, reflected a commitment by the state to positive intervention in the field of training and the levy system gave a financial leverage on firms. However, as the training boards were mainly concentrated in those industries which had few women workers, their establishment did not help many women.[13] Furthermore, it was apparent to observers that the boards did not consider it their role to encourage the training of women and girls.[14] Commercial and clerical training which might have suited women were resisted by employers.[15]

In their failure to identify and come to terms with the specific training needs of women, the training boards reflected the opposition of employers and unions to women's training as well as social constraints. The TUC had issued a charter of aims for women workers as early as 1963 in which the need for the development of training for women was emphasized. In 1972 the TUC was still pressing for the development of training, on the grounds that the impact of the Industrial Training Bill had been negligible. Representatives of the TUC argued that when levy grants were made to firms the boards should insist that a proportion of the training places went to women and that special grants should be made for 'non-traditional' training and for training for those returning to work.[16] Yet at the same time many of the prevailing assumptions about the training of women were also evident in statements of the TUC representatives. These statements, in fact, often contradicted stated TUC goals. For instance, the Expenditure Committee on the Employment of Women noted that:

> The unconscious acceptance of traditional roles and occupations is well illustrated by the TUC evidence which, while favouring equal training opportunities for women, describes 'the vast majority of courses' at Government Training Centres as 'clearly appropriate only for men'.[17]

However it was not that the courses were only suitable for men but that only men were admitted to them. The fact that the majority of places were for the engineering and construction industries was seen as the 'natural' reason for the bias towards male students. However, the unions were not the only ones to show some ambivalence towards the employment and training of women. The National Council of Women gave evidence to the *Expenditure Committee* that:

> a spokesman from the Department of Employment has recently suggested to one of our members that (a) many girls do not want training, (b) the overall employment position should be

considered before training more married women; and that (c) it may not be good for the community that married women should be trained, and that the only circumstances in which more women will be trained is when there is economic need.[18]

Women were doing badly in many areas of training. In 1970 only 110 females were apprenticed to the skilled craft occupations compared to 112,000 males and less than one fifth of those on day-release courses were female. Where girls were in apprenticeships the majority of these were in hairdressing. This situation is clearly related to the kinds of attitudes displayed by the unions and the Department of Employment.

However, further changes in training policy were introduced at the beginning of the seventies which appeared to offer some means of altering this situation. Whilst no specific mention of women's needs were made in either the Green Paper [19] of 1972 or the White Paper [20] of 1973, the Employment and Training Act (1973) initiated developments which were to have relevance for women.

The Act provided for the setting up of the Manpower Services Commission which was to manage public employment and training services through two executive arms, the Employment Services Division and the Training Services Division. The Training Services Division was to be responsible for the Training Opportunities Scheme (TOPS) which was replacing the old vocational training schemes in government training centres. Furthermore, section two of the Act which enumerated the functions of the Commission made special mention of arrangements that could be made to encourage increases in the opportunities available to women and girls.

The Training Services Division made the first important gesture towards a consideration of the special needs of women in the training process. The government had already argued that the introduction of legislation on equal opportunities for women could be expected to be beneficial in this area. In connection with the Equal Pay Act, it had agreed to remove male-female differences in training allowances. The government did not, however, propose to deal with other issues such as the distance of training centres or the absence of childcare facilities which might well have hindered the training of women. Yet the government was prepared to consider some experimental part-time training courses, even if these were only in the female-dominated commercial and clerical fields.[21]

In 1976 the Training Services Division brought out a report on 'Training Opportunities for Women'.[22] This was a result of a

decision by the Commission in 1975, the year of the Equal Pay and
Sex Discrimination Acts, that women were one of the groups
whose training needs should be treated as a priority of special
national importance. The Sex Discrimination Act [23] in fact, had
gone a long way towards encouraging more and wider training
facilities for women by specifically exempting certain forms of
training provision from the terms of the Act. Section 47 allowed
for positive discrimination in the provision of training courses for
men or for women where the number of persons of that sex in the
jobs that the training scheme provided for had been extremely
small in the previous year. It also allowed for schemes in particular
areas. Section 47 also dealt with the needs of those returning to
work after a period of domestic responsibility and permitted both
special training schemes and discrimination in selection for training
programmes.

The report of the Training Services Division, issued against this
background, recognized the inadequacy of existing training
provision for women in every aspect, from day-release and
apprenticeship to government training schemes.[24] It also admitted
that there was an unsatisfied demand for training., and argued that
there were legislative, economic and social justifications for the
provision of training for women. However, whilst the report must
be welcomed as the first major initiative by the state in the post-
war period to consider the specific training needs of women, it
gives the impression of a lack of dynamism and of a failure to
develop a commitment to positive intervention. The emphasis in
the report is on research into ways of assisting women and the
exploration of possible ways of extending training.

The lack of dynamism in training policy is understandable in
terms of the deepening economic crisis in Britain. Training
provision had made no great progress in the late 1960s even
though there had been open encouragement to women to enter
the labour market. In the 1970s policy statements had been made
in favour of women's opportunities but these were seldom put into
practice as economic problems grew.

The provision of training opportunities for women

The full impact of this lack of commitment is evident in the
provisions the MSC made for women. When set up, the Training
Services Division was made responsible for the Training
Opportunities Scheme (TOPS). The programmes in this scheme
were not aimed at school leavers but at those who had been out of
permanent education for more than two years, and were aged at
least 19. The TOPS programmes offered a wide variety of courses

from higher level programmes in management, science and technology to craft courses and provision for the commercial and clerical sectors. Both men and women were eligible for TOPS courses and the number of women on the programme gradually increased. In 1972, before the Manpower Services Commission took over, only 6,000 women trained on the TOPS programme.[25] By 1975 the numbers had increased to 27,000; in 1977 the figure reached 40,881 and the figure was the same in 1978. By then women made up around 43 per cent of those completing TOPS courses and the percentage in 1980 was around 45 per cent.[26] In terms of encouraging numbers of women to train, it is clear that MSC programmes had considerable success. Unfortunately whilst the numbers of women involved increased, the schemes do not represent a change in the range or level of opportunities open to women.[27] Women on TOPS schemes are found mainly in 'female' occupations. Most of them take courses in clerical work, shorthand and typing and they make up the majority on courses concerned with education, office machines, food preparation, hairdressing, cleaning etc. Very few women are to be found in the higher level courses or in the government skill centres where subjects such as engineering, vehicle repair, carpentry and joinery, capstan setting machining and bricklaying are taught. (In 1978 only 658 women were on such courses in skill centres compared to 23,357 men and women on these courses made up only 1.5 per cent of the women taking TOPS courses that year.)[28] Although the actual numbers in these courses may have increased slightly over the years, the overall expansion of TOPS courses means that women represent no greater proportion of the overall student number.

Even though the numbers of women on TOPS schemes appear to have grown so rapidly, albeit in female-dominated occupations, there are still many other drawbacks associated with the schemes. The failure to provide childcare facilities and the fact that there are virtually no part-time training opportunities is a major hindrance. The small training allowance paid to women who also have to pay for childcare is another limitation. The small numbers of women entering courses for areas of work at present dominated by men has been partly blamed on the limited guidance offered by those administering the schemes,[29] and the need for effective occupational guidance is continually stressed by those examining this area of work preparation.[30]

A special development in the TOPS programme has been the introduction of Wider Opportunities for Women (WOW) courses in colleges. These courses are designed, administered and financed by the Training Services Division, and aimed at women who are likely to enter manual or skilled employment. Even though participants can be 19 on entry, the courses have tended to attract older women. The courses are short and are meant to help women formulate realistic re-entry plans for work, as well as providing the information and self-confidence that will help them carry these out. Welcome as such courses are because of their particular concern for the older woman worker, it is clear that the numbers at present attending them are infinitesimal. Even more important, so far as discrimination faced by women on the labour market is concerned, is the fact that an evaluation of pilot courses found that the courses were not leading women to enter into a wider range of jobs.[31]

There is some provision of similar courses for women outside the MSC. New Opportunities for Women (NOW) courses or similar 'return to work' courses are to be found in many further education colleges. These too are mainly concerned with women returning to work after a break and they do not demand any entry qualifications. The courses vary a great deal in content, emphasis and duration. Indeed there is no clear information on how many such courses are available in Britain.

The Industrial Training Boards were also empowered by the Sex Discrimination Act to run positive discrimination and return to work schemes. However, those boards which set up initiatives tended, like the Engineering Industry Training Board, to focus on school leavers rather than older women and dealt with very small numbers.[32] It is clear that despite verbal commitment to the training needs of women, a commitment fuelled by government equality legislation, very little has so far been achieved in practice by state training bodies. This situation would be bad enough in a period of rising employment for all groups. In the current context it presents a gloomy picture. As current unemployment figures rise, many women are being thrown out of work and there has been a more rapid rise in their rate of unemployment than there has been for men.[33] Men's and women's jobs are segregated both vertically and horizontally in such a way that women are found primarily in the lower paid, lower level jobs and in female-dominated sectors of the economy.

Further opportunities for training could at least offer some women the chance to move into male-dominated occupations where there are still employment opportunities or open paths to promotion. Training for women could also help prevent the further 'masculinization' of new occupations that are opening up. This is an important issue when it is expected that current female occupations will be hardest hit by new technology.[34]

It seems clear, however, that many of the training programmes that recognise women's problems are being set up outside the

MSC, although often drawing on sources of state financial assistance. Finance through the Inner City Partnership scheme can be used, for instance, to help establish training courses for women that are part-time and provide nursery facilities, both of which are essential for women with children. Such schemes are most often the ones that aim to open up opportunities in previously male dominated areas of work.[35]

The opening up of training opportunities to women in this way merely juggles numbers within an existing work pattern where the majority of women workers provide a cheap source of labour. If women were to enter male-dominated occupations in large numbers, it seems likely that these would become 'feminized occupations' with associated problems of low pay and status. Women would not necessarily make any major gains in the long term.

The possibility of more radical gains for women comes from an area of state training policy that is highly controversial and which is not aimed solely at women. It is the area of youth policy.

The development of youth programmes

The youth programmes of the MSC developed from the Holland Report, 'Young People and Work' which was published in 1977.[36] This Report marked the start of new developments inside the MSC which have had a major impact on the forms and sites of training offered to young people in Britain. The report was particularly concerned with the phenomenon of rising youth unemployment[37] and led to the establishment of a third agency inside the MSC, the Special Programmes Division which was set up in 1978. The Holland Report described previous efforts to deal with the unemployed in the 16–18 year old age group as 'piecemeal and *ad hoc*', involving a variety of unco-ordinated agencies.[38] The view of the committee responsible for the Report was that youth unemployment could be expected to rise as a result of demographic trends until at least 1981. The numbers of young unemployed were expanding rapidly, especially amongst girls, and as well as the duration of unemployment was increasing. The Report proposed a new and coherent programme to help this group find permanent jobs.

Two kinds of opportunities were to be offered to young trainees. These were work experience schemes and preparation for work courses. Many of the latter were to be offered in Further Education Colleges and consisted of assessment, short industrial and remedial courses. This marked the intervention of the Department of Employment into the specifically educational area since the MSC bought its courses in the colleges. At the same time the development of the courses marked a revolution in the concept of training itself and in what constituted the skills which training courses were to pass on.

The courses were seen by the MSC as a bridge between school and work, a period of transition which had to be situated outside of a school system which so many pupils rejected by leaving as early as possible.[39] The courses were meant to provide those 'skills' which many school leavers were felt to lack and which employers were assumed to require. In the past the notion of skill had been associated with craft work, with a combination of mental and physical dexterity in a particular area of work. Under the aegis of the Special Programmes Division a much wider definition of skill came into use. Skill was regarded more as a way of organizing activity and involved a combination of what are now regarded as individual skills and general skills, that is numeracy, communication and practical skills, together with social and life skills, attitudes to work and a knowledge of working life.[40] Training was, in this respect, given a new meaning which was removed from that traditionally used and evoked in the earlier MSC Reports.

The development of MSC programmes dealing with youth unemployment came against a more general background of political concern with the process of transition from school to work that was part of a redefinition of educational objectives under the Labour government. This in turn was part of wider concern for economic and social problems. James Callaghan's speech[41] at Oxford in October, 1976, had expressed concern about the links between education and the economy. The new political priority expressed there generated a number of consultative papers[42] and initiatives which are still continuing in the 1980s. This concern was not merely British but found expression throughout the European Communities at this period.[43]

The focus on the problems created by 'youth' meant that schemes concentrating on this issue made provision for females as well as males. Widespread action in this area of training could not be seen entirely in male terms, especially as in many areas it was the young women who were suffering most from the effects of unemployment.

In 1979 a report was published on the opportunities for women and girls in the special programmes in the MSC. This report's special concern was with the ways in which women could be introduced into 'non-traditional' areas of work. The report started from the assumption that 'there are practically no jobs which cannot be done by girls, given the opportunity and appropriate training'.[44] It also recognized the specific form of disadvantages suffered by the female work force. These included a lack of confidence to enter new areas and the problem of having different educational experiences. The report thought that girls' lack of technical and mathematical skills could be directly compensated for. Stress was placed on the need to avoid reinforcing female patterns of work in the courses, work experience and temporary schemes by making use of the exemptions allowed by the Sex Discrimination Act. The problems of older women with domestic responsibilities were also acknowledged. However, once again practice failed to match up to stated policy.

The Youth Opportunities Programme (YOP) offered work experience schemes and work preparation courses. In the first year there were 162,000 participants in the scheme.[45] In 1981 around 500,000 took part. This represents a rise from one in ten school leavers to one in two. Female school leavers make up 50 per cent of those participating in YOPs and have maintained this percentage despite the rise in the absolute numbers involved. However, within the programmes the same dispiriting pattern of work opportunities for women is to be found. Far more girls, for instance, go into community work experience schemes, a continuation of women's role in 'caring' areas,[46] whilst more boys enter the training workshops. Work experience places in employers premises make up the majority of opportunities in the YOPs programme and here the tendency is for further reinforcement of occupational segregation. To some extent the MSC can claim that this is out of their control, for the Commission has to rely on the voluntary co-operation of employers. Employers, particularly in small firms, are notorious for their maintenance of segregated work roles. Sponsors can only be encouraged, not forced, to make provision for women in 'non-traditional' areas.[47]

It is clear that in the area of youth programmes the MSC has had no great success in opening up fresh occupational opportunities for women. However, the MSC's emphasis on the individual's lack of saleable attributes has had other effects. The courses funded by the MSC have been based on the premise that school leavers lack the desired attributes that employers require, and this has led to a focus on the need to provide trainees with the 'skills' they are presumed to lack. The definition of skill which emphasizes 'social and life skills' (which is different from the concept of skill embodied in the traditional notion of craft skill), can be of benefit to women. Whilst the traditional concept of skill prevailed, it could be used as a means of devaluing attributes possessed by women. A move to a new definition of skill could allow women to be regarded as equal possessors of 'skills' and therefore cannot be used so easily to exclude them from jobs. It also opens up the possibility of new bases for job evaluation which could transform the present sexual hierarchization of work.

Implementation of such changes would, however, require trade union pressure. This remains problematic whilst there is a male-dominated union bureaucracy. Craft skills represent a way in which groups of male workers have gained control of an area of knowledge and competence which they have used to their advantage in negotiations with employers. This new definition of 'skill' could be used to break down the privileges of male workers which depended on the definition of their work as skilled. However, the new 'skills' are also used by employers to help trainees 'adjust' to the world of work, to a hierarchically organized, disciplined labour process. They are not intended to develop an individual's initiative, independence and creativity. Possible benefits to women from changes initiated through the youth training programmes do not, therefore, come without costs, even for women themselves. Furthermore the gains for women must be weighed against the accusations that young people will be used as a substitute, at lower wages, for older labour.

Further, the plans for the extension of training or educational opportunities to the whole 16—19 age group could mean the development of a new system of stratification similar to that once produced by the grammar and secondary modern schools. YOP trainees could become the permanent occupants of the lower rungs of the social ladder. This may be a high price to pay for what are tenuous gains for women.

Conclusion

It is clear from this account of state training programmes that policies which have increasingly made reference to the needs of women have not been matched by appropriate provision. In practice the concern has been with males and the need to broaden the opportunities available to women has seldom been met. As the situation stands at present, training programmes mainly serve to reinforce the existing sexual divisions within and between occupations. Undoubtedly much more could be done, especially by the MSC, to open up job opportunities for women and to attack sex segregation. The Women's Employment Projects Group, who represent many of the more radical training projects for women, have recently made detailed suggestions to the MSC as to how an equal opportunities policy commitment might be realized. These involved quota places on MSC schemes, the provision of childcare and part-time training opportunities, increased marketing to sell the idea of 'non-traditional' schemes, an explicit code of practice for all levels of staff, and monitoring of schemes to assess implementation of equal opportunities policies. However, as male unemployment continues to rise, opposition to the entry of women into male-dominated occupations seems likely to continue and, whilst women continue to be used as a flexible reserve in many areas of employment, no pressure will emerge from employers for any real equality on the labour market. Women still have a fight ahead if they are to make state training policy mean what it says.

The implementation of the more far-reaching possibilities inherent in changing the concept of skill seems even further away. Not only is opposition from male workers likely, there are also substantial costs for women involved. Those on YOPs courses could be stigmatized and the control of the labour force further intensified, through the emphasis on subjective attributes. Yet if the new training initiatives do succeed in attacking the form of job classification as 'skilled' or 'unskilled', then the gains for women could be considerable. As the recession continues and the employment prospects for women look grim, any struggle to open up job opportunities for women would be worthwhile.

Acknowledgements

I would like to thank Madeleine Arnot and Veronica Beechey for their helpful comments and the Socialist Feminist Social Policy Group, especially Wendy Clark, for encouraging discussion of this area.

Notes

1. CSE Sex and Class Group, Mimeograph, 1981.
2. A. Phillips and B. Taylor (1980) 'Sex and skill: notes towards a feminist economics', *Feminist Review,* no. 6.
3. A. Pollert, *Girls, Wives, Factory Lives* (London: Macmillan, 1981, p. 65).
4. The number of centres fell from 23 in 1951 to 13 in 1962. However, by 1971 the numbers had increased to 1952. House of Commons Expenditure Committee, *Seventh Report* (London: HMSO, 1973).
5. Ministry of Labour, *Training for Skill: Recruitment and Training of Young Workers in Industry* (Carr Report) (London: HMSO, 1958).
6. Ministry of Education, *15—18*, (Crowther Report) (London: HMSO, 1959).
7. Ministry of Education, *Half Our Future* (Newsom Report) (London: HMSO 1963).
8. Hilary Land, 'Sex Role Stereotyping in the Social Security and Income Tax Systems', in J. Chetwynd and O. Hartnett *The Sex Role System* (London: RKP, 1978). H. Land, 'Who Cares for the Family?',

The Journal of Social Policy, July 1978. H. Land, 'The Family Wage', *Feminist Review,* No. 6, 1980. The male breadwinner family makes up 5 per cent of the present workforce. J. Coussins and A. Coote, *The Family in the Firing Line* (London: CPAG, 1981).

9. For example in 1974 in CSE examinations 191,275 girls compared with 185,562 boys passed English; 59,482 girls passed in French compared with 37,127 boys. However, when it came to maths 142,801 girls passed compared to 152,672 boys; in physics the difference was even more notable — 10,221 girls passed compared to 76,074 boys. The GCE results showed similar differences. See R. Deem, *Women and Schooling* (London: RKP, 1978) Tables 3.2 and 3.3, pp. 67—8.

10. *The Industrial Training Bill,* 1964.

11. Frank Cousins of the National Union of General and Municipal Workers is quoted to this effect in P. Perry, *The Evolution of British Manpower Policy* (London: Bacie, 1976), p. 106.

12. M. Woodhall, 'Investment in Women: a Reappraisal of the Concept of Human Capital', *International Review of Education,* Vol. 19, No. 1, 1973.

13. House of Commons Expenditure Committee, *The Employment of Women, Sixth Report* (London: HMSO, 1973). Evidence of the National Joint Committee of Working Women's Organizations, p. 84.

14. *Ibid,* Memorandum of the National Council of Women of Great Britain.

15. Dept of Employment, *Government Observations on three Reports on Youth Employment Services, the Employment of Women, and Employment Services and Training,* Cmnd. 5536, (London: HMSO, 1974).

16. House of Commons Expenditure Committee, *The Employment of Women, Sixth Report* (London: HMSO, 1973) p. 2106.

17. *Ibid.*

18. *Ibid,* Memorandum of the National Council of Women of Great Britain, p. 97.

19. Dept of Employment, *Training for the Future — A Plan for Discussion* (London: HMSO, 1972).

20. Dept of Employment, *Employment and Training: Government Proposals* Cmnd. 5250 (London: HMSO, 1973).

21. Dept of Employment, *Government Observations on Three Reports on Youth Employment Services, the Employment of Women and Employment Services and Training.* Cmnd. 5536, (London: HMSO, 1974).

22. MSC, *Training Opportunities for Women* (Training Services Agency, London: MSC, 1976).

23. *Sex Discrimination Act,* 1975.

24. Type of employment entered by school leavers in 1974:

Class of Employment	Boys (%)	Girls (%)
apprenticeship to a skilled occupation	43.0	6.5
employment leading to recognized professional qualifications	1.3	1.7

clerical employment	7.0	40.5
employment with planned training	17.1	17.3
other	31.6	34.0

Source: Figure 4, *Training Opportunities for Women, op. cit.*

25.   M. Alexander, *Equal Opportunities and Vocational Training* (Berlin: European Centre for the Development of Vocational Training, 1980), p. 9.

26.   These statistics can be found in N. Fonda, 'Current Entitlements and Provisions: a Critical Review', in N. Fonda and P. Moss (eds) *Mothers in Employment* (Middlesex: Brunel University, 1976) p. 43; S. Rothwell, 'United Kingdom', in A. Yohalem (ed.) *Women Returning to Work* (London: Francess Pinter, 1980) p. 197; Alexander, *op. cit,* p. 9; S. Robarts, *Positive Action for Women* (London: NCCL, 1981) p. 87.

27.   These have been the elements the EOC is most concerned about. See EOC, *Review of the Training Opportunities Scheme* (Manchester: EOC, 1978).

28.   Alexander, *op. cit,* p. 9.

29.   Fonda, *op. cit.*

30.   Rothwell, *op. cit.*

31.   S. Stoney and M. Reid, *Further Opportunities in Focus,* report of a project commissioned by the FEU from the National Foundation for Educational Research, 1980.

32.   T. Keil and P. Newton, 'Into Work — Continuity and Change', in R. Deem (ed.) *Schooling for Women's Work* (London: RKP, 1980); A. Cook, 'Vocational Training, the Labour Market and the Unions', in R. Steinberg Ratner (ed.) *Equal Employment Policy for Women* (Philadelphia: Temple University Press, 1980).

33.
Registered Unemployment	*1975*	*1980*
female	141,600	457,400
male	650,200	1031,500

that is a 59 per cent rise for men, a 223 per cent rise for women.
EOC, *Submission of Written Evidence to the House of Lords Select Committee on Long-Term Remedies for Unemployment* (Manchester: EOC, 1980).

34.   Some take a minimising view of the possible impact of new technology, A. Sinfield, *What Unemployment Means* (London: Martin Robertson, 1981), p. 137. Others anticipate catastrophic effects. There appears to be no exact way of calculating the possible effects of technological change, L. Hesselman and R. Spellman 'Responses to the Employment Consequences of Technological Change', paper given to the Production Studies Group Conference on the Employment Consequences of Technological Change, September 1980. However, there is a consensus that it is areas of female employment that will be worst hit. J. Gershuny, 'Technical Innovation and Women's Work in the EEC: A Medium-Term Perspective', mimeograph (EEC Seminar on Women's Employment

Prospects, Manchester, May 1980). E. Bird, *Information technology in the office: the impact on women's jobs.* (Manchester: Equal Opportunities Commission, 1980).

35. J. Fawkes, 'Breaking the Mould', *The Guardian*, December 16, 1981.
36. MSC, *Young People and Work* (Holland Report) (London: MSC, 1977).
37. Between 1972 and 1977, the year of the report, the number of unemployed 16—17 year olds had risen 120 per cent compared to an overall rise of 45 per cent in unemployment.
38. MSC, *Young People and Work* (London: MSC, 1977), p. 7.
39. G. Holland, 'The Youth Opportunities Programme', *Trends in Education,* Summer, 1979.
40. A typology of this new definition of skills is available in Schools Council Discussion Document, *Skills for Employment 1980.*
41. *TES*, 22 October 1976, 'What the PM said'.
42. After that three clear directions for future development emerged. The first dealt with vocational preparation for the employed. See DES, *A Better Start in Working Life,* Consultative Paper (London: HMSO, 1979). The second dealt with schools and work. See *Education in schools: a Consultative Document,* Cmnd. 6869 (London: HMSO, 1977). The third dealt with the area of training. An overview of the latter two was provided in DES, *16—18, Education and Training for the 16—18 year olds: a Consultative Paper* (London: HMSO, 1978).
43. A major European Communities Action Programme was launched in 1976 by a resolution of Council and the Ministers of Education meeting in Council. It included pilot projects, reports on common themes, study visits and workshops, statistical guidelines and information arrangements. The European Social Fund has also been changed to provide assistance in this area.
44. MSC, *Opportunities for Girls and Women in the MSC Special Programmes for the Unemployed* (London: MSC, 1979).
45. MSC, *Annual Report 1978—9* (London: MSC, 1980).
46. MSC, *Review of the Second Year of Special Programmes* (London: MSC, 1980), p. 7.
47. S. Green, 'The Employer's Attitude to Working Mothers', in N. Fonda and P. Moss (eds) *Mothers in Employment* (Middlesex: Brunel University, 1976). MSC, *Opportunities for Girls and Women in the MSC Special Programmes for the Unemployed* (London: MSC, 1979).

PART THREE

The Domestic Sphere

Part Three is concerned with some of the ways in which women's position and experience is structured by the form of the family in our society. One important issue for feminists has been that of questioning commonsense assumptions about the 'naturalness' of the family form as we know it and how far the family is socially constructed, for instance, by the operations of the state. In the first article in this section, therefore, Felicity Edholm takes on board this notion of 'naturalness' by a cross-cultural examination of kinship, marriage practices and child—adult relationships. The ways in which marriage and homemaking are organized in our culture is taken up in the next article in which Lee Comer argues that monogamy and marriage can actually be destructive forces and a major source of women's oppression. This viewpoint is highlighted by Rebecca and Russell Dobash who provide evidence from their research on the ways in which women may be subject to violent assault within the marital relationship. A related topic is that of family law and Julia Brophy and Carol Smart's article considers whether women are its protected and 'spoilt darlings' or, on the contrary, have their dependence on men enforced by *legal* conceptions of appropriate family structures. A further area of concern within feminist debate is the way in which women have been seen as being primarily responsible for housework and childcare. The first of these issues is covered in the article by Christine Bose who discusses whether or not the development of new technology in the home has been liberating for women. This selection of readings on the family and women's position within it is concluded by a piece from Adrienne Rich on the experience of motherhood. This is somewhat distinctive in style compared to many of the readings, being autobiographical in form, as well as more subjective and experiential in content.

3.1   The unnatural family

FELICITY EDHOLM

A recent anthropological text book defines the family as 'a cluster of positions to and through which an individual traces crucial kinship links, particularly links with others which give him/her rights and positions, etc.' (Keesing 1976, p. 292). It is further emphasized that the family is not a necessary social group in either social or economic terms, and that households and families are not identical, similarly bound units. This definition seems to have little to do with any of the elements that we commonly assume to be central to the kinds of family with which we are familiar. There is no mention of gender, none of co-residential units, of domesticity, of marriage or sexual relations. We are only given the idea of rights and positions, and the mystification of 'crucial kinship links' related to these. What, then, has happened to what we commonly conceive of as the family? Why are we given such a removed definition? What are these kinship links?

Anthropologists, in their attempt to understand the ways in which societies other than their own function, have inevitably constructed unfamiliar social relations in terms of those with which they are familiar; they have developed conceptual tools which have been formulated from within the constraints of their own culture, which inevitably relate to their own world.

It was, and still is, widely argued that some form of the family, and, in some cases, of the nuclear family, was universal, and was found in all societies. Only recently has this accepted wisdom been challenged and it has still not been dislodged. One major reason for its resilience in anthropology, apart from the crucial political, economic and ideological significance of the family in the nineteenth and twentieth century western world, is that groups very similar to those which we identify as the family do exist in the majority of societies known to anthropologists. Furthermore, anthropologists have tended to assume that an adequate explanatory definition of any given social or cultural trait can be extended to similar traits in other cultures. But as one anthropologist has commented: 'because the family seems to be the predominant unit

Specially commissioned for this volume

we must not be bemused into thinking that it is the 'natural' or 'basic' one' (Fox 1967, p. 38).

We have to look similarly at the crucial exceptions, to re-examine the seemingly familiar, family-like groups, to question the given assumptions about human relations and social forms that we almost inevitably have. In the light of the new self-consciousness about the dangers of generalization, when all-embracing definitions are given they now tend, as the already quoted definition of the family demonstrates, to become minimalized and abstracted to the point of identifying no immediately recognizable social form. Definitions are now guidelines and tools rather than explanations.

But what are the kinship links referred to as so crucial in the same definition? When anthropologists talk about the family, it is primarily in terms of kinship. At its simplest, kinship refers to the ties which exist between individuals who are seen as related, through birth (descent) and through mating (marriage). It is thus primarily concerned with the ways in which mating is socially organized and regulated, the ways in which parentage is assigned, attributed and recognized, descent is traced, relatives are classified, rights are transferred across generations and groups are formed. Such relationships are seen as constructed within the basic constraints and imperatives on the organization of human life; production and reproduction, mating, dependence, the need for enculturation and the life cycle. Kinship is above all concerned with relationships which are socially constructed; relatives are not born but made.

When we look at the societies studied by anthropologists and at the variation in kinship systems, it is clear that the range of social options is enormous, that the constraints on human behaviour do not produce uniformity, and that those assumptions we make about what is 'natural' in respect of fundamental human kinship relations, are profoundly challenged by the evidence from widely different societies. If we take some of these assumptions, we can then look at some anthropological data on kinship and become aware of the extent to which we are profoundly ethnocentric in our outlook.

It is usually assumed that the family, a co-residential unit containing parents and their own children, is the natural primary unit within which domestic and sexual relations and socialization will take place; that relationships between members of a family are unique and specific, and are recognizably different to relationships with individuals outside the family; that there is, at least for the early years of life, an inevitably deep and necessary dependence between a mother and her children, and that there is some sense of obligation and interdependence between those who are members of the family, particularly between parents and children, that incest taboos operate within the family unit, and that property, status and positions pass within the family. It is also usually assumed that there is considerable interdependence, both social and sexual, between men and women and that this is revealed within the family/the household.

The most critical areas of kinship to examine in order to have some understanding of the family are those which offer the greatest challenge to preconceptions and which have significant effect on the construction of kinship relations in so far as they affect the assumptions we have outlined above. Five areas will be explored: conception, incest, parent/child relations and adoption, marriage, households and residence.

Conception

The question of who our kin, our relations are is answered in numerous ways, even for the primary parent-child relation. Notions of blood ties, of biological connection, which to us seem relatively unequivocal, are highly variable. Some societies of which we have anthropological record recognize only the role of the father or of the mother in conception and procreation. The other sex is given some significance, but is not seen, for example, as providing blood . . . as having any biological connection. Only one parent is a 'relation', the other parent is not. In the Trobriand Islands, for example, it is believed that intercourse is not the cause of conception, semen is not seen as essential for conception (Malinowski 1922). Conception results from the entry of a spirit child into the womb; the male role is to 'open the passage' to the womb, through intercourse, and it is the repeated intercourse of the same partner which 'moulds' the child. A child's blood comes from its mother's side and from her siblings, her mother and mother's brother, not from the father. A child will not be related by blood to its father, but will look like its father since he has through intercourse created its form. Fathers continue after birth to have a very close and intimate relationship with their children and it is this contact which also is seen as creating the likeness, as moulding the child in his/her father's image.

Other societies recognize the crucial importance of semen in the formation of a child, but believe that it is essential for conception that either the semen of more than one man is involved — or that fertility is only possible given a mixture of different semen, thus a newly-married woman in Marind Anim society (in New Guinea) is gang-raped at marriage, and on subsequent ritual occasions (Van Baal 1966). Semen is understood as being necessary for growth throughout childhood and adolescence and elaborate male homo-sexual activities ensure that adolescent boys are in receipt of semen.

The Lakker of Burma on the other hand consider that the mother is only a container in which the child grows; she has no blood connection with her children, and children of the same mother and different fathers are not considered to be related to each other (Keesing 1976). These cases are extreme but have important implications in that they indicate not only that relations which seem to us to be self-evidently biological, are not universally seen as such. 'Natural', 'biological' relations are not inevitably those which organize human relations at a very fundamental level, since what is understood as 'biological' is socially defined and therefore is expressed in different ways.

Incest

Incest is another area of human relations which is widely discussed in terms of some kind of innate, instinctive abhorrence for sexual relations with 'close kin' and is often attributed to a subconscious realization of the genetic danger of in-breeding. (It is not uniformly accepted that in-breeding is inevitably disadvantageous.)

Incest taboos, defined as prohibitions on sexual relations between individuals socially classified as kin, as relations, are nearly universal. But the prohibition does not inevitably apply to the individuals whom we would identify as primary kin. The most dramatic exceptions to incest are found in certain royal dynasties (Egypt, Hawaii) where in-breeding (brother-sister) was enforced in order to keep the purity of the royal line, as well as in Ptolemaic and Roman Egypt where apparently father-daughter and brother-sister sexual relations were relatively common. In most other known societies, sexual relations between those socially recognized as 'biologically' related are taboo. The Trobrianders, for example, do not consider the children of one father and different mothers to be related and sexual relations between those children are thus entirely legitimate, whereas sexual relations with women who have the same mother, or whose mothers are siblings, is taboo. The Lakker of Burma do not consider that the children of the same mother have any kinship links. 'Incest' does not apply to these non-kin and sexual relations are permitted. In other societies in which, for example, the category of mother or sister is extended to include all males or females of the same generation who are descended through one parent from a common grandfather, or great-grandfather, it is frequently this whole group which is sexually unavailable. It is the social definitions of significant kinship relations that are important in defining incest rather than any concept of natural biological imperatives militating against sexual intercourse within a 'natural family unit.'

Parent/child relations: adoption

It is nearly universally accepted in all anthropological texts on the family, however prepared they are to accept the fact that the nuclear family is not ubiquitous, that 'the mother-child tie is inevitable and given', that 'the irreducible and elementary social grouping is surely the mother and her children'. This is seen as determined by the imperatives of infantile dependence and the need for breast-milk, and is also related to other psychological needs on the part both of the mother and of the child. It is in this context instructive to consider the implications of the widespread practice of adoption. In many societies, children do not live with their 'real' parents, but often stay with their mothers until some time after they have been weaned, when as they say in N. Ghana, they have 'gained sense' (at about six). However, throughout Melanesia and Polynesia, children are adopted just after weaning or, in some instances, well before — a phenomenon which is considered as absolutely acceptable. In some instances, babies are adopted and breast-fed by their adopted mother. Margaret Mead (1935) describes such a situation among the Mundugumor in New Guinea: 'even women who have never borne children are able in a few weeks, by placing the child constantly at the breast and by drinking plenty of coconut milk, to produce enough, or nearly enough milk to rear the child, which is suckled by other women for the first few weeks after adoption' (p. 193).

In Tahiti, young women often have one or two children before they are considered, or consider themselves to be, ready for an approved and stable relationship. It is considered perfectly acceptable for the children of this young woman to be given to her parents or other close kin for adoption, while she is freed to continue what is seen as the 'business of adolescence'. The girl can decide what her relationship to the children will be, but there is no sense in which she is forced into 'motherhood' because of having had a baby; 'motherhood' in such a situation can be seen as a status reached by women at a particular stage of development, as involving a psychological and social readiness, not something inevitably attached to the physical bearing of children.

In nearly all the societies in which adoption of this kind is common, (and where anthropologists have discussed it at length), it is clear that the adopted child will still maintain contact with its 'natural' parents, and will know what their relationship to each other is. A Tahitian man (himself adopted) was asked about children's relations to their parents: 'if you are not adopted you are grateful to your biological mother, because she gave birth to you. On the other hand, when you are taken in your infancy by somebody it isn't worthwhile to think anymore about your mother. The woman who took you is just the same as your biological mother. Your gratitude is because you were an infant and you were taken' (in Levy 1970, p. 81). One of the interesting aspects of this definition of the relationship between parents and children is the sense in which it is seen as so critically dependent on gratitude — from child to parent — since it is recognized that adults choose to bring up the child, and do not have a necessary sense of responsibility, or instinctive love for it. The implications of such attitudes for all social relations are clearly considerable.

Again, in most of these societies it is agreed that the adopted child is more the foster father's than the true father's. Margaret Mead (1935), writing on the Manus of New Guinea, describes the very considerable personality similarities she saw between fathers and their adopted children. The relationship between fathers and children is extremely close, fathers feed and spend a lot of time with their children. The 'likeness', of which the Trobriand Islanders speak, between father and children, is also, in many other Melanesian and Polynesian societies, seen as due to the close personal contact between them. The father-child relationship is seen as a crucial, and above all, as a social relationship; one which is created by social contact, not one which exists because of a 'blood relationship'. In Tahiti, it is considered an ultimate shame for adopted children to leave the house of their adopted parents since the relationship between those who have lived together and who have grown 'familiar' ('matau') with each other (the essential ingredient for all good relations) is seen as inevitably far closer than that between biological 'natural' parents.

It is instructive in this context to consider the United Nations' study on the *Adoption of Children in Western Nations*, in which it is argued that in the West, society attributes 'a sacred character . . . to family bonds' (Levy 1970). The extent to which this attribution is ideological is even more evident once we have understood the extraordinary narrowness of our definitions of familiar 'natural' relations.

Marriage

It has been claimed that some form of marriage is found in all human societies. The definitions of marriage, however, again give some indication of the kind of complexity that is involved in the attempt to provide universals. One famous definition by Goodenough (1970) defines marriage in these terms:

> Marriage is a transaction and resulting contract in which a person (male or female, corporate or individual, in person or by proxy) establishes a continuing claim to the right of sexual access to a woman — this right having priority over rights of sexual access others currently have, or may subsequently acquire, in relation to her (except in a similar transaction) until the contract resulting from the transaction is terminated, and in which the woman involved is eligible to bear children (pp. 12—13).

Other definitions stress above all the significance of marriage in determining parentage — in allocating children to different groups. The definitions have to be understood in relation to the kinds of social arrangements which are entirely inconsistent within our notions of marriage.

The Nayar of Northern India provide one of the most problematic cases of 'marriage' (Schneider and Gough 1972). The basic social group among the Nayar is the Taravad, a unit composed of men and women descended through the female line from a common ancestress. Thus it is brothers and sisters, mothers and children who cohabit. A child becomes a member of the mother's Taravad, not the father's. Nayar girls were involved, before they reached puberty, in a formal ritual with a man from an equivalent caste to her own, and then was able to take as many lovers as she wished; the 'husband' — the man who had been involved in the ritual — only had a very minimal ritual attachment to his 'wife', although he too could be one of her lovers. (Not all lovers came from the same caste.) Husbands and fathers, in such a context, are entirely peripheral to the domestic life of their wives and children — and never cohabit.

Among the Nuer of the Nile Basin, one of the most common forms of marriage is what has been called 'ghost' marriage (the anthropologist Evans-Pritchard who worked among the Nuer estimates that nearly 50 per cent of all marriages correspond to this form). Ghost marriage refers to the situation in which a man dies, unmarried, or with no children of his own. If this happens, a close kinsman (related to him through his father's line) will marry a wife 'to his name' and children born of this union will be seen as the dead man's children. A man who has been involved in marrying in this way and bearing children for another man will, when he dies and if he has not contracted a second marriage in his own name — only possible if his wife dies — have to become in his turn a proxy father and a subsequent ghost marriage will be contracted. If a married man dies, his widow then should ideally be married by a brother or close male kin of the dead man and again, children borne of this union will be considered to be those of the dead man, not of the living husband.

The Nuer also have another contractual form of 'marriage' in which an old and important, usually barren, woman may marry a younger woman. Nuer marriages are contracted through the 'husband' giving the bride price (cattle) to the wife's group. The children born to this younger woman will then, for particular purposes, such as inheritance, be considered as the children of the old woman, their 'father'. Marriages of this kind indicate the importance among the Nuer both of becoming a parent, or rather a male parent, in order to become an ancestor — for only 'fathers' with offspring are remembered and have status as ancestors — and also of the inheritance of property. Nuer marriages also demonstrate that the marriage indicates a contract between the group of related 'men' who are seen in some sense as equivalents and a woman married to one of them.

These two widely differing examples illustrate one of the other critical elements in the relations defined by marriage: the difference between the 'legally' recognized father or mother and the person who was involved in conception, or birth. In both the cases cited above, the person we would see as the father, he who had impregnated the woman, is not given any social recognition at all, it is the person, not necessarily male, who is given the social position of father who is recognized through the ritual of 'marriage'. The two males are distinguished in anthropological literature thus: the biological father is the *genitor*, the biological mother the *genetrix*, the 'socially' recognized father the *pater*, the socially recognized mother the *mater*. In cases of polyandry — where a woman is 'married' to more than one man, as is the case among the Toda, one of the men will perform a ritual which makes him the pater, and the child and subsequent children, will belong to his group. In some of the societies (very few) in which polyandry exists, it is a group of brothers who share a wife. In some cases a group of sisters will be 'married' to a group of brothers, and in such situations the children belong to the family group. Individual paternity is thus socially less important than membership of a family unit.

Paternity is of crucial importance in societies in which status, positions and property are transmitted through the male line. The notion of the group, related through the male line, can in some societies have such force that sexual relations between a woman and any male from the same group as that into which she was born (and such a group can include a considerable number of individuals, all the descendents of a common great-grandfather, for example) are regarded as incestuous. We can see with the example of the Nayar (although the Nayar do constitute an exceptional case) that paternity has far less social significance if all important social attributes are gained through inheritance down the female line. (It is important to recognize that such a system of inheritance does not imply that men are marginalized in such an inheritance system, but that it is brothers rather than husbands who are the significant social males.)

Even in situations in which the attribution of paternity is so important we cannot simply assume that the concepts of legitimacy and illegitimacy are clearcut. In many societies of this kind there are all kinds of arrangements for the allocation of children — which are not wholly dependent on the concepts of the determining factor of parenthood.

Household and residence

Our conception of what constitutes the family is dependent not only on what we have called kinship ties but equally in terms of residence, domestic units or households. Given the range of kinship relations that we have briefly explored, it is inevitable that a wide range of different residential patterns exist. Moreover, households will not only be composed of individuals whose relations to each other are based on different criteria, but the size and composition over time of such households will vary, as will their relation to production, to other units and to social positions.

There are three basic forms of residence as isolated by anthropologists: vivilocal, where a married couple and their children live with the kin of the husband; matrilocal, where the couple live with the kin of the wife; and neolocal where the couple live independently of either group of kin. This scheme is however further complicated by the fact that in many societies in which descent is traced through the female line (matrilineal societies), the children might initially live with the mother and father with the father's kin, and then later move to live with their mother's kin; in other words, with their mother's brothers, those from whom they will inherit property, status or position. Often in such societies (such as the Trobriand Islanders) daughters never live with their mother's kin — they stay with their father's until they marry and then move to their husband's kin. The complication of residence patterns is considerable — one of the factors which these different patterns demonstrate is that households as units of parents and their children are not a necessary or permanent social arrangement.

The extent to which individuals are identified with any one household, both as children and as adults, varies considerably. In most matrilineal societies men will circulate and often a man will split his available time and space between kin and conjugal roles. In some societies of this kind, men will live alternately in two places, or will frequently visit two different units, or move at different stages from one to another. In the case of the polyandrous Toda, a woman married to different men will circulate between their different households (Rivers 1906). Children similarly will shift residence in many societies — in many instances, because of the 'institution' of fostering whereby from the age of about 5, children are sent to be brought up by non-parental kin. Claims to have a foster child are formally expressed as the rights held by a man in his sister's children — and by a woman in her brother's daughter — but it is much more extensive than this, and there are many instances of children living with their grandparents' (Goody 1969, p. 192). Households then can often be extremely fluid units, with shifting membership.

In most of the known societies of the world, monogamy is the exception rather than the rule. Some anthropologists claim that over 90 per cent of the world's cultures involve plural polygamous marriages. We have already referred to polyandry, one woman with several husbands, but by far the most common form of polygamy is polygyny — one man with several wives.

In some polygynous societies, almost invariably those in which descent is traced through the male line, households consist of a series of relatively self-contained living quarters, in which a man and his wives, each with her own children, live, one wife in a relatively autonomous domestic unit. In others, domestic arrangements are dominated by a group of brothers, with their wives and their offspring.

The domestic existence of each smaller unit within such a group is determined by the existence of the larger group and is ultimately dependent on the authority of those males who are in control of the unit as a whole.

In such situations it is again difficult to arrive at a useful definition of such a unit if we are concerned to consider households purely as kinship entities. Is such a mother and children unit an entity, or is it a sub-household within a much larger household?

The Tiv of Nigeria provide an example of this latter form of 'household'. Tiv kinship groups live in compounds, a circular arrangement of huts and granaries, in the centre of which is an open space — 'the centre of Tiv family life'. The compound head is the senior, eldest man. He settles disputes, supervises the productive activities of the group and controls magic. His several wives live in separate units in the compound which is also inhabited by his junior children, unmarried daughters and married sons and their families. In addition, there may be a younger brother and his family, and/or outsiders.

As is argued by the anthropologists involved, while in a sense each wife who has a separate hut and her children constitute a separate domestic unit, the larger compound group — a patrilineal extended family augmented by outsiders — is the central domestic unit of everyday Tiv life and of collective economic enterprise (Bohannon and Bohannon 1968).

It is only when we consider the household in terms of this latter — its productive capacities — that we can make sense of this kind of domestic unit usually found in agricultural communities. Households and domestic units are not only an arrangement of people related to each other through parent-child ties, but in societies such as the Tiv, they form units of production and have to be analysed and understood as such.

Kinship ties have thus been seen by some anthropologists as constituting the relation of production. The Tiv compound, for example, is essentially a means of reuniting and controlling necessary labour, both productive and reproductive. Clearly households in many societies have to be analysed as units of production and consumption, and as providers of labour. The form of the household must therefore be analysed in terms of the economic structure of the society as a whole and cannot simply be seen as a unit containing the 'family', essentially defining sets of affective relations. Precisely because the western ideal of the nuclear family is so ideologically and spatially separated from wage labour, the recognition of the profound economic significance of household formation in other societies has posed considerable problems for anthropologists. It has been even more difficult for western sociologists to re-examine the economic role of the family within their own society in the light of the understanding gained through anthropological analysis.

Polygynous households of the kind described above are common in Africa, south of the Sahara, and however different their form, they are usually crucial productive units. In New Guinea, very different domestic arrangements exist and these cannot be analysed in terms of the same economic determinants. In Marind Anim and many other New Guinea societies, domestic organization constructs very considerable separation between men and women. Special men's houses provide the focal point for all male life (often including sleeping and eating) and there are often stringent taboos on women having access to such houses and, in general, on contact between males and females.

Conclusion

The family, particularly the nuclear family, can be seen, through comparative analysis, as just one very specific means of organizing the relations between parents and children, males and females. It is not, as has so often been claimed, some kind of 'natural' instinctive and 'sacred' unit. Even the bond between mothers and their own children, which is seen in almost mystic terms as the fundamental biologically-determined relationship, can be seen as far less important than we are generally led to believe. Universal definitions of human relations must be constantly questioned and the whole notion of the 'natural' must, in terms of human relations, be challenged, and the 'unnatural' — in these terms the social construction of relationships — must be fully recognized.

References

Bohannon, P. and Bohannon, L. (1968) *Tiv Economy,* North Western University Press.

Carroll, V. (1970) *Adoption in Eastern Oceania,* The University of Hawaii Press.

Evans-Pritchard, E.E. (1951) *Kinship and Marriage among the Nuer,* Oxford, The Clarendon Press.

Fox, R. (1967) *Kinship and Marriage*, Harmondsworth, Pelican.

Goodenough, W.H. (1970) *Description and Comparison in Cultural Anthropology,* Chicago, Aldine Publishing Co.

Goody, J.R. (1969) *Comparative Studies in Kinship,* London, Routledge and Kegan Paul.

Keesing, R.M. (1976) *Cultural Anthropology, a contemporary perspective,* New York, Hunt, Rinehart & Winston.

Levy, R.I. (1970) *Tahitian Adoption as a Psychological Message,* in Carroll, V.

Malinowski, B. (1922) *Argonauts of the Western Society,* London, Routledge and Kegan Paul.

Mead, M. (1935) *Sex and Temperament in Three Primitive Societies,* New York, William Morrow & Co. Inc.

Rivers, W.H.R. (1906) *The Todas,* New York, McMillan.

Schneider, D. and Gough, E.K. (1972) *Matrilineal Kinship,* Berkeley, University of California Press.

Van Baal, J. (1966) *The Dema, Description and Analysis of Culture (South New Guinea)*, The Hague, Martinius Nijhoff.

3.2 Monogamy, marriage and economic dependence

LEE COMER

The strongest strand in the connecting thread [between all families, what makes one family substantially like every other family,] is monogamy — one man and one woman loving each other in an intensively exclusive way, and if not, then at least living together. We have no choice but to believe in monogamy, even when we don't or can't practise it. Within the confines of the monogamous principle, it is surprising how many contradictions can be tolerated but how little they affect the principle. [. . .]

The origins of the ideal of romantic love have been well documented. That love and marriage were once anathema to each other, that love could only flourish when it departed from convention is well known. Marriage was a contractual arrangement, largely confined to the propertied classes, and was based on suitability and financial considerations. The partners were expected to respect each other and, hopefully, be compatible. It is not my purpose here to trace the history of romantic love but merely to restate a commonplace. Where once marriage for love was the exception, it is now the rule. In theory, at least, for we are not out of the wood yet. On one level we pity women from other cultures who, despite their education in this country, must still submit to arranged marriages to men they may never have met. On another level, the romantic imagination is still caught by the flowering of unpermitted love, love which flouts convention and is tinged with tragedy. [. . .]

Perhaps not everyone is completely taken in by the ideal. For there is a tacit acceptance that romantic love can perish within the confines of mortgages and domesticity, and that to tie it down is to squeeze the spirit out of it. Adolescents look at their parents, neighbours and family friends and lament the dearth of happy marriages, swearing either that they will never marry or that they will wait until they really do find Mr. or Mrs. Right. They're going to make dead sure that they don't end up like their parents. By the time they're in their twenties, their ideals may have taken a

Source: Comer, L. (1974) *Wedlocked Women*, Feminist Books, Leeds

battering. Apparently, the only alternative is loneliness, or promiscuity, social exclusion and insecurity, all of which closes in on them so fast that marriage appears the only sensible solution, even if Mr. Right was a little wrong. [. . .]

Is it really as bleak as that? Is monogamy inevitably destructive? Given real *choices* I believe it need not be but under the weight of social pressure and expectation, it almost always is. Because monogamy, which leads to responsible marriage, is a fundamental form of *social control*. To be sure, there are many couples who have managed to salvage the best from the situation they have been pressured into. The lifelong union of a man and a woman may well result in a happiness which touches all those with whom they have contact. But it is rare and it is always a testament to their resilience. If we were not conditioned into the monogamous principle, if many more expressions of love and affection were permissible in a more fluid atmosphere of what is, and is not, acceptable (for instance, open relationships between people of the same sex, or with more than one person at a time), then monogamy, instead of being a safety net for loneliness, would merely be one of many alternatives which people might well choose *freely*.

In the absence of real choice, monogamous love is institutional-ized [in marriage and] . . . we don't see that the expectations — the baggage that we all bring to marriage — are impossible to live up to. If we didn't expect to find personal salvation through married love we wouldn't be disappointed in not finding it.

But marriage itself must remain above suspicion. [. . .]

Marriage is the first and basic model of the division of labour and power between the sexes, the legalized sanction whereby society justifies the public separation of men from women by throwing them together in private. Within the institution of marriage, men and women are supposed to resolve the conflicts of the public domain, where the power, education and money are so massively weighted in favour of men — where men treat women as inferiors with impunity, giving orders to waitresses, secretaries, barmaids, cleaners and shop assistants alike, and where the commercial bombardment of nipples and thighs perpetuates the sexual gulf between men and women. Is a man who works on a building site, spending much of his day leering at women passers-by, to come home and treat his wife as an equal? Is a man who gives orders to women at work as habitually and as effortlessly as he pees, supposed to, as soon as he closes his front door, regard his wife as an equal? Is a woman who has deferred to her boss's judgment all day at work supposed not to defer to her husband's? Is a woman who has been conditioned to be a passive sexual object, receiving and occasionally deflecting men's attentions, suddenly supposed to take the sexual initiative when she is married? Is a woman who works all day in close contact with other women in the typing pool, the shop or factory, supposed to reserve her innermost thoughts for her husband whom she sees for only a few hours a day? Are we supposed to neglect the intimacy of the work place in order to concentrate on the home?

Without marriage as the private safety valve for public conflict, women would not tolerate the injustices of unequal pay, power and education and the degradation of sexual objectification — all the things in fact, which make up the sum total of their usefulness. Without marriage, human sexuality would not have to submit to social and physical restraint. Marriage is presented as society's panacea for these ills. Marriage does not solve these conflicts but the fact that it contains them, is what makes it such an effective and useful form of social control.

Any glance round society reveals that the sexes are placed on opposite poles with an enormous chasm of oppression, degradation and misunderstanding generated to keep them apart. Out of this, marriage plucks one woman and one man, ties them together with 'love' and asserts that they shall live in harmony and that they shall, for the rest of their lives, bridge that chasm with a mixture of betrayal, sex, affection, deceit and illusion. While marriage is supposed to heal the rift and while women, out of loyalty and affection, claim that it does indeed lead to harmony (I'm writing to tell you I've got the most considerate husband in the world — considerate?), they are eager players in the game. Like the lone woman on a board of directors, marriage is society's tokenism. It's easy to rationalize the continued division of labour, power and money between men and women by pointing to marriage and suggesting that at *heart*, that is, in the private emotions which have no consequence on the outside world where the game is actually played, relations between men and women are just fine and dandy. From the sociologists' angle, the further apart men and women are in terms of work, education, personal goals and so on, the more popular is marriage. (People are marrying younger, living longer and most divorced people re-marry.) Because there is no real evidence for 'the battle of the sexes' it is assumed not to exist.

There is a battle but it takes place without spectators. Within marriage, it is women's duty to heal the rift between the sexes, to gloss over the differences with love and judgment and a few beguiling tactics. And because it is an impossible task and because failure in it reflects badly on her, she struggles alone and unnoticed. [. . .]

Magically, the power that is vested in men, in all spheres of life, is somehow supposed to be neutralized in marriage, thereby justifying its legitimacy outside the home.

As long as a man is seen to exert influence in his work and his social life, he can smile with the best of them and say that, at home, his wife wears the pants. It costs him nothing to defer to his wife's authority in the home because he has ample compensation outside it and, in any case, it keeps the little thing happy! And, in the total power game, the home is but a tiny part, which any generous and self-respecting man can relinquish. For the man at the bottom of the social ladder the situation is rather different. He is reduced to claiming authority merely on the basis of male authority, a situation which prevails and is condoned everywhere. The Newsomes and other researchers have found that the lower down the social scale, the more rigid are the attitudes towards women's domestic role — i.e. the claim for male superiority. These attitudes are less rigid amongst the professional classes but there is still a great discrepancy between what is preached and what is practised. [. . .]

'Professional men demand deference because of their work. This enables them to accept the doctrine of equality without having to live it' (Gillespie 1972). [. . .] The middle-class man has the same access to power, which accrues to him *as a male*, as does his working-class counterpart. But with great magnanimity he can turn to his wife and maintain that he isn't going to use it. And she is trapped for she can't complain about him dominating her like other men dominate their wives. She can only complain about the amount of time he spends on his work, his neglect of the children, their lack of communication, his boring business friends which she must entertain and the fact that he is always the centre of attention. But she can't say that he is consciously *dominating* her. To the outside world they would both genuinely maintain that theirs is a marriage of equals but, in areas of importance, she is as powerless as she ever was.

All women wage private struggles against male power. Mostly, they can only take the crumbs that men offer and if the battle-ground is over who is going to do the washing up or where they will go for their holidays (and such matters are usually the defining limit of female power), then that is where the struggle will take place. But it is always a partial struggle, for women can never wrest from men the right to determine where the battlegound will be. That is always men's automatic privilege, the nucleus of their hidden power which they can call upon at will. Whether they resort to their maleness, physical strengths and threats or the demands of their work, the result is the same.

To their credit, some men have tried to equalize the stakes. They acknowledge the symptoms of the struggle, locating them at the kitchen sink, without ever seeing the disease itself. They see that their arguments for avoiding housework and childcare are false and that their wife's work is probably harder and more arduous than their own (this is especially true of middle-class men), so they have rolled up their sleeves and 'helped' in the house but in so doing they have invaded the woman's only sphere of influence. Gradually she sees her tiny corner of autonomy ebbing away. For by participating in the home, men bring to their activity their whole apparatus of male prerogative. He can't just get on with the work. He has to have a *say* in it as well. However eager he may be to help in the home, he is still notably reluctant to relinquish his economic and sexual advantage over women.

The man may try to dispense with his overt authority but he can hardly reject the power, so integral is it to the whole marital structure. As Dair Gillespie (1972) points out:

> He is the economic head of the joint household and hence represents it in the view of society. She takes his name and belongs to his class. She follows him where his work calls to determine their place of residence. Their lives are geared to the daily, weekly, annual rhythms of his life.

Equality in marriage, the neutralization of male power, is usually taken to mean that the partners share in decisions about their future, their home and their children. But the authority of the male does not hinge merely on decisions. A couple may decide on their children's education only once or twice in their married life. Similarly, if they decide to move house or change jobs or if they make three or four major joint decisions together, that is no index of equality. [. . .]

It is simply that the patriarchal [family] has taken a more subtle turn — has, in fact, gone underground. [. . .]

> [. . .] it is clear that for a wife to gain even a modicum of power in the marital relationship, she must gain it from external sources, i.e. she must participate in the work force, her education must be superior to that of her husband, and her participation in organizations must excel his. Equality of resources leaves the power in the hands of the husband. The equalitarian marriage as a norm is a myth. Under some conditions individual women gain power *vis-à-vis* their husbands, but more power is not equal power. Equal power women do not have. Equal power women

will not get so long as the present socioeconomic system remains [Gillespie 1972].

The struggle for ascendancy, the fruitless attempts to reconcile the differences, the silent hurts and the wells of resentment are the cracks in every marriage structure which love merely papers over. And when the paper wears thin to reveal the widening cracks, we have, we are told, no-one but ourselves to blame. Imprisoned in our bedrooms and kitchens, we attribute our discontents to the shortcomings of our partner, the bad influences of our mothers or our own private hang-ups which prevent us from coming to terms with marriage. Women will say that they can't communicate with their husbands and men will say that their wives 'don't understand them' and the same situation is played out over and over again in a million households where the story is the same and only the faces are different. The man will clench his teeth and kick the furniture and the woman will bite back her tears and when finally, at bed time, they make it up, the woman will tearfully admit that the children have made her edgy and tired and really it was just a petty quarrel and she promises not to let the 'little things' get her down again, and the man says he will try not to get so angry but he is so pushed at work and does need to relax at home, so if she could just be a little more welcoming when he comes home and not bother him too much with her little problems . . . . and so they fall asleep, in a fragile blanket of love which is stretched past breaking point and which will split open again in a week or a month to reveal another aching crack which they must again strain to close.

The bridge that marriage constructs across the chasm between the sexes is an illusion which most of us are constrained to enact as reality. By disguising the division between the sexes which this society perpetrates, it reinforces the apartheid of public life and removes the battleground to a 'safe' and insignificant place — the home. Our private lives may be disrupted and in many cases, utterly destroyed by it, but all the while the wheels of the system will keep on turning smoothly. And as long as men and women row in private or submerge their differences in silence while putting on a married face to the outside world, the chasm between men and women will continue to serve the society that created it. [. . .]

The suggestion that housewives should be paid for their work offends many people. To pay housewives, paradoxically enough, cheapens their work. When it is reduced to an economic trans-action with all that that implies — definition of work, hours, terms of contract and so on — it brings the hard outside world into the home. In addition, the stranglehold that her labour of love has on her would be released and she would occupy the same economic ground as her husband. Their separate and irreconcilable worlds would merge, depriving the man of his role as provider and severely curtailing his economic power over her. To introduce payment for the woman's work is to taint love with cash. [. . .]

The ethos which surrounds the woman's motivations, imprisoning her in its assumptions, disguises her oppression by elevating it. The prevailing ideology ensures that she will continue to work without reward by entrusting her with motives which transcend economic 'greed'. She is thus not at the bottom of society's pile but, strangely, at the top. She may be denied and deprived of the means of self-realization, of a right to an independent life of her own, of even enough money to take herself out to the cinema once in a while, of enjoying any of the amenities offered to the rest of society (including even her own children whose pocket money is their own to do with as they like), of self respect ('he'd never refuse but I always have to ask for money, even if it's only for tights or something') but, with all this, goes the compensatory knowledge that she holds a special place. If the woman's work and the value attached to it were held in equal esteem as her husband's, there would be no need to place her on a pedestal. It is contempt that puts her there and keeps her there and many women, through long material deprivation, come to realize it, just as they realize that the pedestal they occupy isn't worth the illusions it is built on.

The love that women work for is not the pure selfless kind that men would like to think it is. It is borne of necessity. It's the kind of love which the small tenant farmer feels for his landlord — a sort of forelock touching acquiescence. Because love can only be given under two conditions — genuine equality and where the person who loves is not deprived herself. But with marriage as a system of male patronage in which the man receives the woman's labour in exchange for providing her with a roof over her head, food and clothing, the parallel with colonial slavery is unmistakable.

Oh, but it isn't like that! Isn't it? When the love that so thinly disguises the economics dies, it is like that, which is why so many women will defend their situation very strongly. And because they are trained to find satisfaction in disillusion, they may even boast of their position. ('Oh, he'd never let me go out to work! He says he earns enough for both of us.')

A terrible silence hangs over 'the central horror of the dependence of women on men'. There is a wide-spread and deep-seated belief that housewives are very privileged to be supported by men, and any suggestion that they aren't is instantly howled down. [. . .] How dare they bite the hand that feeds them? And any pity that might have been extended is wiped out. Women must be seen to be grateful. If there is any pity to be shed it is men who receive it for they are the ones who are burdened with working to support women and children; but to push the point a little, do we feel sorry for the slave owner because he has to feed and clothe the slaves who work for him or do we pity the slave for his loss of freedom and economic independence? The silence on the subject is the silence of guilt. [. . .]

The silence on the subject is also due, in part, to the assumption that women are not dependent on men, that in fact the money he earns belongs to them both. The concept of 'our money', with each partner having equal access to it, is a comfortable middle-class myth. According to Hannah Gavron's (1966) study, it isn't even practised by the majority of the middle class anyway. She found that over half her sample of middle-class housewives were given allowances with which they had to make do. Only 44 per cent of these housewives were in the position of 'drawing on money when they needed it'. And of course if the woman does not know what her husband earns, there can be no question of her sharing it. A survey carried out by the Child Poverty Action Group found that 'husbands who earn more than £5,000 a year are as likely to fail to tell their wives how much they get as working-class men'.[1] Hannah Gavron found that over three quarters (77 per cent) of the working-class housewives in her sample had a 'regular amount from their husband's pay packet each week and tried to make do with it'. Only 23 per cent 'just shared it out as needed'. It is clear that equal sharing of the husband's income, with the wife's free and independent access to it, is the exception and not the rule.

But the exception proves nothing. What I want to suggest is that the shared money ideal is precisely that, an ideal. In the modern marriage, which the sociologists assume to be the norm, the equality of the partners is as much of a sop to women as the equality of their access to money. Whatever arrangements and tactics are used to tart up the situation, nothing can effectively disguise her dependency.

> . . . I am getting more and more dissatisfied with being financially dependent, not because my husband has made any difficulties about money or considered my 'contribution' in caring for the children as unimportant, but because I *feel* dependent.

For a long time I made the mistake of assuming, along with everyone else, that when people asserted that in their marriage there was no distinction between his money and 'our' money, that this was true for all couples who subscribed to the ideal. It was only when I thought back over my own experience of such a situation, and when I questioned more deeply, that the politics of financial dependence became apparent. Loyalty and self negation are powerful agents of economic oppression. If any sociologist or interested person had inquired into the financial arrangements in my marriage I would have lain my hand on my heart and sworn that we shared money equally. And, in theory, I would have been telling the truth. In fact, it would no more have occurred to me to spend money on anything but housekeeping as it would for him not to.

Behind the ideal, subscribed to only by a minority of the population anyway, lies the reality, a reality in which the husband can spend his money howsoever he wishes but a reality in which she must hesitate before obliquely suggesting that she really does need a new winter coat, a reality in which she makes do because to do otherwise is to encroach too far into the man's rights. The only money she spends guiltlessly is on food for the family and clothes for the children.[2]

The myth of 'our money' is further emphasized by the ideal of joint discussion. It sounds nice in theory but what it amounts to in practice is the means whereby the woman talks her husband round, gets his *permission* to buy a washing machine, vacuum cleaner and so on. Joint discussion is not evidence of increased mutuality in marriage but merely an acknowledgement that the wife may have some say in how best to spend money on the home. He apportions it and she spends it *on his behalf*. But do they honestly sit down together and discuss how he shall spend money that is not meant for the house? Do they weigh up the relative merits of £2 on a horse or a pub crawl? And if they do, doesn't the ideal of joint discussion lose some of its rosy hue?

Traditionally, the man is supposed to have a better grasp of (non-domestic) financial problems and he can therefore reprimand her for her 'extravagance'. Perhaps she bought herself a new pair of boots for the winter or a gadget that would ease her housework. But would she dare to question whether he really needed a new fishing rod or whether they could really afford for him to go to Wembley? This double standard operates in the majority of homes and anyone who doubts it should be asked to imagine what husband, however wealthy, would fail to ask his wife how much those boots cost?

The woman's economic subordination is matched by her husband's anger and indignance. Righteously he asserts that he gives her everything she needs. He works his balls off all week so that she can have the things she wants and if he isn't entitled to some enjoyment, just what is he entitled to? And the woman, hurt and defeated by such logic, retreats behind a wall of self effacement. All her lines of attack are circumscribed by her dependent position. She, too, works all week, but it doesn't merit the label work because it isn't paid. And, without a moment's hesitation, he can sweep away the nonsense of shared money, merely by stating the truth. He earns it and he *gives* it to her. Faced with the facts, she can only nag or whimper. Such are the politics of economic dependence.

Housewives, old age pensioners, students, social security claimants and single mothers have a lot in common. They are all supposed to undergo some magical reduction in their economic needs at certain crucial points in their lives. People on Social Security form themselves into Unions to fight for better rights, and pensioners, despite the pious statements of politicians, are recognized as an economically deprived section of the community, but housewives are supposed to thrive on having no money of their own. Until very recently, the wife had no legal right to her own money if she hadn't earned it herself. Even if she had managed to save a little each week from her housekeeping, that money still rightfully belonged to her husband. This law has only recently been amended so that now the housewife is entitled to *half* of what she's saved from the housekeeping. In the hard facts of people's lives, this is all very much in evidence.

But the evidence is disguised by the apparatus of women's oppression which asserts that women don't need money for themselves. And the degree to which they internalize their oppression is evident from their statements on the subject: 'I wouldn't dream of spending money on myself'. [. . .] 'You get a lot more sensible about money when you're married. I don't go wasting it on myself'.

No other section of the community turns up its nose at money. The husband allows his wife just enough to feed the family, thereby keeping the lid firmly down on the devil in her that will rise up at the first opportunity and go on a wild spending spree in town. And such mystification eats into women's consciousness so that they will nod and say 'Oh, I don't handle big financial decisions. I leave all that to my husband', ignoring the fact that they looked after themselves very well before they were married, they didn't have to hand over the management of their earnings to anyone else and they probably budget far better than their husbands anyway. The 'I-don't-need-money-for-myself' syndrome is a profound response. It is a telling indication of the depth of the housewife's humiliation. She says she doesn't need money for herself because *she hasn't any money.* [. . .]

The protection that the man's wage affords her is supposed to extend to relieve her of all but subsistence needs. But the material deprivations housewives suffer is not always immediately obvious. For instance, the majority of my questions about the food they ate were dismissed by the working-class housewives I spoke to. Not only did they not sit down to eat meals, they did not eat meals. As with the rest of their lives, they tended to make do, that is, they cooked meals for their husbands and children and nibbled as they cooked and dished them up. Not one of these housewives ate breakfast. They simply took sips of tea as they dressed the kids and served the husband. Their diet consisted, on the whole, of biscuits and their family's leftovers. If one takes notice of the happy family-type advertisements, one can see that the woman is almost invariably shown standing up while the rest of the family are sitting eating around a table.

In very identifiable ways the housewife's economic dependence lays to waste her adulthood. In public he must handle the money. At the cinema or at a restaurant, even in cases where the woman is actually carrying the money, she first hands it over to him so that he can do the actual paying. Men must be *seen* to be in control of it.

Perhaps most oppressive of all is the fact that the housewife is, at all times, dependent on her protector's health and goodwill: 'I know we live quite comfortably but then I also know that it could all disappear tomorrow. I've no illusions about it. I live on a borrowed dream'. She can never forget that the man can withdraw his support whenever he chooses. Similarly she is dependent on his continuing good health which is why those advertisements for life insurance, with a cross on the man's heart, suggesting a coronary at an early age, are so effective. But widowhood is only the tip of the iceberg. It is when the marriage goes sour that the full force of her economic oppression becomes painfully apparent. All her instincts might tell her to leave but her common sense urges her to stay. If her children are small her freedom of choice is restricted to the frying pan or the fire. Her chance of earning more than £15 per week are remote and the possibility of finding satisfactory care for her children while she works is non-existent, to say nothing of finding accommodation for a woman on her own with children. The only other alternative is Social Security which will give her only bare subsistence money and only under extreme duress. They will watch her and question her and can withhold her money at a moment's notice and without explanation. [. . .]

In theory, the husband is obliged to pay maintenance to his wife when she has custody of the children. But the law makes it ludicrously easy for him to evade payment and in a very real sense condones his right not to. If he goes to ground, only token attempts are made to find him. The courts are lenient in other ways. Four weeks can lapse in his payments before any action is taken and there are many cases where men are hundreds of pounds in arrears about which nothing is done.

As long as society refuses to pay women a decent wage, sufficient to support themselves as well as their children, as long as it continues to assert that women should be dependent on men, as long as Social Security departments, employers, Housing Committees and maintenance laws deny women's right to decent food, warmth, clothing and good housing, married women with children will be forced to give way to their common sense. They will be compelled to stay with their husbands for the sake of the children, that is, for their economic security. The Missing Persons Department of the Salvation Army has about four times as many errant husbands on their books as wives. We can only guess at the submerged numbers of women who are desperately unhappy in their marriages but who stay because economics has replaced love.

Notes

1. *The Guardian,* 11 October 1972.
2. I was first struck by this in teaching when I saw children from relatively poor working-class families who were lavishly dressed and where the husband never seemed to be short but where the mother had barely two changes of drab clothing. She feels no guilt in spending money on the children but, like skimping on the housework, it would be immoral to spend money she hasn't earned on herself.

References

Gavron, H. *The Captive Wife,* Routledge and Kegan Paul 1966, Penguin 1970.
Gillespie, D. 'Who has the Power? The Marital Struggle' in H.P. Dreitzel, (ed.) *Family, Marriage and the Struggle of the Sexes,* Collier-Macmillan, 1972.

3.3   The violent event

REBECCA AND RUSSELL DOBASH

[. . .]

The beginning of the violent episode [. . .]

The events described to us were almost always preceded by a verbal confrontation relating to ongoing aspects of the marital relationship, with the husband or wife making demands on their partner or complaining about various transgressions. The majority of these arguments were not trivial but centred on long-standing contentious issues. Whether it was the first, worst, last, or typical violent incident described by the women, the majority of the disputes that preceded the violence focused on the husband's jealousy of his wife, differing expectations regarding the wife's domestic duties and the allocation of money. This pattern also emerged concerning the most frequent source of confrontations throughout the couple's married life. 44 per cent of the women reported sexual jealousy (almost always unfounded) as the major source of altercations, followed by disagreements relating to money (16 per cent) and the husband's expectations regarding the woman's homemaking (16 per cent).

Sources of conflict [. . .]

Many of the women we spoke to told us of similar reactions from their husbands. One woman described how her husband, like Jimmy, was jealous from the very beginning of their marriage.

> From the very start he's always been jealous, if he seen me even speaking to a neighbour and it happened to be a man, it didn't matter if he was nine or ninety, 'what are you talking to him for? What can you have to talk to him about?' I mean, you could just be passing the time of day with somebody. [. . .]

Other women reported that their husbands instigated arguments

Source: Dobash, R. and Dobash, R. (1980) *Violence Against Wives*, Open Books, London, pp. 97—123

regarding domestic duties, such as housekeeping or child-minding activities. [. . .]

One woman recounted an argument over food preparation when discussing what usually happened before an assault:

> I would be in bed and if he was in that kind of mood, he would pull the bedclothes off and say, 'Get out of that fucking bed, come on, get out and get me something to eat'. He might start on about my family or friends — it could be anything that would set him off — he would say: 'Pull your face straight, you miserable bugger', or 'There's never anything in this bloody house to eat. Is that all you've got?' I said we might have a bit of boiled ham or something. He said: 'Right, put that on a sandwich.' Or if there's cheese, 'There's never anything but bloody cheese, cheese, cheese, cheese, all the time.' So you'd get it, and then I might just answer back, and I'd say: 'Well it's good enough for me, cheese, and it's good enough for the children. What's wrong with a cheese sandwich?' It would start off with him being angry over trivial little things, a trivial little thing like cheese instead of meat on a sandwich, or it might be the way your face just looked for a second at him, or something, and then he'd just give you one across the face, always across the face.

The other common focus of disputes leading to attacks was the expenditure of money. The women told us that their requests for housekeeping money and their husband's expenditure of money on his individual pursuits, such as a night out at the pub or gambling, led to verbal confrontations and violence. [. . .] In describing the last time her husband used violence against her, one woman recalled the specific verbal exchange about money that led to the attack.

> Well, I had friends in and he went away out and he came in the scullery and says to me: 'Can I get ten bob for the bookies?' And I says to him, 'I've no got very much money.' So he went out and there was nothing said. The next thing my sister saw him walking back in the living room and she says to me: 'He is coming back in, and he's in a hell of a temper. You can see it on him.' So the next thing we heard the scullery getting smashed up, you see, so I went in and I says to him: 'What's wrong?' 'Don't you f— —ing ask me what's wrong,' he says. I says: 'What is it? What have I done?' So he slapped me across the face.

Although confrontations usually precede violent attacks, confrontations do not necessarily involve verbal exchanges. Some of them may involve only a one-word or one-sentence accusation made by either partner, which is immediately followed by a punch or a kick; other violent events begin without any words having been uttered. [. . .]

The following account illustrates a violent reaction regarding food preparation that began without a verbal confrontation.

He had come home from work and he'd been drinking. He was late and I'd started cooking his meal, but I put it aside, you know, when he didn't come in. Then when he came in I started heating it because the meal wasn't ready. I was standing at the sink, and I was sorting something at the sink, and he just came up and gave me a punch in the stomach. I couldn't get my breath. He'd punched me and the wind was knocked out of me. I just sort of stood there, and I couldn't get my breath. I held on to the sink for ages, and the pain in my stomach and trying to get my breath, and that was the first time I remember that he ever touched me. It was only because his tea wasn't ready on the table for him.

Men who repeatedly attack their wives often do so because they perceive, as in the preceding example, that their wives are not providing for their immediate needs in a manner they consider appropriate and acceptable. These chastisements are sometimes not prefaced by an argument. [. . .]

[The following quotation demonstrates] the reaction of men who thought that their needs and desires should take precedence over those of all other members of the family.

We were having a birthday party and my father was there. . . . Well, I had my son blow out the candles and make a wish and then help make the first cut. I had him give the first piece to my father because he had to go to work. My husband stormed out of the house. . . . He came back loaded that night simply because my father had the first piece of birthday cake instead of him. . . . That was the first time he broke my wrist.[1]

The antecedents of this episode related to the failure of the wife to meet her husband's perceived immediate needs, a failure that threatened his conception of himself as the head of the household. [. . .]

The specific factor or factors preceding the violence may seem insignificant and the violent response totally unrelated to the context in which it occurs when the confrontations are analyzed without due consideration of the ongoing relationship. It is imperative, therefore, that we seek an understanding and explanation of verbal encounters preceding violent episodes in the wider patterns of subordination and domination in the marriage and in the expectations of the men and women involved. In a violent episode it is not necessarily the specific issue that is being contested but the relationship between the husband and wife. Couples usually argue over the same issues during their marriage and though these problems may not explicitly arise prior to a violent episode, they are the background factors that shape the marriage and its violence. [. . .]

The husbands of the women we interviewed, did not like their actions, opinions, and beliefs questioned during a verbal confrontation and quickly responded to such challenges with force. [. . .] Women were required to agree with their husbands and accept their position of authority regardless of its merit. If they did not, they might be summarily silenced through the use of force.

> We were having an argument about something. I think it was money. I'm no exactly sure but probably because we didn't have the money for him to go out — that was what usually caused all the arguments. It was the first time he really hit me. It wasn't just a slap, you know, he didn't give me a black eye at first, but it was really a sore one, you know, a punch. Before then he used to shout and bawl messages, you know; I wouldn't answer back, didn't open my mouth. I used to just sit there or go and wash the dishes or something. But this time I started shouting back at him and that was it. He got angry and made a dive for me and started thumping me about. [. . .]

The verbal exchange and efforts to avoid violence

When and if a verbal exchange preceded the episode the women often attempted to alter the seemingly inevitable course of events by trying to reduce the potential for violence. The primary, and one would think potentially the most successful technique is withdrawing from the situation. This opportunity is usually denied the women. Withdrawing from a potentially violent situation within the home is very difficult for a woman: there is no safe place to go in the home; children have to be attended to; and the husband might very well block her exit. A second alternative, is agreement with the accusations that the aggressor is making. [. . .] A woman who agrees, either truthfully or falsely, to her husband's accusations regarding her supposed infidelity or failure to meet his need may actually guarantee a violent punishment. [. . .]

Women attempt to avoid or divert the violence by other means: they try to reason with their husbands or they seek an alternative, non-violent solution during the verbal confrontation. Some try to withdraw from the argument by not arguing. Other women take the opposite tack and attempt to point out injustices in their husband's claims or put their own point of view. On some occasions such efforts to avoid violence are successful: 'Well, if I thought I had time, you know, I'd sort of slowly back down, and sort of, you know, overcome the situation by changing the subject into something else. But other times, well, usually, I didn't, and I got it.'

Regardless of the reaction from the woman she usually is unable to avoid or prevent a violent response. Almost 70 per cent of the women told us that arguments with their husbands nearly always, or often, ended in an attack. The verbal confrontations were usually short, most lasting less than five minutes. Only a very few women on very infrequent occasions responded to their husband's verbal aggression by initiating violence. [. . .]

The nature of the violence and the reactions of women [. . .]

The men usually employed various forms of violence but on occasion a man would use only one type of physical force as the following example illustrates:

> Well, he just started shouting and bawling and then he just called me names, you know, swearing at me. And he started hitting me, punching me. He kept punching my face all the time — it was my nose. And he wouldn't let me sit down or anything. He made me stand in the middle of the floor. He wouldn't let me go into bed and I was screaming and he just kept punching my face. He'd walk away, maybe go into the kitchenette, come back, and have another punch at me. . . . All night. I wasn't to sit on the chair or the floor. I was to stand there. He fell asleep and I went into bed and he woke up in the morning and he asked me what had happened to my face because my nose was all swollen and bruised. I told him it was him, but he didn't say anything. Then that night he came back and thumped me again, and it was just the same routine.

This account illustrates that being punched can mean much more than one might envisage. [. . .] Many men use their feet in attacks on their wives. Commonly, the woman is pushed or punched to the floor and then severely kicked in the head and body.[2] [. . .]

The dynamic aspects of violence to wives cannot be captured in a gross quantitative manner. Only in the first assault in a marriage, is the violence usually of a singular nature, such as one slap or punch. In the majority of incidents men use various forms of violence, as the following incidents reveal:

> He punched me, he kicked me, he pulled me by the hair. My face hit a step. He had his bare feet, you know, with being in bed, and he just jumped up and he pulled on his trousers and he was kicking me. If he had his shoes on, God knows what kind of face I would have had. As it was I had a cracked cheek bone, two teeth knocked out, cracked ribs, broken nose, two beautiful black eyes — it wasn't even a black eye, it was my whole cheek was just purple from one eye to the other. And he had got me by the neck and, you know, he was trying, in fact, practically succeeded in strangling me. I was choking, I was actually at the blacking-out stage. I was trying to pull his fingers away, with me trying to pull his fingers away, I scratched myself, you know, trying to get his fingers off. He hit me and I felt my head, you know, hitting the back of the lock of the door. I started to scream and I felt as if I'd been screaming for ages. When I came to he was pulling me up the stair by the hair. I mean, I think it was the pain of him pulling me up the stair by the hair that brought me round again. I can remember going up the stair on my hands and knees and the blood — I dinnae know where it was coming from — it was just dripping in front of my face and I was actually covered in blood. I just got to the kitchen door and he just walked straight to his bed. I just filled the sink with cold water, put a dish towel in it, and held it up to my face. I remember I went through to the living room and I fell asleep and I woke up in the morning with this matted dish towel and, God I couldn't move. There wasn't a bit of me that wasnae sore. [. . .]

As these examples illustrate, men who attack their wives often use extreme force and they do not restrain themselves because they are attacking a woman.

The response of women [once violence begins]

Regardless of the severity of the attacks, women usually report that they seldom attempt to respond to violence with force. Often it is impossible to retaliate. The superior strength of men allows them to immobilize their wives' hands and/or feet or enables them to force the woman down to the floor or against a wall. As one woman told us: 'I'd have loved to have been able to hit him back, but I just couldn't bring myself to do it. In fact, I was in situations that I couldn't hit back. In fact, the only thing I've done is bit his finger.' [. . .]

The percentage of women in our study who attempted to hit back was about the same whether it was the first, worst, or last violent episode. When we asked about their typical response only a very small number (four women out of the entire group) said that they always tried to hit their husbands back. The majority said they never (33 per cent) or seldom (42 per cent) attempted to use force. The remaining 24 per cent of the women attempted to use force on a few occasions. [. . .]

The majority of the women we interviewed responded to a violent attack by remaining physically passive. Women learn that it is futile to attempt to match the physical force of their husbands and try primarily to protect themselves during attacks. Two women summed up the experience of most of the women: 'Well, I didn't try to hit him back. It just got worse if I did.' 'I just tried to defend myself, got my arms up to save myself.' A woman who reported receiving only one black eye in all of the attacks she experienced during her married life indicated that this was because she learned to protect herself: 'Just the one, and I never got a black eye again. It was always, I held my hand up to my face. That's the first thing I ever done as soon as he made a move, you know, automatically.' Another common response was to scream or cry but this reaction often led to even greater violence. One woman described how she learned that it was always best to remain silent and passive.

> I found out the best way not to get him into a tirade would be not to cry out loud, do you know what I mean, not to cry out. I know it sounds silly, but if you can just think to yourself, 'I'm going to get two or three and then he'll stop,' that wasn't bad. He could just stop after two or three, but he wouldn't if you cried out or you protested.

Screaming and crying was likely to arouse the curiosity of outsiders, who usually did not intervene but who might learn that the public image of the husband as a decent, upstanding fellow was not the same as his private behaviour. [. . .] Not only do men who attack their wives not like their opinions and desires to be questioned or thwarted, they also do not like their wives to resist punishment. Women are supposed to accept physical abuse because their husbands feel that it is justified.

Physical injuries

The physical consequences of violent events were often visible on the faces and limbs of the women we interviewed. It is difficult to appreciate the seriousness of the injuries received in a particular assault or from repeated attacks over a period of several years. The women reported that the usual assault resulted in bruising of the face, limbs, or body. The bruises ranged from minor discolourations of the skin to severe contusions requiring weeks to heal. [. . .] Bruising usually was coupled with other injuries such as cuts to the face or body, abrasions, torn hair, and fractures. [. . .] Women are sometimes knocked unconscious. [. . .]

One woman described the result of a particularly brutal attack during most of which she was unconscious.

> He grabbed me from the chair, dragged me into the sitting room, to the hall, pulled me halfway up the stairs, then pulled me back down and started to kick and stand on me. And that was in front of his own mum. I was knocked out with the first couple of blows he gave me. He was hammering into something that was just like a cushion on the floor. I had a broken rib, broken leg on the right side, two front teeth knocked out, burst chin — I've still got the scar — I had five stitches, and a broken arm on the right side.

The multiple injuries sustained by this woman were rather unusual. However, nearly 9 per cent of the women reported receiving fractures or losing teeth at some time during their married life. [. . .]

The injuries often required medical attention and even hospitalization. Nearly 80 per cent of the women reported going to a doctor at least once during their marriage for injuries resulting from attacks by their husbands; nearly 40 per cent said that they sought medical attention on five separate occasions. Many women thought they required medical care but were prevented by their husbands from seeking such attention. [. . .] The women we interviewed suffered serious woundings, innumerable bloodied noses, fractured teeth and bones, concussions, miscarriages and severe internal injuries that often resulted in permanent scars, disfigurement and sometimes persistent poor health.

Physical injuries are often coupled with serious emotional distress. Many women are chronically emotionally upset and/or depressed about the attacks and the prospects of the next one. For some women the emotional distress is so severe that medication and even hospitalization become necessary.

Just bang, bang, bang, and me heart used to be going fifty to the dozen. And I used to be shaking like a leaf [days after the attack]. But I hadn't to show him this, [. . .] I was always terrified. My nerves were getting the better of me in the finish, you know. I was getting so I used to shake through bloody fear. He knew this and I think he loved this. [. . .]

Presence of others during an altercation

Violent events like the ones described in the foregoing accounts usually occur in the home but this does not necessarily mean that they are not observed by others. [. . .] We found that 59 per cent of the first violent incidents did occur without anyone observing them, but over 75 per cent of the women reported that the last attack was observed by at least one other person, usually their children. Over the course of a violent marriage there was an increase in the probability that others would be present during an assault. This pattern is not surprising: young married couples are usually childless or have only infant children, who are not thought of as observers, but as the children grow older, it is very difficult for them to avoid witnessing attacks. A majority of women (59 per cent) reported that the children usually were present during an assault, and it was not unusual for some children almost always to observe attacks on the mother.

The reactions of the children were varied. Many of the younger children were frightened, and unable to comprehend what was occurring — 'they just sat quiet,' — but some young children comprehended and reacted: 'Donna used to get hysterical. The wee soul, she'd only be about six and one-half, and she would say, 'come on, dad, you're going to be good and you're not going to fight with mum tonight. Please, dad, you promised".' As the children grow older, they occasionally attempt to intervene either physically or verbally.[3] [. . .] Beatings are sometimes witnessed by friends or relatives, who, like the children, react in various ways. The woman's friends or relations are much more likely to intervene than the husband's friends or relatives: [. . .]

[For example,]

And whenever he's hit you in front of people, what have they usually done?
Well, actually his friend, he sort of said, you know: 'Come on, get a hold of yourself.' This sort of thing. They didn't really tell him off. They didn't want to quarrel with him, too, but they sort of said: 'Get a grip on yourself'. You know, 'Leave her alone' and that. Mostly when I was pregnant, you know. They'd pull

him back, but they never actually fought with him because of it. They told him to calm down.
And how do you think these outsiders felt about you, seeing you getting battered?
I think they were just more embarrassed than anything else that they happened to be there at the time.
And do you think they felt sorry for you and reckoned — did they want to get involved?
I don't think they wanted to get involved at all. I mean most of his friends anyway was doing the same things to their wives. I mean Bruce used to give his wife knockings as well.

As described in the above account, the usual response of friends and relatives is simply to do nothing or to tell the husband to stop. Very rarely do friends or relatives attempt physically to intervene in the violence. [. . .]

Pleas from outsiders seem to make very little difference: 'They used to tell him to stop but he didn't take any notice'. Outsiders may actually touch off or aggravate an assault. If a woman were to question her husband's actions or his supposed rightful authority over her in front of friends or relations, he might consider this a double affront. Not only had she questioned his authority, but she had rebuked him in front of others, a double humiliation. In describing the first violent attack one woman told us about this type of confrontation. Her husband had invited another couple to visit them, but instead of coming directly home from work to help entertain the guests he stopped at a friend's home. When he arrived home with his friend, his wife protested about his late arrival — both in front of his friend and within hearing distance of the visiting couple. He responded by telling her to 'mind her own business, I do what I like'. When she complained that he was inconsiderate, he punched her against the wall and knocked her unconscious. This happened 'simply because I chastised him and there was somebody there in the sitting room'.

Though outsiders do at times inhibit a violent attack, the presence of an audience prior to or during such an episode may help escalate the assault. This depends upon the man involved, the nature of the verbal exchange with his wife, and the orientation of the outsiders to violent behaviour.[4] The presence of others during a verbal altercation is most likely to precipitate violence if the potential aggressor perceives the observers as supportive of his actions or if, as in the example cited above, he feels humiliated in their eyes.

After the violent event

Reaction

After an assault, the typical reaction of both the man and the woman is to remain in the home. Almost all of the women (90 per cent) reported that usually they remained in the house and were unable to do anything immediately after an attack.

> I didn't do anything about it. After he hit me I just cried and tried to keep quiet, hoping he would calm down.

> I just used to sit and cry because I know for a fact that if you start hitting back then you'll get more hitting back, you see. So I just sort of sat back and took it all.

A considerable proportion of the women we interviewed (20 per cent) also indicated that their husbands forcibly kept them from going out. A few women discussed extreme restraints upon their mobility: 'Before he went to work in the morning he would nail the windows shut, and padlock the doors from the inside'.[5] Husbands might physically prevent their wives from leaving the house even to seek help or medical assistance, but usually women were restrained by verbal threats of retaliation.

Women sometimes responded to a violent attack by attempting to placate their husbands: 'I used to ask him if he wanted something to eat. Or I wouldn't say anything, you know, sort of try and get him to cool down more or less'.

Immediately after an attack husbands tended to do nothing, to ignore the act, or to behave as if nothing had happened. Almost 80 per cent of the men usually acted in this manner.

> He just sat and read and that. He didn't talk. We didn't talk to one another.

> He went to sleep. Mind you, he was tired [from beating her]. I've no doubt that he was physically worn out. He was exhausted.

> He didn't feel anything. Most peculiar, [he] just starts talking to you, you know, as long as you're doing as you are told.

The second most common response of the husband following the attack was to go to a pub or just out to cool off. [. . .]

Feelings about the violence

The feelings and emotions expressed by the women we interviewed were complex. Women usually felt very upset after a violent episode, and these feelings persisted for several days and sometimes weeks afterward: 'I was very upset about it. I mean, I had never seen anything like this happening. I'd never experienced violence in a home. I was pretty upset about it. . . . I was crying all the time'. This account aptly describes the typical reaction of over 65 per cent of the women. Women also felt shocked, frightened, ashamed, bitter, and angry after an assault: 'Oh, I was frightened, you know, I was terrified, miserable. I was always sitting on an edge waiting for him to get to sleep.' [. . .]

A woman often feels angry after a violent event because her husband ignores her feelings and concerns, because he reacts to her protestations with violence, because a special event such as Christmas or a child's birthday has been spoiled, or because he has shamed her by attacking her in front of friends or relatives. In our study intense anger was most likely after the worst assault since it was typically both humiliating and severe. [. . .]

Men may also feel angry after a violent episode, but unlike the women their anger is a continuation of the feelings that gave rise to the verbal confrontation and not a response to the attack. However, men usually act, or at least appear to act, blasé after attacking their wives and express little or no remorse. The husbands of the women we spoke to very rarely apologized or showed contrition immediately following an assault.

If there was any expression of remorse or contrition it usually occurred early in the marriage and after the first violent incident: Over 35 per cent of the men apologized after the first attack, whereas only 14 per cent did so after the worst attack. The bulk of the men typically acted as if nothing had happened. Whether it was the first, worst, or last assault, they very rarely expressed any remorse or regret, and if they did apologize it was usually after a few days or weeks. Only a small percentage (8 per cent) of the husbands almost always expressed remorse immediately following the violent event; 22 per cent usually expressed regret after a few days. [. . .]

On a few occasions men showed their contrition by doing something for their wives such as helping with the dishes. One woman described how her husband used this technique several weeks after a violent attack.

Oh, he was sorry. He tried to make it up, you know. He would help me do things in the house that week, which he never did.

And when it came up for New Year he was saying, 'Oh, wait and I'll clean this. I'll do that'. I think that was his way of trying to say he was sorry.

However, whether it was the first, worst, or last violent attack, expressions of regret or contrition, apologies or helpful behaviour were not typical of the men. Instead, they rarely or never expressed remorse or contrition regarding their violent actions.

No, he didn't apologize. He never said he was sorry. I used to say to him sometimes 'Do you not feel sorry about it', and he'd say: 'No, I'd never say I was sorry because if I was I wouldn't do it in the first place'. He always said that.

I never recall him having any remorse whatever, never recall him ever coming to see me and saying, well honey, put his arm around me and say I'm sorry.

Not only did most husbands fail to apologize or show regret after a violent attack, they often continued to argue with, or to act aggressively towards their wives, demanding that she do something for him, threatening to bring in a third party who he thought would take his side and condemn his wife, or threatening to put her out of the house.

Oh, I've seen it after he'd maybe stopped the hitting — the actual hitting would maybe go on for ten minutes or something — but then he would sit and go on for hours. And you're sitting there in a cold sweat waiting on whatever else is going to happen. I couldn't talk. My mouth was shut. I would just sit and he'd maybe make me do things, you know, break something and say: 'Right, sweep that up'.

Men also attempt to rationalize their violent behaviour by denying responsibility for the assault or by arguing that their wife's actions or inactions provoked them.

He'd always just deny it or say it hadn't happened or say it had been an accident. Even to this day he'll argue: 'I never hit you when you were pregnant. That's a lie. That's the last thing in the world I'd do'. He still insists he's not a violent man. He'll say: 'That's one thing I hate is a man that hits a woman'. [. . .]

He would always make out it was my fault. If I hadn't said this or if I hadnae done that, it would never have happened. He always claimed that I provoked him. It was always I provoked him. [. . .]

Although most men were not drunk when they attacked their wives (30 per cent of the men in our police sample were described as intoxicated and 25 per cent of the women described their husbands as often drunk at the time of an incident), some of the men who had been drinking denied that they had hit their wives or maintained that they were not responsible for the beating because they were intoxicated.

He always says that he never hit me, but I know that he knows because sometimes he says things about it.

He would say: 'Look, this isn't me. It's the drink that is making me act this way'.

Men who have only had a small amount to drink and could in no way be considered drunk also use alcohol as an excuse. Women, too, may use their husband's drinking (of even minimal amounts) as a means of making sense of the violent behaviour and of placing blame upon something 'outside' the marital relationship.[6]

Thus, men deny responsibility for their violent acts by asserting that their wife's arguing or perceived inappropriate behaviour led them to behave in a violent manner.[7] [. . .]

Accusations which place the blame upon the victim, may lead a woman to express shame or guilt regarding the violent event. In our study this was especially the case after the first attack since it was seen as a blemish on the marriage. One of the women we interviewed told us that after the first assault she 'was ashamed, I didn't want anybody to know. I was hoping the neighbours hadn't heard.' Women often feel that if only they would try harder, keep the house cleaner, or cook better, then maybe their husbands would not beat them. [. . .] Some women even apologize to their husbands for supposedly provoking the violence. [. . .]

Violent incidents are very rarely discussed by husbands and wives. Usually no explicit effort is made to effect a reconciliation and reconstitute the relationship or to explore and resolve the conflicts that keep surfacing. Couples usually just drift back together again.

I just went about my business normally. It was just a case of talking and no more, like, 'What are you wanting for breakfast? What are you wanting for your tea?' And he wouldn't say what he wanted, 'Just anything will do.' It was just talking and answering and no more. [. . .]

Despite this pattern of letting things ride, women do make it very clear to their husbands that they are upset and dissatisfied with the pattern of violence and with the marriage. It is erroneous to assume because the couple does not talk about the violence that women accept it. [. . .]

[*Rights, authority and violence*

We conclude from the experiences of the women we interviewed that] husbands believe that their wives cannot and should not make certain claims upon them. Claim making is not a two-sided process. Men who use violence consider it their right and privilege as men and as heads of households to make claims of their wives; if their demands are not met, as in the cases of the timing of meals or of responding to sexual advances, the woman may be punished. Conversely, the man does not believe that his wife can make such strong claims relating to his actions; he considers her claim-making to be extraordinary and inappropriate and she might be silenced through the use of force. [. . .]

Violent men often view other people as objects to be exploited in their attempts to meet their own needs. They elevate the fulfilment of their personal desires to the status of a 'natural law', operating on the premise that their own welfare is of primary and exclusive concern to others. In arguments and confrontations preceding their use of violence these men rarely note or admit to the discontent of the other person and to their concerns and needs, and this is especially true in relationships with women. [. . .]

This predisposition is not evident only in men who attack their wives. Many men in Western society learn to expect that their wishes and concerns come first, that because they are males and heads of households they have certain prerogatives and rights that supersede those of women — especially in the family where the rights of males over females are clearly defined from a very early age. The difference between violent men and other males is that the former are prepared to use physical means to enforce or reinforce their own views. When men do use force to chastise and punish their wives for failing to live up to their unilateral standards, they can be very violent indeed. [. . .]

In summary, the violent episode most often is preceded by a short verbal confrontation, although some prefatory arguments may be intermittent and last several hours. The altercations relate primarily to the husband's expectations regarding his wife's domestic work, his possessiveness and sexual jealousy, and allocation of the family's resources. The verbal confrontation may be initiated by either the husband or the wife, but it is usually initiated by the husband. When a husband attacks his wife he is either chastising her for challenging his authority or for failing to live up to his expectations or attempting to discourage future unacceptable behaviour. Men use diverse and often severe forms of physical force. The usual method of attack is slapping, punching, and kicking, which results in bruises, lacerations, and fractures, some of which require medical treatment and even hospitalization. Men commonly fail to react to the consequences of their violent actions — ignoring the violence and acting as if nothing had happened. Although some men eventually may apologize they very rarely do so immediately following an attack. The majority do not express any contrition whatsoever and often deflect the blame for their violent actions onto their wives. Women, on the other hand, do not ignore the violence but they must remain in the home, often detained by the husband or because they have few places to go. Generally, women feel shattered, frightened, ashamed, and angry. Emotions of this nature may continue for days or weeks after the attack.

Notes and References

1. R. J. Gelles (1974) *The Violent Home: A Study of Physical Aggression Between Husbands and Wives,* Beverly Hills: Sage, p. 139.
2. Kicking and standing on women was practised with hobnail boots in Yorkshire during the late nineteenth century and was called 'purring'.
3. See Gelles, *op. cit,* p. 33 *et seq.* Also see J. R. Hepburn (1973) 'Violent behaviour in interpersonal relationships', *Sociological Quarterly* 14 (Summer) pp. 419—29, and H. Toch (1969) *Violent Men: An Inquiry into the Psychology of Violence,* Chicago: Aldine.
4. Faulkner's work on violence among ice hockey players illustrated a situation in which a supportive audience reinforced and indeed demanded the use of physical force. See R. Faulkner (1973) 'On respect and retribution: toward an ethnography of violence', *Sociological Symposium* 9 (Spring) pp. 17—35.
5. S. Eisenberg and P. Micklow (1974) 'The assaulted wife: Catch 22 revisited. (an exploratory legal study of wifebeating in Michigan)', mimeograph, University of Michigan Law School. Also available from Rutgers University School of Law, 180 University Avenue, Newark, N.J. 07102.
6. See Gelles, *op. cit,* pp. 113—18 for a discussion of the role of alcohol in violent events and C. H. McCaghy (1968) 'Drinking and deviance disavowal: the case of child molesters, *Social Problems* 16(1) pp. 43—9, for an example of the use of alcohol in disavowing responsibility for a socially unacceptable form of deviance.

7. G. W. Sykes and D. Matza (1957) 'Techniques of neutralization: a theory of delinquency', *American Sociological Review* 22, pp. 667—70, considered several techniques that adolescents use in dealing with their feelings regarding delinquent acts; two of these are 'denial of responsibility' and 'denial of the victim' or blaming the victim.

3.4 From disregard to disrepute: the position of women in family law

JULIA BROPHY AND CAROL SMART

There is, it would seem, a popular belief that twentieth-century women have now achieved equality with men. In fact this century has been described as the 'woman's epoch' because of the volume of legal reforms which have apparently ameliorated the position of women in the family and in economic and political spheres. In addition, women are perceived as not only achieving equal rights with men but, in some instances, as receiving special treatment from the law. This is particularly the case in the area of family law where women usually receive the custody of children and are usually entitled to maintenance from their husbands. The Law Commission, for example, recently stated:

> We have been told that the continuing financial obligations imposed by divorce often cause severe economic hardship for those who are ordered to pay, normally of course the husband . . . The obligation to maintain an ex-wife is particularly resented if the husband feels that it is his wife who is really responsible for the breakdown of the marriage; and such feelings are further exacerbated where he believes that his ex-wife has either chosen not to contribute toward her maintenance by working, or has elected to co-habit with another man, who might be in a position to support her . . . For many husbands the effect of divorce may seem to involve not only the end of their marriage, but also the loss of home, children and money (1979: 15—16).

The view that the 'pendulum' has swung back too far and, in mitigating the effects of nineteenth-century legislation, has come to favour women unfairly, is now common currency. For example, there is now a growing emphasis on fathers' rights to custody, and pressure groups such as Families Need Fathers (FNF) argue that

Source: Brophy, J. and Smart, C. (1981) From disregard to disrepute: the position of women in family law, *Feminist Review* No. 9, October, pp. 3—16.

men are unfairly denied rights over their children. There is also a growing belief, fostered in particular by the Campaign for Justice on Divorce (CJD), that wives, even common-law wives, can financially exploit men and remain a drain on their economic resources for life. For example recent celebrated cases involving Michelle Marvin, Britt Ekland and Bianca Jagger have helped to create a popular impression that divorce or separation constitutes a financial 'rake-off' for wives and cohabitees.

In this chapter we put forward the view that although the *formal* legal rights of married women have improved, we are not in fact witnessing an equalization of rights. Such a development would not in any case improve the structural position of women. But in addition we wish to distinguish between, on the one hand, an improvement in women's legal position and, on the other hand, the law's continued support of a family structure in which women's dependency is a fundamental feature. We argue that although inequalities of power within the family have been modified, the basic patriarchal structure of the family, which entails dominance and dependency, is sustained rather than undermined in family law. We shall examine briefly the development of family law from the nineteenth century, focusing on divorce, maintenance and custody, in order to locate these contradictory themes in their historical context. We shall also consider contemporary developments in family law and attempt to reveal the complex relationship between law, women and the family.

Nineteenth-century developments

Rights over children

The attitude of the courts in the late eighteenth and early nineteenth centuries was unequivocal; all parental authority over legitimate children was paternal, with total rights being vested in the father. Prior to 1839 the courts did not have any real jurisdiction to *award* children to either party. The ideology of 'father right' was so taken for granted that a father's right to custody was treated as entirely uncontroversial. Even where the father was clearly shown to be unsuitable to have 'possession' of his children, the courts were unable to undermine his rights. Drunkenness and profligacy were viewed as unsufficient grounds on which to prevent him regaining the 'possession' of his child even when combined with destitution. During this period the courts were concerned with upholding what was perceived to be the father's 'natural' rights to his children. These rights were automatically established on paternity and were not conditional upon the quality of care offered nor the degree of attachment felt by the father. Although the courts did occasionally consider the child's welfare as relevant, where this occurred they tended to assume that paternal custody naturally coincided with the interests of the child. For example, in 1883 it was argued that:

> It is not to the benefit of the infant as conceived by the court, but it must be to the benefit of the infant having regard to the law which points out that the father knows far better what is good for his children than a court of justice (*Re Agar Ellis* (1883)).

The 1839 Custody of Infants Act provided the first formal, legal link between a mother and her children and marked the beginnings of a challenge to automatic father right. It allowed a mother to have the physical custody of her children up to the age of seven years, provided that she had not committed adultery, and it permitted her access to her minor children at the discretion of the courts. This was the first statutory recognition of a mother's nurturing role, which has become such an important feature of contemporary family law. The legal concept of the 'unfit' parent also provided a breach in the principle of automatic father right. This concept indicated the extent to which the courts began to recognize that children required a certain level of care in their upbringing which might not be provided by the father in spite of his 'natural' rights. So mothers gained more rights over their children in two ways, firstly through their nurturing role when the children were very young, and secondly through the realization that 'inadequate parenting' was a social problem[1] of sufficient significance to override the natural authority of the father. There was at this time a growing concern over the moral and physical welfare of children (Davin 1978), and the way in which the courts were gradually willing to reduce the autocratic powers of the father over his children was not so much a reflection of the improved status of women as a recognition of the social value of adequate mothering.

Rights over property and income

By the nineteenth century women's relationship to property was already well established. For example common law provided that property should only be passed down through the male line (Harrison and Mort 1980) so that women's access to property and income was nearly always mediated through their relationships to their fathers or husbands. By the end of the nineteenth century, however, legislation gave women rights to property which were formally equal to those of a man or a single woman, but she had far fewer rights in general. For example she had no right to leave her husband without his permission and if she did he could physically restrain her. She had no right to maintenance if she could not prove that her husband had committed a matrimonial offence. Although she could 'pledge her husband's credit' this was of little value to poor women and became increasingly unpopular with creditors. Her right to divorce (which was not extended in practice to working-class women) was also more restricted than her husband's, as he could divorce her on a single act of adultery whilst she had to establish adultery combined with another matrimonial offence. It is therefore quite inaccurate to talk of an equalization of rights between husbands and wives at this time although the principle of married women's rights had begun to enter into law.

If a wife's rights were not greatly improved at the end of the nineteenth century, the growing proliferation of legislation on divorce, separation and maintenance also did little to undermine the husband's authority over her. His authority as head of the household was upheld by the courts in a number of ways. Any challenge by a wife to his authority or to the principle of sexual monogamy resulted in the courts refusing to grant her maintenance. The magistrates' courts, which dealt exclusively with working-class women, took an even more rigid position on adultery than the divorce courts and treated adultery as an absolute bar to maintenance for wives. In fact it was consistently argued at the end of the nineteenth century that it would be contrary to 'public policy' to oblige a husband to pay maintenance for a guilty wife as this would encourage her disobedience and disloyalty (McGregor *et al*, 1970). Such disobedience, it was maintained, would serve to undermine the stability of the family and would provide a threat to the nation as a whole.

The power structure in the family at the end of the nineteenth century had not been radically altered therefore, and the authority of the father over his children was not really jeopardized. This was in spite of the fact that the concern over the welfare of children was beginning to have some effect in the courts. The control of the husband over property was not fundamentally altered either. Men still retained a privileged access to property through inheritance and through their involvement in waged or remunerative work. In practice therefore women of all classes (with few exceptions) remained dependent upon their husbands to provide an income.[2] By the end of the century the courts had firmly established that maintenance to a wife and the custody of children would only be granted where it was *morally* deserved. The courts also consistently reinforced punitive sanctions against women who committed adultery or gave birth to illegitimate children. Although there were considerable class differences between the women using the High Courts and the magistrates' courts, the jurisdictions were broadly similar both in operating punitively towards women who transgressed against the patriarchal family structure, and in reinforcing the authority of the 'head of the household'.

The 'woman's epoch'?

The twentieth century has been depicted in legal texts as the 'woman's epoch' (Graveson and Crane 1957). Reforms to legislation have been treated by many legal academics and practitioners as indicating a wholesale improvement in women's rights and in their status in the family, in employment and in politics. As early as 1930 Judge McCardie maintained that: 'I find privileges given to a wife which are wholly denied to a husband and I find that upon the husband has fallen one injustice upon another' (*Gottliffe* v. *Edelston* (1930)). Whilst in 1950 Lord Denning proclaimed that: 'The fact that women had gained equality with men had tremendous potentialities for civilization, but whether it was for good or bad had yet to be seen', and later that: '(The wife) is now indeed the spoilt darling of the law, and (the husband) the patient pack-horse' (*The Times,* May 13, 1950).

The judiciary has tended to maintain that law has established equality between the sexes. But it has also claimed that it has created a legal system that confers *preferential* treatment on women and wives. A superficial examination of statutory reforms during the early part of this century may indeed appear to support these suppositions. For example an Act of 1923 equalized the grounds for divorce between men and women, while the 1925 Guardianship of Infants Act gave mothers the same rights as fathers to *apply* to the courts for the custody of children. In addition, much of the legislation governing the magistrates' domestic jurisdiction at this time was drafted to protect women and to provide for their maintenance. Husbands were actually prevented from applying to the magistrates' courts on equal terms with wives until 1981. However a closer examination of the underlying principles of the legislation and of the effectiveness of these reforms reveals the poverty of this traditional legal view and casts doubt on the ability of legislation to alter fundamentally the power relationships within the family.

In relation to the Custody of Infants Act 1925, for example, the establishment of formal equality between parents, although important, did not prove to be the most significant feature of the statute. This Act established that the guiding principle in deciding custody disputes was to be the welfare of the child and it was to be this principle, rather than the principle of equal rights, which was to become the most significant feature of the legislation as far as mothers were concerned. The interests of the child had increasingly been a factor to which the courts referred in resolving custody disputes; the 1925 Act made that feature a statutory requirement. In so doing, it legitimated an already ongoing concern about child welfare. But it also marked a shift in the circumstances in which a child's interests were identified as being best served. With the turn of the century the concept of child welfare was subject to a certain amount of redefinition. It came to embrace much broader ideas about the general well-being of children and was no longer narrowly focused upon physical health and moral rectitude. In particular it included a recognition of the importance of mothering for a child's development during the formative years, and it was via this shift that the legal position of women-*as*-mothers improved in custody disputes. In practice therefore the motivating force for improving women's position in custody cases was not the existence of formal legal 'rights' but rather the state's growing concern over children and their need for maternal care. So the mother's claim to custody was essentially legitimated through a recognition of the value of her maternal role, and it was this role which began increasingly to eclipse the rights of fathers in relation to children. By the mid-twentieth century the courts were consistently referring to the value of the role and the 'naturalness' of the child/mother relationship. For example in a custody dispute in 1965 Judge Slamon stated:

> I think there is no doubt — and this is not a proposition of law — that from the point of view of commonsense and ordinary humanity, all things being equal, the best place for any small child is with its mother (*H* v. *H and C* (1969)).

While in 1975 Judge Ormond remarked: 'Unless there were some really good reasons, children of this age (5, 2 and 1 years) should be with their mother. That was the social norm' (*B* v. *B* (1975)).

However, judicial recognition of the importance of the nurturing role continued to be influenced by the courts' evaluation of a mother's 'morality'. Although 'punishment' of the guilty spouse was no longer a formal feature to be considered in deciding custody, in practice when considering what was seen as a wife's errant sexual behaviour, the emphasis on the significance of the mother/child relationship often became of subordinate importance, and adultery could mean the loss of her children. For instance in 1950 Judge Wallington, on awarding care and control of a 2-year-old girl to a father, justified his decision on the grounds that: 'It could never be in the interests of the child to be entrusted to the care of a woman who had committed adultery' (*Willoughby* v. *Willoughby* (1951)). During that period a number of decisions in the lower courts were overturned in the Court of Appeal, and some attempts were made to distinguish between the role of a 'bad' wife (an adulteress) and that of a bad mother, although it appears that the two roles were never treated as mutually exclusive. But there were also some attempts to stem this development, for example in the 1960s Lord Denning argued that:

> This (good mothering) in itself is not always enough; one must remember that to be a good mother involves not only looking after the children, but making and keeping a home for them with their father . . . in so far as she herself by her conduct broke up that home she is not a good mother (*Re L (infants)* (1962)).

However, the general trend in the Court of Appeal was to attempt to distinguish between the two roles if there was sufficient evidence to suggest that the mother adequately cared for her children, and that the matrimonial offence was not indicative of a 'general promiscuity'. It is also important to realize that even though the higher courts were gradually becoming more willing to allow adulterous wives to care for their young children, in cases where a wife's sexual behaviour was an issue, the courts tended to maintain the overall authority of the father by granting 'split orders'. These decisions entailed awarding legal custody to the father, but giving the mother day-to-day care and control. In effect, this meant that whilst the mother had responsibility for the daily care of her children, the father retained the power and authority to make important decisions. So a mother whose morality was questioned by the courts tended (where the concern was with young children) to be given the daily responsibility for her children but no legal power or authority over their upbringing. In this way, the father's ultimate power was maintained not simply over his children but also, indirectly, over his wife.

However, the twentieth century has not been identified as the 'woman's epoch' solely on the basis of developments in child custody. Of equal significance have been the developments relating to maintenance and property. As with the issue of custody, changes in these areas cannot simply be understood in terms of an equalization of rights because, although traditional property rights have been undermined, the 'rights' of women-as-wives have usually been conditional. Such 'rights' have, at various times, been contingent upon a moral evaluation of a woman's sexual behaviour, an economic valuation of her adequacy as a wife and mother. The development of the law and legal practice regarding maintenance payments for wives for example have, until recently, been closely linked with the issue of extra-marital sexual relations. Until 1981 adultery by a wife was an absolute bar to a petition for maintenance by a wife in the magistrates' courts. Moreover a single act of adultery some years after a marital breakdown could mean a wife lost the right to maintenance from her husband. The divorce courts were always less rigid in their response to adultery than the magistrates' courts, but a wife's maintenance (prior to 1969) was routinely reduced as a way of compensating the husband for her infidelity.

In relation to matrimonial property a similar trend can be identified during the fifties and sixties when a wife's security in the matrimonial home improved. Even though her husband might be sole legal owner, under certain conditions a wife might be allowed to stay in the home against her husband's wishes and financial interests. In this way the law intervened in a husband's property rights as he could be prevented from evicting his wife and realizing his capital. However, a wife's 'right' to remain in the home depended entirely upon a legal fiction, namely her innocence and her husband's guilt. This extension of rights to wives was therefore entirely dependent upon the proof that they were 'good' and 'deserving' wives. The faultless wife who had contributed to the accumulation of family assets through thrifty housekeeping, servicing her husband and caring for the children was therefore more likely to be allowed to stay in the home. However where she was not faultless she forfeited this moral right. This trend in case law improved the position of some wives but it also perpetuated the legal and social view that a wife's right to maintenance, to accommodation or to property was dependent upon her moral worth and not her economic contribution to family assets through her domestic labour. This approach was exemplified by Lord Denning in 1969 when he maintained that:

Some features of family life are elemental in our society. One is that it is the husband's duty to provide his wife with a roof over her head; and the children too. So long as the wife behaves herself, she is entitled to remain in the matrimonial home . . . This is a personal right which belongs to her as a wife. It is not a proprietary right. . . . So long as she had done nothing to forfeit that right, the court will enforce it (*Gurasz* v. *Gurasz* (1969)).

Although the higher courts were increasingly willing to curtail the husband's property rights in the post-war period they would not alter the basis on which property rights could be accumulated. Prior to the reform of the divorce law in the 1970s the courts refused to recognize a wife's *indirect* contribution towards the accumulation of property or family assets. The only way ownership or part ownership could be established was through a direct contribution of cash or through title deeds, contracts or receipts. A wife who did not earn a wage was therefore usually excluded from the accumulation process. She might however be said to have earned a 'beneficial interest' in a property if she had engaged in 'men's work', such as building, labouring and carpentry. This work was recognized by the courts as contributing an economic valut to a property which could be recouped at a later stage. But 'women's work' was seen as contributing no value and therefore could not be rewarded economically. As Lord Denning argued in 1968: 'The wife does not get a share in the house simply because she cleans the walls or works in the garden or helps her husband with the painting or decorating. Those are the sort of things which a wife does for the benefit of the family without altering the title to, or interest in, the property' (*Button* v. *Button* (1968)). The only erosion of (men's) property rights that occurred in the fifties and sixties therefore reflected a moral reward for good behaviour or a financial reward for the direct contribution of 'value'. To achieve the former a wife had to be innocent of a matrimonial fault, and to achieve the latter she had to acquire the skills of a crafts*man*. Her structural position of economic dependency within the family was hardly affected by the acquisition of these new, conditional rights.

The introduction of reforms to family law in the early 1970s introduced these 'rights' into legislation; previously they were entirely dependent upon judicial discretion. This change to a large extent removed the contentious issue of a wife's behaviour and its effects upon her claim to maintenance or her right to accommodation. In addition it formally recognized the value of domestic labour as an indirect contribution to the acquisition of assets. A wife's adultery (in theory) could no longer wipe out a consideration of the economic value of her unwaged labour to her husband. In reality, however, there is no simple equation between the economic provision by a husband through his wage and the economic contribution by a wife through her domestic labour. The courts take other factors into account and the most important is not a wife's indirect economic contribution but her status as a mother.

The benefits wives now appear to enjoy on divorce (the custody of children, the occupation of the matrimonial home and the receipt of maintenance) are not benefits or rights that simply

accrue to women-as-wives. They flow from juridicial concern over
the welfare of children. It is because women tend to have the
custody of children, that they also tend to be awarded the

matrimonial home or to have the tenancies of rented accommodation transferred to them. Once again the law is not so much operating to improve the rights of wives against those of husbands, but is acting to protect children and provide them with an 'appropriate' caretaker. So although the economic vulnerability of some wives on divorce has been mitigated to an extent, this protection in practice largely derives from her status as a mother and not from a recognition of her economic contribution to the family.

We are not, however, putting forward the argument that it would be sufficient to simply recognize and reward women's economic contribution, nor are we implying that it unambiguously advantages women when the courts attempt to protect and promote the caring role of mothers. Rather we are trying to establish that the development of law in this epoch has in no sense radically affected the structures of dependency in the family. On the contrary it has improved the conditions of dependents and has preserved the popularity of marriage. This point is particularly important to stress because the current backlash against modern divorce law is based on the fallacy that it is *women* who now receive positive discrimination at a time when the law in other areas insists that women and men should be treated equally. The argument for equal rights is now used against women, wives and mothers irrespective of the fact that they all occupy different positions within the family and the waged economy. Before we discuss this point fully we wish to examine the way in which family law contributes towards the reproduction of the family.

Reproducing the family

We have argued so far that developments in family law cannot simply be viewed as an incremental process of accumulating 'rights'. Moreover we would suggest that an improvement of the position of wives within marriage has occurred simultaneously with an increasing intervention in the family and with the development of more permissive strategies for regulating the members of families. We can, for example, observe that at a time when the economic vulnerability of women-as-wives was being partially ameliorated, the significance of marriage itself began to decline. This decline has two aspects. Firstly, with the changing pattern of married women's work in the post-war period, it was not *marriage* so much as *motherhood* that marked women's entry into economic dependency. Secondly, it was gradually recognized that the family and marriage were no longer the same thing and the state began to relax the strategy of regulating family members through strict controls over marriage and divorce. Instead of retaining a policy of negative control, 'easy divorce' developed. This facilitated the reconstruction of recognized, lawful unions through the availability of remarriage, and this has occurred along with a tendency to extend to the unmarried the duties and obligations normally associated with marriage. As a consequence of this partial dislocation between the family and marriage, and the changing economic position of women within the family unit, many of the strategies employed within family law to regulate the family and to reproduce the economic dependency of family members have been modified. However it would be misleading to suggest a total transformation of legal practice, as contradictions between traditional strategies towards regulating the family and more contemporary practices still exist.

We have argued that the position of the mother improved as a consequence of the concern for children but it is also important to point out that this led to a realignment of power within the family. In effect the mother became an increasingly important figure within the family. However at the same time the construction of mothering disadvantaged women economically because the individual mode of reproduction, prevented most mothers retaining any economic independence. So although the mother's position in the private sphere was enhanced it was at the expense of weakening her position in the public sphere of waged labour (Land 1980). This has remained a disadvantage as there has been no movement towards the socialization of childcare. On the contrary legal discourse celebrates the individual relation between a mother and her child and consistently reinforces ideologies of motherhood in which the biological bond between mother and child is given primacy. However legislation has failed to contribute in a material sense to the economic viability of the mother/child unit outside of a family structure; whilst celebrating motherhood the law has retained the economic dependency on the mother on either a 'wage-earner' or the state. In effect mothers are prevailed upon to provide vital duties with regard to children but the only really viable means for them to do so is within the confines of the heterosexual family unit (whether or not that unit is legitimated by marriage). So it is not motherhood in isolation that is revered by the courts but motherhood within a familial structure.

This approach to 'legitimate' motherhood is particularly evident in relation to the principles underlying the recent Law Commission proposals on illegitimacy[3] and in child custody disputes in which the mother has been identified as a lesbian. In the latter case the courts continue to refuse the mother custody of her children even where the children are very young. In these cases the primacy of the mother/child relationship is completely overruled because of the unorthodoxy of non-heterosexual relationships. Even though the courts do not generally suggest that lesbianism necessarily precludes good mothering, the judiciary are concerned that the child should be in an environment where it can experience heterosexual family relationships. In these cases good mothering is no longer perceived as simply providing care but is placed in a much broader context and made explicitly synonymous with socialization into 'normal family life'. The importance of that socialization as far as the courts are concerned is to ensure that the 'normal family' will be reproduced a generation later and to guard against the possibility that alternative family forms might develop. Consequently the father who can provide a heterosexual environment with a substitute mother or with the child's grandparents is nearly always seen as more desirable by the courts.

In these cases the courts can be seen to be using traditional strategies to regulate the structure of the family. They have denied the mother custody and limited her contact with her children. In this respect the wife who is a lesbian is subject to forms of regulation similar to those employed against the adulterous wife in previous decades. The courts fear her influence, not only on the individual child, but also upon 'the family' and public policy in general. We can, therefore, perceive a continuity in legal practice in these cases but at the same time there have been important shifts in family law which represent the development of alternative strategies for reproducing the family.

One such shift has been the courts' changing focus on individual family members. Traditionally the focus has been on the dependent members of the family, namely wives and children. The head of the household was treated as the authority figure who was accorded powers of control over other members. He was not subject to the same degree of scrutiny as other members precisely because of his position of authority. However, as we have argued, there has been a realignment of power within the family and the law can now directly intervene to curtail the husband's authority. Moreover the (partial) removal of the concept of matrimonial offence has had very important implications for the position of the husband in family law. Essentially it means that he can no longer evade the duty to maintain his wife regardless of her adultery or desertion, and consequently he, and not his wife, has been constituted as the central figure. It is his willingness or ability to maintain his dependents that occupies the law, not the quality or degree of his wife's misbehaviour. Family law no longer argues, as it once did, that it is against 'public policy' to award maintenance to a guilty wife. On the contrary it now argues that it is in the interests of preserving 'public funds' that all husbands should support their dependents. The aspects of family law which used to punish the wife in order to discourage other wives from disobedience is less evident now. Instead it is the husband who is scrutinized.

This gradual shift from a focus on wives to husbands has obscured the law's relation to women. Because family courts now concentrate on, and have gained greater powers to enforce obligations on husbands, wives *appear* to occupy a privileged position. But a wife's economic position is not necessarily improved by this strategy because the policy of the courts is not to benefit wives but to protect the 'public purse' and to deflect the economic costs of the disintegration of the family away from the welfare state and onto individuals. Although this policy is not new it has never been an unconditional policy within family law as it has been in welfare law. Family legislation is now moving closer to welfare legislation and is also adopting interventionist strategies that have been more common to the latter. For example the courts have increasing powers to investigate incomes, to deduct monies at source, to vary property ownership and to investigate the family through the agency of welfare officers. Intervention into and surveillance over the family is becoming more extensive and the prevailing strategy of family law is not to construct a semi-autonomous institution within which one patriarch has absolute power, but to regulate family members (positively and negatively) and to contain economic dependency within the family unit.

The relation of law to the family is therefore complex and it cannot be depicted simply as a negative or conservative force which unambiguously oppresses family members, especially women. On the contrary some legislation, as we have argued, has improved the position of wives within the family, although the structures of economic dependency, which are a defining feature of the family, have largely been preserved.

Conclusions

We have argued that it is a fallacy to describe the twentieth century as the 'woman's epoch' as far as family law is concerned and that it is inadequate to depict recent developments in terms of increments in women's rights. In fact the problem for feminist politics with a concept of rights is that it leaves untouched structural inequalities and makes demands at the level of formal equality. Although the concept of equal rights has traditionally been adopted by the powerless or disadvantaged, it can equally be appropriated by more powerful sectors of society. There is nothing inherently progressive in this concept and although the demand for equal rights has achieved certain benefits for women, anti-feminist groups have also used it in order to undermine advances made by women in improving their social and economic status. In particular the demand for rights is problematic in the area of child custody, since the law has, for some time, been moving away from a position of rights *over* children towards an emphasis on duties and responsibilities *towards* them. Indeed the notion of individual rights over children would seem to be especially problematic for feminist strategy if we are attempting to establish equality of responsibility and caretaking between parents.

Rights therefore pose a difficult problem for feminists, more especially as the concept has been raised yet again in relation to the question of women accruing too many rights and advantages over men within marriage. The idea that marriage favours women is, of course, not new. For example Blackstone maintained in the eighteenth century that: 'Even the disabilities, which the wife lies under, are for the most part intended for her protection and benefit. So great a favourite is the female sex of the laws of England' (quoted in Blom-Cooper and Drewry, 1976: 155).

However the contemporary debate about the disproportionate advantages accorded to women in marriage, which has recently been fuelled by groups such as CJD and FNF, has taken on a new aspect. Harper (1979), for example, argues that the burden that is placed on husbands to maintain their wives is now an anachronism because the legal status of wives has improved so much. He states:

> It seems to be overlooked that these obligations developed at a time when a wife was regarded as a mere chattel . . . Then it was logical that the man to whom she owed total legal and personal submission for a lifetime should be obliged to maintain her . . . Today a husband has no such rights over his wife and it is a case of hunting with the hounds and running with the fox to demand both the modern rights of women and the old obligations of men (*The Guardian*, September 25, 1979).

Although Harper is right in stating that wives are no longer the legal chattel of their husbands, he ignores the fact that the duty to maintain is not simply contingent upon a husband's counterbalancing rights, but upon the fact that the division of labour between husbands and wives places women in a position of dependency upon their husbands. The duty to maintain stems from an economic reality and not an eighteenth century legal right, so that the loss of those legal rights should not automatically lead to a reduction in a husband's obligations as Harper proposes.

There is no consideration of the structural dependency of women as wives and mothers in Harper's argument, nor in the tracts published by CJD, but even where the domestic role of women is considered in the equation (Deech 1980), it is treated as an advantage that *privileges* women. Domestic labour becomes conflated with a concept of the right not-to-work. For example Deech has suggested that:

> It may be argued that women have a right to be full-time housewives and mothers and that this in fact damages their career prospects permanently. Even if this argument is accepted, the right is not in practice exercisable in conjunction with our easy, no-fault divorce laws (*The Times*, January 14, 1980).

Domestic labour in this context becomes a 'luxury of choice' which is exercised by wives to the disadvantage of ex-husbands and their new wives and families.

The problem with the arguments put forward by Harper and Deech is that they conflate law and legislation with the reality of inequality within the family and within wider society. They ignore that women are still in a subordinate position, both in the domestic and waged economy in spite of legislation on equal pay, sex discrimination, domestic violence and matrimonial property rights. They also fail to recognize that law, as well as other social institutions, operates to constitute women as dependent within the family. This level of analysis locates the problem of dependency at the level of individual members of the family.

The current backlash is an example of the way in which the concept of equal rights in family law can operate to obscure the structural inequality between husband and wife, fathers and mothers, within the family. By arguing that on the breakdown of marriage individual men should no longer be held responsible for the maintenance of individual women (since such women should be able to be self-sufficient) they misconstrue the whole development of matrimonial law in recent decades. Legislation has not altered the ability of wives and mothers to be self-sufficient, in fact as campaigns for disaggregation have revealed much legislation supports and reinforces a woman's dependence on a 'head of household'. Moreover family law has attempted to attach the responsibility for the maintenance of wives and children even more securely to individual men. The point is that this development, and the alliance of family and welfare law has not been a process of enhancing individual women's rights but a process of regulating the family structure and reducing the costs of the single family unit to the state. Husbands are increasingly obliged to maintain their wives, not because wives are 'the spoilt darlings' of the law, but because the law attempts to contain dependency within individual, economically viable family units.

Notes

Julia Brophy and Carol Smart are both doing research on Family Law at the Centre for Criminological and Socio-Legal Studies, University of Sheffield. The research is funded by the SSRC.

A fuller version of this paper was presented at the BSA Conference on Inequality held in April 1981. A copy of that paper can be obtained from the authors.

Our thanks to Anna Lutwama for all her help in preparing this paper.

1. The Custody of Children Act 1891 gave the courts the power to make a declaration of parental 'unfitness'. This Act was instigated after a number of cases in which parents who had abandoned or deserted their children, later recovered the children from Dr. Barnardo's home. Under this Act the court could, if it was of the opinion that the parent was 'unfit', refuse to return the child to parental custody.
2. Even in the working-class family, women were dependent on their husband's earning power because the concept of the family wage depressed women's earnings. (Land 1980, Barrett and McIntosh 1980.)
3. The Law Commission's proposals on illegitimacy attempt to deal with the 'stigma' of illegitimacy by giving the biological father automatic rights (to give his nationality to the child, to be entered on the birth certificate and to have equal claims to custody and access as the mother). If these proposals were introduced, it would mean a mother would have to go to court to prevent her child's father exercising these rights. The Commission did not propose to abolish illegitimacy by raising the legal status of women.

Case Notes

B. v. *B* (1975) Family Law, Vol. 6, p. 42.
Button v. *Button* (1968), Weekly Law Reports, Vol. 1, p. 462.
Gottliffe v. *Edelston* (1930), King's Bench, Vol. 2, p. 393.
Gurasz v. *Gurasz* (1969), All England Law Reports, Vol. 3, p. 823.
H v. *H and C* (1969), All England Law Reports, Vol. 1, p. 263.
Re Agar Ellis (1883), Chancery Division, Vol. 24, p. 317.
Re L (infants) (1962), All England Law Reports, Vol. 3, p. 4.
Willoughby v. *Willoughby* (1951), Probate, p. 184.

References

Blom-Cooper, L. and Drewry, G. (1976) *Law and Morality*. Duckworth: London.
Barrett, M. and McIntosh, M. (1980) 'The Family Wage: Some Problems for Socialists and Feminists', *Capital and Class*, No. 11.
Corrigan, P. (1980) (ed.) *Capitalism, State Formation and Marxist Theory*, London: Quartet Books.
Davin, A. (1978) 'Imperialism & Motherhood' *History Workshop* No. 5.

Deech, R. (1980) 'Why maintenance is a bad bargain for all concerned', *The Times*, January 14, 1980.

Graveson, R.H. and Crane, F.R. (1957) *A Century of Family Law*, Sweet and Maxwell: London.

Harper, B. (1979) 'Divorce is a misfortune which befalls both', *The Guardian* September 25, 1979.

Harrison, R. and Mort, F. (1980) 'Patriarchal aspects of nineteenth century state formation', in Corrigan (1980).

Hutter, B. and Williams, G. (1981) (eds), *Controlling Women*, London: Croom Helm.

Land, H. (1980) 'The family wage' *Feminist Review*, No. 6.

Law Commission (1979) *Working Paper on Illegitimacy*, No. 74, London: HMSO.

McGregor, O.R. *et al.* (1970) *Separated Spouses*, Duckworth: London.

3.5 Technology and changes in the division of labour in the American home

CHRISTINE BOSE

[. . .]

Introduction

Popular ideology indicates that 'technology', broadly defined, has 'liberated' women from the home. The theory is so well accepted that it is often assumed to be true and rarely is tested as an hypothesis by social scientists. Various household technologies have been studied, as has the division of labour. However, we have no clear model of the relationship between them. Undoubtedly this is because of the lack of theoretical development given to the ideology, the vaguely-defined key terms, and the contradictory evidence found in sex stratification research literature. Problems abound. Which technologies have liberated women: in-door plumbing, the vacuum cleaner, the yogurt-maker or wire whisk? What is liberation: less physical or mental exertion, cheaper appliances, or less time spent on housework? If women have been liberated, why haven't the number of hours absorbed by housework declined over the last 40 years? [. . .]

Terminology and indicators

When speaking of technologies which impact the home we refer to two broad levels. The first is the process of industrialization which, with increasing urban centralization, has raised the general technological level of American society as a whole. The second referent is to particular home technologies. We distinguish among three major classifications of household technologies, following Hartmann's (1974) typology:

Source: Bose, C. (1979) Technology and changes in the division of labour in the American home, *Women's Studies International Quarterly*. Vol. 2, pp. 295—304, Pergamon Press, Oxford

Utilities such as running water, electricity, gas, sewage and garbage services which form the technological infra-structure.

Appliances, the actual machines used in performing housework. These can be disaggregated by size (large, small), power needs (electric, manual), and durability (durable, non-durable).

[Commodities (purchased pre- or semi-processed goods), notably] foods including those convenience foods produced for use in the home and fast food services where complete meals are purchased, and often consumed, outside of the home.

Imbedded within this classification is the distinction among technologies provided by the public *versus* private sectors, and among those intended for use in the home *versus* those for use outside of the home.

The latter distinction is important in defining aspects of household division of labour. For as services are provided by workers outside of the home (cooking, dry cleaning) we might expect a decline in total amount of work performed in the home. To a certain extent, the only true liberation from housework comes when someone else does the work. How could this liberation be measured?

(1) First, the proportion of all housework tasks done by each household member could be rearranged. In particular, the proportion done by wives would need to decline for women to be 'liberated'. However, we know that women do the largest proportion of tasks in contemporary households and that there has been relatively little change in this division over the last 15 years (Berheide *et al*, 1976). Further, the total time spent on housework has either increased or remained stable between 1930 and the 1950s (Vanek 1974, Cowan 1974). We know relatively little about task-sharing earlier than this time.

(2) Second, some of the work currently performed in the home could be provided by market services. Options include the purchase of domestic help within the home or the use of fast food services, laundries, etc. outside of the home.

We know, regarding this second indicator, that there was a rapid decline in domestic service from 1900 to 1950 (Oppenheimer 1970). Meanwhile recent years have shown a great increase in use of fast food services, such that one in four meals is now eaten outside the home (Vaugh 1976). Does this mean that the loss of help of others has been compensated for by outside services?

Certainly this is a part of the explanation, but there are also other intervening variables.

(3) Third, women's own use of time might be reallocated so that housework absorbs a smaller percentage of our total time. The reduction could occur through smaller family size, lower cleanliness standards, etc. Or, the interference of other roles such as that of paid employee could reduce total time available for housework.

Within this last category some writers also include the change in housework content from heavy production work (ironing, cooking, laundry) to physically 'lighter' consumption work (product maintenance, transportation to stores, purchasing) and family care. We do not interpret this change in content housework as a liberation from it. Consumption work still takes time, is integral to the maintenance of the home, and is carried out by household members. Thus unless consumption/maintenance takes less time than production we cannot interpret the change in housework content as 'freeing' women.

Probably the largest impact has been caused by married women's entry into the paid labour force. On the average, women in the labour force do 3—4 hours per day less of housework than do full-time housewives. Why have women been able to move into paid employment? Is the change facilitated or caused by various levels of technology?

We hypothesize that during the last 100 years, technology has been used to substitute for loss of the labour of non-wives. As domestic service declined, and then household size followed suit, household technology allowed wives to take over the increased work load. Just as wives' workload might have been lightened by some utilities, loss of helpers and new technologies combined to allow women to bear the burden of new tasks. This combination may initially have been more profitable than increasing market services. Of course, we expect these substitution effects to vary with the socio-economic background of families. Wealthier families probably still could afford to pay for outside domestic help.

Now, as housework focuses more on consumption, women can take on labour force jobs when they are available. Further, the decline in the ability of one income to support a family pushes women into the labour force as does the increasing alienation, isolation, and boredom of most household tasks.

Technological impacts

The long-term trend of industrialization has impacted women's roles in several ways. Prior to the industrial revolution the household was a centre (for all its members) of both production and consumption. As industrialization began, the household retained its dual character, producing goods for home consumption and for the market economy under the cottage system. The latter function diminished rapidly as centralized factories developed, leaving the home as a centre of consumption and socialization. Thus production for home and market became physically separated. The market economy produced goods for use in the home, rather than developing food, laundry or child care services to take more functions outside of it (Hartman 1974, Gilman 1966). Strasser suggests that this choice was made between 1907 and 1916 when large capital investors found a more profitable outlet in the automobile than in the washing machine or other home products.

As production moved out of the home, the work of household maintenance did not decrease. If anything, standards of output were raised! Early nineteenth-century attempts to bring market-place 'rationalization' to the home had failed, primarily because building practices, the cheapness of coal, the symbolic value of the open fire, and the presence of servants allowed the existence of households independent of centralized urban functions. The general lack of interest in efficiency and labour-saving contributed to this resistance. However, once the servant crisis occurred and the industrial ethic of efficiency and labour-saving developed, the home became a logical site to apply these values. The rationalization of the home was thus dependent upon the prior industrialization and rationalization of the outside work place.

Two social trends in the early twentieth century make these connections explicit. First, the 'domestic science movement' of the 1920s, which attempted to make housework more like industrial management (see Ehrenreich and English 1975); and second the 'new home economics' which sought to apply microeconomic theory to household production, based on early works of Margaret Reid (1934). These movements illustrate how the principles of scientific management, as developed by Taylor, were extended to the home. Current home economics literature is still full of applications of his time/motion study techniques. [. . .]

We can now look at the classes of utilities, appliances and [commodities]. Utilities clearly changed household work more than any other technical improvement introduced because they eliminated several time-consuming heavy tasks. Hot and cold running water eliminated carrying, pumping and heating water; electricity and gas eliminated coal and wood stoves which had required chopping wood, carrying coal and continuous cleaning or stoking. Yet data on utilities' impact are slim and unreliable. We assume that time was undoubtedly saved, even though total housework time did not decline. Rather time saved was passed to other household activities which were carried on by women. The major utility transformation did not have profound impact on the household division of labour, although it did reallocate wives' time. Time budget studies that compare rural/urban time allocations all show an increase in time spent on childcare, purchasing and management and a decrease in time spent in meal preparation (Vanek 1974, Ogburn and Nimkoff 1955, Robinson and Converse 1972). Over the last 50 years, despite the introduction of 'labour-saving devices', the amount of time which women spend on housework has either remained constant or actually increased. The net effect of these technologies might have been greater if utilities had not fostered second-level effects and if other social changes were not going on simultaneously. In household production as elsewhere we find a tendency to use the time provided by labour-saving machinery, not for more leisure, but for more goods or services. Today, not only rising standards, but also the proliferation of small and medium-sized appliances that are task-extending or — adding rather than task-eliminating have offset many of the original gains made by utilities in decreasing time. It sometimes seems that what technology may give with one hand it can take away with another. New small appliances involve more elaborate cleaning, more storage problems and increased likelihood of maintenance.

It is also possible that some household appliances have been used as a substitute for more equal divisions of labour. As Walker and Woods (1976) note, men do little work inside the home no matter what their wives do. Such studies control only for age, class and number of children and not for equipment. Yet Thrall (1970) found that when families had garbage disposals, wives were more likely to take care of the garbage than in those with no disposal. He found a similar pattern with dishwashers. Task-specific technologies may develop so that women can take over tasks previously done by the other family members rather than *vice versa*. We know that in some middle-class families there is a positive correlation (0.20) between number of appliances and household work time. Apparently appliances either create more work and/or women use the time saved elsewhere in accord with rising standards (Berheide *et al* 1976).

It might be worth exploring why people continue to purchase appliances that do not seem to save time and are often quite expensive. One obvious explanation is that people believe they save time even if there is no proof of time-saving in their daily lives. Another and perhaps better explanation is that household equipment has, apart from its perceived efficiency effects, symbolic value. For the housewife who sees her role as a nurturant one, and who may believe that equipment increases the quality of her work and thus of home life, a well-equipped home is a necessity. For many Americans a well-equipped home is also an indication of social status. For the husband who sees his role as provider, the ability to give household gifts may involve symbolic power and reassure him of his dominance. To date we have little information on kitchen appliances as gifts or on who decides to purchase equipment. Research in this area could help explain the rationality of appliance purchases.

Convenience foods are often claimed to be a major time-saver and therefore a 'liberator' of the household cook. However time saved by convenience foods is seen as something to spend on family or for other purposeful activities — spending money only to lessen work seems to conflict with traditional values. And here again, assessments of time saved must be based on speculations because scratch *versus* convenience food studies do not measure shopping, planning and management time or meal types. So their conclusions that convenience food saves several minutes over preparing from scratch are meaningless, even though the former may save some time. Convenience foods are also more costly, but until recently consumers seemed ready to pay the price. Now we are witnessing a move towards more natural foods. Whether this change means that women will spend more time in the kitchen depends on whether or not convenience foods were a major factor in reducing kitchen time initially.

Family size and age of children have been found to be significant factors in determining overall time spent in housework (Walker and Woods 1976, Vanek 1974) and in meal preparation in particular (Walker and Woods 1976). Furthermore the percentage of employed women has more than doubled in the last 50 years. Thus it is no surprise that smaller families eat out more often than larger ones and that women who work prepare fewer meals at home [...] (Vaugh 1976).

Eating out is a long-run trend which became necessary and acceptable during the Second World War with the mass entry of women into the work force. The long-run trend is supported by several factors: (1) continued increase of married women's labour force participation; (2) cost of eating at home which rose faster than that of eating out between 1972 and 1975; (3) women recognizing the cost of their own time spent in cooking.

However there are also limitations on the ability of market services to replace home food preparation: (1) massive advertising campaigns by supermarkets and appliance industry pointing out that it is now cheaper to eat at home (if the cook's time is not counted as a cost); (2) inflation which will cut back on the ability of mid- and lower-income groups to eat out — if real household income declines more families may be forced to eat at home; (3) among higher income groups, women are combining eating in better restaurants with more gourmet cooking at home.

Thus among higher income and non-employed women, gains in time afforded by eating out may be offset by preparation of more elaborate meals.

Non-technological impacts

Why didn't electrification and indoor plumbing change household division of labour or free women for non-household tasks? The answer lies in several social and economic trends.

Households were becoming smaller by 1900 because of the loss of family members, boarders and servants. The availability of apartments and jobs for single women allowed older and single members of families to live alone, instead of with relatives. Although this increased isolation and the number of household consumption units, the trend did reduce average household size. Decline in number of children also contributed to the trend. The developing ideology of the privatized household meant a decline in the number of people wanting to take in or be boarders. Again, this meant a decline in household size as well as a loss of independent income for some wives. The xenophobic attitudes of the First World War resulted in severe restrictions on immigration which further cut into the demand for boarding situations. Finally, the developing demand of domestic labour for clear service contracts and regular hours reduced the number of household services provided by others. Over a 50-year period the employment of domestic servants dropped to almost one-third its 1900 level (Oppenheimer 1970).

This period of 'servant crises' was an opportune time for the industrial ethic of efficiency to be applied to the home (Ravetz 1968). In theory the process might have occurred using technological solutions in the home or by bringing household functions into labour force production modes. In practice, the former mode prevailed and technology was brought into the home where women could now perform all the work previously done by other family members or servants. The household work-environment became increasingly privatized. Thus utilities helped to foster second-level effects by allowing the development of power driven, single-task home appliances rather than community solutions. With the advent of child labour laws, childcare tasks at home were increased. And after the Second World War and the diffusion of the automobile, consumer tasks were increased.

The continually increasing number of women entering the labour force is the trend which has had the largest impact on *time* spent on housework (Vanek 1974, Ogburn and Nimkoff 1955, Robinson and Converse 1972). Recent studies (Szalai 1975, Thrall 1970) make it clear that housework time reduction is a function of employment and not of the amount of technology available. Employed women substitute non-durable time-savers for their labour (Strober 1977), shop at fewer stores on fewer days, and prepare fewer meals (Vaugh 1976). It should be noted, however, that married women employed outside the home do not do significantly smaller proportions of housework (Berheide *et al* 1976). Thus women's employment changes their own division of time, but does not change the household division of labour.

A non-historical, family variable — stage in life cycle — is also important in explaining technological usage. At least currently, appliance usage and convenience food purchase are primarily determined by years married, and number and ages of children (Anderson 1971). Presence of children changes the content of housework, but not the division of household work (Berheide *et al* 1976). Only older children play some role in reducing wives' proportion of non-childcare tasks (Berk and Berk 1976).

Researchers feel that income or social class is also a major determinant of technological ownership (Thrall 1970).

Technology and working conditions in the home

The clarity in the division between male and female tasks in the home has increased. Technology has been used to privatize work and thus increase the load on many individual women (Cowan 1976b, Gilman 1966). Housework remains within decentralized, inefficient units. In fact, it may now be difficult to move some housework tasks out of the home (Cowan 1976a, Kneeland 1928). First the small scale of household work and technologies is labour-intensive. Second, the work has become so emotion-laden that moving it into a more communalized term may be impossible (Ravetz 1965). Further, women's labour at home is unpaid and thus 'cheap', so our labour has been used for these tasks, retaining the division of labour within the home and keeping home work structurally separated from the paid work system (Davidoff 1976). Ironically, the combination of market goods and women's unpaid labour in the home may have discouraged the growth of comparable market services (Baumol 1967), and increased the type of work and time involved in their use and maintenance. Thus in spite of the increasing entry of women into the workforce, the impact of household technology may have been to make the prescriptive statement 'woman's place is in the home' descriptively true both by increasing the hours required on household tasks and by technologically unemploying working women from paying jobs as domestics, seamstresses or laundresses.

Men do little work inside the home whether or not wives work, and the ratio of female to male tasks remains the same. Technology has not saved time or redefined sex roles. Rather, it has changed the type of work performed and has allowed standards and productivity to rise. So it seems possible that technologies have been used as a substitute for a more equal division of labour.

[Thrall's findings (1970) on the effects of owning garbage disposers and dishwashers cannot be presumed to apply to all other appliances, but certainly] the pattern is consistent with earlier trends of wives (with washing machine aid) taking over the roles of the disappearing laundresses or grandparents.

Improving working conditions in the home is the opposite of freeing women for other tasks. Nonetheless, if women are taking on new household roles, has technology improved the working conditions? One indicator of working conditions is workers' or housewives' satisfaction. There is little data to refer to here. If studies of housewives' attitudes exist at all, they are the private property of market researchers. One study however (Oakley 1974), found that ownership of equipment and other amenities may affect the way particular tasks are performed or add interest to certain tasks, but it does not create satisfaction with housework as a whole. Satisfaction or dissatisfaction with housework was unrelated to the number of appliances owned. Housewives did register dissatisfaction over the lack of social interaction and the monotony inherent in the housewife role. In another study (Berheide et al 1976), we find that middle-class women feel primarily 'neutral' about housework — neither interested nor disinterested — but similar to alienated blue collar workers.

Yet insofar as technologies were designed to be used in the home and reinforce the home system, keeping women economically marginal to the larger society, technologies are related to dissatisfaction with housework. Several studies have documented women's preference for paid employment over housework (Ferree 1976, Mostow 1975, Rubin 1976). And the deteriorating effects of being 'just a housewife' are no longer myth or speculation. The National Center for Health Statistics found that fewer working wives suffered from nervousness, insomnia, trembling hands, nightmares, perspiring hands, headaches, dizziness and heart palpitations than did a matched sample of non-working wives. The monotony of the home setting, the repetition of menial tasks and the isolation and lack of stimulation from other adults were found to be the source of chronic fatigue in full-time housewives (Friedan 1965). The problem is not confined to middle-class women. The preference to be out of the home is also reflected in an increasing incidence of this 'housewife syndrome' among Native American and working-class women (Fogleman 1975).

Working conditions have been affected in other ways as well. The form and content of work in the home have changed, although the hours are the same. First, standards have gone up. Second, the work is not physically as heavy although the burden of monotony has increased. Third, there has been an increase in time spent with children, on purchasing, transportation and management, simultaneous to a decrease in time spent on meal preparation (Robinson and Converse 1972, Vanek 1974). Women's home role has primarily become one of consumer, with the attendant needs for planning purchases, travelling to consumption centres, and making the actual purchase (Weinbaum and Bridges 1976, Galbraith 1973).

Conclusion

Popular ideology would indicate that technology makes all things equal. Popular theory would indicate that technology succeeded in substituting first for lost servant help and later for lost family members' aid. But that substitution has always meant that just when women's work load was declining, new burdens were added. However, the current division of family labour does not even effectively maximize family efficiency (Berk and Berk 1976). It seems that the only real 'convenience' comes when someone else does the work. This could occur in three ways. The first is the reallocation of women's own time.

The changes in women's division of time between home and work force have not been explained by technology itself as an independent variable. Rather the labour force demand for women, reduced household size, home monotony and inflation have drawn women to paid work which has in its turn decreased time available to spend on housework (but can increase total female labour time). The relocation of housework toward consumption, transportation and childcare has facilitated women's move into the labour force, but it is not likely to have caused this re-division of women's time. Nor has technology *per se* caused these changes due to the economic context of its use within the home. While the increased ease of work brought by utilities might have 'freed' women, the second-level effects were in the opposite direction. Appliances in the home often extend women's role therein. Therefore we predict that ownership of increasing amounts of home technologies is likely to be positively correlated with stereotyped division of labour. The underlying assumption is that more technology is purchased as income increases. Beyond a certain income level, not only will technology increase, but women/wives will be less likely to seek paid employment and more likely to fulfil the mother/wife role prescription. Thus home technology and division of labour, though correlated, are linked by the prior variable of income.

The second form of change — re-division of labour among household members — has simply not occurred. The work content has varied, but women's prime responsibility has gone unmodified by utilities and has probably been extended by appliances.

At this juncture, only labour market solutions to housework offer the prospect of relieving women's burden. The proliferation of fast food services indicates that some chores are moving out of the home. Others, such as child or laundry care, remain home-centred. The service sector of the economy is clearly growing. We need to monitor this area to see: (1) which services are provided — are they housework oriented? (2) who provides them — do women move into paid work providing the same services in the labour force as they did at home?

In the past, non-technological changes such as those in labour force or household composition have had the greatest impact on household division of labour, and we can expect future change to emanate from this direction, too.

References

Anderson, Thomas W. 1971. *The Convenience-Oriented Consumer.* Studies in Marketing No. 14. Bureau of Business Research, The University of Texas at Austin.

Baumol, William. 1967. Macroeconomics of unbalanced growth — the anatomy of urban crisis. *Am. Econ. Rev.* 57, 415–426.

Berheide, Catherine W., Berk, Sarah F. and Berk, Richard A. 1976. Household work in the suburbs: the job and its participants. *Pacific Sociol. Rev.* 19, (4), 491–518.

Berk, Richard A. and Berk, Sarah F. 1976. A simultaneous equation model for the division of household labour. Paper presented at AAAS annual meetings, Boston.

Berk, Sarah F., Berk, Richard A. and Berheide, Catherine W. 1976. The non-division of household labour. Northwestern University, unpublished.

Cowan, Ruth Schwartz. 1974. A case study of technology and social change: the washing machine and the working wife. In Hartmann, Mary and Banner, Lois eds. *Clio's Consciousness Raised: New Perspectives on The History of Women,* 245—253. Harper and Row, New York.

Cowan, Ruth Schwartz. 1976a. From Virginia Dare to Virginia Slims: woman and technology in American life, mimeo.

Cowan, Ruth Schwartz. 1976b. Two washes in the morning and a bridge party at night: the American housewife between the wars. *Women's Studies* 3, 147—172.

Davidoff, Lenore. 1976. The rationalization of housework. In *Dependence and Exploitation in Work and Marriage,* 121—151. Longman, London.

Ehrenreich, Barbara and English, Deirdre. 1975. The manufacture of housework. *Socialist Revolution* 5 (4), 5—40.

Elliott, Carolyn M. 1977. Theories of development: an assessment. *Signs* 3 (1), 1—8.

Ferree, Myra Marx. 1976. Working-class jobs: housework and paid work as sources of satisfaction. *Social Problems* 23, 431—441.

Fogleman, Billye. 1975. Housewife syndrome among native American women. *Urban Anthropology* 4 (2), 184 (Abstract).

Friedan, Betty. 1965. *The Feminine Mystique.* Dell Publishing, New York.

Galbraith, John. 1973. The economics of the American housewife. *The Atlantic Mon.* 233, 74.

Glazer, Nona. 1976. Housework. *Signs* 1 (4), 905—922.

Gilman, Charlotte P. 1966. *Women and Economics.* Harper and Row, New York (originally published 1898 by Small, Maynard & Co., Boston).

Hartmann, Heidi. 1974. Capitalism and Women's Work in the Home, 1900—1930, PhD dissertation, Yale University.

Kneeland, Hildegard. 1928. Limitations of scientific management in household work. *J. Home Econ.* 20, 311—314.

McCormack, Thelma. 1975. Toward a nonsexist perspective on social and political change. In: Millman, Marcia and Kanter, Rosabeth M. eds. *Another Voice,* 1—13. Doubleday, New York.

Mostow, E. 1975. A comparative study of work satisfaction of females with full-time employment and full-time housekeeping. *Am. J. Orthopsychiatry* 45 (4), 538—548.

National Center for Health Statistics. 1970. *Selected Symptoms of Psychological Distress.* U.S. Dept. of Health, Education and Welfare, Table 17, 30—31.

Oakley, Ann. 1974. *The Sociology of Housework.* Pantheon Books, New York.

Ogburn, W.F. and Nimkoff, M.F. 1955. *Technology and the Changing Family.* Houghton Mifflin, Cambridge, Mass.

Oppenheimer, Valerie K. 1970. *The Female Labor Force in the United States.* Berkeley, University of California, Institute of International Studies, Population Monograph Series No. 5.

Ravetz, Allison. 1965. Modern technology and an ancient occupation: housework in present day society. *Technology Cult.* 6, 256—260.

Ravetz, Allison. 1968. The Victorian coal kitchen and its reformers. *Victorian Studies* 11 (4), 435–460.

Reid, Margaret. 1934. *Economics of Household Production.* John Wylie, New York.

Robinson, John and Converse, Philip. 1972. Social change reflected in the use of time. In: *Human Meaning of Social Change.* Russell Sage Foundation, New York.

Rubin, Lillian Breslow. 1976. *Worlds of Pain: Life in the Working-Class Family.* Basic Books, New York.

Strasser, Susan. 1977. Never Done: Ideology and Technology of Household Work, 1850–1930, PhD dissertation, State University of New York at Stonybrook.

Strober, Myra. 1977. Wives labor force behaviour and family consumption habits. *Am. Econ. Rev.* 00, 410–417.

Szalai, Alexander. 1975. The situation of women in the light of contemporary time-budget research. Conference Paper: World Conference of the International Women Years, Mexico City.

Thrall, Charles. 1970. Household Technology and the Division of Labor in Families, unpublished PhD dissertation, Harvard University.

Vanek, Joanne. 1974. Time spent on housework. *Scientific American* 231, 116–120.

Vaugh, Charles. 1976. Growth and future of the fast food industry. *Cornell Motel and Restaurant Administration Q.*

Walker, Kathryn E. and Woods, Margaret E. 1976. *Time Use: A Measure of Household Production of Family Goods and Services.* Center for the Family of the American Home Economics Association, Washington DC.

Weinbaum, Batya and Bridges, Amy. 1976. The other side of the pay check: monopoly capital and the structure of consumption. *Mon. Rev.* 28 (3), 88–103.

3.6 Anger and tenderness: the experience of motherhood

ADRIENNE RICH

Entry from my journal, November 1960

My children cause me the most exquisite suffering of which I have any experience. It is the suffering of ambivalence: the murderous alternation between bitter resentment and raw-edged nerves, and blissful gratification and tenderness. Sometimes I seem to myself, in my feelings towards these tiny guiltless beings, a monster of selfishness and intolerance. Their voices wear away at my nerves, their constant needs, above all their need for simplicity and patience, fill me with despair at my own failures, despair too at my fate, which is to serve a function for which I was not fitted. And I am weak sometimes from held-in rage. There are times when I feel only death will free us from one another, when I envy the barren woman[1] who has the luxury of her regrets but lives a life of privacy and freedom.

And yet at other times I am melted with the sense of their helpless, charming and quite irresistible beauty − their ability to go on loving and trusting − their staunchness and decency and unselfconsciousness. *I love them*. But it's in the enormity and inevitability of this love that the sufferings lie. [. . .]

May 1965

To suffer with and for and against a child − maternally, egotistically, neurotically, sometimes with a sense of helplessness, sometimes with the illusion of learning wisdom − but always, everywhere, in body and soul, *with* that child − because that child is a piece of oneself.

To be caught up in waves of love and hate, jealousy even of the child's childhood; hope and fear for its maturity; longing to be free of responsibility, tied by every fibre of one's being.

That curious primitive reaction of protectiveness, the beast

Source: Rich, A. (1977) *Of Woman Born: Motherhood as Experience and Institution,* Virago, London, pp. 21−55

defending her cub, when anyone attacks or criticizes him — and yet no one more hard on him than I! [. . .]

Unexamined assumptions: First, that a 'natural' mother is a person without further identity, one who can find her chief gratification in being all day with small children, living at a pace tuned to theirs; that the isolation of mothers and children together in the home must be taken for granted; that maternal love is, and should be, quite literally selfless; that children and mothers are the 'causes' of each others' suffering. I was haunted by the stereotype of the mother whose love is 'unconditional'; and by the visual and literary images of motherhood as a single-minded identity. If I knew parts of myself existed that would never cohere to those images, weren't those parts then abnormal, monstrous? And — as my eldest son, now aged twenty-one, remarked on reading the above passages: 'You seemed to feel you ought to love us all the time. But there *is* no human relationship where you love the other person at every moment'. Yes, I tried to explain to him, but women — above all, mothers — have been supposed to love that way.

From the fifties and early sixties, I remember a cycle. It began when I had picked up a book or began trying to write a letter, or even found myself on the telephone with someone toward whom my voice betrayed eagerness, a rush of sympathetic energy. The child (or children) might be absorbed in busyness, in his own dreamworld; but as soon as he felt me gliding into a world which did not include him, he would come to pull at my hand, ask for help, punch at the typewriter keys. And I would feel his wants at such a moment as fraudulent, as an attempt moreover to defraud me of living even for fifteen minutes as myself. My anger would rise; I would feel the futility of any attempt to salvage myself, and also the inequality between us: my needs always balanced against those of a child, and always losing. I could love so much better, I told myself, after even a quarter-hour of selfishness, of peace, of detachment from my children. A few minutes! But it was as if an invisible thread would pull taut between us and break, to the child's sense of inconsolable abandonment, if I moved — not even physically, but in spirit — into a realm beyond our tightly circumscribed life together. It was as if my placenta had begun to refuse him oxygen. Like so many women, I waited with impatience for the moment when their father would return from work, when for an hour or two at least the circle drawn around mother and children would grow looser, the intensity between us slacken, because there was another adult in the house.

I did not understand that this circle, this magnetic field in which we lived, was not a natural phenomenon.

Intellectually, I must have known it. But the emotion-charged, tradition-heavy form in which I found myself cast as the Mother seemed, then, as ineluctable as the tides. And, because of this form — this microcosm in which my children and I formed a tiny, private emotional cluster, and in which (in bad weather or when someone was ill) we sometimes passed days at a time without seeing another adult except for their father — there *was* authentic need underlying my child's invented claims upon me when I seemed to be wandering away from him. He was reassuring himself that warmth, tenderness, continuity, solidity were still there for him, in my person. My singularity, my uniqueness in the world as *his mother* — perhaps more dimly also as Woman — evoked a need vaster than any single human being could satisfy, except by loving continuously, unconditionally, from dawn to dark, and often in the middle of the night.

In a living room in 1975, I spent an evening with a group of women poets, some of whom had children. One had brought hers along, and they slept or played in adjoining rooms. We talked of poetry, and also of infanticide, of the case of a local woman, the mother of eight, who had been in severe depression since the birth of her third child, and who had recently murdered and decapitated her two youngest, on her suburban front lawn. Several women in the group, feeling a direct connection with her desperation, had signed a letter to the local newspaper protesting the way her act was perceived by the press and handled by the community mental health system. Every woman in that room who had children, every poet, could identify with her. We spoke of the wells of anger that her story cleft open in us. We spoke of our own moments of murderous anger at our children, because there was no one and nothing else on which to discharge anger. We spoke in the sometimes tentative, sometimes rising, sometimes bitterly witty, unrhetorical tones and language of women who had met together over our common work, poetry, and who found another common ground in an unacceptable, but undeniable anger. The words are being spoken now, are being written down; the taboos are being broken, the masks of motherhood are cracking through.

For centuries no one talked of these feelings. I became a mother in the family-centred, consumer-oriented, Freudian-American world of the 1950s. My husband spoke eagerly of the children we would have; my parents-in-law awaited the birth of their grandchild. I had no idea of what *I* wanted, what *I* could or could not choose. I only knew that to have a child was to assume adult womanhood to the full, to prove myself, to be 'like other women'. [. . .]

I have a very clear, keen memory of myself the day after I was married: I was sweeping a floor. Probably the floor did not really need to be swept; probably I simply did not know what else to do with myself. But as I swept that floor I thought: 'Now I am a woman. This is an age-old action, this is what women have always done.' I felt I was bending to some ancient form, too ancient to question. *This is what women have always done.*

As soon as I was visibly and clearly pregnant, I felt, for the first time in my adolescent and adult life, not guilty. The atmosphere of approval in which I was bathed — even by strangers on the street, it seemed — was like an aura I carried with me, in which doubt, fears, misgivings, met with absolute denial. *This is what women have always done.*

Two days before my first son was born, I broke out in a rash which was tentatively diagnosed as measles, and was admitted to a hospital for contagious diseases to await the onset of labour. I felt for the first time a great deal of conscious fear, and guilt toward my unborn child, for having 'failed' him with my body in this way. In rooms near mine were patients with polio; no one was allowed to enter my room except in a hospital gown and mask. If during pregnancy I had felt in any vague command of my situation, I felt now totally dependent on my obstetrician, a huge, vigorous, paternal man, abounding with optimism and assurance, and given to pinching my cheek. I had gone through a healthy pregnancy, but as if tranquilized or sleep-walking. I had taken a sewing class in which I produced an unsightly and ill-cut maternity jacket which I never wore; I had made curtains for the baby's room, collected baby clothes, blotted out as much as possible the woman I had been a few months earlier. My second book of poems was in press, but I had stopped writing poetry, and read little except household magazines and books on childcare. I felt myself perceived by the world simply as a pregnant woman, and it seemed easier, less disturbing, to perceive myself so. After my child was born the 'measles' were diagnosed as an allergic reaction to pregnancy.

Within two years, I was pregnant again, and writing in a notebook:

November 1956

> Whether it's the extreme lassitude of early pregnancy or something more fundamental, I don't know; but of late I've felt, toward poetry — both reading and writing it — nothing but boredom and indifference. Especially toward my own and that of my immediate contemporaries. When I receive a letter soliciting mss., or someone alludes to my 'career', I have a strong sense of wanting to deny all responsibility for and interest in that person who writes — or who wrote.

If there is going to be a real break in my writing life, this is as good a time for it as any. I have been dissatisfied with myself, my work, for a long time.

My husband was a sensitive, affectionate man who wanted children and who — unusual in the professional, academic world of the fifties — was willing to 'help'. But it was clearly understood that this 'help' was an act of generosity; that *his* work, *his* professional life, was the real work in the family; in fact, this was for years not even an issue between us. I understood that my struggles as a writer were a kind of luxury, a peculiarity of mine; my work brought in almost no money: it even cost money, when I hired a household helper to allow me a few hours a week to write. 'Whatever I ask he tries to give me', I wrote in March 1958, 'but always the initiative has to be mine'. I experienced my depressions, bursts of anger, sense of entrapment, as burdens my husband was forced to bear because he loved me; I felt grateful to be loved in spite of bringing him those burdens. [. . .]

By July of 1958 I was again pregnant. The new life of my third — and, as I determined, my last — child, was a kind of turning for me. I had learned that my body was not under my control; I had not intended to bear a third child. I knew now better than I had ever known what another pregnancy, another new infant, meant for my body and spirit. Yet, I did not think of having an abortion. In a sense, my third son was more actively chosen than either of his brothers; by the time I knew I was pregnant with him, I was not sleepwalking any more.

August 1958 (Vermont)

I write this as the early rays of the sun light up our hillside and eastern windows. Rose with [the baby] at 5:30 a.m. and have fed him and breakfasted. This is one of the few mornings on which I haven't felt terrible mental depression and physical exhaustion.

. . . I have to acknowledge to myself that I would not have chosen to have more children, that I was beginning to look to a time, not too far off, when I should again be free, no longer so physically tired, pursuing a more or less intellectual and creative life. . . . The *only* way I can develop now is through much harder, more continuous, connected work than my present life makes possible. Another child means postponing this for some years longer — and years at my age are significant, not to be tossed lightly away.

And yet, somehow, something, call it Nature or that affirming fatalism of the human creature, makes me aware of the inevitable as already part of me, not to be contended against so much as brought to bear as an additional weapon against drift, stagnation and spiritual death. (For it is really death that I have been fearing — the crumbling to death of that scarcely-born physiognomy which my whole life has been a battle to give birth to — a recognizable, autonomous self, a creation in poetry and in life.)

If more effort has to be made then I will make it. If more despair has to be lived through, I think I can anticipate it correctly and live through it.

Meanwhile, in a curious and unanticipated way, we really do welcome the birth of our child. [. . .]

Before my third child was born I decided to have no more children, to be sterilized. (Nothing is removed from a woman's body during this operation; ovulation and menstruation continue. Yet the language suggests a cutting- or burning-away of her essential womanhood, just as the old word 'barren' suggests a woman eternally empty and lacking.) My husband, although he supported my decision, asked whether I was sure it would not leave me feeling 'less feminine'. In order to have the operation at all, I had to present a letter, countersigned by my husband, assuring the committee of physicians who approved such operations that I had already produced three children, and stating my reasons for having no more. Since I had had rheumatoid arthritis for some years, I could give a reason acceptable to the male panel who sat on my case; my own judgment would not have been acceptable. When I awoke from the operation, twenty-four hours after my child's birth, a young nurse looked at my chart and remarked coldly: 'had yourself spayed, did you?'

The first great birth-control crusader, Margaret Sanger,[2] remarks that of the hundreds of women who wrote to her pleading for contraceptive information in the early part of the twentieth century, all spoke of wanting the health and strength to be better mothers to the children they already had; or of wanting to be physically affectionate to their husbands without dread of conceiving. None was refusing motherhood altogether, or asking for an easy life. These women — mostly poor, many still in their teens, all with several children — simply felt they could no longer do 'right' by their families, whom they expected to go on serving and rearing. Yet there always has been, and there remains, intense fear of the suggestion that women shall have the final say as to how our bodies are to be used. It is as if the suffering of the mother, the primary identification of woman *as* the mother — were so necessary to the emotional grounding of human society that the mitigation, or removal, of that suffering, that identification, must be fought at every level, including the level of refusing to question it at all. [...]

Once in a while someone used to ask me; 'Don't you ever write poems about your children?' The male poets of my generation did write poems about their children — especially their daughters. For me, poetry was where I lived as no-one's mother, where I existed as myself.

The bad and the good moments are inseparable for me. I recall the times when, suckling each of my children, I saw his eyes open full to mine, and realized each of us was fastened to the other, not only by mouth and breast, but through our mutual gaze: the depth, calm, passion, of that dark blue, maturely focused look. I recall the physical pleasure of having my full breast suckled at a time when I had no other physical pleasure in the world except the guilt-ridden pleasure of addictive eating. I remember early the sense of conflict, of a battleground none of us had chosen, of being an observer who, like it or not, was also an actor in an endless contest of wills. This was what it meant to me to have three children under the age of seven. But I recall too each child's individual body, his slenderness, wiriness, softness, grace, the beauty of little boys who have not been taught that the male body must be rigid. I remember moments of peace when for some reason it was possible to go to the bathroom alone. I remember being uprooted from already meagre sleep to answer a childish nightmare, pull up a blanket, warm a consoling bottle, lead a half-asleep child to the toilet. I remember going back to bed starkly awake, brittle with anger, knowing that my broken sleep would make next day a hell, that there would be more nightmares, more need for consolation, because out of my weariness I would rage at those children for no reason they could understand. I remember thinking I would never dream again (the unconscious of the young mother — where does it entrust its messages, when dream-sleep is denied her for years?) [...]

Even today, rereading old journals, remembering, I feel grief and anger; but their objects are no longer myself and my children. I feel grief at the waste of myself in those years, anger at the mutilation and manipulation of the relationship between mother and child, which is the great original source and experience of love.

On an early spring day in the 1970s, I meet a young woman friend on the street. She has a tiny infant against her breast, in a bright cotton sling; its face is pressed against her blouse, its tiny hand clutches a piece of the cloth. 'How old is she?' I ask. 'Just two weeks old', the mother tells me. I am amazed to feel in myself a passionate longing to have, once again, such a small, new being clasped against my body. The baby belongs there, curled, suspended asleep between her mother's breasts, as she belonged curled in the womb. The young mother — who already has a three-year-old — speaks of how quickly one forgets the pure pleasure of having this new creature, immaculate, perfect. And I walk away from her drenched with memory, with envy. Yet I know other things: that her life is far from simple; she is a mathematician who now has two children under the age of four; she is living even now in the rhythms of other lives — not only the regular cry of the infant but her three-year-old's needs, her husband's problems. In the building where I live, women are still raising children alone, living day in and day out within their individual family units, doing the laundry, herding the tricycles to the park, waiting for the husbands to come home. There is a baby-sitting pool and a children's playroom, young fathers push prams on weekends, but childcare is still the individual responsibility of the individual woman. I envy the sensuality of having an infant of two weeks curled against one's breast; I do not envy the turmoil of the elevator full of small children, babies howling in the laundromat, the apartment in winter where pent-up seven- and eight-year-olds have one adult to look to for their frustrations, reassurances, the grounding of their lives.

But, it will be said, this is the human condition, this inter-penetration of pain and pleasure, frustration and fulfilment. I might have told myself the same thing, fifteen or eighteen years ago. But the patriarchal institution of motherhood is not the 'human condition' any more than rape, prostitution, and slavery are. (Those who speak largely of the human condition are usually those most exempt from its oppressions — whether of sex, race, or servitude.)

Motherhood — unmentioned in the histories of conquest and serfdom, wars and treaties, exploration and imperialism — has a history, it has an ideology, it is more fundamental than tribalism or nationalism. My individual, seemingly private pains as a mother, the individual, seemingly private pains of the mothers around me and before me, whatever our class or colour, the regulation of women's reproductive power by men in every totalitarian system and every socialist revolution, the legal and technical control by men of contraception, fertility, abortion, obstetrics, gynecology, and extra-uterine reproductive experiments — all are essential to the patriarchal system, as is the negative or suspect status of women who are not mothers. [. . .]

The institution of motherhood is not identical with bearing and caring for children, any more than the institution of heterosexuality is identical with intimacy and sexual love. Both create the prescriptions and the conditions in which choices are made or blocked; they are not 'reality' but they have shaped the circumstances of our lives. The new scholars of women's history have begun to discover that, in any case, the social institutions and prescriptions for behaviour created by men have not necessarily accounted for the real lives of women. Yet any institution which expresses itself so universally ends by profoundly affecting our experience, even the language we use to describe it. The experience of maternity and the experience of sexuality have both been channeled to serve male interests; behaviour which threatens the institutions, such as illegitimacy, abortion, lesbianism, is considered deviant or criminal.

Institutionalized heterosexuality told women for centuries that we were dangerous, unchaste, the embodiment of carnal lust; then that we were 'not passionate', frigid, sexually passive; today it prescribes the 'sensuous', 'sexually liberated' woman in the West, the dedicated revolutionary ascetic in China; and everywhere it denies the reality of women's love for women. Institutionalized motherhood demands of women maternal 'instinct' rather than intelligence, selflessness rather than self-realization, relation to others rather than the creation of self. Motherhood is 'sacred' so long as its offspring are 'legitimate' — that is, as long as the child bears the name of a father who legally controls the mother. It is 'woman's highest and holiest mission', according to a socialist tract of 1914,[3] and a racist southern historian of 1910 tells us that 'woman is the embodied home, and the home is the basis of all institutions, the buttress of society'.[4] [. . .]

Patriarchy would seem to require, not only that women shall assume the major burden of pain and self-denial for the furtherance of the species, but that a majority of that species — women — shall remain essentially unquestioning and unenlightened. On this 'underemployment' of female consciousness depend the morality and the emotional life of the human family. [. . .] Patriarchy could not survive without motherhood and heterosexuality in their institutional forms; therefore they have to be treated as axioms, as 'nature' itself, not open to question except where, from time to time and place to place, 'alternate life-styles' for certain individuals are tolerated. [. . .]

Most of the literature of infant care and psychology has assumed that the process toward individuation is essentially the *child's* drama, played out against and with a parent or parents who are, for better or worse, givens. Nothing could have prepared me for the realization that I *was* a mother, one of those givens, when I knew I was still in a state of uncreation myself. That calm, sure, unambivalent woman who moved through the pages of the manuals

I read seemed as unlike me as an astronaut. Nothing, to be sure, had prepared me for the intensity of relationship already existing between me and a creature I had carried in my body and now held in my arms and fed from my breasts. Throughout pregnancy and nursing, women are urged to relax, to mime the serenity of madonnas. No one mentions the psychic crisis of bearing a first child, the excitation of long-buried feelings about one's own mother, the sense of confused power and powerlessness, of being taken over on the one hand and of touching new physical and psychic potentialities on the other, a heightened sensibility which can be exhilarating, bewildering, and exhausting. No one mentions the strangeness of attraction — which can be as single-minded and overwhelming as the early days of a love affair — to a being so tiny, so dependent, so folded-in to itself — who is, and yet is not, part of oneself.

The physical and psychic weight of responsibility on the woman with children is by far the heaviest of social burdens. It cannot be compared with slavery or sweated labour because the emotional bonds between a woman and her children make her vulnerable in ways which the forced labourer does not know; he can hate and fear his boss or master, loathe the toil; dream of revolt or of becoming a boss; the woman with children is a prey to far more complicated, subversive feelings. Love and anger *can* exist concurrently; anger at the conditions of motherhood can become translated into anger at the child, along with the fear that we are not 'loving'; grief at all we cannot do for our children in a society so inadequate to meet the human needs, becomes translated into guilt and self-laceration. This 'powerless responsibility' as one group of women has termed it, is a heavier burden even than providing a living — which so many mothers have done, and do, simultaneously with mothering — because it is recognized in some quarters, at least, that economic forces, political oppression, lie behind poverty and unemployment; but the mother's very character, her status as a woman, are in question if she has 'failed' her children.

Whatever the known facts,[5] it is still assumed that the mother is 'with the child'. It is she, finally, who is held accountable for her children's health, the clothes they wear, their behaviour at school, their intelligence and general development. Even when she is the sole provider for a fatherless family, she and no one else bears the guilt for a child who must spend the day in a shoddy nursery or an abusive school system. Even when she herself is trying to cope with an environment beyond her control — malnutrition, rats, lead-paint poisoning, the drug traffic, racism — in the eyes of society the mother *is* the child's environment. The worker can unionize, go out on strike; mothers are divided from each other in homes, tied to their children by compassionate bonds; our wildcat strikes have most often taken the form of physical or mental breakdown.

For mothers, the privatization of the home has meant not only an increase in powerlessness, but a desperate loneliness. [. . .]

Motherhood, in the sense of an intense, reciprocal relationship with a particular child, or children, is *one part* of female process; it is not an identity for all time. The housewife in her mid-forties may jokingly say; 'I feel like someone out of a job'. But in the eyes of society, once having been mothers, what are we, if not always mothers? The process of 'letting-go' — though we are charged with blame if we do not — is an act of revolt against the grain of patriarchal culture. But it is not enough to let our children go; we need selves of our own to return to.

To have borne and reared a child is to have done that thing which patriarchy joins with physiology to render into the definition of femaleness. But also, it can mean the experiencing of one's own body and emotions in a powerful way. We experience not only physical, fleshly changes but the feeling of a change in character. We learn, often through painful self-discipline and self-cauterization, those qualities which are supposed to be 'innate' in us: patience, self-sacrifice, the willingness to repeat endlessly the small, routine chores of socializing a human being. We are also, often to our amazement, flooded with feelings both of love and violence intenser and fiercer than any we had ever known. (A well-known pacifist, also a mother, said recently on a platform: 'If anyone laid a hand on *my* child, I'd murder him.')

These and similar experiences are not easily put aside. Small wonder that women gritting their teeth at the incessant demands of childcare still find it hard to acknowledge their children's growing independence of them; still feel they must be at home, on the *qui vive*, be that ear always tuned for the sound of emergency, of being needed. [. . .]

When I try to return to the body of the young woman of twenty-six, pregnant for the first time, who fled from the physical knowledge of her pregnancy and at the same time from her intellect and vocation, I realize that I was effectively alienated from my real body and my real spirit by the institution — not the fact — of motherhood. This institution — the foundation of human society as we know it — allowed me only certain views, certain expectations, whether embodied in the booklet in my obstetrician's waiting room, the novels I had read, my mother-in-law's approval, my memories of my own mother, the Sistine Madonna or she of the Michelangelo *Pietà*, the floating notion that a woman pregnant is a woman calm in her fulfilment or, simply, a woman waiting.

Women have always been seen as waiting: waiting to be asked, waiting for our menses, in fear lest they do or do not come, waiting for men to come home from wars, or from work, waiting for children to grow up, or for the birth of a new child, or for menopause.

In my own pregnancy I dealt with this waiting, this female fate, by denying every active, powerful aspect of myself. I became dissociated both from my immediate, present, bodily experience and from my reading, thinking, writing life. Like a traveller in an airport where her plane is several hours delayed, who leafs through magazines she would never ordinarily read, surveys shops whose contents do not interest her, I committed myself to an outward serenity and a profound inner boredom. If boredom is simply a mask for anxiety, then I had learned, as a woman, to be supremely bored rather than to examine the anxiety underlying my Sistine tranquility. My body, finally truthful, paid me back in the end: I was allergic to pregnancy.

I have come to believe, that female biology — the diffuse, intense sensuality radiating out from clitoris, breasts, uterus, vagina; the lunar cycles of menstruation; the gestation and fruition of life which can take place in the female body — has far more radical implications than we have yet come to appreciate. Patriarchal thought has limited female biology to its own narrow specifications. The feminist vision has recoiled from female biology for these reasons; it will, I believe, come to view our physicality as a resource, rather than a destiny. In order to live a fully human life we require not only *control* of our bodies (though control is a prerequisite); we must touch the unity and resonance of our physicality, our bond with the natural order, the corporeal ground of our intelligence.

The ancient, continuing envy, awe, and dread of the male for the female capacity to create life has repeatedly taken the form of hatred for every other female aspect of creativity. Not only have women been told to stick to motherhood, but we have been told that our intellectual or aesthetic creations were inappropriate, inconsequential, or scandalous, an attempt to become 'like men', or to escape from the 'real' tasks of adult womanhood: marriage and childbearing. To 'think like a man' has been both praise and prison for women trying to escape the body-trap. No wonder that many intellectual and creative women have insisted that they were 'human beings' first and women only incidentally, have minimized their physicality and their bonds with other women. The body has been made so problematic for women that it has often seemed easier to shrug it off and travel as a disembodied spirit. [. . .]

My own story, is only one story. What I carried away in the end was a determination to heal — insofar as an individual woman can, and as much as possible with other women — the separation between mind and body; never again to lose myself both psychically and physically in that way. Slowly I came to understand the paradox contained in 'my' experience of motherhood; that, although different from many other women's experiences it was not unique; and that only in shedding the illusion of my uniqueness could I hope, as a woman, to have any authentic life at all. [. . .]

Notes

1. The term 'barren woman' was easy for me to use, unexamined, fifteen years ago. It seems to me now a term both tendentious and meaningless, based on a view of women which sees motherhood as our only positive definition.
2. Margaret Sanger, *Motherhood in Bondage,* New York, Maxwell, (Reprint 1956).
3. John Spargo, *Socialism and Motherhood,* New York, 1914.
4. Benjamin, F. Riley, *White Man's Burden,* Birmingham, Alabama, 1910, p. 131.
5. Twenty-six million children of wage-earning mothers, 8 million in female-headed households in the United States by the mid-1970s (Alice Rossi, 'Children and Work in the Lives of Women', a paper delivered at the University of Arizona, February 7, 1976).

PART FOUR

Constructing Gender

The focus of the book now shifts somewhat for in Part Four we include three readings that look at some of the explanations that have been put forward to account for the differences in position and experience for men and women, in terms of their physiological characteristics, their socialization experiences and their sexuality. Else Bartels provides an outline of the main physiological differences between women and men but makes particular note of the large overlaps that are found between groups of women and groups of men in terms of, for example, height and weight. Suzanne Kessler and Wendy McKenna focus on the issue of socialization — the process by which biologically female and male human animals become women and men with socially recognizable genders, feminine and masculine. Their article gives an overview of the main theories which compete in the field of socialization to explain how gender differences arise. One of these theories is that of Sigmund Freud, and the last piece in this section contains extracts from his own writing on the development of female sexuality. Freud was concerned to explore how individuals' sexual desires are shaped by experiences with their early love objects within the family. His attention was also focused on the question of how anatomical sex differences are related to psychic structuring as masculine or feminine. The inclusion of these extracts provides an opportunity to examine one original source which has attracted much attention from some feminists who feel that, while some of Freud's remarks about women have a derogatory ring, his theories actually form a useful basis from which to start answering questions about the implications of sex differences for women's position.

4.1 Biological sex differences and sex stereotyping

ELSE BARTELS

If one asks the question: 'what are the main biological differences between a woman and a man?' everybody will have an answer based on what is looked upon as 'general biological knowledge'. Even so, everyone has slightly different understanding of biological differences, and so we will not easily find two people who will give exactly the same answer.

There are, of course, obvious differences between the sexes as, for instance, the size and shape of the genitals, but there are others which are less obvious. Popular ideas about sex differences in biology are, however, not necessarily based on actual knowledge and understanding of biological data, but are, rather, rooted in the ideology of women's place in Nature. My intention in this chapter is less a concern with ideology, but rather to describe some of the known differences in physiology between the sexes. By so doing, I hope that we might begin to evaluate everyday instances in which alleged sex differences, particularly those related to strength and stamina, are held to be important. We need to know: are these sex differences largely a product of ideology, or do they have some reality in nature? And if the latter, do they have any significance for the sorts of things that women and men do?

Before looking at some data on human beings, we will look at ourselves and our environment from the experimentalist's point of view. A particular experiment is set up all ready to perform and it is difficult to separate the important operative factors from the unimportant peripheral ones. Doing this does create problems — for example, separating the factors may require that we obtain sufficient data, and we have then to be careful not to jump to conclusions from too few data. When we have a great number of data (there are statistical tests to show if the number of data in a particular case is enough to say the results are significant or not), then we may find a difference between the two sexes if there is a

Specially commissioned for this volume
© The Open University, 1982

significant difference *on average* (that is the average, or mean value) between the data from women and that from men. Figure 1a gives an example of data on height from 24-year old British women and men. The distribution of height in human populations gives a bell-shaped curve (the normal distribution curve), in which the *mean* value is represented by the middle of each curve. Thus, for women, the mean is 162 cms, while that for men is 174 cms. Also, 50 per cent of the women or men will be taller than the mean height, while 50 per cent will be shorter. We can compare the mean values, but it is not always enough to know that there is a difference in the mean. It is also important to know how much overlap there is between the two groups. Figure 1b shows another figure for height for two different groups of people. In these two groups, the *mean* values for women or men for height are the same as in Figure 1a, but the extent of overlap is different. (A measure for overlap is the standard deviation, which tells us the spread of the normal distribution curve either side of the mean. From the mean to a distance of one standard deviation from the mean is approximately one third (32 per cent) of the total population described by the normal distribution. So, a third of the women have a height between 162 cms and 168 cms, and another third will have a height between 156 and 162 cms in Figure 1a). This example

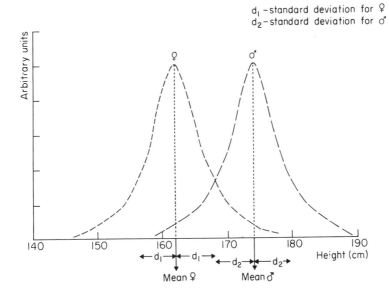

Figure 1a   (a) The normal distribution of height for British women and men (from British population charts)

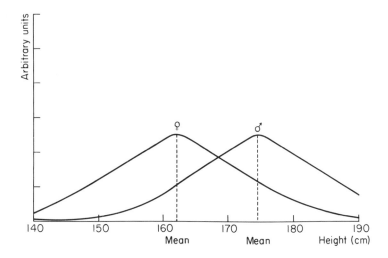

Figure 1b   (b) Another normal distribution of height for men and
women. The distribution is not based on any known
data, but is constructed. The means are the same in
(a) and (b) and the overlap between women's and
men's height is different in (a) and (b).

of height has been chosen because there is a clear difference of the
mean; however, it is important to note that there is also a great
deal of overlap of the data from the two sexes in the example.

Most biological data can be described by a normal distribution
curve, so, when I talk below about differences, I am talking about
differences of the mean.

Childhood

Girls and boys show no significant difference in size at any age,
with the exception of birth weights, for which boys are slightly
heavier (Eveleth and Tanner 1976). Furthermore, there is no sex
difference in strength for body size, although boys tend to have
more strength in hands and forearms (Tanner 1978). The strength
is measured as force produced when jumping, lifting, or doing
other simple tasks involving muscle power. Most biochemical data
which describe metabolism are the same (Eastham 1978), and it is
not before puberty that any major differences in metabolism occur.
In general, children have a higher metabolic rate than adults,
measured by the basic metabolic rate, BMW (the energy consumption of the body per kilogram body weight per minute at rest)

which is 25 per cent higher for a child than for a man (Eastham 1978).

Puberty

Puberty is, on average, reached earlier by girls than by boys, although there is a great variation in the age of start of puberty. This start seems among other factors to be dependent upon the society in which the particular child is brought up. A general trend all over the world is that the age for the start of puberty is decreasing. The decrease from 1860 to 1970 measured by the occurrence of the first menstruation for girls is 2.5 years (Asmussen and Hohwü Christensen 1975). Today the first menstruation occurs on average around the age of 12.

The adolescent growth spurt, the time where a child suddenly increases her/his growth rate over a short interval of time, is earlier in the maturation sequence in girls than in boys, measured in relation to the start of egg/sperm production (Tanner 1978). The earlier start of puberty and the earlier occurrence of the growth spurt during puberty in girls explain the phenomena that girls at a certain age appear to be taller and sometimes stronger than boys at the same age. This may have implications for sport at that age. The visible changes during puberty are:

♀	♂
Growth of body hair	Growth of body hair
Appearance of breasts	Growth of penis
Widening of hips	Widening of shoulders (gives the difference in average carrying angle between men and women)
Increase of the subcutaneous fat layer	Increase of muscle mass
Change in composition of muscle fibres (gives change in muscle strength)	Growth of face
	Growth of vocal chords = Change in voice pitch

(from Tanner 1978, and Asmussen and Hohwü Christensen 1975)

The body changes do of course give men and women a somewhat different shape, but it is worthwhile to keep in mind that there is a wide variation from one individual to another. The stereotyped very 'feminine' women or 'masculine' man with all the stereotyped characteristics related to the sex concerned is hard to find in nature. At the end of puberty all the changes leading to differences described under adulthood have taken place.

Adulthood

Adult human beings do show some sex dimorphism (average differences between individuals of different sex) but not as much as a lot of animal species do. Besides the difference in *shape*, there is, as seen in Figure 1a, a difference in height. Men are on the average taller than women of the same race, society and class (Tanner 1978). Height is influenced by a lot of different factors such as the genetic base, nutrition and hormone balance and possibly training of leg muscles during childhood. There are unknown factors as well. There is no explanation why the average height has increased steadily over the last century all over the world. It seems to have happened both in societies where there has not been major changes in nutrition and in societies where the change in height is known to have been affected by change in nutrition.

Figure 2 shows the average height of men and women from different European countries. It illustrates how difficult it is to talk about differences between the sexes. The figure gives data for people of different professions. If we assume that groups from the same social background have similar living conditions, then we can compare data from one country with data from another country. The figure shows that manual workers tend to be shorter than students.

It is seen that the average Sardinian man is shorter than the average Dutch or Scandinavian woman, so if we pooled data on height from all Europe we may find a higher percentage of overlap between women and men than seen in Figure 1a. Figure 2 gives the average *weight* as well as the average height. Men are seen to be heavier on average than women from the same background. Although weight is generally affected by the same factors as height, height and weight are not necessarily related in a linear way. The tallest populations shown in Figure 2 are not the heaviest. So, to compare the height of women and men, we have to look at women and men from the same society, the same social class and the same height and build. The average man will then be somewhat heavier than the average woman. This is due to the earlier-mentioned difference in muscle mass between men and women. Men tend to have more muscle mass, and women tend to have more subcutaneous fat than men. Since the density of muscle is higher than the density of fat, men will on average be heavier.

In younger people the difference in *subcutaneous fat* between

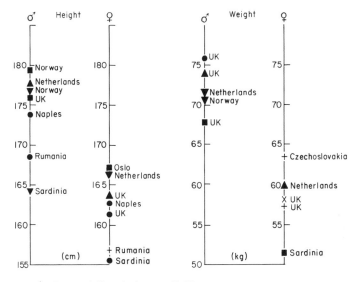

Figure 2   Comparative height and weight means of European
adults according to occupational category
(Selected data from Eveleth and Tanner 1976)

women and men is 10 per cent. When we get older, we tend to put
on weight by adding more fat to our bodies. Although this is not
advisable from a health point of view, it does happen for the
average person. The result is that the average 16—19 year-old girl
shows the same amount of body fat (in percentage of body weight)
as an average 50—72 year-old man (Durnin and Womersley 1974).
The fat/muscle ratio does affect strength because the weight of
the fat adds to the weight carried without adding to the muscle-
produced strength. This leads to the other factor affecting the
difference in weight between the sexes, the muscle mass.

As well as the 10 per cent difference in *muscle mass* in average
between the sexes, there is also a difference in the *distribution of
different types of muscle fibres* in the muscles. There is a variation

of different fibre types in muscles, but what affects muscle strength, the maximal force a person can produce on the spot, and endurance, for how long a time a person can maintain a given force, is whether the fibres are of a fast-twitch type (FT) — strength — or a slow-twitch fibre (ST) — endurance. Men have on average around one third more FT fibres than women (Campbell *et al.* 1979, Gollnick *et al.* 1973). Since some fibres lie between FT and ST fibres in abilities, and since training affects the actual composition of a given muscle by changing these intermediate fibres to either FT or ST (Asmussen and Hohwü Christensen 1975), the difference in fibre composition may not be so much as the present data show in all population groups.

While training can clearly affect muscle composition, the effects of training on strength are more complex. In one study of a group of Scandinavian students undergoing the same physical training, a difference in muscle strength of about 20 per cent was still found. These comparisons were done on the skeletal muscles of arms and legs. However, studies by Dr. Jack Wilmore have shown that women can increase muscle strength by weight training, without altering body shape. This is particularly true for certain muscles such as the thigh muscles. Wilmore suggests that many of the studies of strength have tended to look at college populations (18—25 year-olds). Unless these are specifically studying physical training (as in the Scandinavian example above), then the women and men may not be comparable. As he points out, at that age, many males are active in sports, while most college women tend to lead rather sedentary lives. If, on the other hand, we compare like with like, then the differences in strength are much less, and in certain cases (for example the thigh muscles) may even give women a slight edge. It was earlier believed that there might be a difference in the way that women and men respond to training, but it has now been shown (Pedersen and Jørgensen 1978) that the effect of training as measured by increase in muscle strength is equivalent for women and men.

The difference in the distribution of different types of muscle fibres is not the only explanation for the difference in strength of women and men. If we compare a woman and a man of the same height, build and age, the woman will have a smaller *heart* (which affects the amount of blood circulated per heart beat) and smaller *lungs* (which affect the amount of oxygen the blood is exposed to when running through the lungs). This is to a certain degree compensated by higher resting *heart rate* in women. The smaller lungs give a smaller *vital capacity*, the greatest amount of air that can be expired (used in certain fitness tests), and the percentage of *haemoglobin*, the oxygen-carrying protein in the blood stream, is

14 per cent lower in women (Ganong 1969, Eastham 1978). Muscles need a large quantity of oxygen to work, and it is important to get the oxygen to the working muscles at a high rate of delivery. From this, we could conclude that the average man is slightly better equipped than the average woman to perform this task by the possession of bigger heart and lungs. These differences in heart and lung size between the sexes may, however, not only be a physiological one. Heavy physical training during puberty has been found to enlarge the size of the heart and lungs in girls to a size close to that found in a man of the same height (Astrand *et al.* 1963). These differences, then, may be subject to effects of training such as we noted above, for muscle strength. Women also have a lower *systolic blood pressure* — that is, the pressure of the blood at the point of maximum pressure from the heart's pumping — than men. This may be interpreted either because women on average live a less stressful life (not a physiological difference but a difference created by the environment) or because women are better suited to survive stress (a purely physiological difference). Since it is a difference and since there is no exact definitions of stress which makes stress measurable, the question is more philosophical than biological at present.

The *basic metabolic rate*, BMW, is about 7 per cent lower for women than for men at the same age. Women are therefore more economical to run from an energy point of view. Women eat less per kg body weight. (Remember that children's BMW is 25 per cent higher than BMW for a young adult man.) A woman's BMW goes up to the level of a man during the last three months of pregnancy and during breast-feeding. BMW goes down with age and is 20 per cent lower at the age of 65—70 than at the age of 30 years. The result is that if we eat the same at the age of 70 than at the age of 30, we become fat at the age of 70. Lack of exercise with increasing age is not only to blame for overweight at old age. BMW is not the only factor decreasing with age. Both the muscle mass (MacLennan *et al.* 1980) and the maximal oxygen uptake (Åstrand 1960) decrease with age, and the decline starts earlier in men than in women, although training can slow down the declining processes (Asmussen and Hohwü Christensen 1975).

In the previous pages I have compared women and men at the same age for obvious reasons. The question is, why bother about these differences? We can conclude that the average man from a physiological point of view may be slightly better suited for jobs involving heavy lifting, but the factors like age, height, weight and physical training and so on do affect a person's ability to do physical work. There is therefore no reason to assume that a man always will be the stronger in performing a job involving muscle power. There is a great deal of overlap when averaged over the whole population.

An interesting point is that women and men have nearly the same *working capacity* and that the mechanical efficiency (how much force a machine/person can produce per minute for the same fuel consumption) is the same for women and men (Åstrand 1960). An interesting difference is that women's working capacity is much less affected by altitude than that of men (Wagner *et al.* 1980). We might then ask why mountain rescuing is a nearly 100 per cent male job? Among many other factors, a person's working capacity decreases with age (Åstrand 1960).

There are some differences in biochemical data from men and women, although most data are the same for the two sexes. The most important ones are:

BMW 7 per cent lower in women than in men;
Different quantities of the sex hormones especially during the most fertile years;
Haemoglobin 14 per cent lower in women than in men;
Concentration of waste products from muscles higher in men than in women;
Calcium level in blood 10—15 per cent higher in men than in women (from Eastham 1978).

The difference in concentration of haemoglobin is related in part to blood loss during menstruation, although older women also have lower concentration of haemoglobin than men. The higher percentage of waste products from muscles in men can be related to men's greater muscle mass. There is at present no explanation for the difference in blood calcium. It occurs already in boys at the age of two years.

The menstruation cycle, the cycling of hormone concentrations and the alteration of balance between the different sex hormones and the bleeding that results from this is something unique to the female sex. The male sex does not experience the same kind of regular cycling in hormone balance. The menarche (first menstruation) and the menopause are major events in a woman's life and affect her so strongly both physically and emotionally that it makes a difference in the way women and men experience life. More about this subject can be found in *Why Suffer?* (Birke and Gardner 1982).

There is something popularly called 'the male menopause', but there is no time in a man's life where a physiological change arrives so quickly and so effectually as the menarche and the menopause in a woman's life. The aging process in a man is a much slower series of changes from the age of 35—40 years.

I am not going into the physiological changes during pregnancy and child birth. More about this subject can be found in, for example, *Our Bodies, Ourselves* (Phillips and Rakusen 1979). I just want to say that from a physiologist's point of view, the whole process of pregnancy and childbirth, with all the changes and adjustments of a woman's body over such a short span of time, is impressive and the effect on the individual involved will of course be substantial.

Aging

I have already mentioned the menopause and the changes in physiological parameters during the aging process. There is a major difference found between the sexes in Western society in terms of aging — women live longer. Girls are on average 4—6 weeks ahead of boys in maturity at birth (Ounsted and Taylor 1972) and reach puberty and are fully grown before boys. Even so, the aging process whereby, for instance, muscle strength declines, starts earlier in men. Women reach their maximal strength at the age of 25 and keep this strength until the age of 40, before a slow decline occurs and continues with increasing age. Men reach their maximal strength at the age of 30 and a decrease of strength with age starts right after reaching the maximum. Training does affect decrease of strength, but women seem to keep their maximal strength longer than men, whatever their training condition may be (Asmussen and Hohwü Christensen 1975).

When we look at *The Registrar General's Statistical Review for England and Wales*, we see that there are more boys than girls born every year (around 52 per cent boys to 48 per cent girls). At the age of 19 there are about the same number of boys and girls in the age group, but after 19 the ratio of number of women to the number of men increases with age. The death rates for women and men are shown in Figure 3. All life through, in countries such as ours with good nutrition and medical care, the death rate is lower for women than for men. This means that a woman's chance for living longer is higher than a man's, at least in Britain. The effect is that there are more women old age pensioners than men. This must be taken into account when we discuss how much women use the National Health Service, as old people need more care than younger ones.

The difference in aging is striking within contemporary Western society. However, referring to the average death rate for the two sexes can obscure other sources of variation. Death rates vary, for example, by social class, the area in which a person lives, or ethnic

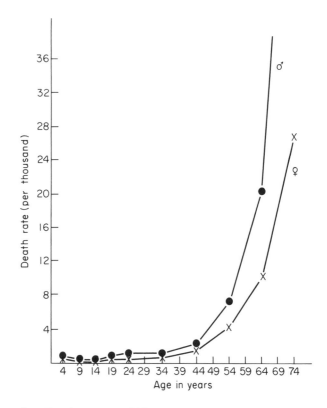

Figure 3   Death rate per 1000 population within sex and age groups
in Britain 1973. Every point represents the death rate in
the age range from the previous point (1—4 years,
5—9 years etc.).
Data from *The Registrar General's Statistical Review of
England and Wales (1975)*

origin. Johansson (1977) paints an interesting picture of variation
in sex ratios in death rates as a product of both social factors and
changes in medical care during the nineteenth century. The sex
difference in death rate has, however, increased overall since the
nineteenth century, which may be due to many contributing factors.

It has been said that the sex difference in death rates can be
explained on the basis that the average woman leads a less stressful
and more protected life than the average man. This is, however,
impossible to judge to what extent a woman — whether she is a
home-working wife with three young children or is also doing paid
work — is exposed to different degrees of stress than men. The
death rates for the next two generations in which more women are

also working full-time may help us to judge whether there is some biological factor which contributes to the sex difference in death rates.

In infancy there is certainly a difference in death rates; that for baby boys is higher than that for girls. One of the reasons for this may be the difference in maturity between girls and boys at birth. It is a fact that premature girls in general have a better chance of survival than premature boys.

Conclusion

I have now mentioned the more important differences between women and men. I have not gone into details because this would involve a whole course on human biology. There are certain statistical differences in many of these biological factors but these are not differences which might explain the present distribution of women and men in jobs involving physical activity. Furthermore, some of the differences are unlikely to be purely biological, but may be related to different social environments of men and women. The only thing which may be said is, that there is surely nothing to classify females as the weaker sex.

References

Asmussen, E. and Hohwü Christensen, E. (1975) *Legemsøvelsernes specielle teori,* Akademisk Forlag, Copenhagen.

Åstrand, I. (1960), 'Aerobic work capacity in men and women with special reference to age', *Acta Physiol. Scand.,* 49, suppl. 169, pp. 1—92.

Åstrand, P.O., Engstrøm, L., Eriksen, B.O., Karlberg, P., Nylander, I., Saltin, B. and Thorén, C. (1963) 'Girl swimmers', *Acta Paediatrica,* suppl. 147.

Birke, L. and Gardner, K. (1982) *Why Suffer: Periods and Their Problems,* (2nd edn), Virago.

Campbell, C.J., Bonen, A., Kirby, R.L. and Belcasto, A.N. (1979) 'Muscle fibre composition and performance capacities of women', *Medicine and Science in Sports,* 113, pp. 260—5.

Durnin, J.V.G.A. and Womersley, J. (1974) 'Body fat assessed from total body density and its estimation from skinfold thickness', *Br. J. Nutr.,* 32, pp. 77—97.

Eastham, R.D. (1978) *Biochemical Values in Clinical Medicine,* Wright and Son, Bristol.

Eveleth, P.B. and Tanner, J.M. (1976) *Worldwide Variation in Human Growth,* Cambridge University Press.

Ganong, W.F. (1969) *Review of Medical Physiology,* Blackwell Scientific Publications, Oxford.

Gollnick, P.D., Armstrong, R.B., Saltin, B., Sambert, C.V., Sembrowich, W.L. and Shepherd, R.B. (1973) 'Effect of training on enzyme and fibre composition of human skeletal muscle', *J. Appl. Physiol.*, 34, pp. 107—111.

Johansson, S.R. (1977) 'Sex and death in Victorian England: an examination of age and sex specific death rate, 1840—1910', in Martha Vicinus (ed.) *A Widening Sphere: Changing Roles of Victorian women*, Indiana University Press, Bloomington.

MacLennan, W.J., Hall, M.R.P., Timothy, J.I. and Robinson, M. (1980) 'Is weakness in old age due to muscle wasting', *Age and Ageing*, 9, pp. 188—192.

Ounsted, C. and Taylor, D.C. (1972) *Gender Differences: Their Ontogeny and Significance*, Churchill Livingstone, London.

Pedersen, P.K. and Jørgensen, K. (1978) 'Maximal oxygen uptake in young women with training, inactivity and retraining', *Medicine and Science in Sports*, 10, pp. 233—7.

Phillips, A. and Rakusen, J. (1979) Boston Women's Health Book Collective: *Our Bodies, Ourselves*, Penguin Books, Harmondsworth.

Tanner, J.M. (1978) *Foetus into Man*, Open Books, London.

The Registrar General's Statistical Review of England and Wales (1975) HMSO, London.

Wagner, J.A., Miles, D.S. and Horvarth, S.M. (1980) 'Physiological adjustment of women to prolonged work during acute hypoxia', *J. Appl. Physiol.*, 49, 3, pp. 367—73.

4.2 Developmental aspects of gender

SUZANNE KESSLER AND WENDY MCKENNA

Jesse (six years old) was asked to draw a picture of a boy and a picture of a girl. When questioned by an interviewer: 'What makes her a girl?' he answered, 'because there is a sun and girls go out on sunny days'. 'What makes this other drawing a picture of a boy?' 'because I coloured it and the man is out tonight. He has to work at night. The moon and he is outside.'

Loren (4½ years old) explained that his drawing of a boy differed from his drawing of a girl 'because it (the boy) has no long hair; 'cause the eyes are different they are rounder; because he is bigger than a girl. She (the girl) has long hair; and she has little curlies in her hair; and she has ears; and because she is smaller.'

Jesse and Loren can also answer the question: 'Are you a girl or a boy?' accurately. They know that they are boys. A child of Loren's age, however, may not be sure whether he will be a man or a woman when he grows up, while Jesse's peers know they will be men if they are now boys. Both Jesse and Loren can list many differences between boys and girls (boys are rougher, girls wear dresses) and were we to observe their choice of toys, ask about their preferred activities, and study some of their behaviours, we would probably conclude that there are definite differences between them and their female peers, differences more evident among the six-year-olds than the four-year-olds.

If we thought of children as nothing but little adults, physically weaker and less experienced but essentially miniature replicas, we might be forced to conclude that Jesse and Loren were mentally defective, or, at least, intellectually slow. Not only are some of their answers to questions about their pictures peculiar, but the reasons they give do not correspond to the actual pictures they drew. Jesse's picture of a boy also has a sun in it; Loren's girl has round eyes and his boy has ears too (see Figures 1–4).

Of course, in the twentieth century we do not consider children to be miniature adults. We accept the reality of development from

Source: Kessler, S. J. and McKenna, W. (1978) *Gender: An Ethnomethodological Approach.* pp. 81–101. © Suzanne Kessler and Wendy McKenna 1978. Reprinted by permission of John Wiley & Sons, Inc, New York

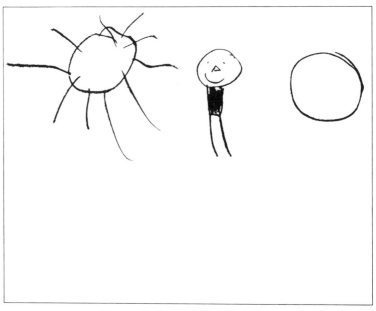

Figure 1   Jesse's drawing of a boy

Figure 2   Jesse's drawing of a girl

Figure 3   Loren's drawing of a boy

Figure 4   Loren's drawing of a girl

child into adult as a process of transformation through stages, each moving closer and closer to mature behaviour and thought processes. We do not expect young children to be rational and responsible, and these expectations are reflected in law, in childrearing practices, and in the scientific study of human development (see DeMause 1975, for an historical review of the concept of 'childhood'). Children do not experience the world the way adults do. They differ from adults not merely in terms of having less experience and knowing less, but also in terms of the way they conceptualize reality, including the reality of gender.

What accounts for the development of gender role behaviour as children grow towards adulthood? How do children learn they are either boys or girls? Is there a learning process in being able accurately to tell girls from boys and women from men?

Unless we assume that the components of gender are completely biological and merely unfold in the course of maturation, it is necessary to seek environmental factors which, at least, interact with biological factors and lead to the acquisition of gender identity, gender role, and gender attribution processes.[1] This has been, and continues to be, the task of psychology, particularly developmental psychology. As a positivist science, like biology, psychology accepts the reality of gender and its components, particularly gender identity and gender role. The 'fact' of masculinity and femininity (adherence to a particular gender role) is as real and objective for psychology as hormones are for biology, and is theoretically as amenable to measurement, quantification, and study. Even the current interest in androgyny (for example Bem 1978) is grounded in the assumption that there are real masculine and feminine traits which can be combined (cf. Rebecca et al. 1976).

There are three main theoretical perspectives in the study of human psychological development: psychoanalytic, social learning, and cognitive developmental. In this chapter we present a general overview of the three theories and discuss their contributions to an understanding of the development of gender identity, role, and attribution. We do not intend this to be an exhaustive critique of the theories.[2] We evaluate, from a traditional perspective, what the theories assert about how children learn there are two genders, how they learn what their own gender is, how they learn what gender others are, and how they learn the behaviours 'appropriate' to their gender. However, our main interest is in presenting psychology as a way of seeing gender.

Psychoanalytic theory

Freud did not write about 'gender role', 'gender identity', or 'gender attribution'. He wrote about 'some psychical consequences of the anatomical distinctions between the sexes' (Freud 1925). His theory is grounded in the premise that people are born with one of two possible anatomies, and he spent a large portion of his intellectual life investigating how these two anatomically distinct groups develop different kinds of mental lives and have different kinds of experiences. There was no question that these psychical and behavioural differences existed. The question was 'why?'

According to Freud, around the age of five, children become aware that they either possess a penis or do not possess a penis. This recognition leads them to develop a particular fantasy involving their genitals (or lack of) and their parents. Out of that fantasy comes a resolution of feelings about the genitals and the parents. This resolution entails identifying with one of the parents and, consequently, internalizing the values of that parent, and eventually exhibiting the same behaviours as that parent. Since the parents' behaviours are (presumably) gender-typed, the child's will be also.

The recognition that one has or does not have a particular set of genitals is, for Freud, tantamount to recognizing that one is a particular gender. 'I have a penis' means 'I am a boy' and 'I do not have a penis' means 'I am a girl.' In this system gender identity is genital identity. If the child fails to accept the reality of her/his genitals (or lack of), then the child has not accepted that she/he is female or male. Freud saw gender identity as so intrinsically tied to genitals that he did not even consider it necessary to provide the theoretical underpinnings of that connection. Nor does he explain how children learn to see *genitals* as the dichotomizing feature by which they distinguish all people and categorize themselves. Why not size, or hair length, or other more public differences?

Recent research draws Freud's equation of genital discovery and gender identity into question. There are children who have male gender identities even though they do not have penises and children who have female gender identities even though they do have penises (Money and Ehrhardt 1972). We do not know how Freud would have dealt with evidence from these cases. Children appear to have fixed gender identities by age three (Money and Ehrhardt 1972), earlier than Freud asserted, and before they show awareness of genital and/or anatomical gender differences (Kohlberg 1966). How would Freud have explained the fact that blind children develop stable gender identities with no apparent difficulty and share cultural ideas about gender (Person 1974), even though they cannot see genital differences? Most of the evidence indicates that awareness of genital differences is not paramount in the development of gender identity.

Freud believed that the recognition that one has a penis or does not have a penis was not sufficient for behaving in a way that is appropriate for people who have penises or do not have penises. Unconscious and semiconscious fantasy is the process that links gender identity to gender role. When children with penises masturbate, they imagine that adults have negative feelings about their masturbation, especially the masturbatory fantasies they have about their mothers, who are their first love objects. They perceive their fathers as rivals for their mother's affections and consequently resent their fathers and would like to get rid of them. They imagine that their fathers would be angered by these feelings and would retaliate in kind with aggression. Specifically, the children fantasize that their fathers will castrate them. Since the children identify with their genitals, this would essentially mean total destruction. The fantasy of castration is given some support when the children with penises notice children without penises and think that those children must have been castrated.

Castration anxiety is unbearable and the only way to resolve it is to relinquish, through repression, all desires for the mother and to identify with the father. In psychoanalytic terms, 'object choice' (wanting someone) is replaced by 'object identity' (wanting to be like someone). By identifying with their fathers they obtain their mothers vicariously. Through identification they assume the values and role behaviours of their fathers. Although the children with penises resolve their castration anxiety by identifying with their fathers, there is typically some identification with both parents, since their first identification has been with their mothers. The amount of identification with each parent, and consequently the amount of male or female gender role behaviour the children display, is, in part, dependent on the relative strength of their masculine and feminine constitutional make-up, a factor that Freud did not explicate in great detail. Nevertheless, by virtue of having a penis, an active sexual organ, the children who successfully resolve their Oedipal desires and castration anxiety, will develop gender role behaviours that are characterized by activity.

Children without penises[3] undergo a different set of fantasy experiences. At around the age of five they become aware of the fact that they do not have penises. Presumably this comes from seeing children with penises and making comparisons. The clitoris, which had been the focus of sexual feeling until this point, and which had been valued for the erotic pleasure it produced, becomes devalued and is now viewed as an inadequate penis. Masturbatory activity is relinquished. According to Freud (1925), penises are valued by children who lack them because penises are '. . . strikingly visible and of large proportions, at once recognize(d) as the superior counterpart of their own small and inconspicuous organ . . .' (p. 252).

The mothers, who had been valued for the needs they satisfied, now became devalued because they, too, lack penises and because they are blamed for the children's deficiency. The children may believe that they had penises but lost them as a form of punishment. Because the fathers have penises, they take on greater value and become the children's object choice.

The children without penises, then, are in the same position *vis-à-vis* their fathers as the children with penises are *vis-à-vis* their mothers. The children without penises must relinquish their fathers and identify with their mothers. Through identification with their mothers, they incorporate ideal female values and the appropriate role behaviours for the female gender. They come to accept their vaginas, rather than their clitorises, as their true genital. Although children without penises are also constitutionally bisexual, and will identify to some extent with both parents, by virtue of having vaginas, passive sexual organs, those children who successfully resolve their Oedipal desires will develop gender role behaviours that are characterized by passivity.

Because there is no strong motivation to resolve their Oedipal conflict (analogous to castration anxiety in the children with penises), these conflicts are never fully resolved. This results in a number of unfortunate consequences. They will have weaker consciences and will never fully give up their desire to have penises, although there will be some ways that that desire can be symbolically fulfilled (e.g, giving birth to sons).

In Table 1 (see p. 281), the development of gender role, according to psychoanalytic theory, is shown arising out of the initial recognition of one's own genitals. For Freud, the study of gender was essentially the study of gender roles. The problem was not how children learn that there exist two genders, or even how they learn that they are a particular gender, but rather (in contemporary terms) how do children develop the appropriate gender role — how and why do boys become masculine and girls become feminine? In the normal course of development, a child would know what genital she or he had, would develop the appropriate fantasy, and would incorporate the values and behaviours appropriate to her/his gender.

It should be clear that gender attribution was not an issue for Freud. Although there is no doubt that, for him, gender equalled genitals, he did not see gender attribution as problematic. Any intrapsychic conflict had to be between gender identity and gender role, rather than gender identity and gender attribution. It is difficult to incorporate, within an orthodox psychoanalytic framework, persons with penises, seen as male by others, who conceive of themselves as really being female, unless this is seen as psychosis or other severe pathology. Presumably, Freud would have considered trans-sexuals[4] people who, because of an unresolved Oedipal conflict, would not accept their own genitals and consequently their own gender. Transsexualism would have been seen as an extreme form of homosexuality, with a masochistic component, accompanied by such severe guilt feelings that the individual could not accept the homosexuality.

Freud's developmental theory has been criticized for several reasons besides his equation of genital awareness with gender identity. It does not take into account the fact that in non-Western cultures children with different genitals may not perform very different role behaviours or may exhibit role behaviours that are the reverse of our own culture's (Mead 1935). In addition, the fantasy that Freud described may be inappropriate in cultures where the child's father is not the authority figure (Malinowski 1932).

The theory is also based on a biological assumption, accurate when Freud was writing but now known to be false, that foetuses were 'constitutionally bisexual', that is, that they had the potential for developing into either gender; one potential was expressed, while the other was suppressed. The contemporary facts are that foetuses develop in a 'female' direction unless something (e.g., prenatal androgens) is added. This knowledge, combined with the belief that boys have to change their identification from their mothers to their fathers, while girls do not have to make any changes, is used to support the contention (contrary to Freud's) that gender development is more difficult for boys than for girls (Person 1974). (Freud concentrated on the idea that boys were the ones who did not have to change the gender of their love object.)

An additional criticism of Freudian theory is that gender development does not end with the resolution of the Oedipal phase. Children continue to learn gender roles throughout childhood, and pre-adolescence and adolescence are important stages in learning masculine and feminine behaviour (Maccoby and Jacklin 1974).

Psychoanalysts who came after Freud[5] varied in the extent to which they supported his views about gender development. Regardless of how far they deviate from the Freudian model, they remain convinced of the sequence: genital awareness leads to fantasy leads to identification leads to gender role (e.g. Person 1974). The modifications they made lie in the following areas:

1. The nature of genital awareness and the role it plays in gender identity;
2. the particulars of the Oedipal fantasy;
3. the role of the social environment;
4. the age at which gender identity and gender role development takes place.

Horney's (1926) explication of the development of gender role focuses on girls and emphasizes quite different aspects of the nature of genital awareness and the content of the child's unconscious fantasy. According to Horney, those children born without penises do not so much experience the lack of a penis as their defining feature, but rather they experience the *presence* of their vaginas. They recognize that they have vaginas and at no point do these children reject their clitorises as inadequate. They are part of their genitals. Anxiety centres around their vaginas, because they cannot be inspected and because the children fear the vaginas will not be large enough to receive their fathers' (fantasized) penises. Children with penises may be envied because it is assumed that they are allowed to masturbate, since they hold their penises when urinating. In normal development, however, this envy disappears when the children with vaginas realize their role in the birth process. There are children with vaginas who continue to envy penises and deny their genitals (and hence their gender), but according to Horney, this is not part of the normal course of development. In sum, she did not see the penis envy as playing the important role in development that Freud claimed.

Horney also discusses how the fantasy of some children with vaginas of wanting a penis is reinforced by a society that values people with penises more than people with vaginas. The penis, then, becomes symbolic of greater power and choice. The incorporation of sociocultural influences has become an integral part of contemporary psychoanalytic theory. Unlike Freud, most psychoanalysts no longer see the child's fantasy as occurring within a vacuum.

Some contemporary formulations of psychoanalytic theory (e.g, Stoller 1975) demonstrate a recognition of the complexities of gender development. Gender identity is not dependent on awareness of one's genitals, but depends on pregenital identification with the mother (for girls) and pregenital separation from the mother (for boys). Identification with the mother is seen as primary for all children, and the development of gender role is also seen as beginning before genital awareness, as a result of the parents' labelling of and interaction with the child. What is hypothesized as arising out of genital awareness and fantasy are the specifics of gender role, particularly such traits as aggressiveness, and dependence/independence (Person 1974). Even these specifics, however, are seen as grounded in a society where males have certain prerogatives which females do not and *vice versa*.

Social learning theory

Psychoanalytic theory postulates a mechanism (identification with the parent having the same genitals) to explain why children learn 'appropriate' gender role behaviours, but the theory does not explain *how* the mechanism works. Identification is defined as the imitation and incorporation of complex values and behaviours without specific external pressures to do this. Evidence for identification comes from studies of parent—child similarities in values and behaviours, but such similarity can be due to factors besides identification (Bronfenbrenner 1958). These factors include direct teaching by the parent in appropriate behaviours, pressure by other people and institutions to behave in certain ways, and genetic factors shared by the parent and child.

With the development of theories of learning in the 1940s and 1950s, psychologists dissatisfied with the lack of emphasis on 'how' in psychoanalytic theory, began to apply principles of learning theory to explain how identification and other psychoanalytic processes can occur. Eventually, a separate perspective developed, called social learning theory.

Social learning theory, while retaining the idea that processes similar to identification are important in the development of gender components, does not retain the basic theoretical postulates of psychoanalysis. Its major assumption, as stated by Mischel (1966), is that the acquisition and performance of gender-typed behaviours 'can be described by the same learning principles used to analyse any other aspect of an individual's behaviour' (p. 56). Gender-typed behaviours are defined as behaviours that have different consequences depending on the gender of the person exhibiting the behaviour. The learning principles include 'discrimination, generalization . . . observational learning . . . the pattern of reward, nonreward, and punishment under specific contingencies, (and) the principles of direct and vicarious conditioning' (p. 57). The emphasis in social learning theory is on observable, antecedent events, rather than on inferred intrapsychic processes, like Oedipal fantasy. The most complete formulation of social learning theory as it relates to the development of gender identity and role is by Mischel (1966, 1970).

In brief, the theory states that through observation children learn behaviours associated with both parents. They learn these behaviours without any direct reinforcement because they see their parents as powerful, effective, and as having control over rewards. (This, according to social learning theory, is the process of identification.) For example, by watching their mother put on lipstick and perfume and observing their father tell her that she looks nice, both sons and daughters learn how to 'dress up'. However, when the children actually perform the behaviours they have learned, they are differentially reinforced. The daughter may be rewarded for 'acting cute', while the son may be disapprovingly told 'boys don't wear lipstick'.

Eventually, through differential reinforcement from parents, teachers, peers, and others, children begin to know what they can and cannot do. They begin to anticipate the consequences of various behaviours, and they begin to value gender 'appropriate' behaviours because they are rewarded and to devalue gender 'inappropriate' behaviours because they are punished or ignored. The child learns the label ('boy' or 'girl') appropriate to the rewarded behaviours, and learns to apply that label to her/himself. Through generalization, the child learns to value that label, since it stands for valued behaviours, and to see the label as an important part of her/his self-concept. Gender identity, according to social learning theory, is just another name for this self-label. The male child thinks: 'I want rewards. I am rewarded for doing boy things. Therefore, I want to be a boy' (Kohlberg 1966, p. 89). Social learning theory makes no assumptions about the age at which any of these processes take place; it only states that this is the sequence in which the development of gender role and gender identity occur.

Social learning theory does not concern itself with the question of gender attribution. There are two genders, and presumably children come to learn about physical gender differences in the same way that they learn anything else. It is taken for granted by social learning theorists that gender labels are applied to people on the basis of objective criteria. There is not a great deal of emphasis on 'ideas' about gender (and how these might develop) since one of the theory's basic assumptions is that although the *acquisition* of gender-typed behaviour may be regulated by cognitive processes, the actual *performance* of these behaviours depends on reinforcement histories. Table 1 (p. 281) summarizes the development of gender identity and role according to social learning theory.

Social learning theory emphasizes the importance of differential reinforcement, but Maccoby and Jacklin (1974) claim that, for the most part, young children are not treated differently by their parents on the basis of gender. If there is differential treatment, it is limited to the parents providing gender-typed clothes and toys, particularly for boys. Others (e.g. Block, 1978) have disagreed with Maccoby and Jacklin, asserting that there is considerable differential treatment in early childhood.

Even if it is true that differential treatment is not strong enough to account for gender differences in behaviour, Mischel's statement of social learning theory could still be useful as a way of describing the development of gender identity. A daughter may or may not wear lipstick when she gets older, but she does learn (because the label is differentially applied) that she is a girl and that girls are expected to behave, in at least certain ways, differently from boys. The specifics of gender role behaviour may not be well accounted for by social learning theory but, according to Mischel, there is not much to account for — there are very few stable and consistent 'sex differences' in behaviour. Whether or not a person eventually exhibits a particular gender-typed behaviour can be predicted only from a study of past and present reinforcement contingencies and environmental stimuli. These factors are different for each individual. Thus, it is not surprising that there are few consistent 'sex differences' in behaviour, or conflicting evidence about differential reinforcement for specific behaviours.[6] [. . .]

Cognitive developmental theory

In contrast to psychoanalytic and social learning theory, cognitive developmental theory (Kohlberg 1966) emphasizes the child's active role in structuring the world, according to the child's level of cognitive development. The theory, based on the work of Piaget, begins with the assumption that the child's reality is qualitatively different from adults' reality. The way the child sees the world changes in discrete stages until, as a young adult, the individual has an 'accurate' view of reality. (From our perspective, children develop until they share the same rules for constructing the world as all other adults. 'Accuracy' is a socially constructed concept.)

Before the age of five to seven, children do not have the concept of conservation of physical properties (Piaget 1952). Adults know that a given amount of water poured from a short, wide glass into a narrow, tall glass remains the same amount of water. Children who have not developed the concept of conservation believe that the amount of water changes when the shape of the container changes. They can give reasons to support this belief (e.g. 'It's taller, so there's more water'). Given Western, scientific constructions of reality, both their belief and their reason are 'wrong'. They have not yet learned the adult rules for reality construction. In Piaget's conceptualization, children are not ignorant, nor have they been taught incorrectly; rather, there is a qualitative difference between the structure of children's and adults' thinking. [. . .]

Kohlberg asserts that gender is a physical category based on anatomy, and until children have the concept of conservation despite transformations, they do not have permanent gender identities. Until they understand that, just as the amount of water does not change when poured from one container to another, gender does not change when, for example, someone who plays with trucks starts playing with dolls, they cannot develop a gender identity.

By the time they are three years old, children can label themselves accurately (e.g. 'I am a girl'). They learn this from hearing others label them, and often can label others accurately, but they do *not* yet know that (1) a person's gender never changes, (2) everyone has a gender, and (3) gender differences are physical/anatomical ones. By the time children are age five or six, they develop the concept of conservation, including the idea that a person's gender is invariant. Not only does the six-year-old know she is a girl, but she knows that she will always be a girl. Only at that point, according to Kohlberg, does it make sense to talk about the child having a gender identity.

Once children develop stable gender identities, they begin to prefer gender-typed activities and objects. This is because children value and wish to be like things that they perceive as similar to themselves. As Kohlberg states it, their thinking is: I am a boy. Therefore I like boy things. Therefore doing boy things is rewarding (p. 89).

As they develop permanent gender identities, boys begin to identify with their fathers because they come to understand that not only are they similar to other boys, but they are also similar to men, of which their father is an example. Thus, they want to be like their fathers.

Girls, by the age of five or six, know they are girls; they like girl things, and want to be like their mothers. However, girls are not as 'typed' in their preferences or identifications as boys, because they identify with their fathers as well as their mothers. In the reality of the young child, 'male' is equated with 'big' and synonymous with 'more powerful'. Consequently, both boys and girls are likely to identify, to some extent, with their fathers and male things in general. Table 1 summarizes the development of gender identity and role according to cognitive developmental theory.

Kohlberg presents arguments for why cognitive developmental theory explains the development of gender identity and role better than psychoanalytic or social learning theory. As we have discussed, psychoanalytic theory maintains that gender identity develops from genital awareness. However, Kohlberg has found that children do not have clear ideas about genital differences until *after* they have developed a gender identity. In addition, psychoanalytic theory asserts that appropriate role behaviours are a result of identification with the same gender parent. Research (Kohlberg 1966) indicates that children are already 'sex-typed' in their behaviour at an age (four years) when, according to psychoanalytic theory, both boys and girls are identified with their mothers. Finally, Kohlberg claims that social learning theory cannot account for why children have such 'unusual' ideas about gender, nor can it account for atypical forms of sexual or gender role behaviours, like homosexuality, despite pressures towards typicality. More importantly, it cannot account for universal similarities in children's concepts and behaviours despite different familial and sociocultural backgrounds.

There are several criticisms that have been made of cognitive developmental theory. One criticism is that being able to label a person 'male' or 'female,' and/or being able to articulate reasons for a label, is not synonymous with being able to make certain distinctions. A psychoanalyst might argue that even if five-year-olds do not say that men and women are different because they have different genitals, they may still know, on some level, about genital differences. A second criticism, as Maccoby and Jacklin (1974) have pointed out, is that it is not necessary for the child to have the concept of gender invariance in order for self-socialization into gender roles to begin. Three-year-olds have clear gender-typed preferences, for example, in toys, and it is impossible to discount the effects of this self-socialization on future behaviour. Thirdly, cognitive developmental theory cannot account for individual differences in the adoption of gender role behaviours without recourse to concepts like 'reinforcement'. In general, the theory tends to ignore individual differences. Nevertheless, there is little argument with Kohlberg's general contention that a child's understanding of 'boy' and 'girl' and the roles associated with these labels are different from adults' understanding, and that that understanding influences the child's behaviour and treatment of others.

Of the three theories, cognitive developmental is the only one concerned with the problem of the development of gender attribution processes. At least in terms of labelling, Kohlberg has been interested in the age at which children can correctly label others 'male' and 'female' and the reasons they give for assigning labels. Implicit in cognitive developmental theory, however, is the assumption that the reasons people give for assigning labels are the reasons they use, an assertion that we question.

Children often give physical gender role characteristics like hair length and dress, as reasons for making gender attributions, while adults give primary and secondary physical gender characteristics like genitals and breasts as reasons. According to Kohlberg, these different reasons indicate a shift from seeing gender as a variable category (anyone could be a woman if the way you know someone is a woman is by hair length) to seeing gender as invariant (one's genitals and secondary gender characteristics do not change). Kohlberg at least indicates an interest in the idea of gender attribution, although he does not see it as primary, nor as a social construction. According to cognitive developmental theory, there are two genders, invariantly dichotomized, which can be labelled on the basis of real, obvious, factual, objective physical characteristics, and that is what everyone does — adults and children alike — but only adults know how they do it.

Table 1 Theories of Gender Development

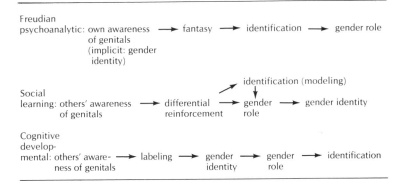

Comparing the theories

An inspection of Table 1 clarifies some of the differences among the three major psychological theories of gender development. The theories vary in their assumptions about (1) whether gender identity precedes or develops from gender role, (2) the age at which these gender components develop, and (3) the ways in which parents, through identification and/or reinforcement, affect the development of gender identity and gender role.

Besides these differences, there are similarities among the theories. Although they all imply that genitals are the criteria for gender attribution, telling females from males is not a concern. This is because for each theory, and for the psychologists and psychoanalysts who work within their frameworks, there is no question about the objective facticity of gender. Gender is as real as height and weight and it can be objectively measured and studied without insurmountable problems. In addition, gender identity and gender role and the processes that lead to their development, like identification and reinforcement, are objective facts. It is assumed that men and women are behaviourally and psychologically different, and the causes of these differences can be found in developmental processes. The incorrigible proposition that there *are* two genders, leads to the assumption that there must be some expression of this dichotomy, even if the differences are not as extensive as formerly believed, and that there is a set of psychological factors leading to an orderly, understandable development of gender differences, including gender identity.

Besides their acceptance of the facticity of gender, the theories, and the research stemming from them, are similar in their emphasis on male development. The theories' treatment of both normal and abnormal development concentrates on boys and tends to offer more satisfactory and complete explanations of male than of female development — even in the eyes of the theorists (see Kohlberg 1966, Freud 1925, Stoller 1975, Heilbrun 1973).

Although Freud (1925) claimed that male development is smoother and less precarious than female development, the evidence (e.g. the higher incidence of 'gender disorders' like transvestism, transsexualism, paraphelias, among men) indicates that male development is more precarious and more sensitive to environmental influences. Thus, in this case, it might be easier to find more orderly relationships between environmental factors (e.g. parental treatment) and gender role development in boys. Girls' development may occur more independently of external influences. This explanation takes it for granted that scientific research and theory is objective and unbiased — a mere uncovering of what is already there.

On the other hand, some explanations for the concentration on male development take into account the fact that psychological theories and data are not independent of the interests of the people doing the science. Such 'accusations' of bias in theory and research have come from a number of sources. Horney (1926), for example, shows how Freud's theory of gender development directly parallels little boys' ideas about gender.[7] The fact that mainly men have created the theories and collected the data may help account for why there has been an emphasis on male development and a relative inability to understand how girls develop. There are several possible reasons: (1) Men are more interested in things like themselves; (2) Men view male development as the norm and try to relate female development to that norm when the developmental processes may be totally different; (3) Men, having been boys, might be able to understand aspects of the development of boys that they cannot in girls.

These criticisms regarding masculine bias share, with the theories being criticized, a belief in the facticity of gender. The implication of the criticisms is that, were the androcentric bias removed from psychology, the 'true' facts about gender could then be discovered. These facts, however, would be no more or less 'true' than the facts we now have. They would simply be grounded in different incorrigible propositions.

There are at least three theories offered to account for the development of gender. Which one is correct? This question is not one that can be answered. All the theories can point to empirical data supporting their assumptions and/or contradicting the assumptions of other theories. Ultimately, there is no way to determine the truth of theoretical formulations (Kuhn 1970). Theories are ways of seeing the world and once one accepts the paradigm of a theoretical orientation, events become interpreted in light of that orientation. Theories may be more or less useful, more or less aesthetically pleasing, more or less 'in vogue', but their claim to truth is, in some sense, a matter of faith in their basic assumptions. Psychological theories of gender development are special examples, because they are scientific and, thus, more explicit in stating their basic assumptions, of the general phenomenon of the social construction of gender. All assumptions about gender, whether scientific or not, are grounded in the incorrigible propositions which we hold about reality. This last statement, is, of course, a statement of *our* theoretical formulation. [...]

Notes

[1. The authors define these terms as follows:
  gender identity — refers to an individual's own feelings of whether she or he is a woman or a man, or a girl or a boy;
  a gender role — is a set of expectations about what behaviours are appropriate for people of one gender;
  gender assignment is a special case of *gender attribution* which occurs once only — at birth, on inspection of the baby's genitals.
  Individuals are routinely attributed a gender on the basis of assignment, behaviour and identity — the three being usually, but not always, congruent (1978), pp. 8—13).]
2. Readers are referred to Freud (1925), Mischel (1966, 1970), and Kohlberg (1966) for the most complete statements of these theoretical positions on gender.

3. We are deliberately referring to this group as 'children without penises' rather than 'children with clitorises' or 'children with vaginas', because in Freud's theoretical framework it is their lack of penises rather than their possession of something else which distinguishes them and influences their psychosexual development in a particular direction.

4. The authors define transsexualism (following Stoller 1968) as the conviction in a biologically normal person of being a member of the sex opposite to the one to which they were assigned (1978, p. 13).

5. This discussion contains only a few examples of modern psychoanalytic treatments of gender development. See Strouse (1974) and Miller (1973) for more complex presentations.

6. Whether there are specific 'sex differences' in behaviour is not the same as whether there are gender roles (i.e. expectations that males and females are supposed to be different). The area of 'sex differences' is too extensive for us to treat it in any detail. (See Maccoby and Jacklin, 1974.) As we have stated before, the question of 'real' differences between the genders is separate from the question of the expectation of differences, the formation of a gender identity, and the ability to label others with the 'appropriate' gender label and to have oneself labelled 'correctly' by others. The assertion by Mischel and others that there are very few 'real' gender differences does not call into question the fact of gender identity or gender attribution. If the 'fact' that there are few 'real' gender differences becomes part of general cultural expectations, there may eventually be changes in gender role expectations. Conversely, as ideas of gender role change, psychologists will find fewer sex differences, not just because socialization practices will change, but also because psychologists, who are first of all everyday members, will change their expectations about what they will find, and will consequently look for and 'discover' very different things.

7. For example, because little boys have penises, they think everyone has a penis. This does not mean, however, that little girls think that they had a penis and lost it as Freud maintained (Horney 1926).

References

Bem, S. (1978) 'Probing the promise of androgyny', in J. Sherman and F. Denmark (eds) *The Psychology of Women: Future Directions in Research*, New York: Psychological Dimensions.

Block, J. (1978) 'Another look at sex differentiation in the socialization behaviours of mothers and fathers', in J. Sherman and F. Denmark (eds) *The Psychology of Women: Future Directions in Research*, New York: Psychological Dimensions.

Bronfenbrenner, U. (1958) 'The study of identification through interpersonal perception', in R. Tagiuri and L. Petrullo (eds) *Person Perception and Interpersonal Behaviour*, Stanford, California: Stanford University Press.

DeMause, L. (ed.) (1975) *The History of Childhood*, New York: Harper Torchbooks.

Freud, S. (1925) 'Some psychical consequences of the anatomical distinctions between the sexes', *Standard Edition,* London: Hogarth Press, Vol. 19.

Heilbrun, A.B. (1973) 'Parent identification and filial sex-role behaviour: the importance of biological context', in J. Cole and R. Dienstbier (eds), *Nebraska Symposium on Motivation,* Lincoln: University of Nebraska Press.

Horney, K. (1926) 'The flight from womanhood', *International Journal of Psychoanalysis,* 7, pp. 324—339.

Kohlberg, L. (1966) 'A cognitive-developmental analysis of children's sex-role concepts and attitudes', in E. Maccoby (ed.) *The Development of Sex Differences,* Stanford: Stanford University Press.

Kuhn, T.S. (1970) *The Structure of Scientific Revolutions,* Chicago: University of Chicago Press.

Maccoby, E. E. and Jacklin, C. N. (eds) (1974) *The Psychology of Sex Differences,* Stanford: Stanford University Press.

Malinowski, B. (1932) *The Sexual Life of Savages* (3rd edn) London: George Routledge and Sons.

Mead, M. (1935) *Sex and Temperament in Three Primitive Societies,* New York: William Morrow.

Miller, J.B. (ed.) (1973) *Psychoanalysis and Women,* Baltimore: Penguin.

Mischel, W. (1966) 'A social-learning view of sex differences in behaviour', in E. Maccoby (ed.) *The Development of Sex Differences,* Stanford: Stanford University Press.

Mischel, W. (1970) 'Sex-typing and socialization', in P.H. Mussen (ed.), *Carmichael's Manual of Child Psychology,* New York: Wiley, Vol. 2.

Money, J. and Ehrhardt, A. (1972) *Man and Woman/Boy and Girl,* Baltimore: Johns Hopkins Press.

Person, E. (1974) 'Some new observations on the origins of femininity', in J. Strouse (ed.) *Women and Analysis,* New York: Grossman.

Piaget, J. (1957) *The Origins of Intelligence in Children,* New York: International Universities Press.

Rebecca, M., Hefner, R. and Oleshansky, B. (1976) 'A model of sex-role transcendence', *Journal of Social Issues,* 32, pp. 197—206.

Stoller, R.J. (1968) *Sex and Gender,* Vol. 1, New York, J. Aronson.

Stoller, R.J. (1975) *Sex and Gender,* Vol. II, New York, J. Aronson.

Strouse, J. (ed.) (1974) *Women and Analysis,* New York, Grossman.

4.3　Female sexuality

SIGMUND FREUD

During the phase of the normal Oedipus complex we find the child tenderly attached to the parent of the opposite sex, while its relation to the parent of its own sex is predominantly hostile. In the case of a boy there is no difficulty in explaining this. His first love-object was his mother. She remains so; and, with the strengthening of his erotic desires and his deeper insight into the relations between his father and mother, the former is bound to become his rival. With the small girl it is different. Her first object, too, was her mother. How does she find her way to her father? How, when and why does she detach herself from her mother? We have long understood that the development of female sexuality is complicated by the fact that the girl has the task of giving up what was originally her leading genital zone — the clitoris — in favour of a new zone — the vagina. But it now seems to us that there is a second change of the same sort which is no less characteristic and important for the development of the female: the exchange of her original object — her mother — for her father. The way in which the two tasks are connected with each other is not yet clear to us.

It is well known that there are many women who have a strong attachment to their father; nor need they be in any way neurotic. It is upon such women that I have made the observations which I propose to report here and which have led me to adopt a particular view of female sexuality. I was struck, above all, by two facts. The first was that where the woman's attachment to her father was particularly intense, analysis showed that it had been preceded by a phase of exclusive attachment to her mother which had been equally intense and passionate. Except for the change of her love-object, the second phase had scarcely added any new feature to her erotic life. Her primary relation to her mother had been built up in a very rich and many-sided manner. The second fact taught me that the *duration* of this attachment had also been greatly underestimated. In several cases it lasted until well into the fourth

Source: Freud, S. (1977) *Three Essays on the Theory of Sexuality*, Volume 7 of *The Standard Edition of Complete Psychological Works of Sigmund Freud* translated and edited by James Strachey, pp. 372—388. Reprinted by permission of Sigmund Freud Copyrights Ltd., The Institute of Psycho-Analysis, and The Hogarth Press, London

year — in one case into the fifth year — so that it covered by far the longer part of the period of early sexual efflorescence. Indeed, we had to reckon with the possibility that a number of women remain arrested in their original attachment to their mother and never achieve a true change-over towards men. This being so, the pre-Oedipus phase in women gains an importance which we have not attributed to it hitherto. [. . .]

And indeed during that phase a little girl's father is not much else for her than a troublesome rival, although her hostility towards him never reaches the pitch which is characteristic of boys. We have, after all, long given up any expectation of a neat parallelism between male and female sexual development. [. . .]

I began by stating the two facts which have struck me as new: that a woman's strong dependence on her father merely takes over the heritage of an equally strong attachment to her mother, and that this earlier phase has lasted for an unexpectedly long period of time. I shall now go back a little in order to insert these new findings into the picture of female sexual development with which we are familiar. In doing this, a certain amount of repetition will be inevitable. It will help our exposition if, as we go along, we compare the state of things in women with that in men.

First of all, there can be no doubt that the bisexuality, which is present, as we believe, in the innate disposition of human beings, comes to the fore much more clearly in women than in men. A man, after all, has only one leading sexual zone, one sexual organ, whereas a woman has two: the vagina — the female organ proper — and the clitoris, which is analogous to the male organ. We believe we are justified in assuming that for many years the vagina is virtually non-existent and possibly does not produce sensations until puberty. It is true that recently an increasing number of observers report that vaginal impulses are present even in these early years. In women, therefore, the main genital occurrences of childhood must take place in relation to the clitoris. Their sexual life is regularly divided into two phases, of which the first has a masculine character, while only the second is specifically feminine. Thus in female development there is a process of transition from the one phase to the other, to which there is nothing analogous in the male. A further complication arises from the fact that the clitoris, with its virile character, continues to function in later female sexual life in a manner which is very variable and which is certainly not yet satisfactorily understood. We do not, of course, know the biological basis of these peculiarities in women; and still less are we able to assign them any teleological purpose.

Parallel with this first great difference there is the other, concerned with the finding of the object. In the case of a male, his mother becomes his first love-object as a result of her feeding him and looking after him, and she remains so until she is replaced by someone who resembles her or is derived from her. A female's first object, too, must be her mother: the primary conditions for a choice of object are, of course, the same for all children. But at the end of her development, her father — a man — should have become her new love-object. In other words, to the change in her own sex there must correspond a change in the sex of her object. The new problems that now require investigating are in what way this change takes place, how radically or how incompletely it is carried out, and what the different possibilities are which present themselves in the course of this development.

We have already learned, too, that there is yet another difference between the sexes, which relates to the Oedipus complex. We have an impression here that what we have said about the Oedipus complex applies with complete strictness to the male child only and that we are right in rejecting the term 'Electra complex' which seeks to emphasize the analogy between the attitude of the two sexes. It is only in the male child that we find the fateful combination of love for the one parent and simultaneous hatred for the other as a rival. In his case it is the discovery of the possibility of castration, as proved by the sight of the female genitals, which forces on him the transformation of his Oedipus complex, and which leads to the creation of his super-ego and thus initiates all the processes that are designed to make the individual find a place in the cultural community. After the paternal agency has been internalized and become a super-ego, the next task is to detach the latter from the figures of whom it was originally the psychical representative. In this remarkable course of development it is precisely the boy's narcissistic interest in his genitals — his interest in preserving his penis — which is turned round into a curtailing of his infantile sexuality.

One thing that is left over in men from the influence of the Oedipus complex is a certain amount of disparagement in their attitude towards women, whom they regard as being castrated. In extreme cases this gives rise to an inhibition in their choice of object, and, if it is supported by organic factors, to exclusive homosexuality.

Quite different are the effects of the castration complex in the female. She acknowledges the fact of her castration, and with it, too, the superiority of the male and her own inferiority; but she rebels against this unwelcome state of affairs. From this divided attitude three lines of development open up. The first leads to a general revulsion from sexuality. The little girl, frightened by the comparison with boys, grows dissatisfied with her clitoris, and gives up her phallic activity and with it her sexuality in general as well as a good part of her masculinity in other fields. The second line leads her to cling with defiant self-assertiveness to her threatened masculinity. To an incredibly late age she clings to the hope of getting a penis some time. That hope becomes her life's aim; and the phantasy of being a man in spite of everything often persists as a formative factor over long periods. This 'masculinity complex' in women can also result in a manifest homosexual choice of object. Only if her development follows the third, very circuitous, path does she reach the final normal female attitude, in which she takes her father as her object and so finds her way to the feminine form of the Oedipus complex. Thus in women the Oedipus complex is the end-result of a fairly lengthy development. It is not destroyed, but created, by the influence of castration; it escapes the strongly hostile influences which, in the male, have a destructive effect on it, and indeed it is all too often not surmounted by the female at all. For this reason, too, the cultural consequences of its break-up are smaller and of less importance in her. We should probably not be wrong in saying that it is this difference in the reciprocal relation between the Oedipus and the castration complex which gives its special stamp to the character of females as social beings.[1]

We see, then, that the phase of exclusive attachment to the mother, which may be called the *pre-Oedipus* phase, possesses a far greater importance in women than it can have in men. [. . .] Our interest must be directed to the mechanisms that are at work in her turning away from the mother who was an object so intensely and exclusively loved. We are prepared to find, not a single factor, but a whole number of them operating together towards the same end.

Among these factors are some which are determined by the circumstances of infantile sexuality in general, and so hold good equally for the erotic life of boys. First and foremost we may mention jealousy of other people — of brothers and sisters, rivals, among whom the father too has a place. Childhood love is boundless; it demands exclusive possession, it is not content with less than all. But it has a second characteristic: it has, in point of fact, no aim and is incapable of obtaining complete satisfaction; and principally for that reason it is doomed to end in disappointment and to give place to a hostile attitude. [. . .]

Another, much more specific motive for turning away from the mother arises from the effect of the castration complex on the creature who is without a penis. At some time or other the little girl makes the discovery of her organic inferiority — earlier and more easily, of course, if there are brothers or other boys about. We have already taken note of the three paths which diverge from this point: (*a*) the one which leads to a cessation of her whole sexual life, (*b*) the one which leads to a defiant over-emphasis of her masculinity, and (*c*) the first steps towards definitive femininity. It is not easy to determine the exact timing here or the typical course of events. Even the point of time when the discovery of castration is made varies, and a number of other factors seem to be inconstant and to depend on chance. The state of the girl's own phallic activity plays a part; and so too does the question whether this activity was found out or not, and how much interference with it she experienced afterwards.

Little girls usually discover for themselves their characteristic phallic activity — masturbation of the clitoris; and to begin with this is no doubt unaccompanied by phantasy. The part played in starting it by nursery hygiene is reflected in the very common phantasy which makes the mother or nurse into a seducer. [. . .]

A prohibition of masturbation, as we have seen, becomes an incentive for giving it up; but it also becomes a motive for rebelling against the person who prohibits it — that is to say, the mother, or the mother-substitute who later regularly merges with her. A defiant persistence in masturbation appears to open the way to masculinity. Even where the girl has not succeeded in suppressing her masturbation, the effect of the apparently vain prohibition is seen in her later efforts to free herself at all costs from a satisfaction which has been spoilt for her. When she reaches maturity her object-choice may still be influenced by this persisting purpose. Her resentment at being prevented from free sexual activity plays a big part in her detachment from her mother. The same motive comes into operation again after puberty, when her mother takes up her duty of guarding her daughter's chastity. We shall, of course, not forget that the mother is similarly opposed to a boy's masturbating and thus provides him, too, with a strong motive for rebellion.

When the little girl discovers her own deficiency, from seeing a male genital, it is only with hesitation and reluctance that she accepts the unwelcome knowledge. As we have seen, she clings obstinately to the expectation of one day having a genital of the same kind too, and her wish for it survives long after her hope has expired. The child invariably regards castration in the first instance as a misfortune peculiar to herself; only later does she realize that it extends to certain other children and lastly to certain grown-ups. When she comes to understand the general nature of this characteristic, it follows that femaleness — and with it, of course, her mother — suffers a great depreciation in her eyes. [. . .]

At the end of this first phase of attachment to the mother, there emerges, as the girl's strongest motive for turning away from her, the reproach that her mother did not give her a proper penis — that is to say, brought her into the world as a female. A second reproach, which does not reach quite so far back, is rather a surprising one. It is that her mother did not give her enough milk, did not suckle her long enough. Under the conditions of modern civilization this may be true often enough, but certainly not so often as is asserted in analyses. [. . .]

When we survey the whole range of motives for turning away from the mother which analysis brings to light — that she failed to provide the little girl with the only proper genital, that she did not feed her sufficiently, that she compelled her to share her mother's love with others, that she never fulfilled all the girl's expectations of love, and, finally, that she first aroused her sexual activity and then forbade it — all these motives seem nevertheless insufficient to justify the girl's final hostility. Some of them follow inevitably from the nature of infantile sexuality; others appear like rationalizations devised later to account for the uncomprehended change in feeling. Perhaps the real fact is that the attachment to the mother is bound to perish, precisely because it was the first and was so intense; just as one can often see happen in the first marriages of young women which they have entered into when they were most passionately in love. In both situations the attitude of love probably comes to grief from the disappointments that are unavoidable and from the accumulation of occasions for aggression. [. . .]

We shall conclude, then, that the little girl's intense attachment to her mother is strongly ambivalent, and that it is in consequence precisely of this ambivalence that (with the assistance of the other factors we have adduced) her attachment is forced away from her mother — once again, that is to say, in consequence of a general characteristic of infantile sexuality.

The explanation I have attempted to give is at once met by a question: 'How is it, then, that boys are able to keep intact their attachment to their mother, which is certainly no less strong than that of girls?' The answer comes equally promptly: 'because boys are able to deal with their ambivalent feelings towards their mother by directing all their hostility on to their father'. But, in the first place, we ought not to make this reply until we have made a close study of the pre-Oedipus phase in boys, and, in the second place, it is probably more prudent in general to admit that we have as yet no clear understanding of these processes, with which we have only just become acquainted.

A further question arises: 'What does the little girl require of her mother? What is the nature of her sexual aims during the time of exclusive attachment to her mother?' The answer we obtain from the analytic material is just what we should expect. The girl's sexual aims in regard to her mother are active as well as passive and are determined by the libidinal phases through which the child passes. Here the relation of activity to passivity is especially interesting. It can easily be observed that in every field of mental experience, not merely that of sexuality, when a child receives a passive impression it has a tendency to produce an active reaction. It tries to do itself what has just been done to it. This is part of the work imposed on it of mastering the external world and can even lead to its endeavouring to repeat an impression which it would have reason to avoid on account of its distressing content. Children's play, too, is made to serve this purpose of supplementing a passive experience with an active piece of behaviour and of thus, as it were, annulling it. When a doctor has opened a child's mouth, in spite of his resistance, to look down his throat, the same child, after the doctor has gone, will play at being the doctor himself, and will repeat the assault upon some small brother or sister who is as helpless in his hands as he was in the doctor's. Here we have an unmistakable revolt against passivity and a preference for the active role. This swing-over from passivity to activity does not take place with the same regularity or vigour in all children; in some it may not occur at all. A child's behaviour in this respect may enable us to draw conclusions as to the relative strength of the masculinity and femininity that it will exhibit in its sexuality.

The first sexual and sexually coloured experiences which a child has in relation to its mother are naturally of a passive character. It is suckled, fed, cleaned, and dressed by her, and taught to perform all its functions. A part of its libido goes on clinging to those experiences and enjoys the satisfactions bound up with them; but another part strives to turn them into activity. In the first place, being suckled at the breast gives place to active sucking. As regards the other experiences the child contents itself either with becoming self-sufficient — that is, with itself successfully carrying out what had hitherto been done for it — or with repeating its passive experiences in an active form in play; or else it actually makes its mother into the object and behaves as the active subject towards her. For a long time I was unable to credit this last behaviour, which takes place in the field of real action, until my observations removed all doubts on the matter.

We seldom hear of a little girl's wanting to wash or dress her mother, or tell her to perform her excretory functions. Sometimes, it is true, she says: 'Now let's play that I'm the mother and you're the child', but generally she fulfils these active wishes in an indirect way, in her play with her doll, in which she represents the mother and the doll the child. The fondness girls have for playing with dolls, in contrast to boys, is commonly regarded as a sign of early awakened femininity. Not unjustly so; but we must not overlook the fact that what finds expression here is the *active* side of femininity, and that the little girl's preference for dolls is probably evidence of the exclusiveness of her attachment to her mother, with complete neglect of her father-object. [. . .]

The turning-away from her mother is an extremely important step in the course of a little girl's development. It is more than a mere change of object. We have already described what takes place in it and the many motives put forward for it; we may now add that hand in hand with it there is to be observed a marked lowering of the active sexual impulses and a rise of the passive ones. It is true that the active trends have been affected by frustration more strongly; they have proved totally unrealizable and are therefore abandoned by the libido more readily. But the passive trends have not escaped disappointment either. With the turning-away from the mother clitoridal masturbation frequently ceases as well; and often enough when the small girl represses her previous masculinity a considerable portion of her sexual trends in general is permanently injured too. The transition to the father-object is accomplished with the help of the passive trends in so far as they have escaped the catastrophe. The path to the development of femininity now lies open to the girl, to the extent to which it is not restricted by the remains of the pre-Oedipus attachment to her mother which she has surmounted.

If we now survey the stage of sexual development in the female which I have been describing, we cannot resist coming to a definite conclusion about female sexuality as a whole. We have found the same libidinal forces at work in it as in the male child and we have been able to convince ourselves that for a period of time these forces follow the same course and have the same outcome in each.

Biological factors subsequently deflect those libidinal forces [in the girl's case] from their original aims and conduct even active and in every sense masculine trends into feminine channels. Since we cannot dismiss the notion that sexual excitation is derived from the operation of certain chemical substances, it seems plausible at first to expect that biochemistry will one day disclose a substance to us whose presence produces a male sexual excitation and another substance which produces a female one. But this hope seems no less naïve than the other one — happily obsolete today — that it may be possible under the microscope to isolate the different exciting factors of hysteria, obsessional neurosis, melancholia, and so on.

Even in sexual chemistry things must be rather more complicated. For psychology, however, it is a matter of indifference whether there is a single sexually exciting substance in the body or two or countless numbers of them. Psychoanalysis teaches us to manage with a single libido, which, it is true, has both active and passive aims (that is, modes of satisfaction). This antithesis and, above all, the existence of libidinal trends with passive aims, contains within itself the remainder of our problem.

Notes

1. It is to be anticipated that men analysts with feminist views, as well as our women analysts, will disagree with what I have said here. They will hardly fail to object that such notions spring from the 'masculinity complex' of the male and are designed to justify on theoretical grounds his innate inclination to disparage and suppress women. But this sort of psychoanalytic argumentation reminds us here, as it so often does, of Dostoevsky's famous 'knife that cuts both ways'. The opponents of those who argue in this way will on their side think it quite natural that the female sex should refuse to accept a view which appears to contradict their eagerly coveted equality with men. The use of analysis as a weapon of controversy can clearly lead to no decision. [. . .]

PART FIVE

Feminism and the Production of Knowledge

This final section of the book contains chapters which we have grouped under the broad heading 'Feminism and the Production of Knowledge'. Whilst the context of these articles is quite varied, they are all linked by a concern for the ways in which knowledge about women has been, and is, constructed, consciously and unconsciously, within and outside the academic disciplines, by government departments and by us all in our daily lives.

The first two chapters, by John Lennane and Jean Lennane, and by Hilary Graham and Ann Oakley, both concentrate on the ways in which the medical profession constructs certain sorts of perspectives about women, based on their definitions of female biology and psychology and how this affects women's own perceptions of their bodies, health and reproduction capabilities. This is followed by an article by Diana Russel which, through an examination of the incidence of rape and its effects on women's lives, provides a further illustration of the categories constructed to describe and explain women's behaviour; in this case, the definitions used by the rapists, the police and the courts.

One problem with establishing how often violent events like rape occur is the inadequacy of available statistics. On a more general level, this issue is explored by Paul Allin and Audrey Hunt in the next chapter. They examine what might at first sight be the most 'objective' form of knowledge and show how the apparently unassailable authority of official statistics can be questioned. Following from this, Hilary Rose considers the construction of knowledge in another field often considered as objective, namely the field of scientific knowledge and suggests ways in which women's specific concerns can help to foster a more humanistic science.

Another way in which current perceptions of women have been formulated is through the construction, in earlier periods, of women's sexuality. Lucy Bland's article looks at how the re-definition of the sexuality of good and bad women came to be thought of in terms of the 'healthy mother', breeding for the good of the race, while the bad woman came to be thought of in terms of promiscuity.

In the final chapter, Penelope Brown and L. J. Jordanova examine a dichotomy around which much of Western thought has been organized, that of 'nature *versus* culture'. Looking at the way in which this dichotomy has structured thinking about the sexes, the article draws together material on scientific thought and various social manifestations of women's subordination. The authors challenge that opposition of categories within which women are assigned to the sphere of 'nature' in a way that obscures the social divisions which give rise to male dominance and female subordination.

5.1 Alleged psychogenic disorders in women — a possible manifestation of sexual prejudice

JEAN LENNANE AND JOHN LENNANE

Abstract Dysmenorrhea, nausea of pregnancy, pain in labour and infantile behavioural disturbances are conditions commonly considered to be caused or aggravated by psychogenic factors. Although such scientific evidence as exists clearly implicates organic causes, acceptance of a psychogenic origin has led to an irrational and ineffective approach to their management.

Because these conditions affect only women the cloudy thinking that characterizes the relevant literature may be due to a form of sexual prejudice.

> Woman is a miserable creature. . . . sick threequarters of her life
> . . . as far removed from man as man is from the forest monkey,
> so that it is a question if it could have any pretensions to being
> human, or whether such pretensions can be reasonably respected.
> Donatien, Marquis de Sade: *Justine.*

The therapy of a disorder is often hampered by imperfect understanding of its pathogenesis. When its cause is definitely known, it may be possible to treat that; if, however, there is no response to this treatment, either because it is inadequate or because knowledge of the cause is in fact incomplete or wrong, there is rarely any hesitation in directing treatment to the relief of the patient's symptoms. It can be justifiably argued that relief of suffering is desirable even in the absence of more definitive measures.

Nevertheless, there is a group of conditions whose management is not based on these principles. They are all physical in their

Source: Lennane, K. J. and Lennanne, R. J. (1973) Alleged psychogenic disorders in women — a possible manifestation of sexual prejudice. Printed by permission from the *New England Journal Of Medicine.* Vol. 288, pp. 288−292

manifestations, but have come to be regarded as psychogenic in origin. It is of interest that many of these conditions directly affect only women.

Four such conditions concern us here: primary dysmenorrhea; nausea of pregnancy; pain in labour; and infantile behavioural disorders. Despite the well documented presence of organic etiologic factors, the therapeutic literature is characterized by an unscientific recourse to psychogenesis and a correspondingly inadequate, even derisory, approach to their management.

Primary dysmenorrhea

This well defined clinical entity occurs in about 50 per cent of women.[1,2] The almost invariable pattern is for the first cycles, often for the first two to four years, to be painless.[2] The condition seldom persists after the birth of the first child, or after the age of 25.[2] Suppression of ovulation with estrogen prevents the occurrence of pain with the following period[1,3,4] prevention of dysmenorrhea being an accepted side benefit of oral contraceptive theory.[4] Ovulation tends to be irregular, or not to occur at all, till 16 to 18 years of age.[5]

It seems, then, that whereas the exact cause of pain may be unknown, it is dependent on the occurrence of ovulation. It may be considered a cultural by-product in that it would rarely occur if marriage followed soon after the menarche, and the first pregnancy soon after the establishment of ovulation.

The condition, however, is commonly considered to be partly or wholly a psychogenic one: 'It is generally acknowledged that this condition is much more frequent in the "high-strung", nervous or neurotic female than in her more stable sister'.[1] 'Faulty outlook . . . leading to an exaggeration of minor discomfort . . . may even be an excuse to avoid doing something that is disliked'.[2] Or more simply, 'the pain is always secondary to an emotional problem'.[6]

There is no valid basis for this attitude. These authors are not referring merely to the effect that the personality of the patient may have on the amount of suffering or complaining occurring in any organic illness, but are implying, or directly stating, that the patients' faulty outlook is causing the condition.

However, a well defined painful syndrome occurring in 50 per cent of those exposed to a particular stress has no parallel in conventional medicine. Battle stress, for example, in which the stress would appear to be very much more severe, is not a specific entity; symptoms vary, and it is relatively uncommon.[7,8] If the pain is the result of 'faulty outlook' one would expect it to start at the time of the initial psychic shock (menarche), and not two to four years later. The pain is dependent on the occurrence of ovulation and is reliably and usually completely removed by suppression of ovulation (92 per cent of severe cases in one study[1]). Perhaps the few who do not respond to ovulation suppression might be psychologically disturbed, but in practice, psychosomatic study and psychometric tests do not confirm this hypothesis.[1]

Quite apart from these objections scientific supporting evidence is completely absent — e.g. a prospective study of pubescent girls, or of menstruating girls who were not yet ovulating. Evidence, when offered, is scanty: '*A dysmenorrheic mother usually has a dysmenorrheic daughter*'[2] (original italics), which, if true (no statistical confirmation is offered), would more usually be taken to indicate a hereditary factor.

The attitude to treatment may also be unusual. The pain 'rarely lasts in a severe form for longer than 12 hours . . . colicky . . . patient looks drawn and pale and may sweat; nausea and vomiting are common'.[2] Any severe visceral colic may be described in almost identical words. However, 'analgesics may be warranted until the diagnosis is established. Ovulation suppression is a valuable temporary expedient . . . management must be directed at the underlying psychodynamics . . . must be prepared to pursue a cure over a long period of time [until the age of 25, or the first pregnancy?] . . . very little can be done for the patient who prefers to use menstrual symptoms as a monthly refuge from responsibility and effort'.[6] The patient with visceral colic is treated with rest and relief of pain; the patient who persists in having severe dysmenorrhea may be denied both.

Nausea of pregnancy [. . .]

It is a well defined clinical entity occurring in 75[6] to 88 per cent[10] of pregnant women. It consists of an unusual type of nausea, which is typically worst when the patient arises in the morning, but may also occur at other times of day,[4,6,9,10] is relieved by food, seldom interferes with eating or causes more than slight weight loss unless it is severe,[4] and may or may not be accompanied by vomiting.[9] It usually begins in the fifth or sixth week, sometimes earlier, and subsides by the 14th to the 16th week.[6,10] It is often more severe in multiple pregnancy.[6] The type of nausea and its usual duration are exactly mimicked by estrogen therapy,[4] and such nausea is a recognized side effect of estrogen-containing oral contraceptives.[4] Estrogen has been shown to be excreted in large amounts during pregnancy.[4]

The exact cause remains unknown, but the nausea is probably due to some substance secreted in excess during pregnancy, and in increased amounts in multiple pregnancy, it seems likely that this substance is estrogen.[4]

The condition is nevertheless commonly held to be partly or wholly psychogenic, again without any scientific supporting evidence. 'Few will deny that the psychogenic factor is of prime importance, and it is probable that the many adjustments demanded of the newly-pregnant women impose a mild condition of stress coupled with an irrationally exaggerated fear of the obstetric hazards confronting her, especially that of producing an abnormal child'.[10] 'Nosologically classified with the neuroses . . . [nausea of pregnancy] . . . may indicate resentment, ambivalence and inadequacy in women ill-prepared for motherhood'.[6]

The percentage of those confronted with this particular stress in which this specific syndrome develops is even higher than that for the dysmenorrheic group. Many of the latter would never see a doctor, but nearly all pregnant women see one, and to classify up to 88 per cent of patients with a particular organic condition (pregnancy) as neurotic is unusual in the extreme. Its occasional occurrence before pregnancy is suspected[9] and its severity in multiple pregnancy contradicts the neurosis theory, unless it is postulated that the patient can subconsciously and definitely diagnose these conditions as early as the fourth week. Its occurrence with oral contraceptive therapy is also contradictory, unless these patients are resentful, ambivalent and inadequate because they are not pregnant. Despite rejection of the neurosis theory for these and other reasons in a paper by Rhodes,[9] it is dogmatically maintained, without reasons, by an author citing that paper as his only reference.[6]

Treatment of the condition has been made difficult by the thalidomide disaster, and drug therapy must now be considered even more hazardous since the discovery of a totally unacceptable side-effect (vaginal cancer) occurring in young women 20 years after their mothers had received stilbestrol in early pregnancy.[11] The observation that these mothers frequently lost their nausea[12] fortunately seems to have been overlooked, perhaps because stilbestrol is not a tranquilizer.

It is interesting in this connection that a genuinely psychogenic factor seems to have been missed. Stale and unpleasant odours, and cooking smells generally, may be nauseating to a sensitive person who is not already nauseated; exposure to a substance, sight or smell that has caused vomiting in the past may also provoke nausea.[13] A married woman, especially if she has children, is likely to have her existing nausea constantly aggravated in this way, and may in effect be undergoing a form of aversion therapy to her house, and particularly her kitchen. Directive psychotherapy of the husband to cope with an extension of the masculine role for a few weeks so as to remove this psychogenic factor might seem safer than any drug can now honestly be said to be, and cheaper than admission to a hospital.

Pain in labour

Pain is defined as an unpleasant subjective sensation, typically associated with nonspecific physiologic and affective responses.[14] Its presence in animals may be inferred from these responses, but in human beings it is usually diagnosed by questioning of the patient, or from the patient's complaints of pain. Such questioning is not often done in labour, and it is therefore difficult to discover what proportion of untreated labours are painless or involve only discomfort. The figure is certainly no higher than 14 per cent.[15]

Again there is a widely held belief that the pain experienced by the large majority is partly or wholly psychogenic in origin, largely because of the theory of 'natural childbirth' by Grantly Dick Read.[16] Blockade of a physiologic response to pain would not be expected to have any effect on the sensation itself, and it is remarkable that prevention of an emotional response should be expected to do so; the theory postulates, however, that the pain usually experienced is due to an increase in muscular tension caused by fear, and that removal of fear will therefore prevent the occurrence of pain.[16] Strong visceral contractions against an obstruction are usually painful, but the theory states that labour, as a 'physiologic function', should be painless.[16] The method seems to work in practice mainly by a refusal to accept that pain is in fact present, even here: 'Women will say that they cannot do any more, they are suffering the most appalling agony. They will ask for anesthesia and demand of their attendant that he shall do something to relieve them. . . .'[16] The use of meperidine hydrochloride in the first stage purports to be merely sedative ('. . . enables a woman to regain her self-control and determination to proceed with confidence and courage, recognizing that pain will be very largely of her own making').[16] Since one injection of meperidine is as much effective pain relief as most conventionally managed patients can expect,[17] and the method has advantages (antenatal education, husband's support during labour, consciousness for the delivery and, possibly, some analgesia for the suggestible), it has been popular with women themselves. Unfortunately, patients undergoing 'natural childbirth' whose pain is intolerable may meet a frankly punitive attitude:

A woman who has neither understanding nor control should be

removed before she disturbs the emotional equanimity of others. One shrieking woman can ruin a dozen labours. There will always be individuals who have no intention of either learning or helping themselves, or accepting any responsibility for their own behaviour. They should be looked upon as a definite menace in a maternity hospital, and treated accordingly.[16]

Conventional management is now often supplemented by 'natural' features, or by the similar 'psycho-prophylaxis,'[18,19] and prospective patients are taught these theories as established fact[20] — even to the extent of such novel (not to say deviant) ideas as antenatal practice in relaxation in the presence of artificially induced pain.[21]

There are other unusual features in conventional methods as currently practised. One is the use of a barbiturate or other sedative in early labour.[17] Besides their lack of analgesic effect, these drugs may cause excitement or delirium, and cannot be relied on to produce sedation in the presence of pain.[22] Another feature — the prevalent method of giving pain relief on the attendants' assessment of the patients' outward manifestations of discomfort, or according to the progress of labour[17] — is completely unreliable. The incidence of severe pain in one study was less than 20 per cent when it was estimated by the attendants, but more than 50 per cent when it was estimated by the patients themselves,[23] whereas other workers found that 50 per cent of patients would have liked more relief of pain than they were given.[24] In a study on the effect of personality on labour, patients with high scores for neuroticism and extroversion suffered more fear, but less pain, than those who were more stable and introverted; the former had been given more relief, presumably because of their greater outward manifestations of discomfort.[25]

Beazley et al.[17] rejected the conventional pattern as demonstrably inadequate, and by basing relief of pain on the patients' assessment, using heroin in preference to meperidine, and giving paracervical blocks to control late first-stage pain, they obtained satisfactory results (assessed by the patient) in 60 per cent. The considerable amounts of opiate used had a negligible effect on the Apgar scores, and the progress of labour was not impaired. Moreover, delay in giving analgesics was often associated with difficulty in obtaining adequate relief of pain later in labour, explaining why patients with relaxation training may find labour more unpleasant than those without it.[25]

Even these results cannot be considered satisfactory. Supplementary possibilities include hypnosis, which is limited by the resistance of a substantial minority of patients,[23] and epidural analgesia. The latter highly effective method (85 to 90 per cent satisfactory[15]) can be used routinely in primigravidas without increasing the forceps rate.[15] It is not widely available, however, and is commonly used only in 'prolonged and difficult' labour[26] if at all.

Thus, the choice for most women faced with the prospect of some hours of severe or intolerable pain lies between the illogical and ineffective 'natural' methods and the irrationally applied and usually inadequate conventional ones.

Disturbance in young babies

Infantile colic

Again, this is a well defined clinical entity, occurring in healthy, thriving babies,[27,28] usually beginning in the second or third week of life and subsiding spontaneously at three or four months,[28,29] and occurring most frequently in the late afternoon or evening.[27,29] The incidence of significant colic in a prospective study was 23 per cent.[29] [. . .]

The origin of the condition is completely unknown. The many current theories and studies are critically reviewed elsewhere.[29] Spock[28] nowhere suggests, in his detailed section on the subject, that it is in any way the mother's fault, but elsewhere it has been attributed to maternal insecurity, anxiety, tension, and conflicts about accepting the feminine or maternal role.[30] It is listed under 'Psychological Disorders' in a standard pediatric textbook.[31]

Evidence against this etiology is, again, that it is a common and well defined condition; treatment with a drug that is in no way a tranquilizer, even of the baby, is effective, and a prospective study of the 146 mothers of newborn infants, using a standardized objective psychologic test (the MMPI), — a study that should surely have been done before the theory was advanced, — showed no relation to maternal emotional factors.[29]

'Distress syndrome' (crossness, disturbed sleep and disturbed feeding patterns in normal young infants for which they were admitted to a baby-care hospital) is the subject of a more recent paper,[32] in which, again, the condition is said to be caused by maternal anxiety despite the following findings: one 'experimental' mother who was not anxious; the occurrence of anxiety in two control mothers; remission of the syndrome in a distressed baby who did not relapse when transferred to the care of a foster-mother who was anxious and tense; and remission of the anxiety of most of the 'experimental' mothers after admission of their babies to the hospital. These findings are easily explained on the alternative theory that the babies' disturbed behaviour would be likely to cause their mothers anxiety, but the authors have nowhere considered this possibility even to discard it. Other criticisms apply. The study is retrospective; eight is a very small experimental group, and assessment of maternal anxiety is subjective and unstandardized.

Vomiting ('spitting,' 'posseting' — the difference is quantitative not qualitative[28]) is extremely common in the early months,[28] and Carne has postulated a relation between it and the not uncommon[33] condition of puerperal depression.[34] The suggestion is not that two common conditions may frequently coincidentally coexist, and that a depressed mother may find a normal amount of vomiting intolerable, but that her depression has caused the vomiting. Evidence for this hypothesis is anecdotal and unsystematic, in that the mother often presented complaining of the baby's vomiting rather than her own ill defined malaise, and when her depression was successfully treated, she usually stopped complaining of the vomiting. It is not recorded whether the vomiting had in fact stopped. Nevertheless, Carne's paper has been cited without comment,[33] and 'statistical confirmation' has been offered, again with the depressed mother as the only observer, and with no follow-up observation.[35]

Discussion

The features common to all the subjects discussed are the ready acceptance of a psychogenic origin without evidence, and the remarkable persistence and damaging nature of such a belief.

The mechanism by which this conclusion seems to have been reached in all these conditions is the reversal of a truism. The reversal is logically unsound, but will still fit in with the observed phenomena often enough to retain an impressive aura of 'truth.' Thus, the severity and duration of the pain in severe dysmenorrhea would be expected to make most patients apprehensive; this has been reversed to say that fear and dislike of menstruation cause or aggravate the dysmenorrhea. Nausea of pregnancy, particularly if severe, may make the subject ambivalent about the state that is causing it (or actively hostile if the pregnancy is not a welcome one) as long as the symptoms last; this is reversed to say that ambivalence or hostility causes the nausea. Pain, by definition, is an unpleasant sensation, which therefore has a marked affective accompaniment;[14] this is reversed to say that the affect (fear) causes the pain in labour. Prolonged bouts of unexplained screaming or other antisocial behaviour in her infant are likely to cause a mother anxiety; this has been reversed to give the theory that infantile colic is caused by maternal insecurity and tension. In fact most normal babies exhibit some kind of disturbed behaviour in the early weeks, and the 'perfect' baby who lies in his crib all day and never cries may have a severe mental defect.[36] Unfortunately, if this possibility were more generally recognized, it would only be a matter of time before a paper appeared on 'Lack of stimulation and overemphasis on 'good' behaviour in the early weeks — maternal factors in severe mental defect.'

The belief in psychogenesis, once reached, is remarkably persistent. The dependence of dysmenorrhea on ovulation, for example, was first demonstrated in 1940.[3] There has been no corresponding demonstration of any dependence of ovulation on 'failure to adapt to the feminine role' (indeed the reverse would seem more likely), but 30 years later, standard gynecologic textbooks still emphasize a psychogenic cause, and this persistence is repeated in the other subjects discussed. The most remarkable persistence, however, is of the Biblical attitude[37] to pain in labour, for which the woman is still held morally responsible,[16] allowing irrational and ineffective treatment of prolonged and severe pain to continue in the otherwise analgesia-oriented 20th century.

An erroneous belief in psychogenesis is damaging to the patient in many ways, though possibly convenient for the doctor. There is an unfortunately widespread view that the patient whose symptoms are psychogenic is not entitled to any symptomatic relief. The terms commonly used to describe the psychic difficulty — 'neurotic' or 'unfeminine' — are, to the laity, simply derogatory, and patients reluctant to be so classified may be unduly dependent, complaisant, uncritical and 'feminine' in their behaviour, and reluctant to report severe symptoms or failure to respond to treatment. The patient who, coincidentally, is neurotic or unfeminine in some real sense is not likely to be helped by being told that the difficulty is the cause of her other unpleasant symptoms. The belief must impede research and retard real progress, and treatment directed at the psychic 'cause' is a waste of time and money.

Illogical, persistent and damaging beliefs constitute prejudice, and in view of the fact that all these conditions affect women, whereas the majority of specialists and textbook authors are men, it is tempting to postulate an underlying sexual basis for this prejudice. There is no doubt that such a postulate could be vigorously debated, but from the practical point of view, it should not be allowed to cloud the central issue, which is clearly the need for the application of normal objective scientific methods to these topics. Whatever the reasons for the present unsatisfactory position, it is surely to be hoped that teachers and practitioners alike will be able to bring themselves to approach these conditions in a properly rational and critical fashion.

Acknowledgement

We are indebted to Mr. Graeme Duncan, F.R.C.S., M.R.C.O.G., for a review and criticism of the manuscript.

References

1. Menaker JS, Powers KD: Management of primary dysmenorrhea. Obstet Gynecol 20: 66—71, 1962.
2. Jeffcoate TNA: Principles of Gynaecology. Third edition. London, Butterworth and Company, 1967, pp. 684—686.
3. Sturgis SH, Albright F: The mechanism of estrin therapy in the relief of dysmenorrhea. Endocrinology 26: 68—72, 1940.
4. Astwood EB: Estrogens and progestins. The Pharmacological Basis of Therapeutics: A textbook of pharmacology, toxicology, and therapeutics for physicians and medical students. Fourth edition. Edited by LS Goodman, A Gilman. New York, The Macmillan Company, 1970, pp. 1538—1565.
5. Kinsey AC, Pomeroy WB, Martin CE, et al: Sexual Behaviour in the Human Female. Philadelphia, WB Saunders Company, 1953, pp. 124—125.
6. Benson RC: Gynaecology and obstetrics, Current Diagnosis and Treatment. Edited by MA Krupp, MJ Chatton. Los Altos, California, Lange Medical Publications, 1972, pp. 377—434.
7. Sargant W, Slater E: Physical Methods of Treatment in Psychiatry. Third edition. Edinburgh, E and S Livingstone, 1954, p. 12.
8. Mayer-Gross W, Slater E, Roth M: Clinical Psychiatry. Second edition. Baltimore, Williams and Wilkins Company, 1960, pp. 133—134.
9. Rhodes P: Hyperemesis gravidarum. Practitioner 192: 229—233, 1964.
10. Barr W: Vomiting, hiatus hernia and heartburn,[26] pp. 202—211.
11. Greenwald P, Barlow JJ, Nasca PD, et al: Vaginal cancer after maternal treatment with synthetic estrogens. N Engl J Med 285: 390—392, 1971.
12. Malleson J: An endocrine factor in certain affective disorders. Lancet 2: 158—164, 1953.
13. Roth JLA: Symptomatology, Gastroenterology. Vol 1. Second edition. Edited by HL Bockus. Philadelphia, WB Saunders Company, 1963, pp. 14—71.
14. Keele CA, Neil E: Samson Wright's Applied Physiology. Twelfth edition. London, Oxford University Press, 1971.

15. Potter N, Macdonald RD: Obstetric consequences of epidural analgesia in nulliparous patients. Lancet 1: 1031—1034, 1971.
16. Read GD: The influence of the emotions on pregnancy and parturition, Antenatal and Postnatal Care. Seventh edition. Edited by FJ Browne. London, J and A Churchill, 1951, pp. 88—113.
17. Beazley JM, Morewood JHM, Leaver EP, et al: Relief of pain in labour. Lancet 1: 1033—1035, 1967.
18. Training for childbirth — meeting of National Childbirth Trust, Lancet 1: 765—766, 1961.
19. Giles AM: Psychoprophylaxis,[26] pp. 548—557.
20. McClure-Browne JC: How a baby starts to grow, You and Your Baby. Edited by T Weston, London, British Medical Association, Family Doctor Publications, 1969, pp. 11—28.
21. Flew JD: The hygiene and management of pregnancy. Practitioner 194: 738—742, 1965.
22. Sharpless SK: Hypnotics and sedatives, The Pharmacological Basis of Therapeutics: A textbook of pharmacology, toxicology, and therapeutics for physicians and medical students. Fourth edition. Edited by LS Goodman, A Gilman. New York, The Macmillan Company, 1970, pp. 98—134.
23. Perchard SD: Hypnosis in obstetrics. Proc R Soc Med 53: 458—460, 1960.
24. Rock TL: Obstetric labour and the hypnotic technique. Pacif Med Surg 74: 105—108, 1966.
25. Furneaux WD, Chapple PAL: Some objective and subjective characteristics of labour influenced by personality, and their modification by hypnosis or relaxation. Proc R Soc Med 57: 261—262, 1964.
26. Practical Obstetrical Problems. Fourth edition. Edited by I Donald. London, Lloyd-Luke, 1969.
27. Illingworth RS: Evening colic in infants: a double-blind trial of dicyclomine hydrochloride. Lancet 2: 1119—1120, 1959.
28. Spock B: Baby and Child Care. New York, Pocket Books, 1957.
29. Paradise JL: Maternal and other factors in the etiology of infantile colic: report of a prospective study of 146 infants. JAMA 197: 191—199, 1966.
30. Stewart AH, Weiland IH, Leider AR, et al: Excessive infant crying (colic) in relation to parent behaviour. Am J Psychiatry 110: 687—694, 1954.
31. Settlage CF: Psychological disorders, Textbook of Pediatrics. Ninth edition. Edited by WE Nelson, VC Vaughan III, RJ McKay. Philadelphia, WB Saunders Company, 1969, pp. 72—92.
32. Ironside W, Lewis P: Anxiety in the mother-infant interactions. Aust NZ J Psychiatry 3: 227—232, 1969.
33. Pitt B: 'Atypical' depression following childbirth. Br J Psychiatry 114: 1325—1335, 1968.
34. Carne S: The influence of the mother's health on her child. Proc R Soc Med 59: 1013—1014, 1966.

35. Dalton K: Prospective study into puerperal depression. Br J Psychiatry 118: 689—692, 1971.
36. Illingworth RS: The Development of the Infant and Young Child: Normal and abnormal. Fourth edition. London, E and S Livingstone, 1970
37. The Bible (revised version). Genesis 3: 1—16.

5.2 Competing ideologies of reproduction: medical and maternal perspectives on pregnancy

HILARY GRAHAM AND ANN OAKLEY

[. . .] In talking about the different ways in which doctors and mothers view pregnancy, we are talking about a fundamental difference in their perspectives on the meaning of childbearing. It is not simply a difference of opinion about approach and procedures — about whether pregnancy is normal or pathological, or whether or not labour should be routinely induced. Rather, we are suggesting that doctors and mothers have a qualitatively different way of looking at the nature, context and management of reproduction. In this chapter, we use the concept of a frame of reference to indicate this difference. 'Frame of reference' embraces both the notion of an ideological perspective — a system of values and attitudes through which mothers and doctors view pregnancy — and of a reference group — a network of individuals who are significant influences upon these sets of attitudes and values. [. . .]

Obstetricians and mothers: contrasts in their frame of reference

The difference in the two frames of reference revolve around divergent views of both the nature of childbearing and the context in which it is seen. Specifically, our data suggest that mothers and doctors disagree on whether pregnancy is a natural or a medical process and whether, as a consequence, pregnancy should be abstracted from the woman's life-experiences and treated as an isolated medical event. These two issues are in turn related to two other areas of disagreement. The first concerns the way the quality

Source: Graham, H. and Oakley, A. (1981) 'Competing ideologies of reproduction: medical and maternal perspectives of pregnancy', in *Women, Health and Reproduction*, Helen Roberts (ed.), Routledge and Kegan Paul, London, pp. 50—74

of childbearing is assessed — in other words what are the criteria of success? The second concerns the way the quality of reproduction is ensured, i.e. who controls childbearing? It is these four issues [. . .] that lie at the heart of the conflict between mothers' and doctors' frames of reference. Anthropologists have discussed questions about the nature, context and control of childbearing in describing the differences in the management of childbirth between Western and non-Western cultures (Mead and Newton 1967, Mnecke 1976, Oakley 1977). The issues of nature, context and control have also been identified as crucial to an understanding of the historical development of Western obstetrics (Oakley, 1976). Interestingly, these dimensions have been less systematically explored in the study of the structure and processes of modern maternity care.

Nature of childbearing

Obstetricians

The key element in the doctor's perspective on reproduction is the status of reproduction as a medical subject. Pregnancy and birth are analogous to other physiological processes as topics of medical knowledge and treatment. The association of obstetrics with gynaecology as a specialism reinforces this lack of distinction between reproduction and the rest of medicine, by setting aside a special area to do with the physiological attributes of womanhood (Scully and Bart 1973).

Mothers

Bearing children is seen by mothers to be a natural biological process. It is akin to other biological processes (like menstruation) that occur in a woman's life. This is not to say that it is a woman's 'natural destiny' to bear children. Rather, for those women who do, the process is rooted in their bodies and in their lives and not in a medical textbook (Graham 1977).

Context of childbearing

Obstetricians

The obstetrician's frame of reference attaches a particular, and a limited, significance to pregnancy and birth as medical events. The doctor views the individual's career as a pregnant and parturient woman as an isolated patient-episode. [. . .] Being a patient is the woman's key status so far as the obstetrician is concerned, although other statuses she might have, for example as an unmarried person, as an engineer or street-cleaner, may affect the doctor's attitudes and behaviour *vis-à-vis* the patient by influencing his/her perception of the kind of medical treatment and patient-communication that is most appropriate (Stoller Shaw 1974, Macintyre 1976, Aitken Swan 1977).

Mothers

A woman views reproduction not as an isolated episode of medical treatment but as an event which is integrated with other aspects of her life. Having a baby affects not only her medical status, it has implications for most of her other social roles. This is seen most clearly during first pregnancy and birth when a woman becomes a mother. [. . .] But even in subsequent births, her role can change as her pregnancy affects her occupational standing, her financial position, her housing situation, her marital status and her personal relationships. As Hart (1977) has shown, the new baby impinges permanently and comprehensively on a woman's life-style.

Criteria of success

Obstetricians

The obstetrician's frame of reference gives a particular and again restricted meaning to the notion of 'successful' reproduction. Here the reference point is perinatal and maternal mortality rates, and to a lesser degree certain restricted indices of morbidity. A 'successful' pregnancy is one which results in a physically healthy baby and mother as assessed in the period immediately following birth, i.e. while mother and child are still under the obstetrician's care (Haire 1972, Richards 1974).

Mothers

Because of the holistic way in which women view childbearing, the notion of successful reproduction is considerably more complex than the simple measurement of mortality and morbidity. Though in almost all cases the goal of the live birth of a healthy infant is paramount, success means primarily a satisfactory personal experience. This applies not only to the pregnancy and birth but to the subsequent mother-baby relationship and to the way in which motherhood is integrated with the rest of a woman's life. Unlike the obstetrician's criteria of success, these criteria — pregnancy/

birth experiences, experiences with the mother-baby relationship, and experiences with integrating motherhood into a woman's life-style — are not separable or easily observable, but can only be assessed in the weeks, months or even years following birth (Kitzinger 1972).

Control of childbearing

Obstetricians

The medical frame of reference defines reproduction as a specialist subject in which obstetricians are the experts, possessing (by virtue of their training) greater expertise than any other social group. This expertise is not limited to any one particular area, for example, the mechanics of the birth process, but is held to extend to the entire symptomatology of childbearing (Scully and Bart, *op. cit;* Kaiser and Kaiser 1974).

Mothers

Mothers view themselves as knowledgeable about pregnancy and birth. This knowledge stems not primarily from medical science, but rather from a woman's capacity to sense and respond to the sensations of her body. Rather than being an abstract knowledge acquired through formal training, it is thus an individualized and to some extent intuitive knowledge built up from bodily experiences (Boyle 1975, Goldthorpe and Richman 1976, McKinlay 1973).

Conflicts in the frames of reference

How do the conflicts we have seen between medical and maternal frames of reference manifest themselves? In trying to explain this, we concentrate on data relating to interaction in the antenatal clinic as this is the main forum in which mothers and medics meet. We have selected dimensions of doctor-patient interaction which illustrate and substantiate the differences between doctors and mothers already identified. These four dimensions are: (1) conflict over the status of reproduction as health or illness; (2) the question of the doctor-as-expert versus the mother-as-expert; (3) the issue of who makes the decisions about reproductive care; and (4) the kind of communication doctors and mothers see as appropriate to their joint interaction.

Health or illness?

One important norm within the culture of the medical profession is that judging a sick person well is more to be avoided than judging a well person sick. This 'medical decision rule' is applied to obstetrics as it is to other branches of medicine; every pregnancy and labour is treated as though it is, or could be, abnormal, and the weight of the obstetrician's medical education acts against his/her achievement of work-satisfaction in the treatment of unproblematic reproduction (Scheff 1963). The 'as if ill' role was a recurrent feature in the observed interactions between doctors and patients. It was made explicit when doctors needed to explain or justify particular medical attitudes and routines to their patients. Such explanations and justifications might be called for when a doctor discussed the type of antenatal care he/she felt most appropriate for his patient, when advising on a woman's employment and domestic commitment or when prescribing medical treatment.[1] For example:

> *Patient:* I'm a hairdresser. I only do three days a week — is it all right to go on working?
>
> *Doctor:* Up to twenty-eight weeks is all right on the whole, especially if you have a trouble-free pregnancy as you obviously have. After that it's better to give up.
>
> *Patient:* I only work three days a week, I feel fine.
>
> *Doctor:* Yes, everything *is* fine, but now you've got to this stage it's better to give up, just in case.

But the most common way in which the 'as if ill' rule is manifested in antenatal care today is through the routine prescription of various tests and procedures such as ultrasonic scanning, twenty-four hour urine collection for the measurement of placental function, and frequent internal examination to assess the competence of the cervix. The subject of tests and procedures occupies an important place in the antenatal encounter. In nearly half the encounters observed in the London hospital, there was at least one reference to technology — to one testing procedure or another. Of the questions asked by patients, 29 per cent concerned medical technology — ultrasound, blood tests, induction and so on, and another 5 per cent concerned prescribed drugs. For some women these sophisticated procedures and forms of treatment are the hallmark of a 'proper' pregnancy. Other women felt less happy about this medicalization of childbearing, unaware perhaps of the equation between pregnancy and illness until they began their careers as antenatal patients. The first antenatal visit thus comes as a considerable shock, disturbing long-held notions about pregnancy as a natural process. One London mother put the case succinctly:

> I though, okay, first baby, the best thing to do is to have it in hospital, because it's far more of an unknown quantity . . . but it's this concern with medicine that seems to override everything else — the natural process, I mean. I mean it is something that women have always been brought up to do; everybody knows that, okay, it's painful, having labour and everything, but it's very rewarding; it's the one pain we've been brought up to expect and not to be scared of. Before the hospital thing pregnancy was a normal, nice condition. I'm not sure it isn't an illness now.

Apprehension about medicalized reproduction is greatest among primiparae (first-time mothers), two-thirds of whom expressed anxiety about antenatal checkups. The focus of this anxiety is often the vaginal examination, and, for more than half of the York and London primiparae, this was their first experience of this examination.

> I'll tell you what terrified me, the internal, cos I'd never had one before and the very thought of it, oh God! For a week I was so nervous, I thought I'd get desperate diarrhoea, I was all colly wobbles and I was like that for a whole week.

The vaginal examination is of course an important part of antenatal work. Of the encounters observed in the London hospital, 28 per cent included an internal examination but rarely was the medical rationale for the examination made explicit. Again, the 'as if ill' rule is rarely articulated by medical staff unless a procedure or a prescription is questioned or challenged by a patient. This is illustrated in the following consultation, where a patient refuses an internal examination. She has had a previous termination and her cervix is being assessed fortnightly as part of a research project designed to see whether regular internal examinations are of any use in preventing abortion due to cervical incompetence. On this occasion she refuses the examination and the doctor asks why:

Patient: The doctor last time, he hurt me, and I had a lot of bleeding afterwards — he promised he wouldn't do it again.

Doctor: I don't care a damn what the doctor promised last

time. If you lose the baby it's up to you. Do you know why we do these examinations?

Patient: I thought it was to tell the size of the baby.

Doctor: No, it's nothing to do with that. You've had a termination and this can cause prematurity, and we look to see if the womb is opening up. If it is, we put a stitch in.

The purpose of the regular internal examinations had clearly not been explained to the patient — until she challenged medical dictate.

Who is the expert?

A second way in which the differences between doctors' and mothers' frames of reference is manifested is in conflicts over expertise: in conflicts between doctor-as-expert and mother-as-expert. The definition and interpretation of significant symptoms was a common area of divergence between mothers and doctors. To the doctor, symptoms of importance are those that betray the patient's clinical condition: swollen fingers or ankles, blurred vision, bleeding and so forth. But the patient may very often report symptoms which worry her but which do not worry the doctor. She is reacting to her subjective experience of pregnancy, to her feelings about the physical and emotional changes that pregnancy has brought about. For example:

Patient: I get pains in my groin, down here, why is that?

Doctor: Well, it's some time since your last pregnancy, and also your centre of gravity is changing.

Patient: I see.

Doctor: That's okay. (Pats on back.) [. . .]

Differences in symptom-description are of course a general characteristic of doctor-patient interaction (Stimson and Webb 1975). This kind of medical response which may evoke considerable anxiety in the patient was far from rare: of the 677 statements made by patients during the series of antenatal clinic encounters observed in London, 12 per cent concerned symptoms of pain or discomfort which the doctor ignored or dismissed as clinically unimportant. Mothers also state their feelings about the pregnancy and the birth, sometimes relating these to their social circumstances — a bad marriage, poor housing, for instance and 8 per cent of the statements made by patients were of this kind. Very rarely did the doctor respond seriously to such statements:

> *Patient:* My doctor gave me some tablets for vomiting earlier on but I was reluctant to take them.
> *Doctor:* Are you still reluctant?
> *Patient:* Well I feel so depressed, I'm so fed up. . . .
> *Doctor:* (interrupting) Shall I give you some tablets for vomiting?

Mothers' and doctors' different fields of expertise also compete over the dating of the pregnancy. [. . .]

The routinization of these questions acknowledges their importance, but medical attitudes to the reliability of women's information on these points tend to be sceptical. For example:

> *Doctor:* How many weeks are you now?
> *Patient:* Twenty-six-and-a-half.
> *Doctor:* (looking at case notes) Twenty weeks now.
> *Patient:* No, twenty-six-and-a-half.
> *Doctor:* You can't be.
> *Patient:* Yes, I am; look at the ultrasound report.
> *Doctor:* When was it done?
> *Patient:* Today.
> *Doctor:* It was done today?
> *Patient:* Yes.
> *Doctor:* (reads report) Oh yes, twenty-six-and-a-half weeks, that's right.

Perhaps it is significant that increasingly the routine use of ultrasound is providing an alternative medical technique for the assessment of gestation length; a medical rationale for the inflation of medical over maternal expertise is thus provided. During consultations in the London antenatal clinic, 6 per cent of the questions asked and 5 per cent of the statements made by mothers concerned dates, mothers usually trying to negotiate the 'correct' date of expected delivery with the doctor who did not see this as a subject for negotiation or as a legitimate area of maternal expertise.

Who controls reproduction?

The women interviewed both in York and London reported very few areas in which they were able to exercise choice about the kind of maternity care they had. From the moment they first saw a doctor about the pregnancy, decisions were made for them. As one mother in York put it:

> Well, when I went to see my doctor, he's ever so nice, he said he advised me to have it in hospital. I'm more or less putting my foot down, he said, that you have it in hospital. So I really didn't have any choice.

This lack of control experienced by mothers extended right through their antenatal careers. One sign of mothers' desires to feel in control of their reproductive care is the number of questions they ask about the progress of their pregnancy. Of all questions asked in the London antenatal clinic, 20 per cent concerned the size or position of the baby, foetal heart sounds, maternal weight and blood pressure. A further 20 per cent were questions about the physiology of pregnancy and birth in general or about related medical procedures. These are serious requests but are often casually treated by doctors with resulting confusion and anxiety in the mother.

Actual conflict between mother and doctor over medical decisions was rare in the research series, but it did characterise some encounters, and was particularly likely to do so when decisions about delivery were being made. These confrontations between mothers and doctors thus illustrate one way in which some women express a desire to control what happens to them in childbirth.

A registrar, examining a woman towards the end of her first pregnancy, does an internal examination and comments:

Doctor: It'd be difficult to get you off now — I think you ought to come in for the rest and to do some more water tests and then we can start you off. The baby isn't growing as fast as it was.

Patient: What do you mean, come in?

Doctor: Really it's a matter of when you come in, Sunday, I should think, and then stay in.

Patient: Stay in until it's born, you mean.

Doctor: Yes.

Patient: I don't fancy that very much.

Doctor: If you'd been ready I would have started you off today. You see on the ultrasound it's not growing as well as it was, and on the water tests the oestriols are falling — it's not bad, but you should come in and have some water tests, get some rest, and then we can start you off

> sometime next week probably, when you're ready.
>
> *Patient:* If my husband wanted to come and talk to you about inducing me, can I make an appointment for him?
>
> *Doctor:* I don't think anything your husband said would affect our decision one way or the other.
>
> *Patient:* No, but he would like to talk to you.
>
> *Doctor:* Yes, well he can talk to whoever's on duty, but there's nothing he can say that will affect us: it's a medical question.
>
> *Patient:* Yes, but he'd still like to talk it over, find out what's going on.
>
> *Doctor:* What it amounts to is that we won't be browbeaten by *The Sunday Times*.[2]
>
> *Patient:* No, I understand that.
>
> *Doctor:* If we explained to everyone, and everyone's husband, we'd spend all our time explaining. *I think you've got to assume if you come here for medical attention that we make all the decisions.* In fact I think you should come in today, but I've already been browbeaten into saying Sunday, which is another forty-eight hours.

Here the doctor refuses to 'discuss' the proposed induction with the patient, taking it as axiomatic that the most that should be expected of him is an explanation of the reasons why he wants to induce labour. Interestingly, cases in the series where patients objected to induction all met with hostility from the doctor, whereas when the patient either explicitly or implicitly requested an induction this met with a very different response: in some cases the patient's request was granted, but even where it was not, the plea for induction was accepted as legitimate patient-behaviour. In asking for an induction the patient is subscribing to two important norms in obstetric treatment: the idea that technological childbirth is 'good' childbirth, and the notion that while the doctor's superior expertise may be challenged by *refusing* medical decisions, it is *confirmed* by polite requests for them; 'begging for mercy' is how the doctors often described such requests.

The communication gap

Problems in communicating with doctors were commonly reported in both York and London. Mothers' comments pick out the following related themes:[3] [. . .]

Asking questions

In the London hospital observations, questions asked by patients averaged slightly more than 1 per encounter and statements made by patients (i.e. not in response to anything the doctor said) slightly less. Of the women interviewed in York, 80 per cent said that they had learnt nothing from their antenatal checkups; 40 per cent felt they couldn't ask questions — and of those who did feel they could in theory, many didn't in practice:

> The nurse says 'now do you want to ask the doctor anything?' And more invariably than not you say 'no' because you just don't feel you can. The way they ask you, 'Right, do you want to ask the doctor anything?' you think, no. All you want to do is get up and get out.'

Getting explanations

When mothers do ask questions they usually require much fuller information than the medical staff are prepared to give. A quick 'that's normal' or 'that's nothing to worry about' is not sufficient. Take the disquiet experienced by one London mother:

> I've been getting really bad stomach pains like I'm coming on. I said that to the doctor — I said I had bad stomach pains, he said it's usual but I mean they're getting worse. I said I'm getting pains like I'm coming on. He said you do get this. But they're getting worse. It might *be* usual, but. . . .

Being treated as ignorant

These complaints relate to medical definitions of mothers as ignorant about medical aspects of pregnancy. One York mother, worried about contact with rubella, said:

> I mean you don't need to have done midwifery to know the complications and I wanted an answer. I think my own GP sent my blood off on the Friday and this was Tuesday or Wednesday so I knew the results were there [at the clinic]. But, 'Oh you might hear in the next few days'; it wasn't good enough for me, every hour I was thinking about it. . . . Some nurses and doctors are terribly condescending. And this girl irritated me, so I said, 'When will I know the results of this rubella test?' 'It's out of your hands now, deary, the doctor knows all about it' and I did

feel very irritated by that, I'm an intelligent woman and it annoyed me.

The assumption of ignorance may be a common component in doctors' attitudes to patients (Kaiser and Kaiser *op. cit.,* Davis and Horobin 1977) but patients in antenatal clinics are always women and the doctors are predominantly men[4] (Ehrenreich 1974). Typifications of women as women are certainly articulated in antenatal consultations; for example:[5] [. . .]

> *Doctor:* This is twins . . . they're growing well, but you need more rest . . . I'd advise some good books and a quiet life for three months. You're not working.
> *Patient:* No.
> *Doctor:* Just normal exercise — I want you to have a walk every day, but no gardening, no heavy work, postpone moving or decorating the house. If you do rest, you'll grow yourself slightly bigger babies. After all, it's this (pats her abdomen) that's your most important job isn't it?

And women, it is implied, are inherently unreliable sources of information:

> *Doctor:* (reading case notes) Ah, I see you've got a boy and a girl.
> *Patient:* No, two girls.
> *Doctor:* Really. Are you sure? I thought it said . . . [checks in notes] oh no, you're quite right, two girls. [. . .]

Seeing different doctors

The problem of unsatisfactory communication with doctors is compounded by seeing a different face at every clinic visit. One London mother describes her experience:

> The thing is you get such *varied* opinions — one of them says about your weight and the next time you go I think this is it: I'm going to be told off about my weight again, and then I go and I see somebody completely different and nobody says a thing about it . . . I come out feeling completely confused.

In the York sample, 81 per cent of mothers said they would prefer to see the same doctor every time.

Being on a conveyor belt

All these communication difficulties are related to the organization of antenatal clinics which tend to resemble assembly lines, if only because a small number of doctors must see a large number of patients in a short space of time. In the London antenatal clinic the average time per doctor-patient encounter was 3.9 minutes. It is rarely possible within this framework for mothers to feel that they have been treated as individuals or that they have had a 'good' experience — and such is the emotional meaning of pregnancy to women that many have high expectations of their maternity care. A York mother:

> You sort of feel I've waited all the time, and you're just sat there . . . and I don't know, they treat you like you were just an animal, and yet it's a big thing to you. The first time in nineteen years that something happens, it's a new experience to you although it may be everyday to them. Some of them just don't realize this.

Of all statements made by patients in the London antenatal clinic, 8 per cent were statements of worry or anxiety reflecting dissatisfaction with the kind of communication offered by doctors. Another symptom of patient dissatisfaction is the unanswered (or unasked) question that is posed to the researcher. Indeed in the London project this was a frequent theme of the interviews. Sometimes the unanswered question is a very basic one and a source of great worry to the mother:

> *Researcher:* Did you ask any questions?
> *Patient:* No I didn't. You see when it comes to that I'm very shy in asking questions.
> *Researcher:* Did you want to ask any questions?
> *Patient:* Yes. Is it dangerous like? Can anything happen to you? That's the most I think I wanted to ask. I'm very frightened. I just pray. They asked me — 'any questions?' I just said no. I'm frightened if anything will happen. You know a lot of people in Ireland they used to die having children. . . . There's one question I'm very worried about. And I didn't like to ask it. Since I got pregnant I can't have intercourse at all. I just can't. I don't know why. It hurts. I just can't have it. . . . Is it natural, I wonder? I've got a little baby book there and it says in that book that you should have no problem. It says you should have intercourse with your husband up until seven or eight months.

Patients' difficulties in communicating with doctors are rooted in medical definitions of the ideal mode of interaction with patients in which patient-passivity is central; the patient asks no questions and co-operates with the doctor in all the procedures defined medically as necessary. For example:

> *Doctor:* (entering cubicle) Hello.
> *Patient:* Hello.
> *Doctor:* (reading notes) Mrs Watkins?
> *Patient:* Yes.
> *Doctor:* Well, how are you?
> *Patient:* Fine, thank you.
> *Doctor:* Can I feel your tummy? (He undoes the buttons on her dressing gown and does so.) Any complaints?
> *Patient:* No.
> *Doctor:* (filling in notes) Have you felt the baby move yet?
> *Patient:* Yes.
> *Doctor:* How long have you felt it?
> *Patient:* Two weeks.
> *Doctor:* (feels patient's ankles) All the tests we did last time were good.
> *Patient:* Good.
> *Doctor:* Okay. (Leaves cubicle.)

This mode of interaction is facilitated by the layout of many antenatal clinics, including those described by women in the York and London research projects. A cubicle system for examining patients, and the requirement that patients lie on couches ready for the doctor, militate against doctor-patient interaction as equals. In the London hospital, patients who were found by doctors sitting rather than lying on the couch were regarded as deviant; significantly, patients who began their medical encounters in this way asked more questions and were given more time by the doctor.

The most typical way in which doctors themselves exceed the kind of minimal interaction demanded by the passive-patient model is by offering certain restricted kind of explanation to the patient. The subject of the doctor's explanation may be the physiology of pregnancy, clinic procedure or the technology of ultrasound. Particular kinds of language are used in these explanations.[6] Technical language in explanations is reserved for cases where a doctor wants to encourage a patient to agree to a particular procedure (and perceives her as unwilling to do so). Thus, in the example quoted earlier of a conflict over induction, the doctor referred to 'oestriol' tests as 'water' tests until the patient expressed hostility to the idea of intervention in her pregnancy, at which point he informed her that 'the oestriols are falling'. For other types of explanation, a form of 'lay' language is used. Examples are 'tail', 'feeling inside', 'start you off' (for induction) and terms such as 'tickling' and 'stirring up' for sweeping the membranes as a covert method of inducing labour. This lay language seems to be used fairly indiscriminately, although the doctor's perception of the social class or medical status of the patient may affect his/her choice of words. Thus one houseman regularly used the phrase 'vaginal examination' for patients with middle-class occupations, reserving the phrase 'examine you down below' for those whom he saw as working class.

In addition to this dependence on a form of lay language, the doctor also trivializes and is deliberately non-specific in his description of medical procedures. A thorough and probably uncomfortable internal examination may be trivialized to become 'a little examination' or 'a gentle examination'; induction may be given the label 'a push downhill' or 'marching orders'. For example, one patient asked, 'What do they usually do when they start you off; my last baby I had normally?' The doctor replied, 'It's nothing terrible. They do an internal and break the waters and then drip some magic stuff into your arm.' Such 'explanations' are based on an underlying typification of patients as anxious. Indeed, there seemed to be a widespread supposition among the doctors observed that the reason patients asked questions was anxiety and that, therefore, the main aim of medical explanations was to allay anxiety (rather than to give information). As the following exchange shows, joking is often used as a device for supposedly reducing patient-anxiety, although, as we have seen, it does not necessarily do so:

First Doctor: You're looking serious.
Patient: Well, I am rather worried about it all. It feels like a small baby — I feel much smaller with this one than I did with my first, and she weighed under six pounds. Ultrasound last week said the baby was very small as well.
First doctor: Weighed it, did they?
Second doctor: (entering examination cubicle) They go round to flower shows and weigh cakes, you know.
First doctor: Yes, it's a piece of cake really.

We have briefly outlined here some of the main features of medical and maternal perspectives on pregnancy and birth which emerged during two research projects. We have attempted to 'explain' certain conflicts between the two perspectives by rooting these conflicts in the particular frames of reference employed by the providers and users of maternity care. The frames of reference have been described primarily in terms of the differing social positions and perspectives of these two groups as they interact as *doctors* and *patients*. In outlining these conflicts in present-day maternity care, we have left unanswered the crucial question of what should be done. There appear to be two basic kinds of solution available — one which works within the existing organization of maternity care, the other which involves working towards alternative patterns of care. The first type of solution would involve, for example, redesigning antenatal clinics so that the sense of rush and anonymity is minimized, educating doctors to be less dogmatic about the 'needs' of maternity patients, and encouraging mothers to be more articulate and more reasonable about the kind of maternity care they want. But more fundamental changes may be felt necessary to ameliorate the conflicts between doctors and mothers. It may be that changes *of* the system itself, rather than changes *in* the system are required. Such changes might entail the development of neighbourhood maternity centres, a move back towards home delivery, a transfer of medical responsibility from doctors to midwives, and less task-oriented and more patient-oriented maternity care.

Notes

1. Maternal employment *per se* is of course not related to reproductive causality, although other variables that are associated with it, for instance low socio-economic status, do show some such relationship (Illsley 1967).
2. The doctor is referring to two articles written by L. Gillie and O. Gillie (1974) in *The Sunday Times.*
3. It is interesting to note the similarity between these themes and those picked out in the Standing Maternity and Midwifery Advisory Committee document *Human Relations and Obstetrics,* HMSO, 1961.
4. In September 1977, 25.4 per cent of the gynaecologists and obstetricians in England and Wales listed as hospital medical staff by the DHSS were women (DHSS 1978).
5. A similar pattern of attitudes and treatment regarding female patients has been found outside gynaecology and obstetrics. See Barrett and Roberts (1978).
6. Emerson (1970) has described the medical language used in vaginal examinations.

References

Aitken Swan, J. (1977), *Fertility Control and the Medical Profession,* Croom Helm, London.

Barrett, M., and Roberts, H. (1978), 'Doctors and their Patients: the Social control of women in general practice', in C. Smart and B. Smart (eds), *Women, Sexuality and Social Control,* Routledge & Kegan Paul, London.

Boyle, C.M. (1975), 'Differences between Patients' and Doctors' Interpretations of Some Common Medical Terms', in C. Cox, and A. Meads (eds), *A Sociology of Medical Practice,* Collier Macmillan, London.

Cartwright, A. (1977), 'Mothers' Experiences of Induction', in *British Medical Journal,* 17 September.

Davis, A., and Horobin, G. (eds) (1977), *Medical Encounters: Experience of Illness and Treatment,* Croom Helm London.

Donnison, J. (1977), *Midwives and Medical Men,* Heinemann, London.

Ehrenreich, B. (1974), 'Gender and Objectivity in Medicine', *International Journal of Health Services,* vol. 4, p.617.

Emerson, J. (1970), 'Behaviour in Private Places: Sustaining Definitions of Reality in Gynaecological Examinations', in H.P. Dreitzel, (ed), *Recent Sociology,* no. 2, Macmillan, New York.

Gillie, L., and Gillie, O. (1974), *The Sunday Times,* 13 and 20 October.

Goldthorpe, W.O., and Richman, J. (1974), 'Maternal Attitudes to Unintended Home Confinement', *Practitioner,* no. 212, p.845.

Goldthorpe, W.O., and Richman, J. (1975, 1976), 'The Gynaecological Patient's Knowledge of her Illness and Treatment', *British Journal of Sexual Medicine,* December 1975 and February 1976.

Graham, H. (1976), 'The Social Image of Pregnancy: Pregnancy as Spirit Possession', *Sociological Review,* vol. 24, p.291.

Graham, H. (1977), 'Women's Attitudes to Conception and Pregnancy', in R. Chester and J. Peel (eds), *Equalities and Inequalities in Family Life,* Academic Press, London.

Haire, D. (1972), *The Cultural Warping of Childbirth,* International Childbirth Education Association News.

Hart, N. (1977), 'Technology and Childbirth — a Dialectical Autobiography', in A. Davis and G. Horobin, *op. cit.*

Illsley, R. (1967), 'The Sociological Study of Reproduction and its Outcome in S.A. Richardson and A.F. Guttmacher (eds), *Childbearing: its Social and Psychological Aspects,* Williams & Wilkins, Baltimore.

Kaiser, B.L., and Kaiser, I.H. (1974), 'The Challenge of the Women's Movement to American Gynaecology', *American Journal of Obstetrics and Gynaecology,* pp. 652—65.

Kitzinger, S. (1972), *The Experience of Childbirth,* Penguin, Harmondsworth.

Kitzinger, S. (1975), *Some Mothers' Experiences of Induced Labour,* National Childbirth Trust, London.

Macintyre, S. (1976), 'Who Wants Babies? The Social Construction of Instincts', in D. Barker and S. Allen (eds), *Sexual Divisions and Society: Process and Change,* Tavistock, London.

Macintyre, S. (1976), 'Obstetric Routines in Antenatal Care', paper given at the British Sociological Association Medical Sociology conference, York.

McKinlay, J. (1973), 'Social Networks, Lay Consultation and Help-Seeking Behaviour', *Social Forces,* no. 51, pp. 275—92.

Mead, M., and Newton, N. (1967), 'Cultural Patterning of Perinatal Behaviour', in S. Richardson and A. Guttmacher (eds), *childbearing: its Social and Psychological Aspects,* Williams & Wilkins, Baltimore.

Mnecke, M.A. (1976), 'Health Care Systems as Socialising Agents: Childbearing the North Thai and Western Ways', *Social Science and Medicine,* no. 10, pp. 377—83.

Oakley, A. (1975), 'The Trap of Medicalised Motherhood', *New Society,* vol. 34, p.639.

Oakley, A. (1976), 'Wisewoman and Medicine Man: Changes in the Management of Childbirth', in J. Mitchell and A. Oakley (eds), *The Rights and Wrongs of Women,* Penguin, Harmondsworth.

Oakley, A. (1977), 'Cross Cultural Practice', in T. Chard and M. Richards (eds), *Benefits and Hazards of the New Obstetrics,* Heinemann, London.

O'Brien, M. (1977), 'Home and Hospital: a Comparison of the Experiences of Mothers Having Home and Hospital Confinements', paper given at the Second Seminar on Human Relations and Obstetric Practice, 30 July, University of Warwick.

Richards, M. (1974), 'The One-Day-Old Deprived Child', *New Scientist,* 2 March, pp.820—2.

Royal College of Obstetricians and Gynaecologists (1975), *The Management of Labour,* Proceedings of Third Study Group.

Scheff, T.J. (1963), 'Decision Rules, Types of Error and Their Consequences in Medical Diagnosis', *Behavioural Science,* vol. 8, pp. 97—105.

Scully, D., and Bart, P. (1973), 'A Funny Thing Happened to Me on the Way to the Orifice: Women in Gynaecology Textbooks', *American Journal of Sociology,* vol. 78.

Stimson, G., and Webb, B. (1975), *Going to See the Doctor,* Routledge & Kegan Paul, London.

Stoller Shaw, N. (1974), *Forced Labour: Maternity Care in the United States,* Pergamon Press, New York.

Walker, J.F. (1972), 'The Changing Role of the Midwife', *International Journal of Nursing Studies,* pp. 85—94.

Walker, J.F. (1976), 'Midwife and Obstetric Nurse? Some Reflections of Midwives and Obstetricians on the Role of the Midwife', *Journal of Advanced Nursing,* vol. 1, pp. 129—38.

5.3   Rape and the masculine mystique

DIANA RUSSELL

Many people continue to believe that a woman cannot be raped. Many years ago Clarence Darrow allegedly attempted to demonstrate this in court by holding a cup in a mobile hand and instructing someone to try to insert a pencil into the cup. I was subjected to the same game on a TV programme in 1972. Of course one could easily get the pencil into the cup if one were armed, or if one were to beat the person in the face so that he stopped focusing on moving the cup away, or if one twisted an arm behind the cup holder's back until pain achieved the same end. But these points were missed, presumably because they contradict the myth that women cannot be raped.

It is remarkable that so many people retain that myth in the face of the increasing incidence of reported rape, and despite bloody cases of rape that make headlines. It may be that people cannot contend with the enormity of such a crime and prefer to believe, on the same principle as ' you can't cheat an honest man,' that rape only happens to victims who ask for it.

But it should be noted that men benefit from the wishing-away of rape. For if women cannot be raped, it must mean that women really want intercourse with men whenever men want it, in spite of any woman's claims to the contrary. Ultimately the penis is irresistible. This fantasy is expressed in movies like *Hospital, Straw Dogs,* or *Little Sisters,* to say nothing of standard pornography.[1] But most women require more than the old 'in-and-out' as the hero of *A Clockwork Orange* calls it, in order to enjoy sex. Ignorance and the force of sexual myth prevent many men from realizing this fact.

If women cannot be raped, it is not surprising that men who rape often see themselves as lovers, not as rapists. They believe so strongly that women really want intercourse with them, that they are unable to hear women's protests to the contrary. Women's physical and verbal resistance is seen as part of the female game of

Source: Russell, Diana E.H. (1975), *The Politics of Rape.* Stein and Day, New York, pp. 257—265

pretending reluctance, or as an expression of a desire to be overcome. For example, one woman reported that her date finally succeeded in raping her after a two-hour struggle, but he could not understand why she was so upset, and he was unable to comprehend why she accused him of raping her. He considered himself a lover in the tradition of forceful males and expected to have a continuing relationship with her.

This expectation is quite common when rape occurs in a dating situation and is apparent sometimes even when the rapist is a complete stranger. Two victims reported receiving marriage proposals from their rapists. Some of the men who raped women they knew apparently *were* able to see their acts as rape, though most were not. But even then, the victims report that some rapists did not appear to think that the act of raping would necessarily count against them. After all, since the man had felt sexually turned on to the victim, hadn't she provoked it? Wasn't she asking for it? In any case, don't women like to be raped?

After being raped by two men, a few victims, for example, were asked by their rapists which of the two they enjoyed most. Another woman reported that her rapist was 'furious because I wasn't getting turned on.' One woman who was raped by one of her best friends, whom she had known for over a year, but with whom she had never related sexually, reported that he had to beat her up to achieve his goal. That was the end of their friendship, but a year or so later she reported that he expressed resentment toward her for not having had more compassion for the 'forceful trip' he had been into.

Ms. White, who was hospitalized for three days after she was attacked and raped by an apparent Good Samaritan, was asked by a male psychiatrist at the hospital. 'Haven't you really been rushing towards this very thing all your life?' and then returning home from the hospital she was asked angrily by her husband, 'If that's what you wanted, why didn't you come to *me?*' The myth that women who are raped must want it appears to have been so powerful for this man that he subsequently raped her himself.

In a society dominated by men, it would be difficult for women's view of rape to differ greatly from that of men. Therefore it is not surprising that many women also accept the myth that there is no such thing as rape. But it serves a different function for them. Women have always been dependent on men. It is much more comfortable for women to deny that men are really brutal toward women.

One of the consequences of accepting the myth that there is no such thing as rape is that in situations which fit the definition of rape used in this study, many women, like many rapists, do not see themselves as rape victims. For example, it was only several months after a woman had been working on this study that she re-evaluated earlier experiences and realized that she had been raped twice.[2] The difficulties of realizing that rape has occurred are clear for women who accept the myth. For if rape cannot happen, then the experience of forcible intercourse must be something else. I have come across many such cases, particularly when the woman was not subjected to much violence, or if her rapist was not a stranger.

Unfortunately the myth that women cannot be raped is far more dysfunctional than functional for women. While the myth generally protects men's image in the eyes of women, one of the consequences is that women, like men, often 'put down' raped women by disbelieving them, or by seeing them as responsible for their victimization. (The increasingly popular field of victimology contributes to this view.) And if these unbelievers themselves are raped, they have to struggle with the incredulity of others and their own sense of guilt at somehow having caused it. Often it seems easier to deny the whole experience, but this is hardly a healthy way to deal with the problem.

Even most of those who do realize that they have been raped do not report it, as they do not expect to be believed. Several women, for example, stated that they had always believed that it was impossible for a woman to be raped until it happened to them, and they were convinced that if they told their friends, their colleagues, or the police, they would not be believed, since the victims expected others to subscribe to the myth as unquestioningly as they had done. Unfortunately, this conviction is often borne out. If the woman was raped by a friend, a date, a lover, an ex-lover, an employer, a teacher, a doctor — in fact, if the rapist was not a complete stranger — the police and many other people are unlikely to believe the victim's story. In my study, with three exceptions, only victims who are raped by strangers reported it to the police.

Fortunately, the myth of unrapable women is not as popular as it once was. A less extreme and more widely held belief is that rape *does* happen, but very rarely. This view is supported by the fact that most people have read about the odd case in the newspaper. But few have ever wittingly associated with a woman who was raped. Most people believe that the women they know have never had such experiences. Another myth is that the few rapists who exist are crazy, sadistic psychopaths — freaks of society. This myth is perpetuated by the fact that these are largely the kinds of cases we read about in the newspaper, and we don't hear of any others.

One function of the myth that rape is only perpetuated by society's freaks is that rape then appears to have no further implications for the rest of society. All the sane men must protect 'their' women from the few insane ones, and women without men must watch out. Yet rape is *not* exclusively the act of sadistic psychopaths and is much more widespread than most people realize. Indeed, the view that emerges from this study is that rape is not so much a deviant act as an overconforming act. Rape may be understood as an extreme acting-out of qualities that are regarded as supermasculine in this and many other societies: aggression, force, power, strength, toughness, dominance, competitiveness. To win, to be superior, to be successful, to conquer, all demonstrate masculinity to those who subscribe to common cultural notions of masculinity, *i.e.* the *masculine mystique*. And it would be surprising if these notions of masculinity did not find expression in men's sexual behaviour. Indeed, sex may be the arena where these notions of masculinity are most intensely acted out, particularly by men who feel powerless in the rest of their lives, and men whose masculinity is threatened by their sense of powerlessness.

The desire to prove oneself is very different from a desire for enjoyment. Several of the victims commented that their rapists didn't seem to be enjoying themselves. Some were reported as having difficulty getting erections. These observations suggest that some rapists are not motivated by a sexual urge; the assertion of power over a woman seems more important. At least two of the rapists interviewed by Jack Fremont are cases in point. It is in this sense that rape is sometimes referred to as a political act. A compliant woman doesn't satisfy some men's desire for power, which can only be exercised when there is opposition. Sometimes, then, rape is intended to keep women in their place — beneath men. The men who raped Ms. Davis, for example, told her that she was only getting what she deserved for walking on the street without a man at night. They saw themselves as decent for letting her get away so lightly. She felt they did not particularly enjoy the rape, but were behaving in a way they saw as natural to men when women give them the opportunity, by being unprotected, that men are not supposed to be given. And Ron, one of the rapists interviewed, explained his decision to rape a woman as follows: 'I really didn't feel the urge. As a matter of fact, I had a hell of a time getting an erection. . . . But I forced myself to do it to prove a point to her, to prove that she wasn't as big as she thought she was.'

The view of rape as the natural outcome of opportunity is even more clearly revealed where rape of enemy women is seen as natural soldierly behaviour. This view indicates a widespread acceptance of men's capacity to express aggression and hatred through sex. The recent behaviour of soldiers in Bangladesh, where an estimated 200,000 Bengali women were raped, may have received more publicity than the rape of women by American GIs in Vietnam because the rapists were not Americans.[3] In Vietnam, according to Smail, one of the few members of Charlie Company who talked frankly about rape, 'That's an everyday affair. You can nail just about everybody on that — at least once. The guys are human, man.'[4]

If men can express their hatred and aggression through wartime rape, it would be remarkable if they could not do it at home too. For many men, it seems, aggression and sex are closely related. The unconscious thinking seems to go as follows: being aggressive is masculine; being sexually aggressive is masculine; rape is sexually aggressive behaviour; therefore, rape is masculine behaviour.

Of course, the connection that exists between sex and aggression does not necessarily express itself in rape. Conscience gets in the way for some. Less extreme ways of expressing the connection are more common. For example, some men prefer women to be passive, leaving all the action to them. These men *do* things to women; it is not a mutual act. The men have the power. They are the boss. They do as they will, using women. This is not rape. It is a different kind of power trip. But if one were to see sexual behaviour as a continuum, with rape at one end, and sex liberated from sex roles at the other, the classic pattern just described would be near the rape end. The similarity is clear.

An interesting study by Kirkpatrick and Kanin at Indiana University illustrates the commonness of male sexual aggression. Of the female student respondents, 20.9 per cent reported that they had been offended by 'forceful attempts at sexual intercourse in the previous year,' and 6.2 per cent by 'aggressively forceful attempts at sexual intercourse in the course of which menacing threats or coercive infliction of physical pain were employed.'[5] The incidence may be even higher than these percentages indicate, since the authors report that 'there is no reason to think that offended girls had merely a single unpleasant experience with one partner.'[6] It is interesting that seven out of the ten most violent episodes involved girls in 'regular dating, "pinned", or engaged relationships'. Comparable figures for seniors at high school were obtained in a later study by one of the same authors.[7]

It could be argued that since it is customary for males to take the initiative sexually with women, it is to be expected that they will often go beyond what the woman wants and 'offend' her in this way. In other words, these studies simply reveal the hazards accompanying men's role as initiators. While it seems to me that the traditional masculine role is burdened by such hazards, such a view does not fully explain the findings of these studies. Taking the initiative but being even minimally sensitive to the other person's wishes would not, I believe, result in so many 'offensive' experiences, particularly not at the more extreme levels of aggression nor in the more intimate relationships.

Gagnon's work on female child victims also illustrates the commonness of male sexual aggression. Gagnon says that in the course of gathering data for *Sexual Behaviour in the Human Female*, women were asked whether they had ever experienced sexual contact or approaches as a child by an adult male (defined as a person at least five years older and postpubertal while the female was prepubertal).[8] 24 per cent of the 4,441 women reported having been so victimized.[9] Referring to these data in his study of female child victims, Gagnon concluded that 'it is possible to estimate that between twenty and twenty-five per cent of children reared in a middle-class environment will experience a victim experience in childhood and that the bulk of these will be minimal in character such as exhibition and genital touching,'[10] and that children in a lower-class environment will be exposed to a higher risk of such experiences, probably between one in three and as high as two in five, and the higher risk of exposure will include offenses of greater seriousness. 'If these crude estimates are correct', Gagnon continued, 'the number of children exposed will be in the range of 500,000 per year.'[11] It is common, then, for females of all ages to be subjected to the imposition of male sexual desire at varying degrees of intensity. Imposition is necessarily aggressive. But to be aggressive, domineering, controlling, and powerful is considered masculine.

There are many ways in which the sexual socialization of males predisposes them to rape. That is to say, beyond the masculine mystique, there is a more specific *virility mystique*, which focuses on the sexual domain. For example, males are expected to be able to separate their sexual responsiveness from their needs for love, respect, and affection. They are expected to be able to get an erection in the presence of an attractive 'sexy' woman or upon seeing pictures of naked female bodies. A man is not supposed to be impotent if he is with a prostitute, if he is a participant in a gang rape, or if he is angry with his wife or lover. He is supposed to be able to perform despite any chilling circumstances. One of the reasons why some men are so threatened by women who take the initiative in sexual relations or who want a lot of sex is that it forces men to realize that they *can't* perform whenever the opportunity arises. This fact is less apparent if men always take the initiative. Hence many men feel 'castrated' by women who demand equality in making sexual overtures.

The experience of a woman who was the victim of an attempted rape makes the point. Her would-be rapist felt very embarrassed when he could not get an erection. 'Play with me,' he commanded, to which she contemptuously replied, 'Who's raping who here? That's ridiculous, man!' According to the informant he then felt very foolish and ashamed. 'I had the upper hand from then on. . . . I gave him a hell of a time. He drove me to town. He was very frightened that I would phone the police, and I told him I sure would, and that if he ever did it again, I'd find out. He had to swear many times that he'd never do it again.' Since he had had the physical strength to pin her down and remove her pants, he could also have made her 'play' with him. But it seems that she was able instead to play on his feelings of being unmanly for not being able to rape her without assistance. It is a sad commentary on the consequence of subscribing to the virility mystique that a man feels bad about not being brutal enough to rape a woman.

One of the consequences of being trained since childhood to separate sexual desire from caring, respecting, liking, or loving is that many men regard women as sexual objects, rather than as full human beings. And since the virility mystique stresses the importance of having access to, and keeping score on, many women, the more the better, this approach dominates the perspective on women. Indeed, simply viewing women in this way, and making it clear to male companions that he does, is important for the man who wants to appear virile. One of the rapists interviewed said, for example, 'It was a difficult thing for me to admit that I was dealing with a human being when I was talking to a woman.' After she requested that he not hurt her, 'All of a sudden it came into my head, my God, this is a human being!' Subsequently, he wished he could tell her that his desire to rape her was completely impersonal, as if that would somehow. make her feel better.

Many of the rape victims expressed the feeling that they were viewed by their rapists simply as available cunts. As Roy, another of the rapists interviewed, put it when asked why he had raped his first victim: 'I wanted a piece of ass.' Such observations suggest that if men were not taught to separate sexual feelings from feelings of warmth and caring, rape would be unthinkable, and fewer men would impose their sexuality on unwilling women in other less extreme ways too.

The virility mystique, expounded by magazines like *Playboy*, has no place for the inexperienced or virgin male, when experience is determined by the number of partners and their attractiveness as sexual objects rather than the attractiveness of their personalities and the quality of the total relationships. The crux of a would-be rapist's explanation of his desire to rape a nurse was that he felt bad about being a virgin at the age of seventeen and wanted to prove that he was a man. According to the virility mystique, until a man has 'made it' with a woman, his manhood is in question. How he 'made it' is not so important. And a man must continue 'making it' with women. 'It's better to commit rape than masturbate,' said Norman Mailer,[12] while according to Ogden Nash, 'Seduction is for sissies. A he-man wants his rape.' With such values to guide men, it is not surprising that so many are strongly tempted to rape, and that more than we may care to believe succumb to the temptation.

The virility mystique, then, predisposes men to rape. If women were physically stronger than men, I do not believe there would be many instances of female raping male, because female sexual socialization encourages a woman to integrate sex, affection, and love, and to be sensitive to what her partner wants. Of course, there are many women who deviate from this pattern, just as there are men who have managed to reject their socialization for virility. But cultural trends make these cases exceptional. If our culture considered it masculine to be gentle and sensitive, to be responsive to the needs of others, to abhor violence, domination, and exploitation, to want sex only within a meaningful relationship, to be attracted by personality and character rather than by physical appearance, to value lasting rather than casual relationships, then rape would indeed be a deviant act, and, I would think, much less frequent. Among the Arapesh of New Guinea, males are reared to be gentle and nurturant, and according to Margaret Mead, 'of rape the Arapesh know nothing beyond the fact that it is the unpleasant custom of the Nugum people to the southeast of them.'[13]

If lynching is the ultimate racist act, rape is the ultimate sexist act. It is an act of physical and psychic oppression. It is an act in which a woman is used against her will sometimes because she is seen as just another piece of ass, and sometimes because the act of dominating her provides a sense of power. Like lynching, it is cowardly, and like lynching, it is used to keep individual women, as well as women as a caste, in their place. And finally, as with lynching, the rape victim is blamed for provocation.

Rape is an abuse of power, and the increase in rape shows that men are increasingly unable to handle their excessive power over women. As one of the rapists, Jimmy, says, men rape 'with no more feeling involved and no more neurosis than just "I want you, and I can't have you".' Ray, another of the rapists interviewed, revealed his willingness to take advantage of his physical capacity to rape merely because a woman irritated him. He was also taking advantage of the freedom society gives him by making it virtually impossible for a woman who had behaved toward him as she had to press charges of rape. Eradicating rape requires getting rid of the power discrepancy between men and women, because abuse of power flows from unequal power.

I have argued that rape is consistent with the masculinity and virility mystiques and, in fact, is promulgated by them. Intrinsic to these mystiques is the sexist notion of the biological superiority of males, which justifies their domination of women. Since concepts of strength and superiority are relative, the notion that men should be strong, independent, superior, and domineering implies that women should be weak, dependent, inferior, and submissive. If women were also strong and independent men would presumably regard them as masculine, which would undermine men's own sense of masculinity. The fundamental notions of masculinity and femininity are therefore part of the sexist ideology of this culture. Hence, it would be as accurate to relate rape to sexism as to the masculine mystique, for the maculine mystique is a sexist mystique that serves to maintain the power of men over women.

Notes

1. Aljean Harmetz points out that 'at least 20 films during the last two years served rape to their audiences', and quotes the explanation of MGM's vice-president in charge of production, Daniel Melnick: 'It has something to do with the fantasy life of the men who make movies. They seem to want to believe that at some point the woman stops struggling and starts moaning, that all women really love it, really want to be raped'. 'Rape: New Hollywood Game — An Ugly Movie Trend', *San Francisco Examiner*, October 28, 1973.

2. Briefly, one of her experiences was as follows: A man she had met once recently at a social gathering turned up uninvited to see her. It was obvious that she was ill, and at first he seemed solicitous of her health. Then, realizing she was alone in the house, he made some sexual advance toward her. She made it clear that she had no desire in that direction. Not discouraged, he picked her up, carried her to a bed, and pulled off her pants. She had very little strength and was unable to push him away. After an initial attempt to do so, she just lay back motionless. He had a hard time getting an erection and became very annoyed that she was so unresponsive. He finally was able to work himself up to a weak erection. He entered her, but could not ejaculate. This made him very angry, and he finally left in disgust. Though intercourse had certainly been imposed on her against her will, and her lack of interest in having intercourse was obvious, she did not see this as an experience of rape until very recently.

3. 'Women of Bangladesh,' *Ms.*, August 1972, p. 84.

4. Seymour M. Hersh, *My Lai 4: A Report on the Massacre and Its Aftermath* (New York: Vintage, 1970), p. 185.

5. E. J. Kanin and C. Kirkpatrick, 'Male Sex Aggression on University Campuses', *ASR*, 22 (1953): 53.

6. *Ibid.*
7. E. J. Kanin, 'Male Aggression in Dating Relations', *AJS,* 63 (1957): 197—204.
8. J. Gagnon, 'Female Child Victims of Sex Offenses', *Sexual Behavior in the Human Female,* p. 179.
9. *Ibid.,* p. 180.
10. *Ibid.,* p. 191.
11. *Ibid.*
12. *The Realist* (1962), p. 20.
13. *Sex and Temperament in Three Primitive Societies* (New York: Dell, 1935), p. 110.

5.4   Women in official statistics

PAUL ALLIN AND AUDREY HUNT

Looking at the large number of official publications containing statistics, one might think that there were no problems in obtaining sound and comprehensive statistics to follow the changing experience of women. After all, every woman in the country was included, as ever, in the Census of Population in April 1981 and many statistics which are published do not relate only to men.

We aim to show here that there are a number of factors which at least reduce the appropriateness of official statistics for looking at women's position in society and more probably indicate that official statistics usually describe a man's world rather than fully reflect modern society. First we look generally at the role of statistics. Then, widely-used statistics about women at work and about household structure are considered, along with a brief review of the sources. Finally we put together the two main types of problems, which is first that there is an incomplete statistical picture and, secondly, that the conceptual basis to much gathering of statistics is unsound or, at least, out of date.

The Guardian, 9 December 1981

Specially commissioned for this volume
© The Open University, 1982

Why does it matter which statistics are collected and presented?

We argue that we do not only need statistics about women but we need statistics which are conceptually and practically established on a firm basis. These ideas are, of course, neither new nor unique to this field. The sociological groundwork has been laid out, for example by Hindess[1] and by Irvine and others.[2] We are looking at these general themes therefore to develop the use of statistics in examining the role and position of women, both those who work outside and inside the home.

We should avoid thinking in terms of a textbook application of statistics, where statistics would be called upon — or interpreted as — a body of precise information together with ways of analysing and presenting results. In drawing back slightly from this position we recognize that statistics should form one of the main tools of the social observer or the social policy maker. The power of statistics is best demonstrated where the precision and exactness of the data cannot be disputed. For example, in the Industrial Tribunal case of *Hurley* v. *Mustoe*, statistics were used from the General Household Survey to support successfully the complainant's argument that many women with children go out to work, and that she had been discriminated against while applying for a job because the employer would not accept women employees who had children.

However the general demand for statistical data is to build up a picture to compare women with men, so that social policies can be discussed and enacted, particularly to remove discrimination. The Equal Opportunities Commission has outlined how statistics are vital in carrying out its statutory duties, as laid down in the Sex Discrimination Act.[3] In particular, good and wide ranging statistical material is needed to seek and analyse indirect discrimination, under which, for example, disproportionately large numbers of women may be affected by employment practices even though women are not discriminated against individually. Also, the Commission monitors the Equal Pay Act, needing statistics on earnings and other labour force data, as part of the general assessment of the effects of job segregation and working arrangements such as the distribution of overtime etc. We should note at this stage that the use of statistics may not provide a complete answer, because of deficiencies in this case in the information about part-time earnings, and because it is impossible to compare jobs nationally where equal pay might be sought. Research and enforcement may be tackled more successfully by other techniques, such as job evaluation and work study in local workforces.

We should also briefly consider the strength of the converse argument, that some statistics should not be produced, in terms of the reaction to the US Census Board report that marriages in which couples had sons were less likely to break up than marriages in which couples had daughters. At least one commentator in the UK has supported the view of the women's movement in the US which wants such information suppressed.[4] Opposition is on the grounds of, first, to ask why carry out such an analysis and to question the validity of the statistical results as a mirror of the real world. However, it is the implications of the analysis which appear to have attracted most adverse comment, being seen as a devaluation of women as children and parents. In arguing, as we do later, that the UK Census of Population is a valuable source for statistics on the changing experience of women, we note that this may give scope for a similar analysis, if not similar results, for UK households.

During 1980 all government ministers reviewed the statistical services in their departments. The White Paper which was published in April 1981 (Cmnd. 8236) to report on the results of the reviews, was widely criticized as outside users re-examined their needs of official statistics. The White Paper stated as a leading principle that 'information should not be collected primarily for publication. It should be collected primarily because government needs it for its own business'. The general and forceful response to this was that the collection and publication of official statistics could not be judged solely on the narrow grounds of departmental costs and benefits, however defined: the right of the public to ready and not unreasonably expensive access to information must be considered.

Finally on the demand for statistics we should recognize the need to monitor trends and changes. This is sometimes seen as conflicting with the production of consistent 'time-series'. For example, the official monthly statistics of unemployment have for many years been based on a count of the numbers registered with various state schemes. However, as well as administrative changes which may particularly affect the propensity of unemployed women to register, there have been social and cultural shifts in attitudes towards work and towards unemployment. These are not recognized in the monthly time-series statistics. Also, the questions asked in regular household surveys may still be phrased to maintain some consistency over time. One way out of this would be to allow for the career histories of different generations of women to be surveyed regularly to identify trends and changes.

What statistics are available?

We give some details here of some of the statistics and sources relevant to the changing life styles of women. We make no apologies for concentrating on employment rather than, say, education, although the general tenor of the argument applies to statistics on every aspect of life.

The following statistics and sources are covered:

  (i)   economic activity rates
 (ii)   unemployment
(iii)   sick leave
 (iv)   occupational classifications
  (v)   social class
 (vi)   household structure and characteristics
(vii)   Census of Population
(viii) General Household Survey
 (ix)   Labour Force Survey

(i) Economic activity rates

A person is normally defined as economically active who is either:

 (a) in paid employment
 (b) sick, intending to return to paid employment
 (c) unemployed, seeking work

This definition is obviously based on the traditional masculine life style of continuous 'economic activity' from the time of finishing full-time education to the time of retirement. It does not take account of the markedly different work pattern of many women's lives so that economic activity rates both may underestimate the current extent of activity among women and will be deficient in describing women's life-styles.

Many sources of information under this heading (for example, the Census of Population, the General Household Survey, the Labour Force Survey) relate to a point in time, for example, a recent 'reference week'. Nearly all men can be defined as economically active or not according to the definition but a number of women can not. For example, women (apart from teachers) who work only during school terms because of their children's needs, if interviewed during school holidays, might well be classed as 'inactive'. Another example is that of the married woman who has not worked for some years but is actively seeking work. It is unclear, at the very least, how this woman would be treated under (c) above.

The application of this masculine norm distorts a number of the statistics relating to women's participation in the labour force, which may be further complicated by the method of collecting statistics.

One main source is the Census of Employment which 'provides the accurate benchmark figures with which the Department of Employment re-aligns the industrial and regional employment estimates obtained from the monthly and quarterly sample enquiries'.[5] Obviously, inaccuracies in these benchmark figures will be perpetuated in all related statistics.

The Census of Employment consists of a statutory return made by all employers, apart from HM Forces and private domestic service. Self-employed workers are also excluded. The exclusion of private domestic service undoubtedly results in the omission from the statistics of a great many women workers, particularly part-time workers. The category of self-employed includes home workers, i.e. people who work in their own homes. Apart from professional people (e.g. doctors and writers) the majority of these are people who are given work to do by someone who is an 'employer'. Very little accurate information exists about them but the great majority are known to be women, many of them disadvantaged (lone mothers, physically handicapped, ethnic minorities). A Trades Union Congress enquiry in 1978 found that many of these home workers are severely exploited and that existing legislation which requires firms to supply local authorities with lists of such workers is more honoured in the breach than in the observance. Questions in the 1981 Census of Population might provide some information about this group of women workers (of whom, according to some estimates, there are about 300,000).

Finally we see that the statistics of economic activity give very little information about individual occupations or about the personal background to labour force participation, although the General Household Survey (see below, p.347) gives some analyses by the age of women and by that of any dependent children. The official estimates of economic activity by age, sex and (for women) marital status were given in the April 1981 *DE Gazette* for each year from 1971 with forecasts to 1986.

(ii) Unemployment

Monthly unemployment statistics are derived from registrations for benefit and examination of the history of benefits will reveal the serious deficiencies in the statistics. Prior to World War II flat rate National Insurance contributions (unemployment and sickness) were paid by all employed men and women earning less than a certain amount (the amount increased from time to time, but always excluded better paid workers). Men's contributions were higher than women's, to take account of men's dependents (wives, children). All payers of contributions were entitled to unemployment and sickness benefit and to an old age pension at the age of 65. Men and single women received the same rate of benefit: a married man could claim benefit for his wife if she was not working and for dependent children. Married women, however, received a lower rate of benefit than single women, although their rate of contribution was the same.

The 1948 National Insurance Act introduced a new system, based on much higher contributions. Men's contributions were higher than women's, and working married women and widows were allowed to 'opt out' of all of the contributions except of that part which covered industrial injuries. The advantage to a married woman of paying the contributions was, briefly, that she was entitled to unemployment and sickness benefit for herself and to a pension in her own right when she became 60 (higher than the rate obtainable by virtue of her husband's contributions when he reached the age of 65).

The advantages of opting to pay the full contributions did not appear sufficient to many married women (particularly when women's rates of pay were so low). As a consequence a majority of married women 'opted out' (the exact proportion is not known but some estimates put it at around two-thirds).

These married women and widows had no right to sickness or unemployment benefit and therefore would probably not register for either. It is of particular concern that they would therefore not appear in the monthly unemployment statistics derived from registrations. Opting out was not finally abolished until new legislation came into force in 1978. However, those who already opted out were allowed to continue to do so, and for many years an appreciable number of married women will be excluded from sickness and unemployment figures derived from registrations for sickness and unemployment benefit.

The post-1978 scheme perpetuates the deficiency in another way because there is a lower income limit below which contributions are not paid. The majority of these low paid workers are women, particularly married women working part-time; further changes will be made in 1982 when registration becomes voluntary. We have seen that the monthly unemployment statistics, based on registrations, underestimate the number of unemployed women. The extent of underestimates is increased by the masculine concept of 'economic activity'. Thus, a woman who has been at home for some years raising a family but in urgent need of work, and actively seeking it, would not necessarily be classed as unemployed.

Some information about both registered and unregistered unemployment can be obtained from the General Household Survey, but the size of the sample is inadequate for month-by-month or regional analyses. Another source of information is the Labour Force Survey. These surveys consistently show a greater rate of unemployment among women than the monthly DE figures, because women are, to some extent, able to describe their labour force status without reference to the administrative systems. However, there is still concern that the category of 'housewife' overrides that of 'unemployed' in some cases in these surveys especially during a recession.

(iii) Sick leave

The operation of the state sickness benefit scheme has been described above and we note here just that statistics on registrations for sickness benefit are again distorted for women by their propensity to register. Absence from work because of personal illness is one area where statistics are clearly needed to combat widely-held, but unsupportable, views on the relative unreliability of women. Again by asking men and women themselves, rather than relying on administrative systems, a clearer picture emerges. In this case it is that the proportions of working men and women who are absent at a given time because of accident or illness are the same (General Household Survey questions). Moreover, women tend to be off work for shorter lengths of time.

(iv) Classification of occupations

A principle of most systems of classification of occupations is that a person doing a particular type of work is classified in the same way whatever the nature of the workplace in which the job is done. Thus, a clerk is classified in the same way whether he or she works in a bank, a factory or a garage. Obviously some kinds of job can only be done in one place but this does not affect the overall principle.

Most of the detailed classifications of occupations were devised when women formed a comparatively small proportion of the workforce. Consequently, predominantly male occupations continue to be identified in great detail. For example in the HMSO Classification of Occupations 1980 used for the Census, there are 93 detailed occupations plus foremen and apprentices listed under the major group 'processing, making, repairing and related (metal and electrical)' whereas under 'clerical and related' there are only

23 titles, which run from clerks to office machine operators to postmen (*sic*).

Both in this Classification and in the list of Key Occupations for Statistical Purposes (KOS) we see that occupations tend to be identified by the type of work without much regard to the level of responsibility, beyond identifying supervisors.

The effect of using these classifications can be seen from analyses of employment. The 1977 Labour Force Survey attributed employees to one of 18 major occupational groups. Over 40 per cent of full-time female employees were classified to one order (clerical and related) and a further 40 per cent were put in four other groups. The distribution of full-time men was more evenly spread across the groups. Over 40 per cent of part-time women were classified to one group, of 'personal services', which ranges from catering to hairdressing.

There is therefore a need for a revised system of occupational classification which takes into account the importance of the jobs currently being done by women and classifies them in greater detail. This would be particularly useful to monitor the experience of women returning to the labour market say during their 30s because from the existing statistics it is unclear how well, if at all, they can build on the skills and experience gained when they were first at work.

(v) Social class

In Censuses of Population and other government statistics, social class has a limited meaning. It is based on occupation for working people and usually on former occupation for retired people. Table 1 is derived from the 1971 Census Economic Activity Table.

Table 1 Social class composition of economically active and retired people aged 15 and over (1971)

			Men %	Women %
Social class				
I	(non-manual)	Professional and managerial occupations	5	1
II	(non-manual)	Intermediate non-manual occupations	18	17
III	(non-manual)	Junior non-manual occupations	12	38
III	(manual)	Skilled manual occupations	38	10
IV	(manual	Semi skilled manual occupations	18	26
V	(manual)	Unskilled manual occupations	9	8
		Total	100	100

This is at best only a broad classification which tells us very little about the actual types of work done. For example, the majority of women workers (64 per cent) are concentrated in two social classes (junior non-manual and semi-skilled manual) each of which covers a wide variety of occupations. Junior non-manual, for example, includes clerks, shop assistants and typists of all kinds and many others. Semi-skilled manual includes factory workers of many kinds, agricultural workers, bus conductors and many more.

In addition to this, the definition, being based on occupation, precludes non-workers from having any social class in their own right. Virtually all men are either working or have retired from work but roughly half the female population are not working at any one time and most elderly women have not retired from gainful employment.

It is common practice to classify households on the basis of the social class of the head of household (see below, this page). The head, by standard definition, is usually the husband of a married woman, who, if she is working, loses her identity by this method of classification. Non-working lone mothers, of whom there are at least a quarter of a million according to recent estimates, have no social class in the sense of this definition.

It should be clear from this that while social class has only limited use in categorizing occupations, it has no direct relevance in describing life-style. Studies of 'social mobility' should therefore be treated with caution while continuing to seek better statistics to follow life-cycle events for men and women.

(vi) Household structure and characteristics

Many tabulations in the Census, General Household Survey and other Government and social statistics have used the concept of *Head of Household* for analysis by social class and other attributes. The definition of Head of Household is unashamedly sexist and obviously was first established when only a few married women worked in paid occupations. The definition is:

The head of household is a member of the household and is, in order of precedence, the husband of the person, or the person who:

(i) owns the household accommodation or
(ii) is legally responsible for the rent of the accommodation
(iii) has the accommodation by virtue of some relationship to the owner in cases where the owner or lessee is not a member of the household.

Where two members of different sex have equal claim, the male is taken as head of household. When two members of the same sex have equal claim the elder is taken as head of household.

The characteristics of the Head of Household are used in many analyses to 'define' the household as a whole. Although the Census has in the past introduced a further concept, namely, the 'Chief Economic Supporter', this is also sexist in its definition, males being taken before females at all stages. The General Household Survey (and much social and commercial research) still uses the Head of Household definition.

This concept takes no account of the changing features of family life. More than two out of five married women are economically active at any one time and the great majority of married women will be working at some time in their married lives, before and after the births of their children. For as long ago as 1965 a survey[6] showed that 45 per cent of all married women under 65 years of age were economically active and only 16 per cent had not done any paid work since marriage.

By classifying families and households entirely or almost entirely on the basis of the husband's occupation, the very real contribution made by a working wife to a family's standard of living is ignored. There is a great deal of evidence that working wives' earnings are almost entirely used for family purposes (the 'pin-money wives' myth was exploded long ago).

Alongside the Head of Household definition is that of 'Housewife', used in much social research, including Government Surveys. In simple terms the housewife is the person other than a domestic servant, who is responsible for most of the household duties. Subsidiary parts of the definition ensure that the housewife is almost always female, e.g. if domestic duties are shared, the female is the housewife.

The picture presented by these definitions is of a family with a working husband and a non-working wife who does virtually all the domestic chores. If by chance she does have a paid job, that is of negligible importance. In passing, we note that the taxation laws relating to married couples still perpetuate that myth.

Some forms of classification of households are undoubtedly necessary for many purposes in social research. However, classifications based on the situation as it existed many years ago are inadequate for present day purposes. A classification based on the characteristics of both husband and wife (or of all household members) without the outmoded concept of the 'Head' might be more difficult to devise but would present a truer picture of what actually exists and be more in keeping with present-day thought.

Some progress in this way might follow from the 1981 Census of Population, which was addressed to the 'Head or Joint Heads. . . . of the Household'. The processing of Census data will thus be in terms of relationship within the household to one adult 'reference' person, no longer necessarily the stereotyped male Head. Census '81 material has yet to appear on this.

(vii)   The Census of Population

A full Census of the UK population has been carried out at 10-yearly intervals since 1801 (apart from 1941). It is legally obligatory for Heads of Households to complete the Census Form. (From 1981 this onus was laid on one of the joint heads of the household.)

The 1981 Census included questions on demographic character-istics, accommodation, employment and education. Full tabulations take months or even years to produce. While there are some variations, one aim has always been to preserve continuity of data from successive Censuses.

There is a limit to the amount of information which can be obtained by means of a self-completed compulsory questionnaire. Political pressures often influence what is and is not included. The value of published Census data is affected by some of the definitions and means of classification commonly used, as has been described here. However, with these *caveats* the Census data clearly should not be ignored as a source for research. Unpublished tabulations can be obtained and the system of Small Area Statistics (SAS) may prove useful for work in local areas, or for aggregating over a wider region.

(viii)   The General Household Survey (GHS)

The GHS is a continuous sample survey among households in Great Britain. It is carried out by the Office of Population Censuses and Surveys on behalf of a number of government departments. Basic questions including some relating to demographic character-istics, accommodation and employment are always included, while other topics e.g. smoking habits are covered from time to time.

The male-oriented definitions (similar to those used in the Census) reduce the value of the GHS somewhat as a source of some data relating to women. Another disadvantage is that it is designed to produce reliable annual figures for major population groups, but the sample size is too small for detailed analysis over a shorter time-period. The sample size (about 12000 households annually) is likely to be reduced as a consequence of current cuts in public expenditure, which may seriously limit its usefulness as a source of information about such topics as unemployment among women or single-parent families.

(ix) The Labour Force Survey (LFS)

The LFS sample survey has been carried out at two-yearly intervals since 1973 in the member countries of the EEC. It is confined to residents in private households and covers economic activity and unemployment in some depth. Supplementary questions have been included in some years, for example on working conditions and receipt of pensions. It is a useful source of information about the labour force throughout the EEC. However, it suffers from the same deficiencies as the GHS in respect of small groups etc.

The main problems and how they have arisen

Having looked at these statistics in particular, it might be seen that there are two main problems. First, information is not collected, or is collected only partially. Second, the statistics are based on a conceptual model which is unsound or, at least, out of date. In the latter case we may find that statistics are collected in the same form over time, to maintain a time-series, even though this no longer reflects the world outside. Aspects of both of these main areas have been identified and discussed elsewhere (see the chapter by Ann and Robin Oakley in *Demystifying Social Statistics*,[2] but it is worthwhile considering them briefly here.

First, we recognize that parts of the statistical mirror which we want to hold up to reflect society have still to be silvered, and there is some missing information! This missing information affects women to a greater degree than men, for example where statistics on unemployment are collected through an administrative system with which many women are not involved. Similarly, statistics on earnings from the New Earnings Survey exclude some part-time workers, mainly women, because the survey covers only those employees recorded as paying National Insurance contributions through pay-as-you-earn (PAYE) schemes. The earnings limits for 1979–80 were £19.50 per week or £84.50 per month, so that part-time workers earning less than this were excluded from the 1980 survey. We have seen how homeworking is unrecorded.

Many topics for which there are no statistics concern work or responsibilities undertaken traditionally or for some considerable time, by women. Thus statistics on childcare or the care of elderly or infirm friends and relatives are generally not available. Muriel Nissel[7] and others have drawn attention to the lack of information on income distribution and housekeeping arrangements within the household. In recognizing that information is missing, it soon begins to be more important to turn to the second main area of concern, that statistics are collected according to a conceptual model with which we can find much to disagree.

Thus the second, and the predominant, area of concern can be attributed to the production of statistics within a gender-divided society so that they might conceptually reflect such divisions. It would be easy to argue that if, after all, statistics do reflect society, then there is nothing more to be sought. That conclusion is not reached here. Rather, we see that the changing experience of women, for example in trends in labour force participation since between the World Wars, has not been tracked in statistics about households and work, so that statistics which now, for example, allocate social class on the basis of husbands' occupations are conceptually unsound. This applies both within households which actually contain a husband and as a basis for all households, including the many which are different from a 'traditional' family of working father and non-working mother.

These criticisms apply whether our sociology gives importance to families as the central unit of stratification or not because if, for example, we are studying the health and welfare of individuals we find that many (i.e. married) women are described anyway by what Delphy[8] has called 'association by marriage'. It was reported in August 1981 that the Royal College of General Practitioners was calling for medical statistics to classify married women by their own social class and occupation.

Our critique of the concepts behind many official statistics goes further to bring in what Gershuny and Pahl[9] and others have seen as three connected economies: to add to the 'formal' economy of gross national product the 'household/communal' economy as well as the well-known 'black' economy. That much of the work in the household/communal economy has been the prerogative of women is hardly an astounding principle, but that caring for the elderly or washing and cooking for a family are excluded from our conceptual model of society is of great concern not least when social policies are being formulated or cuts are planned to meet the recession in the formal economy. The stratification by gender (and by class) of domestic and market work has been set out fully by many writers including Murgatroyd.[10]

Looking for improvements

While we accept that we can not avoid indicating how we think improvements should be made, we intend to give only brief suggestions here. The review of government statistics referred to earlier (Cmnd. 8236)[3] has put severe constraints on proposals for expanding the body of official statistics, which is effectively the only source for data of the kind we have mentioned, and the Equal Opportunities Commission will be following this up.

The first improvement is the basic expediency of 'filling the gaps', which is an exercise to be carried out in a variety of ways. For example, many statistics are not published in official volumes but can be obtained, say in the form of copies of computer output, from government statisticians. The Labour Force Survey is disseminated largely in this way.[11] Secondary analysis of surveys deposited with the SSRC Survey Archive may again fill some gaps in the published statistics.[12] On the other hand additional questions could be included in existing surveys for example to review childcare arrangements and, finally, *ad hoc* surveys on women should be carried out or followed-up every few years. Results from the latest official survey 'Women's Employment' are unlikely to be available until towards the end of 1982, leaving far too large an interval since the previous similar survey.[6]

The second suggestion for improving the statistics is to seek wider research into problems such as defining labour force attachment, social class, household structure: problems which have been mentioned often in this article. We recognize that the government's statistical service is the only source of data in many fields and we can see no alternative to their involvement and close liaison with all users of the statistics, particularly those who continue to press for better statistics with which to explore the changing experience of women.

Notes and References

1. Barry Hindess *The Use of Official Statistics in Sociology*, Macmillan, 1973.
2. Ed John Irvine, Ian Miles and Jeff Evans *Demystifying Social Statistics*, Pluto, 1979.
3. EOC document *Government Statistical Services: The Response of the Commission to White Paper Cmnd. 8236*, August 1981.
4. Mary Kenny 'Sexism and Statistics', *Sunday Telegraph*, 11 January 1981.
5. Dept. of Employment 'A review of unemployment and vacancy statistics', *DE Gazette*, May 1980.
6. Audrey Hunt *A Survey of Women's Employment*, Government Social Survey, HMSO, 1968.
7. Equal Opportunities Commission *Women and Government Statistics*, Research Bulletin 4, Autumn 1980.

8. e.g. quoted in 'Women, social class and IUD use' by Helen Roberts, *Women's Studies Int. Quart,* 1979 vol. 2.

9. Gershuny and Pahl 'Britain in the decade of the three economies', *New Society,* 3 January 1980, and in the reader *Unemployment and the Black Economy.*

10. Linda Murgatroyd 'Domestic labour in a class society: stratification inside and outside the home', in E. Derow (ed.) *The Social Construction of the Household Economy,* Croom Helm, to appear.

11. OPCS *Labour Force Survey 1973, 75, 77* Series LFS No. 1, HMSO, 1980. (Contains details of unpublished 1977 tables available at the cost of photocopying.)

12. SSRC *Survey Archive Bulletin* from SSRC Survey Archive, University of Essex, Colchester CO4 3SQ.

5.5　Making science feminist

HILARY ROSE

The need for a new science

'Science it would seem is not sexless; she is a man, a father and infected too.' Virginia Woolfe *Three Guineas.*

The case for the creation of a new science and technology has never been so urgent. Whatever our attitudes to this or that social and political system, or our personal position of domination or subordination, it is becoming difficult to escape the conclusion that the human experiment is fragile. Science and technology penetrate our lives at every point. While antibiotics, polyester fabric and the television — when the programmes are good — are part of the benign aspect of science, other elements, from the mechanization of childbirth through routine induction, massive pollution of the environment to the ultimate terror of nuclear holocaust, increasingly dwarf this. The situation is so serious that if we risk contemplating it, then all too easily we enter a kind of wish-thinking. It is as if, by some gigantic act of faith, we could consensually propel ourselves into a new and better future. In this unimaginable utopia we would be doing a different and other science which would be 'radical', 'serve the people', be of 'human scale', in some way realize and overcome our present discontents and fears. Indeed, the present growth of religious and cult beliefs suggest that many see faith as at least as practical as politics as a way of re-ordering not only the hereafter but also the here and now.

While every sane person is afraid of nuclear war, to oppose it, or indeed any of the other inhuman faces of science, is twice as difficult for women as for men, since, though few men are scientists, women are virtually excluded from directing the production and planning the utilization of scientific knowledge. Of course women do work in scientific laboratories, but only a small minority work as scientists and technologists, most serve as technicians, cleaners and secretaries — tasks which in many ways echo the work they do

Specially commissioned for this volume
© The Open University 1982

at home. This exclusion means that as women we also rarely understand this science and technology which dominate our lives. Thus we may seek to oppose a particular part of science; we may for example, not like the pill with its unpleasant side-effects — but there are not enough women in biology to develop an alternative safe form of contraception. Excluded from science, even in this matter of basic importance to themselves, women can only protest and seek to mobilize humanistic men to develop an alternative.

The exclusion of women from this powerful form of knowledge is all too often portrayed as 'natural'. So profound is the cultural belief that women doing science is unnatural, that even the victims of the exclusion, women, frequently believe it. Opposition to this 'natural' exclusion of women often seeks to explain the process in terms of child rearing practices and schooling, or in terms of the sexist attitudes of male scientists. While these are not unimportant I want to argue in this chapter that the reasons for women's exclusion from science are more profound and rest in the division of labour between men and women, whereby women are assigned nurturant caring tasks involving people — reproductive labour, whereas men are assigned the task of the manufacture of things — productive labour. (The distinction I have used here between productive and reproductive labour should be seen as a first approximation. Reproduction in particular is a term embracing biological reproduction, the transmission of ideas and values and also the renewal of the worker. However, at this stage of the argument the distinction will serve.) Much of women's labour is carried out within the home and unpaid, and only grudgingly recognized as of economic value, while men's labour is usually done for pay in a market-bargaining situation outside the home and is generally considered to be of economic importance. The work of doing science has been constructed in our society as concerned essentially with the masculine, i.e. with the productionist side of human labour. This one-sided productionist emphasis shuts out the interests and potential contribution of women. Only when women in sufficient numbers can appropriate and make over science in a feminist way will we achieve a liberatory science. This argument goes further than the critique of science mounted by the radical science movement since the sixties, which has concentrated on attacking science as an instrument of war and class oppression but ignored gender. The radical science movement, like the feminist movement began with anger against injustice and cruelty. Nonetheless, in order to explain how scientific knowledge and technique were increasingly part of a system of domination, and decreasingly helpful to humanity, it required theory. Because these new radical movements wanted not only to understand the world but to change it, it was almost inevitable that they would turn to the writings of Karl Marx as the theorist of human liberation. It goes without saying that Marx's theories did not immediately explain or indicate how to transform the position of women in a capitalist and patriarchal society — not least because Marx himself was more than slightly patriarchal. Nonetheless marxism — which includes much more recent work developed from Marx's original texts — is a liberatory way of viewing the world and as such, is of great importance to the feminist struggle. Feminists wishing to distinguish their work from that of main stream marxism have often spoken as this chapter does, of 'materialism' rather than of 'marxism' as the source of this theoretical inspiration.

Alternative science for a new society

Over the past dozen years the critique of science and technology has focused attention on the ways in which science and technology are locked into capitalism and imperialism as systems of domination. The denunciation of this present science has served two purposes: negatively, it has facilitated the growth of anti-science, which refuses all of science carried out under any conditions and at any historical time. More positively, it has set itself the difficult task of pointing towards the forms and the content that a different, alternative science might take. This alternative science sets itself no lesser task than anticipating the kind of science and technology which would be possible in a new society. At the same time, through this innovatory practice it contributes to the realization of that society. This chapter is part of this venture in all its difficulty, its false starts, its achievements, and its perilous balancing between concentrating on *doing* something without any theoretical explanation as to how or why and the academic pursuit of theory devoid of practical engagement in political struggles.

Such a project is not without its contradictions and difficulties, for feminism is only just beginning to recapture the full force of Virginia Woolfe's insight. Science it would seem — to rephrase her — is neither sexless nor classless, it is a man, bourgeois and infected too. The trouble with science and technology from a feminist perspective is that they are not only integral to a system of capitalist domination but also to one of patriarchal domination. To try to discuss science under both these systems of domination is peculiarly difficult. Marxism is a highly refined social theory with considerable analytic power: feminist theory with its distinctive conception of knowledge which seeks to include the specific experience of women's oppression is still developing its categories. Hartmann[1] has spoken of the 'Unhappy Marriage of Marxism and Feminism' and she is surely right, for marxism's very clarity and analytic power threatens to overwhelm and deny women's experience of oppression. It comes uncomfortably close to asserting that, where experience speaks of the oppression of racism, nationalism or sexism, and experience fails to fit the theoretical categories, then it is experience not theory which most yield. Thus marxism's long preoccupation with production, and prioritization of productionist struggles has either excluded or trivialized reproduction and its associated struggles.

It has historically been women outside science, such as the novelist and essayist, Virginia Woolfe, or the ex-scientist, now writer, Ruth Wallsgrove,[2] or the sociologist Liliane Stéhélin[3] who have dared to speak of science as male, as part of a phallocentric culture. For women inside science it has been much more difficult. One of the new voices breaking through from within the laboratory is that of Rita Arditti[4] who, having worked in the competitive and macho world of genetics[5] was radicalized by the American anti-war movement. Becoming a feminist within this experience she now argues that nothing less than a 'new' science will serve. The sheer paucity of numbers of women in science and engineering has meant that challenging the existing dominant ideology has been peculiarly difficult, numbers are few, so developing the network between isolated women, is an intractable exercise. Yet, as we enter the eighties, an invisible college of feminist scientists is beginning to assemble.[6]

Apart from a handful of pioneering papers, feminists in the early days of the movement often retreated into anti-science, or avoided the discussion of science, regarding science as monolithically the enemy. Doing science then became an activity in which no serious feminist would engage. But there was a growing political threat as during the 1970s a new wave of biological determinism sought to renaturalize women. The claims of the feminist movement for women to enter the labour market and to share domestic labour equally with men, were met by biologically determinist arguments which claimed the natural subordination of women in both paid and unpaid work. It has required women biologists — or women who will enter the terrain of biological knowledge — to contest its claims. Doing biology is thus no longer seen as hostile but as helpful to women's interests. Increasingly, it is possible to go forward from this essentially defensive purpose to the much more positive goals of seeking to show how a feminist knowledge of the natural world offers an emancipatory rather than an exterminatory science. The task of developing a feminist critique of science, and of moving towards a feminist natural science is at once more difficult and more exciting than the entirely academically respectable activity of reporting descriptively on women's position within science. For feminist analysis, interpretation has constantly to be tested not simply against the demands of theory but always and incessantly against the experience of the specific oppression of women. A materialist feminism returns to the conception of power as rooted in the division of labour, but goes beyond an analysis of class to include the sexual division of labour. For this reason a materialist feminism claims that the attempt to bring together the analysis of both the systems of production *and* reproduction is to carry out the original materialist project of human liberation which Marx and Engels proposed.[7]

What feminists rightly point to is the one-sided materialism — the exclusive preoccupation with production — of both Marx and Engels themselves and indeed the dominant tradition of marxist thought. Here then I shall first, all too cursorily, set out the theoretical achievements of the radical critique of science, making plain the weaknesses which stem from its one-sided materialism. Secondly, drawing on the fast developing feminist analysis of the links between women's paid and unpaid labour, I shall suggest not only why women are by and large excluded from science, but also what kind of science the exclusion produces.

The radical critique of science

The radical critique of science was to explode into practice and to struggle into theory during the late sixties and early seventies. There was an immense wealth of issues contained in the class and social struggles of the movement, but these were frequently narrowed and constrained as the theoreticians filtered the wealth of lived experience through the abstract categories of theory. Against an early rhetoric which attacked the class society, imperialism, racism and sexism (although those who were black, colonized or women might well have had doubts about their equal prioritization in practice as well as in rhetoric) the theoreticians developed two main lines of analysis.[8] The first was the political economy of science, and the second the science and ideology question. While the two are linked at many points, work in political economy was more coherently developed, whereas work on the science and ideology debate was and remains more problematic. The need to reply immediately to the ideological attacks of a racist or sexist science accelerated as the crisis deepened, making it difficult to resist the attack *and* simultaneously to analyse the issues. Indeed, at the time the hostility to science was such that science and ideology became conflated in a way that aided the growth of anti-science.[9]

We must not fail to comprehend, and to endorse the strength of popular hostility and resistance to capitalist science. The arms race, with its SS20s, Cruise and Pershing missiles, the plastic bullets and CS gas of domestic repression, catastrophes such as Three Mile Island or the birth deforming chemicals released through the explosion at the chemical plant of Seveso have all helped to mobilize a popular resistance to existing science and technology. The anti-nuclear movement is yet another manifestation. These movements stand opposed to the forms of rationality imposed by a bourgeois science and a bourgeois society, instead they urge a re-conception of science and technology, one whose rationality is geared to human survival. These new movements are equivocal about science. The apparently necessary link between science and social progress which lay at the heart of the construction of socialist orthodoxy has been thrown into question by the politics of contemporary experience.

The socialist tradition, at least up to the 1960s, believed that the advances of science would automatically throw up problems that capitalist society could not solve: hence in some way science was at least 'neutral', and at best it was on the side of making a new and socially just society. It is this belief in the neutrality of science that the experiences of the 1960s and 70s have overthrown. Such a 'neutral' science was seen as uninfluenced by class, race, gender, nationality or politics; it was the abstract accumulation of knowledge — of facts, theories and techniques — which could be 'used' or 'abused' by society. What the 60s activists discovered in their campaigns against a militarized and polluting science, was that those in charge of this 'neutral' science were overwhelmingly white, male and occupying privileged positions in advanced industrialized society. The antihuman technologies that science generated were being used for the profit of some and the distress of the many. The activists, because they were initially uninterested in theory, had no *explanations* of how this came about, even while particular campaigns revealed to them the non-neutral character of science.

The myth of the neutrality of science

The making of a theoretical critique became urgent. While here I have deliberately focused on the writing of those who were influential within the radical science movement, there has been over the last decade or so, a dramatic shift in more mainstream history, philosophy and sociology of science. A sophisticated form of externalism (that is the thesis that scientific knowledge is structured through its social genesis) has become common to all three, so that much social research is concerned to show how interest shapes knowledge.[10] Books such as Goldberg's *The Inevitability of Patriarchy* constructed scientific theories in order to explain — and justify — men's dominant position. Psychologists such as Jensen in the USA or Eysenck in Britain were concerned to explain — and justify — the dominant position of whites. Science had become a social problem.

Ravetz, a mathematician, historian of science and political radical[11] was the first to pose seriously the issue of just why and how. His answer involved examining the circumstances in which scientists actually produced scientific knowledge. He argued, through an examination of the production of science from the seventeenth to the nineteenth century, that whereas for the early period science was produced on a craft basis, as science entered the twentieth century it increasingly adopted industrialized methods of production. Where the craft worker had worked alone, or with a couple of apprentices, the new system required substantial capital, a large group of scientists, a clear division of labour between them, and common goals to be set and managed by a scientific director.

For Ravetz, it is this industrialization of science which has produced its uncritical character. His political response to this analysis of the new industrialized science is an essentially romantic libertarian one. He calls for the deinstitutionalization of science. He believes that a science tied to the state and industry must lose its initial force and inevitably become an agent of oppression. If science is to re-achieve the liberating role it had in the time of, say, Galileo, it must, like Galileo, once more stand in opposition to institutionalized science. It must become 'critical'.

Another strand within the radical science movement, revolted by the genocidic science employed by America in the war in South East Asia and the fast expanding new technologies of urban repression at home, asked how science could possibly cover itself ideologically with its claims of being 'pure', 'value-free' and above all 'neutral', when even a well regarded book *The Scientific Method* could use as an example with no sense of there being an ethical or political problem involved the making and testing of napalm on a university playing field. From the 'use' and 'abuse' model in which science remained 'fundamental', 'basic' and 'pure' (however its findings might be used or abused further down the line) the new left laid siege to 'the myth of the neutrality of science' itself — the concern of both the scientific establishment and traditional socialism.[12]

A new political economy of science (associated with the physicist marxists Cinni, de Maria and Cicotti[13]) was to argue that bringing science into the capitalist mode of production — that is its becoming industrialized — meant that knowledge itself, as the product of scientific labour, had *itself* become a commodity with a commercial value. Scientific knowledge, in this analysis, is no longer timeless but has value only at a particular time and a particular place. For industry, the patent laws that are presently reaching out to determine and render profitable the burgeoning area of biotechnology for instance, are designed to control the ownership of knowledge in the interest of profit.[14] For the 'basic' sciences the rewards go to those who publish the knowledge first. Diffusion then reduces the value of the knowledge, typically produced in the 'élite' institutions in the metropolitan countries as it becomes transferred to the 'non élite' institutions in the periphery. The value of the knowledge as it passes eventually from the centre of production to the periphery going down as surely as the sale of a second to third hand car.

This approach argues that the natural sciences most closely tied into the power structures of contemporary society are those which are most intensely industrialized. It is the physical sciences — above all physics itself — which is at once the most arcane and the most locked into the capitalist system of domination. We should note that it is these which more or less successfully exclude anything more than very small numbers of women. These industrialized sciences would appear to be highly resistant to feminist reworking, not least because the success of feminist studies have lain in areas — history, philosophy, sociology — characterized by little capital equipment per worker and craft methods of production.

The social origins of science as alienated knowledge

Sohn Rethel[15] following in the traditions of a school of neomarxist intellectuals centred initially in Frankfurt (including Marcuse and Habermas) sought to explain the social origins of the highly abstract and alienated character of scientific knowledge. He argued that it arises out of the profound division of intellectual and manual labour integral to capitalism. Scientific knowledge and its production system are of a piece with the abstract and alienated labour of the capitalist mode of production itself. The Cultural Revolution in China with its project of transcending the division of mental and manual labour was seen by Sohn Rethel (and indeed many or most of the new left) as offering a vision of immense historical significance. They saw within this huge social movement the possibility not only of transcending hierarchical and antagonistic social relations, but also a means of creating a new science and technology, which was not about the domination of nature, or of humanity as part of nature. Today when the experience of the Chinese Cultural Revolution is problematic to assess, it is equally important to affirm our need of such a project to create a new science.

In a world where the alienation of science and technology confront us in the pollution of the seas, the cities, the countryside, to say nothing of nuclear holocaust, such a longing cannot be dismissed as merely romantic. Its realization may rather be a guarantor of our survival.

Certainly aerospace workers in Britain — not easily equated with romantic intellectuals — have in their practice come to very similar conclusions. Beginning in their opposition to the threat of redundancy and a moral distaste for being so deeply involved in the manufacture of war technology, the workers went on to design, and in some cases make, 'socially useful' technologies such as the road-rail 'bus. In this they have simultaneously both contested the division of mental and manual labour in the production of technology and, through the unity of 'hand' and 'brain', begun the long struggle to transform the 'commodity' itself.[16]

The second system of domination

Despite the advances made through the critique of science forged during the 1970s, it is in a theoretical sense 'sex-blind'. It is not that the critics are insensitive to the problems of sexism and racism and many have honourable records in trying to contest them. It is rather that the theoretical categories make it impossible for them to explain why it is, to go back to Virginia Woolfe, that science is 'not only bourgeois but male'. For it is unequivocally clear that the élite of science, its managers and the constructors of its ideology are men. Within science as within all other aspects of production, women occupy subordinate positions, and the 'exceptional women' who 'make it' in this man's world only go to prove the rule. Yet this exclusion of half of humanity means that the 1970s critics of science, while they grappled with the structuring of science and technology under capitalism, failed to grasp or even to guess at the significance of its structuring under patriarchy, that second and all pervasive system of domination. Indeed the radical science movement itself was to reflect in its practice much of the sexism of the social order it opposed.[17]

The critique of science laid successful seige to the claims of science and technology to be 'above history' and had made plain the class character of science within a capitalist social formation. Science came to be analysed as an ideology having a specific historical development within the making of capitalism. Demystifying science involved opposition to the myths which had served to integrate science and to mask its internal contradictions and external functions. Yet there remained a disjuncture between the radical critique embodied within actual struggle during the sixties and early seventies, and *theoretical* explanations developed by the radical science movement. It is difficult not to feel that as the critical work became more theoretical, more fully elaborated, so women, and women's interests receded.

Thus there is no systematic explanation of the sexual division of labour within science, nor despite the denunciation of 'scientific sexism' does the existing critique explain why science so often works to benefit men. By explaining the exclusion of women as occurring through 'ideology', the possibility that there is a materialist explanation, (i.e. that it is in the interests of men to subordinate women within, as well as without, the production system of science) is avoided. It is taken for granted that the domination/subordination, oppressor/oppressed relationship between men and women is either irrelevant or is explained through the production process.

Feminism as materialism

Yet this prioritization of the production process is to ignore that other materialist necessity of history — reproduction. The preoccupation with production as a social process, with a corresponding social division of labour, and the neglect of reproduction as a corresponding social process with a corresponding social division of labour, perpetuates a one-sided materialism. Such a one-sided approach cannot help us either understand our circumstances, let alone transcend them.

It has been precisely reproduction which has been a central focus of the feminist movement in both social struggle and theoretical explanation. It is not by chance that the movement has been concerned with abortion, birth-control, sexuality, housework, childcare; indeed, with all these matters which had been trivialized into silence in the long period since an earlier wave of feminism.

Even now, while most left journals will find space for the

occasional or even regular article by feminists, the exercise remains relatively tokenistic; the 'important' articles which deal with the present economic and political crisis show few signs of integrating feminist theorizing into their work. More than ever, feminists must insist on the significance of the division of labour and not permit the 'renaturalization' of women's labour. Economic political and ideological pressures wish to restore woman to her 'natural' place. Science as the great legitimator, is as usual offering its services.

Housework as a labour process

In this situation feminists must return to the sexual division of labour within the household, which finds its ironical echo in paid labour (in science as elsewhere) if we are to understand the character of a science denied the input of the experience of women's lives. Here, I want to focus on the labour process of domestic labour that secures the production and reproduction of this generation and also of the next.[18] Not only is the housewife in late capitalist society the primary domestic labourer in terms of cleaning, shopping, cooking, or washing, she is also responsible for the childcare so that the next generation is guaranteed. And whatever claims the state socialist societies of Eastern Europe have of changing ownership of the means of production by or rather on behalf of the proletariat, patriarchal relations (as reflected through time budget studies of the domestic division of labour) remain untouched there too.

Time budget of domestic chores for men and women[19]

Samples from cities in:	Average time per day spent on household chores by employed men and women:		Absolute difference:
	Men	Women	
France (6 cities)	3 hr. 19 m.	5 hr. 26 m.	2 hr. 07 m.
UK (London)	2 hr. 42 m.	4 hr. 55 m.	2 hr. 13 m.
USA (44 cities)	3 hr. 02 m.	5 hr. 15 m.	2 hr. 13 m.
USSR (Pskov)	3 hr. 05 m.	6 hr. 55 m.	3 hr. 56 m.

Thus, it is evident that it is not only capitalism which benefits from women's domestic labour. Despite an attempt within Western socialist thought to demonstrate how the domestic labour of the wife/mother reproduces workers in the cheapest possible way for capital, it is clear that *men* have benefited too. Despite a variety of arrangements in the pattern of the ownership of the means of production, there is a consistency in the division of domestic labour which systematically works to the advantage of men. Women's labour within the home remains a form of unfree labour[20] within advanced industrial capitalism (which Marx, for example, saw as moving towards a society of free labourers). It is unfree labour, not simply because it is unpaid, but because she is not free to choose not to do this work but to do some other. A man (except in circumstances like the present economic crisis) can choose, albeit within a narrow range, what job he will do. He can work in production or in service work, tend a conveyor belt or mend cars, in his leisure time he can choose how much he 'helps' his wife. He may be a socially progressive husband and spend a good deal of time on household chores and on the children, but it is 'helping'. The responsibility, whether she works outside the home as well or not, is hers. She has no choice. Indeed if she falls down on the job, the welfare state is likely to find her 'mad' or 'bad' and treat her accordingly.

Not only do women have no choice in this work, it is work of a particular kind which, whether menial or requiring the sophis-ticated skills which are often involved in childcare, always demands personal service. Perhaps to make the nature of this caring, intimate, emotionally demanding labour clear we should use the ideologically loaded term of 'love'. For without love, without close interpersonal relationships, human beings, and it would seem, especially small human beings cannot survive. This emotionally demanding labour requires that women give something of themselves to the child, to the man. The production of people is thus qualitatively different from the production of things. It requires 'caring labour'. In the social division of labour it is this which has been allocated to women and it is this caring dimension of women's labour, originating within the household, which manifestly benefits men. This is probably why women, even when housework and childcare is apparently being equitably shared, remain less convinced than men that justice is being done. Caring labour which secures the reproduction process is trickier than merely seeing whether John or Mary have done their share of the washing up.

If we return to Sohn Rethel's emancipatory project of over-coming the division between mental and manual labour, the significance of woman's caring labour for the production of science becomes clear. He sees the division of labour which lies *between* men, yet takes for granted, in an entirely 'naturalized' way, the allocation of domestic caring labour to women. For while a minority of men are allocated to intellectual labour, the majority are allocated to manual highly routinized labour. For women, the division of labour is structured along different lines, for even that tiny number who become intellectuals are, *in the first instance,* allocated to domestic labour in which 'caring' informs every act. Thus, while both the emancipatory theoretical project of Sohn Rethel and the emancipatory practice of the aerospace workers seek to overcome the division of labour and urge both a new science and a new technology, nonetheless the claim still lies *within* the production of commodities. They seek the unity of 'hand' and 'brain' but exclude the 'heart'. A theoretical recognition of 'caring' labour as critical for the production of people is equally necessary for any adequate materialist analysis of science, and as a crucial precondition for that alternative way of knowing and doing which will help us construct a new science and a new technology. Thus, while Sohn Rethel's proposal seeks to overcome capitalist social relations, it leaves untouched the patriarchal relations between the sexes. In the production of knowledge this carries within it the implication that even if knowledge thus produced would be less abstract, and less oppressive, it would still reflect only the historically masculine concern with production. The historically feminine concern with reproduction would remain excluded.

Sohn Rethel's neglect of the caring labour of women means that the emancipatory theorist of the transcendence of the division of labour implicitly joins forces with the far from emancipatory programme of sociobiology, which would argue that women's destiny is in her genes. If we return to Marx's vision of the socialist society, in which he sees people fishing and hunting before dinner and enjoying social criticism after dinner, we see that even if we forget the issue of whether fishing and hunting are the relevant activities for a socialist future, by not specifying who is to cook the dinner, Marx takes it for granted that it will be the usual invisible labourer, the woman, doing the work. Marx in his conception of utopia, and Sohn Rethel in his analysis, simply do not see women's work as part of the social division of labour, instead, it is 'natural'.

Nor is it enough merely to add a feminine dimension to a basically productionist argument by seeking to bring in the caring contribution of women. Such an additive process runs the danger of denying the social genesis of women's caring skills which are extracted from them by men primarily within the home but also in the workplace, and moves towards biological determinist thought that women are 'naturally' more caring. The problem for materialists is how to admit biology in a realistic but not overwhelming way, while giving priority to the social forces which determine women's lives. Rather than juxtaposing biology *or* culture in explaining women's nature, materialists seek to grasp the relationship between the two. The explanation lies in the relationship between both systems of production, the production of things and the production of people. This explains not only why there are so few women in science, but also, and of equal or even more importance, why the knowledge produced is so abstract and depersonalized. But first, it is necessary to explore briefly those features of the segregated labour market, in which there are 'man's jobs' and 'women's jobs'. This is not to give long lists of the sexual division of labour within the general economy or specifically within science, but rather to look for explanations of how this segregated labour market has historically come about, and to examine the connections between women's paid and unpaid labour.

The social origins of the segregated labour market

Examining this problem within capitalist society, feminists point to the central practice of the 'family wage'[21] in which the man becomes the 'breadwinner', and receives from capital sufficient, not only to reproduce himself, but also his wife and his dependents. Indisputably, the family wage as it emerged during the nineteenth century in the most unionized and better paid sectors of the economy, served to improve the conditions of that entire class fraction, but at the price of enforcing women's and children's dependence on men.

A cumulation of protective legislation[22] excluding women and children from certain kinds and conditions of work (ostensibly for their sake), led to their systematic exclusion from the leading sectors of the economy where the organized 'breadwinners' and capital could battle out the higher wage levels together. Although during the nineteenth century, many women were, in fact, breadwinners (not least because of the high rates of widowhood, to say nothing of the many single women), they were ideologically marginalized in their claims for equal participation and equal pay within the labour market. Today, despite the growth of the single mother family through choice, desertion and divorce, and the necessity for both parents to earn wages in most two parent families, the 'family wage' retains its ideological grip. Indeed, in a world crisis where unemployment grows apace, the ideology of the 'family wage' and the need to defend the 'male breadwinner' looks to make a come-back.

Science and technology as a labour market are part of this general segregated form. Nor, despite some gains here and there, has educational reform, equal opportunity and pay legislation, the ritual invocation of Marie Curie or the photograph of half a dozen smiling women engineering students overcome this structuring of the scientific labour market. The segregated labour market means that scientists are mainly male, which is at once both almost always beneficial to men and, according to the trade cycle, a matter of manipulable convenience to capital.

While it is true that capital in conditions of boom, such as Western capitalism in the 1960s, looks to women (and/or migrants) as a source of labour power,[23] and talks of opening up the entire labour market to women, in practice the labour market remains intensely segregated. Even in the years of expansion women remained in an exceedingly narrow range of clerical and service occupations. In Britain, for example, segregation within the labour market is more marked in 1971, than it was in 1871.[24] Nor is a segregated labour market necessarily to capital's advantage — in the post-Sputnik years, the American state, anxious to boost its numbers of qualified scientists and engineers looked to women as a possible supply source. Focusing on resocialization strategies and publicizing successful 'role-models', the state was nonetheless by and large unsuccessful. It seems to take little less than a nation state at war for the dual labour market to be significantly eroded. A relatively buoyant labour market plus pressure from below, as in the early, even middle seventies produces some (but not radical) concessions. In present conditions of recession, women are losing employment faster than men, and within many occupations there are, as in science, proportionately more unemployed women than men. Yet it is hard to see a male-dominated trade union movement defending women's paid labour with the same energy they give to defending that of men. Even research on unemployment constructs it as almost exclusively a problem of men. Almost no studies of unemployed women have been made,[25] while media accounts focus almost entirely on the male workers' loss of work, self respect and economic difficulty.

Science, as a production system in miniature, faithfully reflects the segregated labour market in general. It excludes women — except for those with exceptionally favourable circumstances — from occupying élite positions within the production of knowledge. Most women in natural science and engineering are relegated to those tasks which most markedly reflect their primary task as wife-mother.[26] Even in those individual laboratories which pride themselves on having a good record on women, if we examine the full labour force, not just the scientists but also the technicians, secretarial and cleaning staff — the majority of women are still carrying out menial and/or personal service work. It is not by chance, nor by biology, that it is overwhelmingly the case that men occupy the leadership positions within science. Only the most exceptional women from highly privileged class backgrounds —

who can, therefore, transfer their domestic labour to other women — are able to get into science. And even then as a number of biographical studies of successful women in science make clear, often only through the personal influence of men, typically husbands, fathers or lovers. While patronage is an important mechanism of advance within science for both men and women, a woman has a much more narrowly defined set of potential patrons, linked to her through her sexuality.

Women scientists in the men's laboratories

Women who manage to get jobs in science have to handle a peculiar contradiction between the demands on them as caring labourers — and as abstract mental labourers. Many resolve this by withdrawing or letting themselves be excluded from science, while others become essentially honorary men, denying that being a woman creates any problems at all.[27] This sex-blindness is particularly evident in the autobiographical accounts of successful women in the sciences, such as the 1965 symposium on *Women in the Scientific Professions*. It has taken Anne Sayre's passionate defence of the molecular biologist Rosalind Franklin whose work was central to understanding DNA, to demystify this sexlessness and to insist that the woman scientist is always working in the men's laboratory.[28]

Evelyn Keller[29] writing of her experiences as a student physicist and later as a research worker echoes this theme of the continuous, subtle and not so subtle exclusion mechanisms deployed against women scientists. She writes how, as a student, she had to be careful to enter a lecture room with or after other students, if she entered first and sat down, men students found it threatening to sit near this low status person — a woman student — and she was often surrounded by a 'sea of seats'. She describes how once she solved a mathematical problem, the possibility that a woman student had done this was so antithetical to the male university teacher's definitions of women's mathematical capacities, that she, like Naomi Weisstein[30], was quite gently asked: 'who (i.e. which man) did it for her, or where did she get (i.e. steal) the solution from'. Keller's experiences are not, however, unique — what is new is that they are discussed.

Thus a woman scientist is cut in two. The abstraction of scientific practice as it has developed under capitalism and patriarchy is in painful contradiction with the other half of her caring labour. As Ruth Wallsgrove[31] writes: 'a woman, if she had any ambition or education, receives two kinds of messages: the kind that tell her what it is to be a successful person, and the kind that tell her what it is to be a "real" woman'. Small wonder that women, let alone feminists, working in natural science and engineering are rare to find, for it is easier to suppress half of oneself than to seek to pursue knowledge of the natural world as a woman let alone to develop a feminist theory of knowledge.[32] Part of that feminist way of understanding is to develop a practice of integrating feeling, thinking and writing, which opposes the abstraction of male and bourgeois scientific thought.

Reconceptualizing science

Feminist theorizing about science is of a piece with feminist theoretical production. Unlike the alienated abstract knowledge of science, feminist methodology seeks to bring together subjective and objective ways of knowing the world. It begins and constantly returns to the subjective shared experience of oppression. It is important to stress shared, as the purely personal account of one individual woman's oppression, while casting some brilliant insights, may tell us more about the essentially idiosyncratic character of her unique experience than the generality of the experience of all or even most women. Nonetheless, within feminist theoretical production, experience, the living participating 'I', is seen as a dimension which must be included in an adequate analysis.[33] Through this process, issues such as menstruation, childbirth, lesbianism, menopause, heterosexuality, incest, male violence, prostitution, homework, childcare become taken out of the margin and put into the central focus.

It must be stressed that the feminist movement did not, and could not, begin with theory — there were no study groups to read a feminist *Capital*. It began with the consciousness raising groups which celebrated lived experience. In these women shared the diffuse and interconnected everyday living out of common oppression. This method defined and developed the theoretical framework itself. What Betty Friedan had earlier described as 'the problem which had no name', which later was increasingly analysed as the specific oppression of women, did not appear as a problem formulated through abstract scientific theory, but out of women talking together and sharing their common experiences. Out of this sharing came feminist theory and methodology. New work about, for example, menstruation, is continuously checked out not only against objective but also subjective ways of knowing. Feminists are interested both in hormones and in how women feel; each is valid. It is not surprising that biology and medicine have been the areas where feminists have both sought to defend women's interests and advance feminist understanding.[34] Abstract theorizing fades in the light of the personal experience of bleeding, pain and tension.

Even within the science and technology of a society which is both patriarchal and capitalist, the movement has begun to develop alternatives. Prefigurative forms not only of organizational structures but also of knowledge serve as a nursery in which to develop feminist natural science. We have in both knowledges and forms achieved important fragmentary gains, the problem is how to go beyond them.

Making visible and contesting the two systems of domination in science and their interconnections and contradictions is no easy task. Socialist critical thought of the seventies had available to it well honed tools of analysis which made it possible to expose the division of mental and manual labour and its implication for knowledge, and also to construct a political economy of science and technology. Feminists have not had such tools nor indeed because of their alienating abstraction are they unequivocally helpful. Instead feminist work must continually return to the baseline of experience of the specific oppression of women. Yet this analysis and its way of constructing social and biological reality on the basis of participation in caring labour are critical for a transformative programme equally within science and within society.[35] Human existence, balanced precariously on the risks of pollution, gigantic accidents, but above all on the logic of nuclear exterminism is too vulnerable for either science and technology to be left unchanged or for the critique to be frozen into a one-sided analysis of domination.[36] However difficult it is to integrate a feminist and a socialist critique of science, it must be made in both theory and practice. The price of failure to achieve the transformation of science and technology needs no emphasis.

Acknowledgements

I would like to thank Pauline Jennings for her typing, Lynda Birke and Diana Leonard for their detailed and helpful comments and Steven Rose for his intellectual and nurturant support.

Notes and References

1. Heidi Hartmann, 'The Unhappy Marriage of Marxism and Feminism', *Capital and Class,* No. 8, 1979.
2. Ruth Wallsgrove, 'The Masculine Face of Science' in *Alice Through the Microscope,* (eds) Brighton Women and Science Group, Virago 1980.
3. Liliane Stéhélin, 'Sciences Women and Ideology' in *The Radicalisation of Science,* H. Rose and S. Rose (eds), Macmillan, London, 1976.

4. Rita Arditti, 'Feminism and Science' in *Science and Liberation,* (eds) Rita Arditti, Pat Brennan, Steve Carrak, South End Press, Boston, 1979.
5. James Watson's *The Double Helix* was to provide an even more demystified account of how science really is, than perhaps he himself had intended.
6. See for instance: Ethel Tobach and Betty Rosoff, (eds) *Genes and Gender,* Gordian Press, 1978; Ruth Hubbard and Marion Lowe (eds) *Genes and Gender,* Gordian Press 1979; *Signs* 4:1, 'Women, Science and Society', 1978, pp. 1—216; Ann Arbor Science for the People Collective, (eds) *Sociobiology as a Social Weapon,* Burgess, Minneapolis, 1977; Lila Leibowitz, *Females, Males, Families: a Biosocial Approach,* Duxbury Press, Mass, 1978; Brighton Women and Science Group, *op. cit*; Ruth Hubbard, Mary Sue Henifer and Barbara Field (eds) *Women Look at Biology Looking at Women,* Schenkmann, Camb., Mass., 1979. (This last book has an invaluable 52 pages bibliography and an appendix).
7. Maureen Mackintosh, 'Reproduction and Patriarchy', *Capital and Class,* 2, pp. 119—27, 1977; Roisin McDonough and Rachel Harrison, 'Patriarchy and Relations of Production' in *Feminism and Materialism,* (eds) Annette Kuhn and Ann Marie Wolfe, Routledge and Kegan Paul, London, 1978.
8. Much of the theoretical work developed within a marxist framework. Here, for reasons of brevity, I have included all the non-feminist theoretical approaches within the broad term 'radical'.
9. Hilary Rose and Steven Rose, 'Radical Science and its Enemies', in *The Socialist Register,* (eds) R. Miliband and J. Saville, Merlin, London, 1979.
10. Feminist scholarship adopting this approach: Elizabeth Fee, 'Nineteenth Century Crainiology: the Study of the Female Skull', *Bull. Hist. Med.,* 53, 1980, pp. 415—33; Donna Harraway, 'Animal Sociology and Natural Economy of the Body Politic' *Signs,* 4, 1978 pp. 21—60.
11. J. R. Ravetz, *Scientific Knowledge and its Social Problems,* Clarendon, Oxford, 1971.
12. Hilary Rose and Steven Rose, 'The Myth of the Neutrality of Science' *Impact of Science on Society,* 2, 1971, also in Arditti *et al. op. cit.*
13. M. Cinni, M. de Maria and G. Cicotti, 'The Production of Science in Advanced Capitalist Countries', in H. Rose and S. Rose (eds) *The Political Economy of Science,* Macmillan, London, 1976, also *L'Ape e L'Architetto,* Feltrinelli, Roma, 1976.
14. David Noble, *America By Design,* M.I.T., Cambridge, 1979.
15. Alfred Sohn Rethel, *Intellectual and Manual Labour,* Macmillan, London, 1978.
16. Mike Cooley, *Architect and Bee,* Hand and Brain Press, Slough, 1980.
17. Rita Arditti's description of being categorized as 'difficult' certainly corresponds with my own experience within the radical science movement. Arditti *et al. op. cit.*

18. I have deliberately not followed the debate about surplus and use values. This debate was spread over a wide range of journals and was particularly sharply developed within the UK. It has been usefully brought together by Ellen Malos, (ed), *The Politics of Housework,* 1979; and by *Donna Woman Femme,* special double issue 'Lavora/ Non Lavoro' 1979, pp. 12–13. At one stage as in Jane Humphries *DWF* article, it was difficult to see the relevance of the debate for feminism. Christine Delphy's intervention as a radical feminist, *The Main Enemy,* Women's Research and Resources Centre, London, 1976, and Heidi Hartmann's intervention as an American marxist feminist, 'Housework as the Locus of Class and Gender Struggle', *Signs,* Spring, 1981, unquestionably moved the debate back into feminist terrain.

19. Data derived from I. Cullen. 'A Day in the Life of . . . . ', *New Society,* 28, 601, 1974. pp. 63–5.

20. Phillip Corrigan, 'Feudal Relics or Capitalist Monuments', *Sociology,* 11, 3, 1977, pp. 411–63.

21. Hilary Land, 'The Family Wage', *Feminist Review,* 6, 1980, pp. 55–78.

22. Jane Humphries, 'Protective Legislation, the Capitalist State and Working Class Men: the Case of the 1842 Mines Regulation Act', *Feminist Review,* 7, 1981, pp. 1–33.

23. Sheila Kammerman, and Alfred Kahn (eds) *Family Policy: Government and Families in 14 Countries,* Columbia University Press, N.Y. 1978.

24. Catherine Hakim, 'Sexual Divisions Within the Labour Force: Occupational Segregation', *Department of Employment Gazette,* Nov. 1978.

25. To be fair, this is beginning to change, within a year or so a number of studies carried out by feminists on women's unemployment should be published.

26. I regard the evidence that there is no or little institutionalized sexism in Jonathan Coles' *Fair Science,* Free Press, 1979, as too weak to modify this argument. Gaye Tuchman's review summarizes the weaknesses of Coles' work neatly in *Social Policy,* May/June, 1980, pp. 59–64.

27. This view is held by most of the natural scientists contributing to either the New York Symposium of 1965 or the recent one held by Unesco. However, it is my impression that in private discussion distinguished women scientists often have another interpretation, they thus perhaps hold public and private accounts according to which domain they are in. See: *Women in the Scientific Professions,* New York Academy of Science. Alice Rossi's paper in this otherwise within ideology collection contains a remarkable pioneering discussion of the importance of choosing the 'right' partner if a woman is to have an academic career and enter marriage.

28. Anne Sayre, *Rosalind Franklin and DNA: A Vivid View of What it is like to be a Gifted Woman in an Especially Male Profession,* Norton, New York, 1975.

29. Evelyn Keller, 'The Anomaly of a Woman in Physics', in *Working it Out* (eds) S. Ruddick and P. Daniels, Pantheon, New York, 1977.
30. Naomi Weisstein, 'Adventures of a Woman in Science' also in *Working it Out*, and in Ruth Hubbard *et al, Women look at Biology Looking at Women*, Schenkmann, Cambridge, 1979.
31. Ruth Wallsgrove, *op. cit.*
32. Feminism has been quick to spell out its methodology, but slow when it comes to developing its theory of knowledge, e.g. Helen Roberts *Feminist Methodology*, RKP, 1981. It is unclear whether feminism is prepared to argue that its way of knowing the world is 'better' than sexist ways, or whether it adopts a position of such reflexivity that knowledge is reduced to relations of power. See H. Rose, 'Hyper-reflexivity: a new danger for the counter movements' in H. Nowotny and H. Rose, (eds) *Counter Movements in the Sciences*, Reidel, Dordrecht, 1979.
33. See Ruth Hubbard's discussion of evolutionary theory as an example of this. Hubbard *et al.* (1979) *op. cit.*
34. There has been a real cultural advance here, a mass of pamphleteering, discussion and bookwriting are constituting new biomedical knowledges and practices, in which women not only refuse the exclusive power of the expert, they also seek a new relationship with nature. References are too abundant but must include B. Ehrenreich and D. English, *Witches, Midwives and Nurses: a History of Women Healers*, Feminist Press, Old Westbury, N.Y., 1973; Boston Women's Health Care Collective, *Our Bodies Ourselves*, Random House, 1971.
35. Since writing this paper Elizabeth Fee has sent me a paper, 'Is Feminism a Threat to Scientific Objectivity' which pursues parallel themes. Unpublished but given at AAAS, January 4th, 1981.
36. Even Andre Gorz, *Ecology as Politics*, South End Press, Boston, for all the freshness of his approach, still naturalizes the division of labour within the family. It is Caroline Merchant who has pressed the case for the importance of ecology for feminist culture, *The Death of Nature: Women, Ecology and the Scientific Revolution*, Harper & Row, San Francisco, 1980.

5.6 'Guardians of the race', or 'Vampires upon the nation's health'?: Female sexuality and its regulation in early twentieth-century Britain

LUCY BLAND

Introduction

In December 1917 a letter, signed only with the initials M.D. was published in *The Times* on the subject of promiscuous women. They were described as 'sexual freelances', who 'stalked through the land, vampires upon the nation's health, distributing and perpetuating among our young manhood diseases which institute a national calamity'.[1] In the same period, women and girls were being enjoined to plan for rational, responsible and healthy motherhood; women were seen as having a *duty* to fulfil their role as 'guardians of the race'. This image of the healthy mother was not only a maternal image but also, I shall argue, a sexualized one. The early twentieth century thus saw the development of two contrasting images of women's sexuality — the 'promiscuous woman' or 'amateur', and the 'healthy mother'.

It may sound strange to suggest that the identity of 'ideal mother' involved a *sexual* identity, alternative to that of promiscuity, but consideration of sex education in the period supports this view. Sex education developed in such a way that it became organized to guide the girl and young woman towards motherhood and away from promiscuity. These were seen as two possible competing courses for the development of girls' sexuality. Through this construction of female sexuality around the choices of monogamy-with-motherhood, or promiscuity, sex education has continued to inform the regulation of women's sexuality through the twentieth century.

Specially commissioned for this volume
© The Open University, 1982

One interesting feature of this development of sex education in the Edwardian period was the new conviction that a certain degree of sexual knowledge acted to *protect* girls and young women. This is in contrast to the Victorian era where the 'virtuous' ideal was that of asexuality or chastity, thought to be best maintained through a state of complete sexual ignorance or 'innocence' in girls. In both periods, girls and women were thought to need protection against falling into sexual 'vice', though this article will argue that such a concern with 'protecting' women was ambiguous and often also involved a desire to *regulate* women's sexuality. As will be shown, this could, at times, take the form of active supervision.

The Edwardian ideal of motherhood was thus accompanied by a perceived need for active intervention to direct a girl's developing sexuality towards this ideal and away from the highly undesirable pursuit of promiscuity. As well as 'sexualizing' the image of the virtuous woman, the early twentieth century also saw a shift in understanding and representing the sexuality of the adolescent. It has been argued that the Victorians lacked a notion of adolescence as a distinct period of development.[2] Youth was seen in terms of stages marked by social dependency. However, by the turn of the century, new ideas were developing concerning adolescence as a crucial period of biological, sexual, psychological and social development.[3] From this new 'knowledge' came the belief that if you 'got them while young', you had them for life, (with the corollary that if you failed to 'win' them, you'd lost them for ever). Adolescence for both sexes was believed to be stressful and difficult, but a girl's adolescence was believed particularly dangerous.[4] Girls of all classes needed 'protection' both from themselves and from 'loose' company, for 'innocence' was no longer felt to convey protection, but rather a vulnerable ignorance. But although this period saw virtuous womanhood starting to be conceptualized as sexual, there was widespread ambivalence about any *display* of women's sexuality, especially from those keen to 'protect' women. Women were in no way to be allowed a sexual identity on the same terms as men.

I now want to suggest why it was that the early twentieth century saw this change of definition and regulation of female sexuality. Space does not permit more than a brief indication of the wider context of Edwardian society to which the conceptualization of the 'healthy mother' was related. I have mentioned that this new ideal mother was spoken of as a 'guardian of the race'. This racial emphasis was a distinctive feature of the time, where concern was with responsible breeding in the interests not so much of individuals as of the 'race' and nation. 'Race' tended to refer to the 'human race', the 'white' race, or the 'British race', according to the context. This reflected the contemporary influence of social darwinism and in particular eugenics, (itself a brand of social darwinism). 'Social darwinism' was a loose-knit doctrine applying concepts from the new evolutionary biology of the late nineteenth century, (such as 'survival of the fittest', struggle for existence), to the study of social institutions. Eugenics, concerned that natural selection in modern conditions had gone off the tracks and that it was no longer the 'fittest' who were surviving, sought active intervention in favour of methods for breeding 'better' people. It saw itself as the 'scientific study of all agencies by which the human race may be improved'[5]. It was above all the 'science of selective breeding', and within this it saw *women's* role in breeding for the nation as central. As one eugenist typically put it: 'the pregnant woman is pregnant with the destiny of races'.[6]

At the turn of the twentieth century a number of developments set the wider context within which to understand the rise of a concern with motherhood in this period. Britain could be seen as undergoing a series of crises — internationally, a challenge from Germany, the USA and Japan to its place as number one imperial power, nationally, the challenges of feminism, an emergent organized working class, and Ireland. It is in the light of these wider crises that we can locate a series of converging anxieties: a growing obsession with the falling birth rate, (the fall being greater among the upper and middle classes), the high infant mortality, the 'rediscovery' of poverty by Booth and Rowntree's surveys and the revelation of the physical deficiency of army recruits to the Boer War, all contributing to a rising fear that national degeneracy had firmly taken hold. Improving the methods and conditions of mothering appeared to many a crucial means of improving the nation's health. Similarly, we can understand the wider context of concern with the promiscuous woman as partly related to anxiety over national health — in this case, alarm just before, during and immediately after the war over rates of venereal disease among civilians and troops, (the fear again of military unfitness), and the spiralling rate of illegitimacy.

To understand the specific forms that the definition of 'ideal mother' and 'promiscuous woman' took, we need to see why this dichotomy came to be formulated firstly in *racial* or national terms, and secondly in terms of *health*. We therefore need to recognize the interconnections on the one hand with emergent definitions of sex and love in terms of race, and secondly with the development of ideas and practices concerning bodily hygiene. The first section of the chapter will set out these interconnections and then I will look in more detail at the way promiscuity and, by contrast, ideal motherhood came to be defined, at the role of sex education in that process and also at the role of the moral panic surrounding VD during the First World War, which was the particular focus for concern over promiscuity.

Race: maternity, sex and love

As already indicated, evolutionary thinking in general was very prevalent in this period. In relation to sex it was widely held that part of our evolved humanity had involved the development of an additional specific *human* aspect — the capacity to love.[7] Sex was increasingly seen as the physical basis of love. 'Love is the flower of which sex is the root.'[8]

In this period we also find the sexualizing of women *in terms of* their maternal instinct, that is, a frequent ideological convergence of woman's sexual and maternal instincts. As the popular medical writer Dr Elizabeth Sloan Chesser expressed it:

The longing of every normal woman to find happiness in sex union and to exercise her functions physically and psychically in marriage and motherhood is an ineradicable instinct.[9]

Since ideal motherhood already stood as the embodiment of selfless love, love, sex and maternity were inextricably bound within the ideology of motherhood. But sex was not only to be subsumed to love and procreation, for under the influence of social darwinism, it had also become seen as a *racial* instinct, to be directed to the needs of race and nation in the pursuit of healthy breeding. In a chapter headed ' A Girl's Duty to the Race', Chesser remarked: 'The attraction between man and woman . . . exists not only for purposes of personal happiness, but for the continuation of life, so we might call love the "racial instinct".'[10] Here we see the equation of sex and love, with both of these subsumed under the concept of racial instinct. Since human sex had been deemed as essentially and naturally related to love and procreation, we can see immediately how this framework would render *promiscuous* sex as *subhuman,* (since believed loveless, thus lacking the 'human' side to sex), *purposeless* (seeking merely immediate gratification, rather than long-term satisfaction of love and procreation), and *unnatural.* During the nineteenth century promiscuity had been generally seen as 'natural' for men. However, by the late nineteenth century many moralists and medics were questioning this assumption and claiming that promiscuity was unnatural for *both* sexes. Nevertheless in practice this did not lead to widespread condemnation of the double standard, for it was always promiscuity in *women* which was seen as particularly undesirable and unnatural, partly because it did not appear to be related to the pursuit of a woman's 'natural' desire for motherhood. It was also seen as fundamentally unclean. It is at this point that we must turn briefly to consider the developments within preventive medicine — the focusing on hygiene of the body as a moral and racial duty. So as well as thinking about sexuality in the context of *racial* concerns, we must also look at it in terms of the contemporary concern with bodily *health*.

Social hygiene

At the turn of the century, the language of religion and social purity, with its emphasis on 'man's' capacity for self-control and will power for moral ends, became combined with that of medicine. There arose a new movement for 'social hygiene' which involved both a combination of the rhetoric of medicine and morals, ideologically, and politically a new coalition of medics and moralists. On the one hand medics claimed moral underpinnings to health 'laws'[11], on the other hand social purists, (including many feminists), pounced on science and certain medical 'facts' as the backing for moral positions. The categories 'health/illhealth' overlaid those of 'virtue/vice'. At the core of this new social hygiene movement lay an *holistic* view of health and hygiene: that hygiene should deal with 'Man' in his/her entirety: physically, mentally, morally, and genetically. Above all, through *education* in hygiene, the individual was conceived of as an active agent in the acquisition and maintenance of his/her health and thereby the nation's. Health was now believed to be controllable and transformable, through the training of individuals, especially youth, in laws of hygiene and self-control in all things.

Reference to 'racial' hygiene again reflected the central influence of eugenics. The period's great enthusiasm for eugenics was primarily due to the appeal of the science's rationality: 'the possibility that man could control a new aspect of his environment — his own body'.[12] The new knowledge of heredity and genetics brought to the fore the question of parental 'fitness', for although procreation was seen as a public duty, it had to be *responsible* breeding — i.e. healthy and 'fit'. It was eugenists who tended to define 'fitness' — namely as 'good' hereditary qualities including not simply *physical* fitness and absence of hereditary diseases, but also absence of mental deficiency.

The *mother's* health was of especial importance, since in addition to contributions genetically, she also carried the foetus. Thus health teaching stressed not only a woman's duty to apply rules of hygiene to the raising of her children, but also her obligation to keep her body healthy and gear it for her future childbearing role.

For a woman to risk her health through risking VD was to violate this moral and national duty; it was also to risk the health of her partner. In nineteenth-century Britain, VDs were construed as God's retribution for sinful impropriety; in the twentieth century they were seen more as incumbent on the 'unnaturalness' of human promiscuity. (Various commentators were quick to point out that VD was absent among all animals save 'man'.) In both periods, the promiscuous act was unclean *and* immoral as demonstrated by the resultant repellent diseases. However, as will be demonstrated, the promiscuous girl or woman of the early twentieth century was perceived primarily in terms of an exorbitant health risk, (as purveyor of VD) over and above her moral condemnation.

Sex education

The 1911 manifesto of what was to become a highly influential morality group, the National Council for Public Morals, (NCPM), believed the solution to the nation's moral decline was to be found in sex education: education of the young in physiological knowledge and high ideals of marriage, and, above all, parenthood.[13] NCPM's membership ranged from clerics and moralists (including a few feminists involved in social purity movements), through to medics, eugenists and fabians. It represented *par excellence* the new medical-moral coalition.

The NCPM was not alone in viewing sex education as a crucial moral preventive: the demand for sex education formed a central strand within the emergent social hygiene movement. As we have seen, both concern with motherhood and with female promiscuity were centrally defined in terms of health of the body, including health rendered by *sexual* purity. In relation to motherhood, I am not arguing that the move for sex education was motherhood's main regulator. (The early twentieth century saw an enormous growth of state intervention into the regulation of maternal duties, including instruction of mothers and girls in mothercraft.[14]) However, sex education material represented an important directive of the girl and young woman both *into* motherhood and *away from* promiscuity.

Sex education in the form of leaflets, pamphlets and books directed either at the child or adolescent, or at the various educators (parent, clergy or teacher) of the child and adolescent, started to proliferate from the end of the Edwardian period. Most of these tracts assumed a gendered (and often class-specific) reader: the girl, the middle-class boy, the 'working mother', the public school master. Although there were certain continuities from Victorian tracts, (notably a stress on self-discipline/self-control, now extended to girls as well as boys, and in those texts on boy's sexuality, a continued, if toned-down obsession with the dangers of masturbation), a number of *new* themes were in evidence. As already indicated, the proclamation that the greatest prevention of and protection from sexual vice lay with the removal of sexual *ignorance,* was a common preamble. Armed with sexual knowledge, no boy or girl would commit, let alone think, sexual impurity. It was time to 'speak out' frankly about sex, to banish silence and ignorance for ever. To be forewarned was to be forearmed.

This 'knowledge' was both to protect and to direct. It consisted of certain biological and ethical 'facts of life' set within an evolutionary context. Thus the sex instruction was presented as integral to our evolution, thereby 'explaining' both the *origin* of sex, and its purpose (namely procreation, and for humans, also love — the distinctly *human* aspect of sex.) Seeing sex as having a purpose by implication gave sex's 'natural' (and hence desirable) direction. Marital monogamy was sometimes additionally claimed as a 'natural' law of humanity, similarly attained through long aeons of evolution, or more frequently in the early twentieth century, as necessary for the stability of the nation and race. To 'keep' yourself pure and clean for the 'racial task' of healthy child production entailed chastity, now believed as desirable and *possible* for young men as well as women, succeeded at marriage by sexual continence. To direct the adolescent girl into motherhood and away from the perils of promiscuity, sex education was essential, for 'an awakened motherhood, by *right instruction* .... will see to it that the reproductive power is not dissipated in vice, but conserved for the service of love' (my emphasis).[15]

But although girls were to be given sexual knowledge, there was great ambiguity over the idea of a girl's protection and capacity for responsibility. For their own protection, girls must be warned of dangers, but despite explicit statements that innocence equals fatal ignorance, these texts also retained a desire to *maintain* such innocence in girls — again in the name of protection. It was necessary, somehow to 'get rid of our ignorance while keeping our innocence'.[16] The medical journal, *The Lancet* too was enquiring 'how to dissipate this ignorance . . . and to replace it by necessary knowledge without sacrifice of modesty. . . .'[17] Girls in particular must be told only so much. Thus Clare Goslett, a feminist, although instructing 'working mothers' to warn their daughters of 'men — vile creatures who were on the lookout for . . . an innocent girl'[18], didn't suggest that mothers actually inform girls as to what such men might *do*. She also advised alerting girls to the dangers of flirting. Important here is the idea of a girl's partial *responsibility* for any subsequent action by the man. However, unlike Goslett, who also warned of unscrupulous men, who 'may talk of *love*, but . . . all they want is to amuse themselves and satisfy their desires at [a girl's] expense',[19] another and not untypical sex educator believed girls should expect the very best of all men, while simultaneously watching themselves 'lest we make it harder for any man to be a true knight'.[20] By implication, the responsibility for any 'unknightly' behaviour was laid at the feet of the girl. Thus we find the contradictory ideal of a girl to be kept in partial innocence-cum-ignorance while also assumed *responsible* for both her own sexual behaviour and *that of the man*.

The 'amateur'

So far I have said nothing of the government's attitude towards the teaching of sex education. It is only with the hysteria over promiscuity, and in particular VD, during the war, that the state was prompted to sanction a semi-official sex education body called the National Council for Combatting VD (NCCVD), set up in the Winter of 1914. As will be indicated, the signs of panic as to the incidence of VD *predated* the war, but real concern with promiscuity arose only in early 1915. Panic initially took the form of wild stories of thousands of 'war babies'. McNeill, a Tory MP, announced to the press in April 1915 that wherever troops were stationed, large numbers of girls were about to become unmarried mothers. (Incidentally, 1915 actually showed an exceptionally *low* illegitimate birth rate, and a phenomenally *high* marriage rate, although the illegitimacy rate soared in subsequent years). Yet McNeill and others were keen to stress that no shame should attach to 'mothers of our soldiers' children', nor to the children themselves.[21]

Although the promiscuous girl as *mother* was not necessarily vilified, the thought of women and girls seeking sex ('war nymphomania'), sent waves of shocked horror across the country. I am not arguing that there *was* necessarily an enormous increase in young women seeking sex; the important point here is that there was widely *believed* to be such an increase. The label 'amateur prostitute' (or simply 'amateur') sprang up as if overnight.[22] People were not always entirely clear as to its definition. McPherson of the War Office was asked if by an 'amateur prostitute' he meant 'a girl who had two or three personal friends or . . . who though not habitually soliciting was prepared for promiscuous intercourse'.[23] He wasn't sure but thought that probably the latter definition was most accurate. The term 'amateur prostitute' reflected a difficulty in understanding active female sexuality outside the institution of prostitution. Yet it was the amateur's distinction *from* the professional prostitute which disturbed. Not only did she seek and give sex 'for free', but unlike the professional (assumed to be working class), the amateur was thought to be drawn from all classes.[24] Amateurs also appeared to be much *younger* than professional prostitutes.[25]

However, the distinction between the amateur and the professional which was of most concern related to VD; the amateur was claimed to be 'the real centre of venereal infection'[26], for apparently it was 'a well known fact that girls and young women are often more dangerous than regular prostitutes'.[27] The letter which I quoted at the beginning of this article is but one example amongst many of the portrayal of the amateur as a hideous disease-carrying threat to the health of the nation's manhood.

The VD panic

Anxiety as to the extent of VD had been building up for some years. The beginnings of this particular wave of panic can be dated back to 1908 when, at the initiative of certain suffragists, the so-called 'conspiracy of silence' was forcibly broken with the publication of Dr Louisa Martindale's *Under the Surface.* This pamphlet and subsequent feminist writings on the subject, (the best known being Christabel Pankhurst's *The Great Scourge,* 1913) claimed that the vast majority of women were the unsuspecting victims of VD imposed by their philandering husbands. The source of the so-called 'woman's disease' they claimed, lay not with the pathology of women's bodies but the insidious effects of VD. Feminists were far from alone in such assertions; many medics followed suit in declaring the horrific extent of syphilis and gonhorrhea among the civilian population.

Why was there such widespread concern with VD? Medical figures for the period revealed no actual *increase* in VD rates, although it was the case that various serious illnesses which until then seemed to be discrete complaints, were being revealed as manifestations of the later stages of syphilis. Thus it seemed that syphilis's true extent had been greatly underestimated.

However, I would argue that the main reason for the focus on VD was that it stood for many as a metaphor, condensing and 'carrying' many of the fears of the period — the concern with the falling birth rate (VD contributing to sterility, still-birth and infant mortality), concern with national efficiency and physical deterioration of troops and civilians (VD often seen as both cause and effect of physical and mental degeneracy), and, for feminists, VD, in its imposition by husbands on wives above all represented the double standard writ large. By 1913 public outcry had reached a crescendo, compelling the establishment of a Royal Commission. In its report of 1916, sex instruction 'based on moral principles' warning of the perils of VD, stood as the core to its preventive strategy, while government-subsidised treatment centres were to be set up to treat, rather than medically prevent VD cases. Its platform was *moral* not medical prophylaxis (prevention) and hence it stood centrally within the medico-moral hygiene movement that embraced many eugenists, medics, moralists and feminists alike.

The regulation of the 'amateur'

The Royal Commission had been set up in 1913 primarily to examine the VD problem amongst the *civilian* population. Once war was under way, the health of the military became a far greater governmental concern, and as I have suggested, the 'amateur prostitute' became the scapegoat for the incidence of VD amongst the troops. Initially, however, the Home Office simply relied on the educative work of the NCCVD, and on the feminist-initiated women patrols to deal with the 'amateurs'. The patrols aimed 'to warn girls who have been speaking to men on duty or behaving unsuitably'[28], although they also intended to make friends with the girls. Nevertheless we can see here an ambivalence towards displays of female sexual initiative and the double-sided nature of the desire to 'protect' — its underside being the supervision of women's sexual behaviour.

As the war progressed, various pressures, in particular from commanders of Colonial forces stationed in Britain, eventually pushed the government towards more repressive measures looking suspiciously like the widely reviled Contagious Diseases Acts of the 1860s. [29] There were various repressive proposals in the Criminal Law Amendment Bills of 1917 and 1918 and the Sexual Offences Bill of 1918, opposed by a wide cross section of feminists. (However, feminists did support the SOB clause raising the age of consent from 16 to 17, which had implications for the control of the young 'amateurs'.) In March 1918 the government introduced regulation 40d under the Defence of the Realm Act (DORA), making it an offence for a women with transmittable VD to have, solicit or invite sexual intercourse with any member of HM forces. That the offence included a diseased women simply *having* sexual intercourse obviously allowed for the 'amateur'. A massive campaign, spearheaded by feminists, sprung up to oppose the new regulation. Feminists may have supported surveillance in the form of women patrols, but in no way would they support state surveillance which scapegoated the woman for the actions of the man.

At the close of war, DORA 40d was rescinded. However, concern with the rates of promiscuity and VD, and with the 'amateur' continued, and the NCCVD correspondingly expanded its educative work across the country. It is perhaps in the nature of this teaching and in the debates and practice in relation to medical prophylaxis for VD, that the contradictions and ambivalences around 'protection' of women and the enjoining in women of rational sexual behaviour, become most apparent.

Prophylaxis and women

It is clear from looking at the debates over prophylaxis (medical prevention) for women that VD control implied the need to protect *healthy* men from *diseased* women; the obverse (i.e. a need to protect healthy women from diseased men) was never contemplated, save as a possible grounds for divorce for the 'innocent' wife. In relation to VD, 'prophylaxis' generally meant the application of certain disinfectants immediately before or after sexual intercourse to protect from infection. Sheaths were also sometimes referred to and used as prophylaxis against VD. The immediate post-war years saw a protracted wrangle between two societies — the NCCVD and the Society for Prevention of VD — over the question of such prophylaxis, and it was prophylaxis for *men* that was largely being considered. NCCVD, the only society with government backing, held out against prophylaxis, both for moral reasons — that provision would be seen as a sanctioning of sexual vice — and medical reasons, though it was not so much the medical effectiveness of prophylaxis as the removal of treatment from the hands of the medics into those of the individual in his self-application of preventives that was of concern. The whole issue was so contentious that even the Lambeth Conference of Anglican Bishops in 1920 passed a resolution, condemning 'distribution or use, before exposure to infection, of so-called prophylactics, since they cannot but be regarded as an invitation to vice'.[30]

Nevertheless, a wide cross-section of groups and individuals supported the provision of prophylaxis, including the NCPM. Witnesses to their special committee on VD[31] discussed prophylaxis for women, but rejected it on various grounds: that any prophylaxis for women would also prevent conception and thus be 'equivalent to race suicide'; (note that the provision of sheaths to troops in the war for VD prevention was never opposed on these grounds); that efficient self-disinfection was very difficult for women, (though no effort was suggested to overcome this greater difficulty); and that provision of such would encourage vice so that 'a phase of society would be produced as vicious and degenerate as any of which history has record'. Male prophylaxis was meanwhile being condoned. Marie Stopes, to her credit, despite referring to 'amateurs' as 'ignorant and very dirty', did recommend prophylaxis for women, though her zeal for disinfectant is somewhat startling: 'this should be a *general rule* for everybody. Even if you know yourself to be *impregnably virtuous, never go out of the house without carrying some disinfectant* (for use) . . . . if unforeseen circumstances place you at the mercy of those passions of the body which you are too little evolved or too weak to master. Then your disinfectant *must* be used' (her emphases).[32] Stopes aside, the general tone of the debate is yet again to deprive the woman who has transgressed the boundary of respectable womanhood of both protection and the capacity to act responsibly. Her image as an irresponsible, unclean slut is thereby inexorably reinforced.

NCCVD and sex education

From the war on, and into the inter-war years, the threat of VD lay at the heart of most sex education material. For the period 1915–25, this is unsurprising given that the main national body involved in sex instruction was the NCCVD. But even with NCCVD's change of name in 1925 (to the British Social Hygiene Council (BSHC)), and the corresponding expansion of its aims, to include both eugenical and wider moral objectives in relation to 'preserving the strength of the family as the basic social unit', the abolition of VD through moral suasion remained central. It propagated its moral philosophy through leaflets, pamphlets, books, numerous lectures in youth clubs, public halls etc, and most popular of all, the showing of films, with names like *The End of the Road, The Flaw, Damaged Goods, Marriage Forbidden,* and *The Girl Who Doesn't Know.* The scale of its work was massive. In 1931, for example, BSHC had given 24,000 meetings attended by 5 million people, 3,000 conferences and 700 courses of lectures, excluding those to soldiers.[33] In one two-week period in 1924 in Manchester alone, NCCVD had given 21 meetings, with an audience of nearly 9,000. Until the introduction of sex education into schools (an extremely gradual process), such lectures, films, leaflets and pamphlets were likely to be one of the main ways that girls obtained a modicum of sexual knowledge.

However, examination of NCCVD/BSHC commissioned material reveals a clear gender-differentiated approach to the question. For instance, compare one of their leaflets *From Man to Men, by one who knows from experience* with their film *The End of the Road.* The leaflet, for men, was written in a chatty reassuring style: 'do not be afraid of meeting at the clinic someone you know. Rest assured he will not "blow the gaff" . . . as he is in the same boat himself'. You are left with the impression that 'us men' have been up to a bit-of-a-naughty-prank, but it will all turn out fine in the end. In contrast, nearly all of their films were based on scare tactics. However, in *The End of the Road,* it was the women who were given by far the most fear. The film reviewer of *The Shield,* a feminist journal commented: 'all the principal women except the heroine come to a bad end . . . We think that the natural conclusions of any ordinary person seeing this film would be that women have no character, no common sense, and no endurance, and that VD is a disease from which men are immune but which they can pass on to the women.' In the hospital scene 'again all the victims are women. The pictures were horrible and revolting . . . and will probably make many people. . . . quite ill'.[34]

Responsibility and protection

This brief examination of an important form of regulation applied to two stereotyped female sexual subjects — the ideal mother and the 'amateur prostitute' — has illustrated some of the ambiguities in operation in such regulation. It appears that two concepts in particular, that of *responsibility* and *protection*, were centrally deployed in discussion of regulation and most open to ambiguity. Arguably, these two concepts remain central to definition and regulation of female sexuality today.

In the nineteenth century women were thought to lack the capacity to reason or be morally responsible for their behaviour. (This was encoded in law, for until the Criminal Justice Act of 1925, a husband was deemed legally responsible for any criminal act of his wife's committed in his presence.) One could say that the twentieth century 'gave' reason to women, though in a highly contradictory manner. Women were thought to be simultaneously both *more* responsible and *less* responsible than men. The idea of women being *less* responsible informed the belief that a girl's need for 'protection' from 'loose' company was greater than boys' due to girls' greater gullibility. This acted to 'rationalize' forms of surveillance of young women and girls never imposed on boys, such as the women patrols in the war. The idea of women being *more* responsible than men took different forms: firstly, women were responsible as breeders — 'guardians of the race'; secondly, women were also partially responsible for *male* sexual behaviour.

This was both as mothers, in their duty to give sex education to their sons and daughters, and as instigators of male sexual behaviour.[35] The last point drew on the belief that women were more able to control their sexual passion than men because of lesser sexual drives — the continuing rationale for the double standard.

As we have seen, attitudes towards 'protecting' the promiscuous woman/girl were contradictory. Although many moralists desired to 'protect' her, in the sense of rescuing her from her vice, as reference to the debate over venereal prophylaxis for women has shown, there was explicit demand from various groups and individuals (*including* feminists) that medical *protection* from VD should not be granted to such women. Such a withholding of protection from disease, (and note that VD often permanently damaged a woman's reproductive organs), contradicted the express desire of many of the *same* groups and individuals, to protect a woman's health for 'fit' maternity. Once tarnished, women were no longer such desirable breeders. We have also seen, in the example of women patrols in the First World War, that a desire to 'protect' can tip over into a desire for active supervision of women's sexuality.

Conclusion

In conclusion, I would like to pose the question: what relevance does the study of the sexual identities given to women in the early twentieth century have for an understanding of the defining and regulation of female sexuality today? I would argue that this period was crucial for subsequent definitions and regulations in several respects. Firstly, the mode of sex instruction developed within this period, such as its moralizing nature, its stress on sex's purpose lying in reproduction and its stress on VD as the peril of promiscuity, set the terms for subsequent sex education.

Secondly, although the particular Edwardian concerns with 'race' and 'social hygiene' made VD into the most potent symbol of the undesirability of promiscuity, which is perhaps no longer the case, today condemnation of the promiscuous woman continues. The sexual polarity around monogamy/promiscuity, as established in the Edwardian era, still organizes sexual life today and is still sharply gender-differentiated. Even if women are now expected to be sexually active, it is still seen as immoral for a woman to separate sex from love, if not from motherhood. There is no female equivalent to the harmless or flattering 'Don Juan'. Women are still caught, as one commentator has put it 'within the double bind of the double standard'.[36]

Notes

1. *The Shield,* December 1917, 'Sources of infection'.
2. See Gorham, D. 'The Maiden tribute of modern babylon re-examined', *Victorian Studies,* Spring 1976.
3. See Stanley Hall, G, *Adolescence,* Appleton, New York, 1904.
4. See Dyhouse, C, *Girls Growing up in Late Victorian and Edwardian England,* Routledge & Kegan Paul, London, 1981.
5. Ellis, Havelock, *The Task of Social Hygiene,* 1912, p. 29.
6. Kenealy, Arabella, *Feminism and sex extinction,* 1920, p. 197.
7. See Geddes and Thomson, *Sex* 1914, and see raging debate in feminist journal *Freewoman,* 1911—12, over the definition of sex.
8. Thomson, J.A, *Education and Social Hygiene,* 1925.
9. Chesser, Elizabeth Sloan, *Woman and Womanhood,* 1912.
10. Chesser, Elizabeth Sloan, *From Girlhood to Womanhood,* 1914, p. 122.
11. E.g. see the works of Dr. Elizabeth Blackwell.
12. Freeden, M, 'Eugenics and progressive thought; a study in ideological affinity', *The Historical Journal* 22, 3 (1979).
13. NCPM in *The Times* 31 May 1911.
14. See Davin, A, 'Imperialism and motherhood', *History Workshop Journal,* No 5, Spring 1978; and Lewis, J, *Politics of Motherhood,* Croom Helm, 1980.
15. Chesser, E. Sloan, *Women, Marriage and Motherhood,* 1913 p. 219.
16. Bulley, *A Talk on Questions of Sex,* 1911.
17. *The Lancet,* 4 January 1913.
18. Goslett, *Things We must Tell our Girls (for Working Mothers),* 1911.
19. Goslett, *Ibid.*
20. Trench, Violet, *Queens: A book for girls about themselves,* 1912.
21. Marwick, A, *The Deluge,* Macmillan, 1933, pp. 107—8.
22. Although the term had been around for many years, e.g. see *The Shield* December 1899.
23. Evidence to the Joint Select Committee of Both Houses on Criminal Law Amendment Bill 1918 and Sexual Offences Bill 1918.
24. E.g. Ettie Rout, a witness to the Special Committee on VD, spoke of 'the promiscuous immorality' that 'invaded all classes of women in this country' during the war. NCPM *Prevention of VD,* 1921.
25. The feminist Alison Neilans estimated their age as 16—19 years, ('Disorderly women' *The Shield,* February 1915) although one woman doctor had heard they were as young as 14—15. (Lady Barrett's evidence to Special Committee on VD *op. cit.*).
26. Nielans, *op. cit.*
27. *The Shield,* April 1913.
28. *The Shield,* 1915.
29. These acts had provided for the compulsory inspection and detention of the diseased prostitutes of certain garrison towns. The opposition, especially from certain feminist groups, had led to the Acts' repeal in 1886.
30. Reprinted in *The Shield,* November—December 1920, p. 103.

31. NCPM, *Prevention of VD,* 1921.
32. Stopes, Marie, *The Truth about VD,* 1921, pp. 38—9.
33. Bristow, *Vice and Vigilance,* Gill and Macmillan, Dublin, 1977, p. 151.
34. *The Shield,* December 1919/20.
35. See Edwards, Susan, *Female Sexuality and the Law,* Martin Robertson, 1980.
36. Pierson, Ruth Roach, 'The double bind of the double standard: VD control and the CWAV in World War II', *Canadian Historical Review,* LXII No. 1, March 1981.

5.7 Oppressive dichotomies: the nature/culture debate

PENELOPE BROWN AND L. JORDANOVA

Introduction

The distinction between nature and culture is basic to recent Western thought. It has so many varied manifestations that it takes considerable effort to make them explicit. Since the mid-nineteenth century, the opposition between nature and culture has become central to evolutionary theory and allied sciences, to debates on heredity and environment, nature *versus* nurture, the measurement of intelligence and educational methods. All these areas are informed by a distinction between unmediated, intractable nature, and a realm of human mastery where conscious social and individual action is accorded an important measure of power. The belief in human capacity to control nature is, in our culture, linked to the development of science, medicine and technology, and to the rational, refined analysis on which they are based. Our science based culture depends on abstract studies, mostly in the physical sciences, and on techniques relating to engineering skills. Both science and engineering are identified with male accomplishments, with the capacity for mathematical and logical reasoning, with mechanical skills; they are literally and metaphorically masculine activities. Women by contrast, are stereotypically identified with so-called caring jobs, nursing, teaching and social work. They are deemed to be uniquely gifted in the realm of human relationships by virtue of their greater emotional sensitivity. The model for female accomplishments is motherhood. The corresponding popular imagery is of soft, tender sympathy overriding reason and intellect. In the common emphasis on the unity of mother and child, the identification of women with nature is suggested. The biological functions of bearing and suckling children imply the privileged status of women with respect to nature. This is further reinforced by their care of defenceless, unformed children who are not yet fully social beings.

Source: Brown, P. and Jordanova, L.J. (1981) 'Oppressive dichotomies: the nature/culture debate', in *Women and Society: Interdisciplinary Essays* Virago, London, Chapter 13

It would be possible to devote an entire chapter to detailing the various ways in which the nature/culture polarity functions both explicitly and implicitly in contemporary society. Our purpose here is different. We simply wish to note the pervasiveness of the dichotomy in our culture, and the power it has, and go on to suggest that we can learn a valuable object lesson from examining the history and use of these ideas, particularly as they are found in anthropological theories. Current debates in anthropology, like those in the natural sciences, rely on a certain approach to the interpretation of sex differences which we feel demands critical scrutiny. And it helps to realize that the presuppositions scientists and anthropologists use have a long and complex history. In what follows we shall outline the principal anthropological arguments, indicate some of their main problems and then briefly place these debates in their historical context in Western thought.

An anthropological debate as object lesson

As we shall make clear later in the chapter, the association of women with nature and men with culture is by no means new. The recent debates within academic anthropology draw on assumptions and stereotypes which have been deeply embedded in our culture for several centuries. Currently, debate centres on the dichotomy between women being seen as closer to nature and men as closer to culture, and its use to 'explain' the apparently universal secondary status of women in all societies. The controversy is of interest to feminists for two reasons. First, it sheds light on the difficulties of generalizing about alleged universals in the position of women. Second, it illustrates the prevalence and the persuasiveness of what we shall call *essentialist* thinking about the sexes. By this we mean the common conviction that sex differences in the sense of gender ultimately refer to concrete, biological distinctions between men and women. We contrast this with a *relativist* position where, while granting biological sexual differences, emphasis is placed on the social construction of sexuality. From this latter perspective there is no such thing as woman or man in asocial terms; women and men, or rather femininity and masculinity, are constituted in specific cultural settings according to class, age, marital status and so on. We further contend that essentialist thinking about the sexes is part of a dominant ideology which is an impediment to our understanding of the ways societies construct the sexes.

The nature/culture debate has taken many different forms within twentieth-century social theory. Among the most important contributions is the work of Claude Lévi-Strauss. For him the human mind works through series of binary oppositions such as nature/culture, wild/tame, raw/cooked. He alleges that the nature/culture distinction is a universal folk concept, based on the equally universal human propensity to bound society off from non-society. [. . .] He also assumes that the human mind is specifically constructed to perceive binary oppositions. For him these dichotomies are in the unconscious; they need to be decided by the anthropologist, so that his model of what it is that social scientists do is of rational, logical deciphering.

A number of critiques have been made of Lévi-Strauss on the grounds that he bases culture in biology. They point out that nature and culture are not value-free terms which can safely be used to explain any phenomenon, for they carry the cultural biases of the meaning attached to them. Western ideas of nature and culture have, since the eighteenth century, focused on the origins and evolution of the human species. Thus, we take the 'natural' to be innate in our primitive heritage, while the 'cultural' is arbitrary and artificial. Furthermore, as will be made clear later, Western traditions lay particular emphasis on controlling nature by means of culture, especially through science, medicine and technology. But ideas of nature and culture can be entirely different in non-Western societies. So, in using our ideas of nature and culture to explain the beliefs and behaviour of other societies we run into the danger of confusing our theories with the cognitive structures of other societies.

The nature, culture and gender debates are best known to English speaking people through two articles published apparently independently in the early 1970s by Ardener and Ortner. They sparked off a heated argument which has resulted in a challenge, on both empirical and theoretical grounds, to the contention that women are universally seen as nearer to nature, men to culture. Critiques have come from two angles: theoretical ones which attack the logic of the arguments and the premises from which they start, and empirical ones using detailed ethnographic descriptions to show that in particular societies these concepts either do not exist in the forms claimed, or are not consistently associated with gender.[. . .]

Neither Ardener nor Ortner argue that women *are* closer to nature. Rather they try to explain how and why women are *seen* to be nearer to nature by members of very different societies. They agree in attributing the source of such a view of women to female biology as perceived by men, and to women's restriction to the domestic sphere. Both rely on the presumed readiness of human beings to attribute symbolic significance to female anatomy.

The underlying logic of both Ardener's and Ortner's arguments moves from the premise that the only unalterable sexual difference is reproductive structures and roles, to the conclusion that this must therefore be at the root of social differences based on the social identification of the sexes, i.e. gender. As we have already stressed, this is not a crude biological determinism where biology causes sex differences as sociobiologists might argue. Both Ardener and Ortner dissociate themselves from this position. But in fact what they do is simply add an extra link to the chain of causation. *Biological differences* provide a universal basis for *social definitions* which place women closer to nature than men, and this provides the basis for the *universal subordination* of women. Indeed both writers simply assume that women are universally subordinate to men, and see their task as explaining this 'fact'. [. . .]

As we mentioned earlier, ethnographic material has also been used to attack the identification of women with nature (MacCormack and Strathern, eds, 1980). Recent accounts show that nature and culture are *not* universal native categories, at least not in the form in which they are conceptualized in our society. The notion of culture as superior to and dominant over nature is not universal. Not in societies which do have such concepts, is there necessarily a simple or consistent relationship with male and female. In both empirical and theoretical critiques of the debate, there is an implicit denial of the value of a rationalist discourse. Nature and culture are relativized concepts, their meaning derives from their place within a particular metaphysics; neither has a unique meaning either within Western thought or cross-culturally.

Many people dislike the ways in which the pair nature/culture has been associated with woman/man in anthropological theory. But it is not the belief that social groups tend to define themselves as 'us' and others as 'not us' which they object to. It is the assertion that 'not us' is equivalent to nature, and is therefore inferior, that they take issue with. The split between 'us' and 'not us' can be into two symmetrical halves rather hierarchically ordered.

Of course we now have to study the formation of 'not us' groups. It is plausible to suppose that at least some of the criteria differentiating 'us' and 'not us' will be sex based, but in gender, not in strictly biological terms. The placing of marginal persons such as childless women, widows, 'hermaphrodites', men who opt out of male activities, is highly culturally variable, and biological sex is not necessarily the determining factor.

Many of the comments we have made relate to the extraordinarily difficult questions of the use of dichotomous pairs in social theory as both explanations and descriptions of social behaviour. In part this brings us to the heart of philosophical disagreements about the form social theories should take, and of psychological disagreements about the way the human mind works and how psychoanalysis and theories of language are used. We are concerned here, however, with some rather simple errors which we believe are commonly made in analysing women. Even if we granted that there was a universal association of the form women are to nature as men are to culture, that would not sanction slipping into assertions about universal judgments of *value* (good/bad, superior/inferior), nor from there into issues of *control* (superordinate/subordinate). And this danger is not confined to anthropology.

The slippage referred to above is possible because of the way we conceptualize women and men as each possessing common features which constrain their lives. The feminist argument against this view is that what cultures make of sex differences is almost infinitely variable, so that biology cannot be playing a determining role. Women and men are products of social relations, if we change the social relations we change the categories 'woman' and 'man'. On both political and intellectual grounds we would argue that to put it at its bluntest, social relations determine sex differences rather than biological sex producing social divisions between the sexes.

The idea that biological differences between men and women cause social ones is, of course, extremely pervasive, and it has gained prominence through the recent spate of writings on sociobiology. Earlier we called it a dominant ideology. Now we want to argue that it is grounded in Western thought, and especially in science, medicine and technology; hence its dominance.

Science and sexuality

For many centuries there have been attempts to separate out what seemed intractable in the environment (nature), from what could easily be altered by human agency (culture). This division was bound up with notions about the form of God's power over both the natural world and over human beings. Only relatively recently it has been argued, did the idea that human beings had mastery over their surroundings assume more importance than the belief that they were impotent by comparison with the deity and were merely guarding the natural world on his behalf (Glacken 1967). The examples we use are drawn from the mid-eighteenth century on, the period when a secular and self-consciously scientific language began to be employed and when interest in the study of the physical and social aspects of 'man', nature and the environment began on a large scale (Jordanova 1979). During the nineteenth century, the nature/culture distinction seems to have applied more consistently to sexual divisions, with the result that stereotypes of women became more rigid. The ways in which this hardening of the divide between the sexes came about are of great interest, and all the more so as the rigid stereotypes were closely linked with a biological definition of sexuality.

As the anthropological material alluded to in the previous section suggested, the relationship between the metaphors people use and the aspects of lived experience they allegedly express are extremely complex. The metaphors contain contradictions, tensions or even what strike us as logical inconsistencies, but these in no way undermine the historical power of the images. For example, the eighteenth century use of women to symbolize truth in the sense of natural reason, virtue and clarity, coexisted with their simultaneous use to symbolize feelings and sentiment, also analogized to nature, but associated with irrationality and superstition. The nature/culture distinction has operated in Western traditions at many different levels. In addition to myths, pictures and symbols of all kinds, a coherent scientific self-consciousness played a crucial role in reinforcing and redefining the identification of female with nature and male with culture.

The scientific endeavour was linked with masculinity, while passive nature, unveiled and revealed by male science, was identified with femininity. The personification of nature as woman and as mother is prominent in much writing in English during the eighteenth and nineteenth centuries. Furthermore, the very process of constructing a scientific culture was conceived of as a struggle between the elements of male reason and female superstition. For civilization to progress, in other words, the forces of intellectual and social order had to triumph over the ignorant mysticism which kept back the human race. Men, in the name of science would assert their culture over women and their religious creeds. For many people the battle for power between traditional and modern forces could be seen in the attempts by the intellectual élite of philosophers, savants and enlightened medical men on the side of science and reason to undermine the authority of superstitious and irrational practices exemplified by the Catholic church, and its main clientèle — women. [. . .]

The struggle between the sexes was, for Enlightenment thinkers, part of the history of the human race. The ideology of progress so deeply entrenched in Enlightenment thought suggested the importance of the growth of a rational, humane and civilized society with the development of knowledge and science as motors of change. Allowing the male value system to prevail was therefore an integral part of the process of developing culture with which nature, raw and unmediated, would be controlled. Human *mastery* over nature should ever increase, this was history, this was science.

Women, as nature were to be controlled, or rather channelled into the correct role for nature in the history of the human race.

Although we are concerned with the manner in which men and women were conceptualized as opposite and complementary using the nature/culture dichotomy, it is important to stress that nature and culture were *not* seen as necessarily incommensurable categories in the eighteenth and nineteenth centuries. Obviously, for human beings to have culture, nature has to yield to their manipulations. Nature, including human beings, is modified as a result of culture. We must be careful therefore not to construe the concept of nature as implying simply a view of the world as composed of intractable, innate qualities. Although nature was distinguished from environment, culture, civilization and society, a continual interaction between them was envisaged. It is certainly true that what we have called essentialist thinking about the sexes is linked with a scientific view of nature, but it would be a drastic over-simplification to equate this with a crude deterministic position. In the natural philosophical and medical literatures of the eighteenth century there were extensive discussions on the ways in which behaviour, what we might call lifestyle, became incorporated into the body through diet, exercise, habits, occupation and so on. As a result, culture is continually affecting natural objects, particularly the human body; culture was identified as a major determinant of health and disease at both physical and moral levels. Both men and women were seen in terms of this continual dialectic between nature and culture.

Far from being defined exclusively in terms of their sex organs, women were, physiologically speaking, distinguished by the occupations and task of womanhood. Although these tended to be closely linked with their reproductive role, the emphasis on lifestyle as a determinant of the characteristics of the human body, provides important clues to the nature/culture relationship in the eighteenth and early nineteenth centuries. The emphasis on occupation as a determinant of health led to a radical boundary being drawn between the sexes. The theoretical basis for this was a physiology which recognized few boundaries; it conflated moral and physical, mind and body, and created a language capable of containing biological, psychological and social considerations. Physicians in late eighteenth-century France used these physiological presuppositions to argue that women were physiologically and automatically quite distinct from men (Kniebiehler 1976). The total physiology of woman could, they argued, only be understood in terms of their lifestyle and the roles they ought to fulfil if they weren't doing so already. The occupational model of health tightly linked jobs performed in the social arena (for women, the production, suckling and care of children, the creation of a natural morality within the family) with health and disease. Of course the occupational model was applied to both men and women, but for the latter permissible occupation was tightly defined according to 'natural' criteria. Women's health therefore depended on their fulfilling a restricted social role which appeared to be an inevitable consequence of their ability to bear children. Men were members of the broadest social and cultural groups, while women's sphere of action was limited to the family — the ultimate guarantor of human stability since it was the essential *biological* unit of *social* life. These arguments led to women being conceptualized as physically feeble, unable to survive without male protection, frivolous and irrational. Women's minds worked differently from men's in making emotive associations rather than logical connections, a belief that became elaborated into a complex psychological theory in the nineteenth century which asserted women's incapacity for rational scientific thought and their superior talent for affective sentiments (Ploss *et al* 1935). [...]

There is no doubt that the question of power is the crucial one and it holds the key to the apparently contradictory ways in which women were associated with nature. As we stressed above, femininity was commonly equated with superstitions, that is, with irrational, illegitimate, mystical power. But it was also associated with moral regeneration; women as natural creatures held within them the possibility for growth and improvement, for the transcendence over evil by the forces of virtue. To be sure this feminine harnessing of positive power also, by implication, involved mystical elements, notably the special bond between mother and child, but here it was safe, even desirable. [...]

Nineteenth-century interpretations of the nature/culture oppositions which extend the argument into an evolutionary framework were sometimes quite explicit about the struggle for power between men and women. These concerns came to the surface in a number of mid-nineteenth century works which dealt with the development of human society and attempted to grapple with the problems of whether all societies go through matriarchal stages (Fee 1974). Such works considered the economic foundations of sex roles and were closely related to prevalent beliefs about women's limited capacities for participation in the labour market.

Late nineteenth-century debates about the entry of women into the medical profession employ the same sexual polarities of nature and culture in an economic sense, for it was considered unseemly for women to compete publicly with men. The argument that women could not become doctors because of their inherent lack of scientific ability is now well known. It was also claimed that only married women had the necessary 'experience' for the job, but they were the very ones who were excluded by virtue of their childbearing and other family-based duties. Unmarried women, on the other hand, might have the life style compatible with a profession, but lacked, by definition, the 'experience' required (Donnison 1977, Delamont and Duffin, 1978. pp.46—7).

The division between married and unmarried women is of great importance. At the end of the eighteenth century the medical literature emphasized the superior health of married women, and contained pleas to married women not to leave the home but to consider motherhood their occupation. At the same period, working women came increasingly from the ranks of young, unmarried girls. In terms of work the division was not just between women and men, but between men and single women on the one hand, and married women who were reproductively active, on the other. Women who worked presented a problem, for by selling their labour power, they entered a male world of abstract commodities with objective values. They violated the neat category distinction. The common nineteenth-century concern for the modesty of women workers should be seen in this context. A working woman carried with her, through her sexuality, the associations of a private, mystified arena connected with feelings in the family, not the public routines of work. She brought the potential for uncontrolled emotion into an arena of life which was held to epitomise control and objectivity, or put more concretely, men and money.

The economic inactivity of women was justified by the idealization of the home and family life as women's preserves. The dominance of women in the family was itself explained in terms of their reproductive and nurturing role which had arisen during the course of human evolution. There was thus a pleasing harmony between the biological, psychological and social division of labour. Female biological rhythms, especially the menstrual cycle, were taken as examples of natural laws at their most beautiful. Women had to submit to the fluctuations and changes of their bodies which were watched over by the benevolent eye of the husband and the physician.

In its application to sexual divisions, the nature/culture distinction mediated forms of power. But perceived distribution of power was not simply a question of male strength and female submission. In fact, two forms of power were envisaged and both had their positive and negative aspects. The first, identified with women, was potency in the realm of feeling which made women good wives and mothers and general upholders of morality. These praiseworthy features were matched by destructive ones; the tendency to be over-emotional, superstitious and credulous made women vulnerable to dogmatic religious and political practices. These two sides of female power express an ambivalence towards nature itself: it was the source of all knowledge, the ultimate ethical arbiter, and at the same time, capable of unpredictable destruction. Male domination, on the other hand, came into its own in the public rather than the private sphere. It was based on an understanding of natural laws and abstract relationships; it was ideally suited to surviving in the complex economy of nineteenth-century Europe. Male power expressed contemporary notions of culture, that it had penetrated nature's laws, understood them and was now in a position to manipulate them. Its negative aspect was a lack of sympathetic identification with others.

One of the most noteworthy features of this ideological construction was the association of each sex with universal biological categories, as if all women and all men were really the same regardless of class or other social differences. In fact class differences are explicit denied in this view, which we characterized earlier as an *essentialist* approach to the sexes. Furthermore, the ways in which the behaviour of men and women were spoken about implied the life style of a bourgeoisie as the fundamental human standard not that of the working people. A basic question remains: what interests were, and are, served by elaborating a set of biologically based, opposed categories which deliberately ignored (or conveniently obscured) social divisions? We argued earlier that during the eighteenth century, male dominance was expressed through an area of human activity, science, which stands, then as now, for the capacity to control and manipulate the natural world. In this sense men possessed power through their identification with scientific knowledge. Simultaneously, women were conceptualized as the passive recipients of scientific manipulation. The dichotomy had implications for many areas of social life: the organization of work, the division of labour, the ways in which political and social stability were envisaged, and the respective roles of husband and wife in marriage and childbearing.

We are not suggesting that scientific thought was conveniently co-opted in the service of male domination, but that scientific theories and practices have provided our culture with one of the most fundamental ways in which sexual divisions were perceived and understood. We would also say that notions of sexuality were basic to the ways in which science as an activity was thought about. These divisions between male and female, science and nature, did not remain at the level of theorizing but set the terms for a whole range of concrete struggles which are still being enacted today in the Western world. It remains a task for feminist study to discover the situation in other cultures, and to be alert to the misuse of such ideas as the nature/culture dichotomy in the area of sexuality.

Bibliography

Delamont, S. and Duffin, L., (eds) (1978) *The Nineteenth-century Woman: Her Cultural and Physical World,* London: Croom Helm.

Donnison, J. (1977) *Midwives and Medical Men: A History of Inter-professional Rivalries and Women's Rights,* London: Heinemann.

Fee, E. (1974) 'The sexual politics of Victorian social anthropology.' In M. Hartmann and L. W. Banner (eds), *Clio's Consciousness Raised,* New York: Harper & Row.

Glacken, C. (1967) *Traces on the Rhodian Shore: Nature and Culture in Western Thought from Ancient Times to the End of the Eighteenth Century,* Berkeley, Cal: University of California Press.

Jordanova, L.J. (1979) 'Earth science and environmental medicine: the synthesis of the late Enlightenment.' In L.J. Jordanova and R. Porter (eds), *Images of the Earth: Essays in the History of the Environmental Sciences,* pp. 119—46, Chalfont, St Giles: British Society for the History of Science.

Knibiehler, Y. (1976) 'Les médecins et la "nature feminine" au temps du Code Civile.' *Annales: Economies, Sociétiés, Civilisations* 31 (4): 824—45.

MacCormack, Carol, and Strathern, M., (eds) (1980) *Nature Culture and Gender,* New York: Cambridge University Press.

Ploss, H.H. and Bartels, M and P. (1935) *Woman: An Historical, Gynaecological and Anthropological Compendium,* 3 vols London: Heinemann. (First published in German in 1885.)

Further Reading

Ardener, S. (ed.) (1975). *Perceiving Women,* London: Dent.

Ardener, S. (ed.) (1979), *Defining Females,* London: Croom Helm.

Caplan, P. and Bujra, J. (eds) (1978), *Women United, Women Divided.* London: Tavistock.

Chodorow, N. (1974), 'Family structure and feminine personality,' in Rosaldo, M. and Lamphere, L. (eds), *Woman, Culture and Society.* Stanford: Stanford University Press.

MacCormack, C. and Strathern, M. (eds) (1980), *Nature, Culture and Gender,* Cambridge: Cambridge University Press.

Rosaldo, M. and Lamphere, L. (eds) (1974), *Woman, Culture and Society,* Stanford: Stanford University Press.

Index